THE RECORD-SETTING TRIPS

THE RECORD-

SETTING TRIPS

By Auto from Coast to Coast, 1909–1916

Curt McConnell

STANFORD GENERAL BOOKS
Stanford University Press
Stanford, California 2003

Stanford University Press
Stanford, California

Printed in the United States of America
on acid-free, archival-quality paper.

Library of Congress Cataloging-in-Publication Data

McConnell, Curt
    The record-setting trips : by auto from coast to coast, 1909–1916 /
Curt McConnell.
        p.   cm.
    Includes bibliographical references and index.
    ISBN 0-8047-4396-7 (cloth : alk. paper)
    1. United States—Description and travel.   2. Automobile travel—
United States—History—20th century.   3. Adventure and adventurers—
United States—History—20th century.   I. Title.
E168 .46   2003
796.7'0973—dc21   2002003101

Original Printing 2003
Last figure below indicates year of this printing:
12   11   10   09   08   07   06   05   04   03

Designed by Mark Ong
Typeset by James P. Brommer
in 12/16 Granjon and Fenice display

This book is dedicated to Stan Morris,

who thinks that he merely found

an old jalopy for a teen-age boy,

but who actually provided a timely

spark that ignited my lifelong passion

for automobiles.

CONTENTS

ACKNOWLEDGMENTS

For their help editing drafts, I'd like to thank my father, Campbell R. McConnell, and my sisters, Lauren McConnell Davis and Beth McConnell. My special thanks go to my mother, Marilyn McConnell, Aiyana and Mariah McConnell-Beepath, Ben and Holly Davis, Stephen and Audrey Broll, and Linda Paulson.

For assistance with general research or help with specific questions, I gratefully acknowledge the contributions of David L. Cole, Ralph Dunwoodie, Beverly Rae Kimes, David Smith, and Karl S. Zahm, as well as:

- Kim Miller of the Antique Automobile Club of America's Library & Research Center, Hershey, Pennsylvania.

- Peggy Dusman, Dan Kirchner, and Karen Prymak of the former American Automobile Manufacturers Association, Detroit.

- Louis G. Helverson, Stuart McDougall, and Bob Rubenstein of the Automobile Reference Collection, Free Library of Philadelphia.

- Serena Gomez and Mark Patrick of the National Automotive History Collection, Detroit Public Library, and Tom Sherry, the collection's contract photographer.

- The staffs of Bennett Martin Public Library, Lincoln, Nebraska, and Love Library, University of Nebraska–Lincoln.

I wish also to issue a blanket "thank you" to the many helpful persons who were willing and able to answer the various questions, large and small, that cropped up while I was writing this book.

INTRODUCTION

DURING THE LATE 1800s and early 1900s, decades before the creation of four-lane interstate highways, coast-to-coast automobile trips were far from the easy, unremarkable matter they are today. At that time, the dirt roads linking cities were snow-clogged in January, muddy in March, and pockmarked with deep and dusty ruts by July. To motor beyond the safety of paved city streets was considered as noble and adventurous—and as foolhardy—as setting sail on an Arctic expedition.

Not surprisingly, the press paid close attention to the experiences of the earliest transcontinental explorers. In 1899 two reporters, John D. Davis and Louise Hitchcock Davis, blazed a trail westward from New York City to Chicago in the first serious attempt to drive across the country—an undertaking billed by one San Francisco newspaper as "an experiment in the interests of the public."[1] Arriving exhausted in the Windy City after three months of travel and dozens of breakdowns, however, the Davises abandoned their "experiment." Not until four years later was the experiment concluded successfully, when, in 1903, Dr. H. Nelson Jackson of Burlington, Vermont, and co-driver Sewall K. Crocker of Tacoma, Washington, became the first persons to drive from coast to coast. Their arduous journey from San Francisco to New York City in a 2-cylinder Winton automobile took them nearly 64 days, 19 days of which they were forced to spend idle owing to breakdowns.

Mechanical failures were a daily feature of two other successful 1903 treks. In the first, a 1-cylinder Packard piloted by Thomas Fetch and Marius C. Krarup required frequent adjustments and an infusion of 28 new parts to complete its 62-day crossing.

Trailing them by a matter of weeks, Lester L. Whitman and Eugene I. Hammond replaced some 50 parts or sets of parts to keep their 1-cylinder Oldsmobile mobile on its 72-day coast-to-coast schedule.

Other successful crossings from 1904 to 1906 steadily lowered the coast-to-coast crossing time and established a variety of other records. For instance, driving a Franklin runabout—the first 4-cylinder and first air-cooled auto to essay the long journey—Lester L. Whitman and co-driver Clayton S. Carris in 1904 crossed the country in 33 days, nearly halving the year-old record of 62 days. In late 1905 and early 1906, a 2-cylinder Reo driven by Percy F. Megargel and David F. Fassett completed the first coast-to-coast round trip and the first wintertime crossing. In 1906, Whitman, Carris, and three relay drivers in a 6-cylinder Franklin lowered the speed record to 15 days. Such a brisk pace over roads as rough as wagon trails "establishes the high perfection to which the construction of the American automobile has attained," the *New York Herald* noted approvingly.[2]

Why would anyone attempt to drive such long distances in a crude machine along primitive trails? Some trip organizers were thirsting for adventure or personal glory. Jackson bought his Winton and paid Crocker's salary merely so that he might claim the honor of driving the first automobile across America. But it was publicity-conscious automakers who sponsored the other record-setting coast-to-coast auto trips between 1903 and 1906. Although primarily intended as advertising stunts, these trips were widely reported and offered valuable data about automobiles and roads. It was usually professional drivers (not ordinary motorists) who were behind the wheel on these treks, often driving slightly modified vehicles—autos stripped of fenders and extra seats, and fitted with oversize gasoline tanks. The deluge of articles in the popular press indicates that Americans followed such exploits closely and thus soon came to appreciate the automobile's utility—although the cost of these trips, both in dollars and in personal suffering, initially discouraged imitators.

That changed in 1908, when Pennsylvania lumberman Jacob M. Murdock, an average motorist in an ordinary, unmodified touring car, became the first person to drive his family from coast to coast. His 32-day journey also marked the first time women and children were passengers on such a trip.[3] Suddenly, the automobile presented owners with seemingly limitless possibilities. "Mr. Murdock proved a transcontinental automobile tour to be pleasurably possible and took a journey across the continent out of the category of abnormal stunts," *Automobile*, one of the auto industry's leading journals, declared. "He demonstrated that no path on this continent presents difficulties not surmountable by the pluck and patience of a tourist."[4] The automobile was quickly evolving from a novelty to a necessity.

Murdock's trip ended the first phase of long-distance motoring, a pioneering era during which successive attempts had proven, first, that transcontinental journeys were possible and, later, that they could be conducted speedily and safely.[5] *The Record-Setting Trips* explores the second phase of coast-to-coast automobile travel: the period from 1909 through 1916, the last full year before America entered World War I. Gone were the days when an automaker sent its product from coast to coast simply to prove that "the automobile is a reliable means of locomotion and no longer a plaything of the rich."[6] Because this point was no longer in question, other factors lay behind the high-profile trips that took place during the eight-year period beginning in 1909. Some of the coast-to-coast journeys during this period demonstrated the commercial possibilities of the automobile, presaging the rise of long-distance bus lines and the trucking industry—both of which came at the expense of the railroads. Other transcontinental trips hinted at the automobile's military usefulness, as well as alerting American citizens and Congress to the country's "crying need" for better roads,[7] with motorists taking up a call for good roads that had originated with bicyclists in the late 1800s.

The eight coast-to-coast auto trips described in this book both reflected and spurred the development of the American automobile in the years preceding World War I—a period we might term the automobile's age of acceptance. According to *Motor Age*, nothing demonstrated the practicality of the automobile like a coast-to-coast trip: "In an industry whose greatest success is founded upon reliability in hard, useful road service, a transcontinental trip over the kind of routes that grace the western section of our country is of more real value than the winning of a half-dozen pure speed races."[8] What's more, for sheer adventure and excitement, coast-to-coast trips captivated Americans like no other motoring event of the day.

Why, then, have automotive historians been so slow to explore these milestone long-distance trips? Or, to rephrase the question, why has this rich vein of automotive history remained unmined for so long? The main reason is the enormous effort necessary to research a single coast-to-coast trip, much less several. *The Record-Setting Trips* is the culmination of thousands of hours spent poring through photo archives, automobile journals, and weekly and daily newspapers. The rare photographs reproduced here, along with the news articles and first-person accounts, readily illustrate both the pleasures and the hardships that these pioneering motorists encountered as they made their way from coast to coast.

All in all, the record-setting transcontinental auto trips that took place between 1909 and 1916 went a long way toward establishing the automobile as the mainstay of American life it is today. I hope that you will find the eight long-forgotten stories that unfold in the pages ahead both enlightening and inspiring: they represent some of most exciting tales of discovery and adventure from the early automobile era.

MITCHELL "RANGER" SPEEDS SECRET WAR MESSAGE TO COAST

1

Rain, bridgeless rivers, fordless streams, washouts and general execrable conditions made the battle to Rawlins [Wyoming] one long to be remembered by the khaki clad dispatch bearers.

—Racine (Wis.) Daily Journal

LATE IN THE SUMMER of 1909, veteran endurance racer Frank X. Zirbes drove two companions in a new 1910 Mitchell "Ranger" from New York City to San Francisco in 31 days. Joined by Private Malcolm E. Parrott and Lieutenant B. B. Rosenthal, Zirbes was engaged in delivering the first U.S. war dispatch sent across the country by auto. He drove only by daylight, in a run designed "to test the practical use of the modern motor car for purposes of warfare in this country."[1] Zirbes struggled with muddy roads in three states, hot weather in Nebraska and washouts and snow in

Wyoming; in both Nebraska and Wyoming, he avoided some hard going by driving short distances over the Union Pacific's railroad tracks.

The dispatch had been sent by Major General Leonard Wood of New York City, "commanding the Department of the East," to Major General John F. Weston, "commanding the Department of California," at the Presidio in San Francisco. According to the *New York Times*, the transcontinental trip was "the outcome of Major Gen. Wood's desire to see the establishment of an automobile service in connection with the regular and volunteer forces."[2] In selecting an automobile for dispatch service, Wood had spurned "heliographs, wireless, Western Union and Postal [telegraph companies], the United States mails, long-distance telephone, aeroplanes, dirigibles, dispatch boats, submarines, and numerous other methods of communication," noted *Motor World*, evidently taking a dim view of the experiment. "In effect he will show that it is a simple thing to hand a motoring courier a dispatch in New York and tell him to deliver it on the Pacific Coast, with a feeling of assurance that the thing will be done."[3]

The Army had for some time been investigating the automobile's military potential, although some doubt existed as to which kind of engine would best suit its needs. As early as 1904, after tests of autos propelled by electricity, steam, and internal-combustion engines, the Army had indicated a preference for the internal-combustion model. But the danger of accidental fires sparked by leaks of highly volatile gasoline was of concern to military leaders. Consequently, according to one of its annual reports, the U.S. Signal Corps had delayed its purchase of an automobile fleet because "this country has not as yet developed a satisfactory vehicle of the internal-combustion type which can use crude oil," or kerosene, a less-volatile substitute for gasoline. Such an engine was not forthcoming, and by 1909 the Signal Corps was evidently ready to use gasoline autos to help carry out its mission of "furnishing the means and the men to transmit military information in order to insure coordination of command and unified action."[4]

During the summer of 1909, just prior to the trip with Zirbes, Wood acted as umpire in a clash of Blue and Red army forces on maneuvers in Massachusetts, one that involved the use of both steam- and gasoline-powered autos. Wood himself used a White steamer, made by the White Company of Cleveland; other White steam cars were used as ambulances and for hauling supplies. "The preference shown the White steamers is explained by the fact that they can be run on kerosene in places where the use of gasolene cars is prohibited by the military regulations," *Motor World* explained. The issue of fuel notwithstanding, the fact that troops using rapid-fire guns mounted on cars and trucks easily routed their horse-drawn opponents demonstrated "the possibilities of the automobile as an adjunct in time of war," the journal observed.[5]

Wood shrewdly timed the 1909 run of the Mitchell Ranger to his advantage, "as application is soon to be made to Congress for a large appropriation for the establishment of an automobile service in connection with the U.S.A. [U.S. Army] Signal Corps," the *New York Times* reported, "and the success of the long motor car journey will be a strong argument in favor of such a service." Indeed, one of the two passengers on the trip, Lieutenant B. B. Rosenthal, told the *Chicago Inter Ocean* that "the primary object of the present trip is to demonstrate that the automobile may be depended upon in time of trouble to make long flights."[6]

PARROTT, ZIRBES, AND ROSENTHAL

Conflicting accounts exist with regard to some of the details of the 1909 Mitchell run. Evidently, it was Private Malcolm E. Parrott, of Poughkeepsie, New York, an infantryman in the 10th Regiment of the New York National Guard, who carried the dispatch, although a few reports award that distinction to Frank Zirbes' other companion, Lieutenant B. B. Rosenthal. Some press accounts, mostly from early in the journey, also claim that Parrott was in charge of the trip; this seems unlikely, given that he shared the car with a lieutenant (although Rosenthal, a veteran of the Spanish-American War, may no longer have been on active duty).

According to the *Racine Daily Journal*, of Racine, Wisconsin, home of the Mitchell Motor Car Company, Parrott "alternated as pilot with Frank X. Zirbes," although it was Zirbes "who piloted the car most of the way." *Motor Field*, however, flatly stated that Zirbes "will hold the wheel of the war car all the way from New York to San Francisco."[7] A few newspaper photographs taken at the conclusion of the run show Parrott in the driver's seat, but these may have been staged: other photos clearly show Zirbes driving the car into San Francisco. Although it is certainly possible that Parrott drove at times, in the Mitchell company's 32-page post-run publicity booklet, *From Ocean to Ocean: How the Mitchell Ranger Carried the First Transcontinental War Dispatch*, Zirbes is behind the wheel in nearly every photo. Although a civilian, Zirbes joined Parrott and Rosenthal in wearing a khaki Army uniform on the ocean-to-ocean trek (see Fig. 1).

According to most accounts, Zirbes—a name often misspelled "Zirbies," even in

Fig. 1. The coast-to-coast Mitchell Ranger and its crew. Left to right: Rosenthal, Zirbes (at wheel), and Parrott. The government-issue canteen and knapsack reveal the car's military mission. (Motor Age, August 26, 1909)

the factory's *Ocean to Ocean* booklet—also acted as mechanic. Zirbes was clearly an experienced driver, whose occupation was listed in the 1910 Racine city directory as "expert, Mitchell Motor Car Co." He was especially familiar with the first thousand miles of the transcontinental trail, "having piloted a car from New York to Chicago several times."[8] According to the *Racine Daily Journal*, the Mitchell employee was "a well-known Racine boy, a driver who has attracted national attention as a successful contestant in twenty-four hour races, and who was practically brought up in the local factory."[9]

Zirbes was also "well known as the pilot of the Mitchell car in the 1908 'around the clock' endurance race at Milwaukee and other big events."[10] As early as July 1903, Zirbes had entered a three-day, 392-mile motorcycle-reliability contest from New York City to Worcester, Massachusetts, and back. Thirteen of the 32 riders dropped out on the first day's run—among them Zirbes, who "lost the lubricating oil petcock off his motor between New Haven and Meriden," *Automobile* reported.[11]

The numerous 24-hour races that Zirbes entered in 1907 alone included one in late June at St. Paul, Minnesota. In that contest, he drove a Mitchell 918 miles to finish second behind a Matheson auto that had traveled 1,037 miles. In July, at a 24-hour race in Chicago, held despite "wretched track conditions," Zirbes rolled up 719 miles to place fifth behind a Thomas (846 miles), a Matheson (842), a Haynes (813), and a Cadillac (794). "The surface was so soft that deep furrows were plowed in the dirt, and the drivers were obliged to follow these tracks to make any speed at all," *Automobile* reported. "To remain in the game any length of time called for almost super-human efforts on the part of the drivers."[12]

In August 1907, Zirbes and a co-driver placed fourth in a 24-hour race at the Brighton Beach track in Brooklyn, New York, behind a Thomas, a Lozier, and a Jackson, but ahead of two French machines—all more powerful than the Mitchell. According to an account published in *Automobile*, about an hour into the race the Mitchell "drove to its stand and had the coil changed, a new radiator fan put in, the bracket of the original one having snapped off, and a new radiator fitted, the fan blades having caused a serious leak." The Mitchell crew also stopped later because of the breaking down of the wooden platform on which were carried the storage batteries. As nine of the fifteen starters fell by the wayside, the 4-cylinder, 30-horsepower Wisconsin-made auto plugged steadily onward to finish with 774 miles—223 miles behind the winning Thomas. Though underpowered in comparison to its competitors, *Automobile* noted, the Mitchell nonetheless "ran a consistent race."[13]

Zirbes' companion on the transcontinental trip, Lieutenant B. B. Rosenthal, of Chicago, belonged to "the Veteran Corps of Engineers of the Spanish-American war brigade," according to the Mitchell company's *Ocean to Ocean* booklet. Almost universally referred to by his initials—only the *Omaha (Neb.) Daily News* gives his first name, Ben—Rosenthal was also a veteran of the Signal Corps. An article in *Motor World* noted that during the 1909 Mitchell run Rosenthal would be "taking observations of the performance of the car, for the War Department," while the *New York Times* further indicated that Rosenthal would "have charge of any temporary bridge building or road making which may be necessary in the Western country."[14]

Quite apart from the 1909 trip, Rosenthal had in fact had an earlier brush with fame, the *South Bend Tribune* told its readers. "Because of his knowledge of construction work, Lieut. Rosenthal was selected by Mme. Sarah Bernhardt, a few years ago, to take charge of the tour which she played under circus tents in the west and southwest." The transcontinental expedition eventually did require his services in the West when "several bridges that had been swept away by washouts had to be rebuilt." According to the Mitchell company, Rosenthal's size made him "the ideal engineer pilot—the big man who would have sufficient physical strength to move the machine by sheer body power upon a hastily constructed army bridge."[15]

VOLUNTEERING THE MITCHELL

How Wood—for whom was named a U.S. Army training center for engineers, Fort Leonard Wood, near Rolla, Missouri—happened to choose a Mitchell auto for his test is open to speculation. He may have been approached by James W. Gilson, sales manager of the Mitchell company, who accompanied the Ranger across the country by train and who reportedly "volunteered" the use of the car.[16] Or perhaps Wood knew Mitchell company President William T. Lewis, a native of Utica, New York, and a former Army officer, who served as a telegrapher during the Civil War. (As late as 1909, the Racine newspaper called the Mitchell president simply "Capt. Lewis" on first reference.)[17] The factory's post-trip publicity booklet, however, gives Parrott

> great credit . . . for seizing upon the psychological moment for demonstrating to Major-General Wood that an automobile could be depended upon to act as an important adjunct to extensive military operations involving a transcontinental "forced march." Private Parrott saw an opportunity to prove the ability of a Mitchell Ranger to do things. Obtaining the permission of the Mitchell Motor Car Company, to proffer the services of the first 1910 model turned out, to the government leaders for the experiment, the militia man volunteered to pilot the expedition across the continent.[18]

Gilson realized that a successful crossing would boost sales. Thanks to the distinctive new look of its 1910 models, the company reaped a press bonanza even before the start of the trip. "To New York automobiledom . . . there was wide interest in the Mitchell car itself, when it first appeared on Broadway," *Automobile* wrote. "The entirely new line of the 1910 product of the Mitchell Company was a surprise. . . . The radiator, and consequently the hood, are materially different in shape from other Mitchells, and the alteration has included the body also."[19]

The coast-to-coast trip won a good deal of free publicity for the Mitchell in the East's biggest cities. "New York, Philadelphia, Boston and, in fact, all the papers have devoted much space on the results each day," the *Racine Daily Journal* remarked. "New York papers are full of the undertaking."[20] One eastern agent who saw the Ranger before the start of the trip requested that his order of 1910 Mitchells be increased by 300 cars, Gilson told the *Chicago Daily News*. But he was obliged to turn down the request:

> We are completely sold out for 1910 and it is going to keep the factory on the hump to fill the orders we have. I wish our factory was twice as large as it is, for then we could make and sell twice as many cars. The trip of the Ranger through the country is making a hit and I expect it will be even more of a sensation when it reaches the Pacific coast.[21]

The automaker, with 1,800 employees in a 500,000-square-foot factory in Racine, announced plans to build 6,012 autos for 1910, double its 1909 production. But if its entire output of 1910 autos had already been spoken for, how could the Mitchell Motor Car Company have filled a U.S. government order for Army cars? One possible answer lies in what the automaker advertised as the "new factory already on the edge of completion" in Racine.[22] With the improved facilities, the company could likely have increased its output to fill a large government order.

"A WARLIKE APPEARANCE"

Sending war messages by auto was nothing new, as the *Nevada State Journal* of Reno correctly observed. "For a long time the government has been trying out the auto under all conditions, preparing for time[s] of strife when railroad and telegraph are liable to be out of commission or in control of the enemy."[23] The Army's experiments began at least a decade earlier, when in summer 1899 Alexander Winton arranged to drive one of his Cleveland-made Winton autos from Chicago to New York City "to demonstrate the efficiency of the motor carriage for carrying messages and mails in time of war."[24] Winton had likewise carried greetings from one Army general to another during a 1901 coast-to-coast attempt that began in San Francisco but stalled in the sands of Nevada.[25] After many experiments during the intervening years, the first of twenty-two autos in "the greatest relay race in history" left Chicago on June 18, 1906, to speed another war message to New York City.[26]

On February 18, 1908, six days after contestants in the New York–Paris auto race left Gotham on a nearly round-the-world journey, a Studebaker "war car" started out along the same route. Driven day and night by relay drivers who shrugged off what *Motor Age* called "the most severe blizzard that has visited this country in years," the dispatch-bearing Studebaker beat the leader of the round-the-world race into Chicago by twenty minutes. Despite grinding to a halt in many snowdrifts and mud holes, the war car subsequently reached Fort Leavenworth, Kansas, in just over 18 days to end its 1,600-mile trek. The Mitchell auto that set out the following year sought to improve on the Studebaker's feat by carrying the first war dispatch between coasts.[27]

The car selected for the task was the first 1910 Mitchell that emerged from the Racine factory, a product of designer John W. Bate, according to press accounts. The new model "has reached the limit of Yankee genius," Sales Manager Gilson boasted to the *Racine Daily Journal.* "There's a million dollars' worth of experience in that machine." Or, as the folksy Captain Lewis put it, "That's a bully car, boys, that 1910 model."[28] Equipped with a Jones speedometer and Hartford tires, the 4-cylinder touring car "had no special mechanical equipment and weighed exactly 2,200 pounds," Zirbes reported. "However, with our military paraphernalia, axes, ropes, planks, luggage and ourselves, it weighed when en route 4,050 pounds, and that was some tonnage to pull."[29]

The Mitchell company offered two 4-cylinder models for 1910—a Model R runabout and Model T five-passenger touring car—along with a 6-cylinder Model S seven-passenger touring car. As a Model T, the Mitchell featured in the 1909 run developed 28.9 horsepower, which, for convenience, both the Mitchell company and automobile journals rounded to 30 horsepower. Its cylinders, cast in pairs, had bore and stroke measurements of 4¼ x 5 inches. The car used a 3-speed sliding-gear transmission, mounted amidships (between the engine and rear axle), and a leather-faced cone clutch. According to automobile journals, the car had a 112-inch wheelbase, expanding and contracting brakes on the rear wheels, and a gasoline capacity of 15½ gallons. In addition, "a sheet steel pan, held by ingenious and easily and quickly manipulated spring hooks, protects motor and clutch from dust and mud." The car was painted olive drab, and a sign on its hood proclaimed it a "Dispatch Car / U.S. Army."[30]

The load included tents and camping outfits, *Motor Age* told its readers, and "a rapid-fire rifle will be mounted on a special platform in front of the driver," although photos do not show a rifle in place. In addition to shovels and picks, "canteens, haversacks and revolvers hung on the sides of the new touring car," *Automobile* noted. Because of such baggage, the otherwise stock Mitchell—nicknamed the Mitchell "Ranger" before the start of the run—"presents a very warlike appearance," a reporter from Indiana observed.[31] A few newspapers even referred to the transcontinental crewmen as "Rangers." "In the estimation of the trained soldiers who are making this long trip," the Mitchell was "especially adapted to the diversified highways and trails that will be used," declared a news report that probably originated in the Mitchell publicity department. "With its clearance, roadability, and time tried motor and [braking] features, the dispatch car may be depended upon to go through with a 'perfect score' each day."[32]

THEY'RE OFF ON A "STRENUOUS TRIP"

Besides traveling "entirely by daylight," the Mitchell dispatch bearers would "travel twelve hours and rest twelve," reported the *Goshen (Ind.) Daily News–Times*. According to another source, the car "travels without pilot or any accompanying party," a reference to the so-called pilot car that many transcontinental drivers hired to guide them.[33] Zirbes, Parrott, and Rosenthal planned to travel through New York, Pennsylvania, Ohio, and Illinois to Chicago, then across the Plains states to Wyoming, before finishing their journey through Utah, Nevada, and California (see Table 1). The men set Thursday, September 16, as their goal for reaching San Francisco, although because of unusually bad roads west of Chicago and a crew member's illness, they were ultimately three days late in arriving.

In preparation for the trip, the Mitchell company shipped the Ranger to New York City on Monday, August 16. The automaker also distributed photos, taken a day or two before the start of the run, showing Zirbes, Parrott, and Rosenthal in the Ranger at Poughkeepsie (see Fig. 2). There, members of Parrott's Company B, 10th Regiment, of the New York National Guard, presented the autoists with an American flag, which adorned the Ranger when it left New York City on Thursday, August 19. As *Automobile* reported:

> With the plan of a definite schedule to follow, about 3,693 miles to cover, and probably much more, the new car is essaying one of the most strenuous trips ever attempted. No records will be aspired to, for the car will deviate from the direct route a number of times in order to visit army posts en route. . . .

TABLE 1. The Mitchell Ranger's Route from New York City to San Francisco, 1909

New York City start:
    12:00 P.M., Thursday, August 19, 1909

New York	*Colorado*
Poughkeepsie	Julesburg
Albany	*Nebraska*
Schenectady	Sidney
Utica	*Wyoming*
Batavia	Pine Bluffs
Buffalo	Cheyenne
Pennsylvania	Laramie
Erie	Hanna
Ohio	Fort Steele
Cleveland	Rawlins
Elyria	Creston
Toledo	Thayer Junction
Indiana	Rock Springs
Ligonier	Granger
Goshen	Evanston
Mishawaka	*Utah*
South Bend	Echo
La Porte	Ogden
Valparaiso	Kelton
Illinois	*Nevada*
South Chicago	Montello
Chicago	Winnemucca
Dixon	Hazen
Iowa	Wadsworth
Clinton	Sparks
Cedar Rapids	Reno
Belle Plaine	Carson City
Tama	Glenbrook
Marshalltown	*California*
Boone	Lakeside
Dunlap	Meyers Station
Council Bluffs	Placerville
Nebraska	Sacramento
Omaha	Stockton
Kearney	Hayward
North Platte	Oakland

San Francisco finish:
    2:00 P.M., Sunday, September 19, 1909

Fig. 2. Parrott greets a fellow member of the New York National Guard in Poughkeepsie, New York. Zirbes is at the wheel, Rosenthal in the back seat. (NAHC)

Preliminary to the actual start was a trip to Governor's Island for the official despatch, and at exactly noon the party, accompanied by a number of Mitchell cars from the Mitchell branch, and a delegation of private owners, assembled at Columbus Circle to witness the beginning of the rigorous jaunt. Private Parrott carried a large flag presented to him by Capt. W. L. Burnett, of his regiment, as well as the pennant of the Hudson Valley Automobile Club of Poughkeepsie, of which he is a member.[34]

According to a Mitchell official, the car was also "rigged out in U.S. pennants." The robust Rosenthal occupied the tonneau, or back seat, which he shared with five suitcases and a number of smaller bags, "while hanging from the tonneau doors were several haversacks," *Automobile Topics* reported.[35]

Cheering on the Mitchell Ranger was "one of the largest throngs that ever gathered to dispatch a motor car on a long journey," according to one of three nearly verbatim reports, evidently based on either a wire story or a factory press release (see Fig. 3).[36]

COAST TO COAST BY AUTOMOBILE

These accounts did not name an attendance figure, although certainly the estimated 200,000 spectators who jostled for position at the start of the 1908 New York–Paris race far outnumbered the Mitchell well-wishers. If press attention reflects crowd size, the crowd must have been quite small: the *New York Herald* and *New York Tribune* devoted just one paragraph apiece to the Mitchell start; the *New York Times* wrote two paragraphs. *Automobile Topics*, perhaps the only publication to name a figure, estimated the crowd at "several hundred persons."[37]

Gilson, the Mitchell sales manager, who witnessed the departure of the Mitchell Ranger from New York, indicated to the *Racine Daily Journal* that during its five-day trip to Chicago the car and its occupants made overnight stops in Poughkeepsie, Utica, and Buffalo. The other overnight stops between New York City and Chicago were at Elyria, Ohio, and Ligonier, Indiana. The Ranger reached Poughkeepsie in 4½ hours during the first day's short run. According to Gilson, on Friday, August 20, the

Fig. 3. Leaving Columbus Circle in the Mitchell Ranger are Zirbes (driving), front-seat passenger Parrott, and Rosenthal in the back seat. (From Ocean to Ocean booklet/NAHC)

Ranger traveled 180 miles from Poughkeepsie to Utica over "muddy, sticky roads" in 9½ hours, while Saturday saw the crew travel 10 hours to Buffalo, 480 miles from New York City.[38] For its running time of 24 hours to Buffalo, the Mitchell averaged an even 20 mph.

FAST TIME TO CHICAGO

"It was a bronzed and dust-covered, khaki-clad trio which motored up to the Reed House" in Erie, Pennsylvania, on Sunday morning, August 22, the *Erie Dispatch* reported. Right on schedule, the Mitchell "departed westward after a brief stop in this city," subsequently arriving at Elyria for the night.[39] According to the factory's *Ocean to Ocean* booklet, the 246-mile dash from Buffalo to Elyria was the greatest distance covered in one day during the trip. Zirbes, Parrott, and Rosenthal—who reached Chicago two days ahead of their rosiest expectations—were probably already well ahead of schedule at Erie.

Heading west on Monday, August 23, Day 5 of the trip, the Ranger traveled from north-central Ohio to Ligonier in north-central Indiana, arriving there 36 hours ahead of schedule. The Mitchell crew left Ligonier at 5:40 A.M. Tuesday, August 24, and at 6:25 A.M. reached Goshen, Indiana, 935 miles from New York City, according to the *Goshen Daily News–Times*. "The party took breakfast at the Hascall in Goshen. The car left at eight o'clock for Chicago where it expects to arrive at 2 o'clock this afternoon. The car followed the Fort Wayne road from Goshen to Mishawaka not touching Elkhart, and will go from La Porte to Valparaiso."[40]

The Mitchell crew reached South Bend, Indiana, later in the morning, 41 hours ahead of its scheduled arrival time, the *South Bend Tribune* reported. "The car stopped only a short time in the city, long enough to leave an account of their journey. The machine was surrounded by an interested crowd attracted to the knapsacks and firearms in the tonneau."[41] From Ligonier the previous evening, the autoists had telegraphed their plan to reach Chicago at 2:00 P.M. Tuesday. At South Bend, however, they were predicting a Chicago arrival time of noon.

Nevertheless, it was 2:00 P.M. when the dispatch bearers finally reached South Chicago, "where they were greeted by local motorists, who escorted them to the South Shore Country club," the *Chicago Inter Ocean* reported (see Fig. 4). In the newspaper's account:

After an impromptu reception the cavalcade continued to the down town district. All along the route pedestrians cheered the war car, which was easily distinguishable because of its dusty appearance. Lieutenant Rosenthal held a large American flag overhead when the tourists reached the business center. The flag was presented to Private Parrott by members of his regiment at Poughkeepsie, N.Y., before the war car left that city for New York to start on the long journey last Thursday noon.

Although scheduled to make a leisurely trip, stopping nights and making side jaunts to visit such military posts as Private Parrott received instructions to call at, Driver Zirbes found the roads so good after leaving Utica, N.Y., that he disregarded the schedule and proceeded with all speed to Elyria, Ohio, many hours ahead of time and reached Ligonier, Ind., Monday evening. . . .

Leading the procession of Chicago automobilists who drove out to South Chicago to greet the tourists . . . were James W. Gilson, sales manager, and Designer Bate of the Mitchell Motor Car company.[42]

The procession of greeters, who included "a number of the automobile and motor club members, as well as owners of Mitchell cars,"[43] reached the Chicago Automobile Club headquarters at 3:00 P.M.

Fig. 4. Left to right: Rosenthal, Zirbes, and Parrott arrive at Chicago's South Shore Country Club. (From Ocean to Ocean booklet/NAHC)

According to the *Chicago Inter Ocean*, "fifty-five hours of actual running time were consumed between the Atlantic seaboard and this city, just seven hours behind the record, which was made by day and night driving." But the record holders had traveled roughly 1,000 miles between New York City and Chicago, while the Ranger crew, in addition to driving only by daylight, "found it necessary to make many detours because some of the roads were being repaired" and thus traveled 1,600 miles between the two cities, reported the *Chicago Daily News*.[44] Given those figures, the Ranger averaged 29 mph for its running time.

In the Mitchell *Ocean to Ocean* booklet, however, Gilson confused the Ranger's elapsed time (5 days, 3 hours from New York City to Chicago) with its 55-hour running time and therefore falsely contended that "the best mark of inter-city record seekers who traveled with relay crews of drivers was shattered."[45] Even if its elapsed time had been only 55 hours, the Mitchell would still have fallen far short of the New York–Chicago speed record. Two years earlier, on August 21 and 22, 1907, four relay drivers in a 6-cylinder Franklin drove between the two cities in 39 hours, 53 minutes, and the record had perhaps been lowered since.[46] But even if the Mitchell posed no threat to existing speed records, it reached Chicago 50 hours ahead of its own schedule, the *Inter Ocean* said. Rosenthal, the trip's chronicler, put the figure at 48 hours, while also pointing out that "we made no attempt at record-breaking."[47] For his part, Zirbes boasted that, whereas the Ranger would in fact spend the night in Chicago on Tuesday, according to its schedule it should be back in Toledo, Ohio.

A MOST DELIGHTFUL (BUT MUDDY) TRIP

Gilson had referred to "muddy, sticky roads" between Poughkeepsie and Utica that the travelers encountered on Day 2. But Rosenthal's comments to Chicago reporters clashed with Gilson's account: "We have had a most delightful trip. We have not had a drop of rain, and we found the roads in excellent condition. We expect to reach San Francisco at least a week ahead of the schedule, although we are not out for speed, and intend to visit various army posts and encampments en route." Parrott offered his own conflicting weather report, remarking that "only a few moments of rain marred our trip to Chicago." Zirbes declared that "the car has not had an adjustment nor a moment's delay from tire trouble" (although the factory's own *Ocean to Ocean* booklet states that the Ranger had its first puncture in Ohio).[48]

Rain the next day, Wednesday, August 25, presumably caught the attention of all three crew members, who at 9:00 A.M. "were given a rousing farewell at the Chicago Automobile club," the *Chicago Daily Tribune* reported.

Capt. Healy and a squad of his mounted police escorted the tourists over the Jackson boulevard bridge. Waving the American flag, which was presented to Private Malcolm E. Parrott . . . the party bid "good-by" to Chicago. After traveling for a couple of hours the tourists were caught in a heavy rainstorm, which continued all during the day, making the roads heavy and progress slow. They arrived at Dixon, Ill., during the evening and will try to make Clinton, Ia., before noon [on Thursday].[49]

Although Zirbes had planned to reach Clinton by nightfall Wednesday, muddy roads limited the Mitchell's progress to 100 miles, or two-thirds of the distance to Clinton. The Ranger would also wallow through mud for the two days following. In the meantime, "so enthusiastic was Dixon over the arrival of the Ranger," Gilson reported, "that it was with difficulty that the eager 'serenaders' were induced to give the couriers their allotted period of sleep. The car was parked out in the open where thousands inspected its mechanism and equipment."[50]

"A MASSIVE MUD BALL"

"On the next day the war car passed many automobiles stalled in the mud before reaching the Mississippi river," the *Racine Daily Journal* recounted. "Dashing through Iowa to take advantage of a lull in the rainstorm," the car reached Cedar Rapids at 6:30 P.M. Thursday.[51] "The car rolled into Cedar Rapids last evening looking like a massive mud ball," according to Friday's *Cedar Rapids Daily Republican*:

Mud completely covered the front lamps, and the hood over the front had to be pried loose from the thick coating of Illinois mud, through which the Mitchell had to plow all the way from Chicago. "We had the most terrible experience getting into Clinton," stated Lieutenant Rosenthal last evening after he had eaten his dinner at the Allison. "The mud was almost impassable, and it is a wonder to me that we performed the feats in the mud that we have." Under the diligent work of Driver Zirbies [*sic*], however, the Mitchell Ranger was cleaned up in fine shape, ready for the next lap today of its long trip.[52]

"I find it a good plan to make a speedy schedule across Iowa and Nebraska to escape threatening downpours, and thereby get good roads," Parrott told the *Daily Republican*. "There is little probability of rain west of Julesburg, Colo. The engine is running so sweetly, despite the big load of human and dead freight, that I'm inclined to believe that we may safely lower the schedule figured out for us by several days and deliver the important dispatch of General Wood to the government post at the Presid[i]o at least a week before it is expected."[53]

On Friday, August 27, Day 9 of the trip, the three men drove from Cedar Rapids through Belle Plaine and Tama on their way to Marshalltown. Unfortunately, though, one of Iowa's fearsome rains spoiled Parrott's speedy schedule. Leaving Cedar Rapids, "Driver Zirbes was almost blinded by lightning, the rain turning the black earth roads into quagmires," reported the *Daily Journal* of Racine, where telegrams kept the Mitchell company posted on the Ranger's progress. "Passing a serious road obstruction—a team of horses struck and killed by lightning—the little car plowed its way through the mud to Tama City."[54]

The car reached Marshalltown at 5:20 P.M. on Friday, according to the *Evening Times-Republican*. "Muddy roads were encountered east of Belle Plaine, and delayed the trip somewhat. . . . The party stopped at the Eldridge-Beebe garage only long enough to secure gasoline and have the car looked over and a few bolts tightened. The trip west was started at 5:40, and it was expected that Boone would be the stop-over point for the night," 50 miles west of Marshalltown.

The car reached Omaha, more than 150 miles beyond Boone, Iowa, at 6:30 P.M. Saturday, August 28, local newspapers reported. Dick Stewart of the Coit Automobile Company, the Omaha Mitchell agent, "went out to meet the car in a Mitchell, and escorted it into Omaha," the *Omaha World-Herald* reported. The Ranger spent the night at the Coit garage. Though still a day ahead of schedule, it had fallen behind its earlier pace. "The car was not able to make as fast time through Iowa," noted the *Daily Nonpareil* of Council Bluffs, Iowa, situated just across the Missouri River from Omaha.[55] According to the *Racine Daily Journal*:

> On the run to Council Bluffs the dispatch bearers were met by a delegation of Indians and cowboys from the Buffalo Bill Wild West show and escorted across the Missouri river to Omaha. Both Buffalo Bill and Pawnee Bill rode alongside the military car for miles, the former remarking that had there been an automobile in the service of the government scouts when the frontier reached almost down to Omaha Limits, the "winning of the West" would have been a much more simple operation. In Omaha the largest delegation of Mitchell cars encountered on the transcontinental run acted as escort to the Henshaw hotel, where the Nebraska motoring enthusiasts gave a banquet in honor of the dispatch bearers.[56]

After spending the night, the trio left Omaha on Sunday afternoon, the *Omaha Daily News* reported. "Continuing the route to North Platte, the military party made exceptional speed. The first tire trouble of the run was encountered there," the Racine newspaper stated, without elaborating. "After being almost fried on the burning sands" of western Nebraska, Zirbes and his companions, following the Union Pacific route, dipped briefly south of the state line to arrive in Julesburg, Colorado, on Tuesday, August 31, Day 13. "The sun in Nebraska baked us to a crisp," the *Ocean to Ocean* booklet quotes one of the three as saying. "When the sun was not burning our lips until they swelled to three times their normal size the wind was busy puffing up our cheeks and cracking the skin."[57]

PARROTT PAUSES, APPENDICITIS PENDING

"Although the elements were entirely antagonistic," the dispatch bearers reached Julesburg "twenty-five hours ahead of schedule," the *Kansas City Star* reported. According to *Motor Age*, Parrott "was taken ill at Julesburg, Colo., and an attending physician cautioned him to give up the trip on account of threatening appendicitis. Private Parrott wired to headquarters to send on relief, but before his would-be successor arrived at Julesburg he had recovered sufficiently to resume the journey." Although his illness, possibly brought on by exposure to the elements in Illinois and Iowa, delayed the car five days at Julesburg, the auto journal recounted, the delay "will not necessarily prevent the men from reaching their destination on scheduled time, as they will double their running time until they catch up."[58]

Parrott, however, evidently recovered in fewer than five days, according to a newspaper in Cheyenne, Wyoming, a day's drive from Julesburg at the Ranger's pace. The trio, who had reached Julesburg Tuesday, arrived Friday in Cheyenne and registered at the Inter Ocean Hotel, according to Friday's *Wyoming Tribune* of Cheyenne. "The car is undergoing repairs here and expects to leave tomorrow," indicated the paper, while neglecting to specify the repairs. In traveling northwest from Julesburg to Cheyenne, the autoists again entered western Nebraska. "The run from Sidney, Neb., to this city [100 miles] was made in less than 3 hours and 30 minutes over very bad roads," related Cheyenne's *Sunday State Leader*, which concurred with Rosenthal in saying that the Ranger arrived on Saturday.[59] Curiously, Rosenthal made no mention of Parrott's illness:

> After entering Colorado we made a detour of 30 miles because of washouts, during which we visited the scene of the attack on Julesburg by the Sioux and Cheyennes some years

ago. Our next stop was at Pine Bluffs, Wyo., which we reached just after the sheriff had rescued a horse thief from a mob that wanted to string him up to a telegraph pole. That night we had to sleep in the mountains. Eleven miles from Cheyenne an irrigation ditch burst and the rushing waters washed out the roads tributary to it. We reached Cheyenne Saturday and were visited by several officers and soldiers from Fort Russell.[60]

The crew camped in the mountains rather than staying in Pine Bluffs, Parrott explained, because "we thought it no place for war couriers—might excite the throng into further acts of violence." Earlier in the day, at Sidney, he said, "the street fair was on, but the flood had descended, turning the place into a mud hole. Some of the tents were taken down and the Mitchell Ranger was permitted to make a detour to the Union Pacific tracks, which we had to use for more than six miles."[61] The route through mountainous southern Wyoming was the usual one for transcontinentalists, Rosenthal said— west from Cheyenne through Laramie, Hanna, Fort Steele, Rawlins, Creston, Thayer Junction, Rock Springs, Granger, and Evanston. The late-summer weather was, however, decidedly unseasonal: heavy rain, and then snow.

Earlier in 1909, another transcontinental traveler had made an equally sodden trip across Wyoming, Parrott later observed. Edward Payson Weston, 71, left New York City on March 15, and by June 9 had walked 2,828 miles to Wamsutter, Wyoming. "The wind is blowing and it is very evident it will rain again," read Weston's telegram to the *New York Times*. "These sudden changes and the daily drenching that I get are becoming monotonous." Weston spent June 13 stranded near Granger, waiting for a new pair of shoes to arrive.[62] Paraphrasing Parrott's own description, the *Reno Evening Gazette* reported that the Mitchell motorists "made excellent time until they hit the roads of Wyoming which Pedestrian Weston found so bad. There they were several times mired in the mud and spent several nights sleeping in the rain. He [Parrott] says that some days in Wyoming they drove only a distance of five or six miles but that once leaving the roads of Wyoming they had very little trouble."[63]

WYOMING'S "GELATINOUS" ROADS

Assuming that the car left Cheyenne on Saturday, September 4, when the *Wyoming Tribune* said it would, the Ranger took five days to travel the approximately 175 miles to Rawlins. The factory's *Ocean to Ocean* booklet remarked that highways between Cheyenne and Hanna resembled "mortar troughs,"[64] but the Mitchell finally arrived in

Rawlins at 3:30 P.M. on Wednesday, September 8, according to the *Rawlins Republican*. "Rain, bridgeless rivers, fordless streams, washouts and general execrable conditions made the battle to Rawlins one long to be remembered by the khaki clad dispatch bearers," the *Racine Daily Journal* recounted. "Time and time again the technical knowledge of Lieutenant Rosenthal had to be called into execution to get the car over streams that were over their banks. Near Creston permission had to be obtained from the Union Pacific railroad to use the company's bridges in crossing torrents."[65]

In fact, the Ranger traveled most of the way across Wyoming, from Laramie to the Utah line, in a steady downpour, Rosenthal later told the *San Francisco Chronicle*. This produced "soggy, gelatinous roads," the newspaper said.[66] To top it off, at Evanston, just before leaving Wyoming, the car ran into what *Automobile* called a heavy snowstorm. "Words are inadequate to describe the conditions we encountered," said Rosenthal, who nevertheless ventured this description:

> We encountered the worst rains in Wyoming's history in this section [Cheyenne to Laramie], as it had been pouring continuously for 5 days. We next poked along from Laramie to Hanna in a downpour, and so many bridges had been washed away that we had to borrow rails from beside the railroad tracks to make corduroy roads.
>
> Outside of Hanna we were stuck in the mud for 3 hours and had to commandeer some teams to haul us out. After reaching Fort Steele bridge we found the approach to the county bridge and the bridge itself, 100 feet long, washed out, and we were then forced to get an order from the Union Pacific superintendent to use the Fort Steele [railroad] bridge. The next 18 miles to Rawlins was along the foothills in a heavy rain.
>
> Thayer Junction, which was our next halt, and which is known as Death Valley, we went through at a snail's pace, using canvas to cover the alkali ditches and get traction. By going through Rock Springs, which is said to be the biggest coal mining town in the west, we were able to make up some time on the way to Granger, because the sun bakes the red desert top and gave us some fair going occasionally. We hit a severe snow storm about 30 miles outside of Granger before we reached Evanston, which we left next morning almost at zero.[67]

Eight days after leaving Cheyenne, Parrott, Rosenthal, and Zirbes pulled into Ogden, Utah, on Sunday night, September 12, Day 25. "All are in good health, and after rounding the corner of the Great Salt Lake look for a speedy and uneventful dash across the desert land of Nevada to Reno," *Automobile* said. But according to Monday's *Racine Daily Journal*, "a telegram received from Mr. Zirbes this morning is dated at a little town near Ogden, Utah[,] and says that the car and party are passing through a raging blizzard." The *Reno Evening Gazette* also reported that at Ogden Rosenthal temporarily left the party "to meet certain government officials."[68]

FLYING THROUGH THE DESERT

The car made much better progress now, because "the roads flattened out into parallel strings of packed sand so that much of the time lost . . . was made up between Ogden and Reno," the *San Francisco Chronicle* said. Parrott and Zirbes crossed the sands of northern Nevada, still traveling without Rosenthal. He nonetheless later described his companions' pleasure at encountering the desert sands between Montello and Winnemucca, Nevada, which represented "easy going as compared with the mud of the further eastern states. . . . although some sandy spots made us take to the sagebrush now and then." On Wednesday, September 15, Parrott and Zirbes "stopped the car a short distance the other side [east] of Hazen . . . slept on the desert all night and then drove into Wadsworth," said the *Reno Evening Gazette*.[69]

Sometime later in the day on Thursday, September 16, Zirbes stopped the car in Sparks to visit an uncle, with whom he "discussed the best roads across the mountains and the finest highways in California." There, Zirbes and Parrott also met A. E. Hunter, "San Francisco agent of the Mitchell car company," and E. E. Elliott, of Carr & Elliott, the Reno Mitchell agency. The agents had driven to Sparks, accompanied by two city councilmen, to escort the "mud-bespattered, road-scarred" transcontinental car into Reno (see Fig. 5). It reached Reno at 2:00 P.M., two days behind schedule, according to the *Nevada State Journal*.[70] Thursday had been the Ranger's original deadline for reaching San Francisco.

"Chauffeur Parrott says the machine fairly ate up the sand on the Nevada desert and made time that compared favorably with that reeled off across New York state. More than 3280 miles have been traveled by the party so far, with 244 miles to come before San Francisco is reached," the newspaper observed.[71] Rosenthal arrived by train to rejoin the car in Reno, and Hunter, too, would ride the Ranger into San Francisco. According to the *Reno Evening Gazette*, the travelers, who lodged at the appropriately named Overland Hotel, planned to leave for the west at noon Friday, September 17, Day 30.

Eager to reach the coast, however, the autoists left Reno early enough Friday to reach Carson City, 30 miles south, "shortly before noon." Arriving "with a flag gaily fluttering from a staff on the front seat," the Ranger was more than the previously reported two days behind time, said the *Carson City News*. Nonetheless, the travelers spoke "very highly of the roads in Nevada and stated that if the others over the country were as good they would have been several days ahead of their schedule instead of be-

Fig. 5. The dusty Mitchell as it arrived in Reno. Left to right: Zirbes, Parrott, and Rosenthal. (From *Ocean to Ocean* booklet / NAHC)

ing four days behind."[72] According to the *Carson City Daily Appeal*, "the party stopped here about ten minutes, inquiring [about] the roads and took on some supplies, leaving by way of King's Canyon road," on a route that would take the Mitchell south of Lake Tahoe through Glenbrook, in Nevada, and then Lakeside, Meyers Station, and Placerville, California. "The last seen of the machine, which travels without pilot or any accompanying party, it was flying up King's Canyon 20 miles an hour."[73]

Beyond Carson City, "we encountered a rise of 3,000 feet to the summit of the Sierra Nevada—one entire rise from the water level being over 7,000 feet," Rosenthal said. "Then there came 50 miles over a magnificent state road into Placerville—all down grade and the finest kind of traveling. From Placerville we pushed along over good roads to Sacramento and Stockton."[74]

PARADE GREETS DISPATCH BEARERS

"Dust covered, weary with the strain of travel in which they encountered all sorts of weather, and anxious to complete the remaining miles of their cross-continent test trip," the Mitchell reached Sacramento at midnight Saturday, reported Sunday's *Sacramento Union*. Even the last leg of the trip from Carson City had had its adventures, according to the *San Francisco Chronicle*, which noted that while the party was crossing the Sierra Nevada, "several small mishaps occasioned long delays." The *Chronicle* did not elaborate, but the *San Francisco Examiner* was more specific: "After leaving Carson City they got lost in the mountains, which delayed their arrival for almost a day."[75] The *Sacramento Union* also related a Wyoming incident that other publications had overlooked:

> Lieutenant Rosenthal says that the worst part of the journey was equally divided between the stretch over the Sierras and in Wyoming, where they broke the frame of the machine and had to resort to a railroad hoisting crane to lift them out of the mire.
>
> On the trip over the Sierras[,] the lieutenant says, he passed automobile after automobile that was broken down or disabled. The last twenty-two miles between this city and Folsom the lieutenant referred to as being "like rolling a baby carriage over a dining room table." He said all the wear and tear of the three thousand miles was amply repaid by a few miles of good travel.[76]

Acting on War Department orders, Colonel C. L. Hewes, commander of the California Coast Artillery, dispatched Lieutenant W. H. Homer and twelve soldiers in two cars to drive east to meet the Ranger, according to the *San Francisco Chronicle*. A photo in the *Ocean to Ocean* booklet, however, shows three cars in the escorting party. "Arriving at Hayward," the *Chronicle* said, "they found that the New Yorkers had been delayed and wheeled on to Stockton, from which place they acted as an official army escort to the military transcontinental machine." Joining the escort were "Mrs. W. T. Lewis, wife of the President of the Mitchell Motor Car Company of Racine, Wis., and her daughter, Mrs. George B. Wilson of Searchlight, Nevada," added the *San Francisco Examiner*.[77]

"The men bore the trip very well and were as brown as berries when they reached their destination," the *Examiner* declared, although elsewhere in the same article the paper said that Zirbes appeared "sun-burned, dust-begrimed and fatigued" as he drove the Mitchell Ranger up Market Street. *Automobile* observed that Parrott, Rosenthal, and Zirbes were "in good condition, although days of battling with rain and mud in Wyoming, following the scorching heat of Nebraska, had left their imprint on both

faces and uniforms."[78] During the entire trip, said the *Chronicle*, "the Stars and Stripes, which had been nailed to a hickory stick and fastened to the tonneau just before leaving New York, floated to the breeze as an official emblem that the automobile was engaged in serious business and was wheeling its way upon an official errand." So attired, the war-dispatch car arrived in San Francisco with its escort at 2:00 P.M. Sunday, September 19, *Automobile* and the *Chronicle* agreed (see Fig. 6).[79]

"The mud-covered car arrived here in first-class order," the *Chronicle* told its readers, "and took its place of honor in the long parade of automobiles up Market street, out Golden Gate avenue to Jackson street, and from there to the Presidio gate." Gilson estimated that "thousands of spectators thronged the streets to see the parade to the Presidio." First, however, the car stopped "at the United States army headquarters in the *Chronicle* building," *Motor Age* said.[80] According to the *Chronicle*'s own report:

> The parade formed at the foot of Market street and contained about twenty-five machines, many of them from the Mitchell factory. In the first car were Lieutenant W. H. Homer, his chauffeur and trumpeter, J. W. Gilson, sales manager of the Mitchell Motor Car Company, from Racine, Wis., and a "Chronicle" reporter.

Fig. 6. The crowds that greeted the Mitchell Ranger, right, when it arrived in San Francisco included sailors from a U.S. Navy battleship. (Motor Age, September 30, 1909)

TABLE 2. The Mitchell Ranger's Travel Time from New York City
to Cities Along the Route

Cities	Elapsed Time
NYC – Chicago, Ill.	5d-02h-00m[a]
NYC – Cedar Rapids, Iowa	7d-07h-30m
NYC – Omaha, Neb.	9d-07h-30m
NYC – Rawlins, Wyo.	20d-05h-30m
NYC – Reno, Nev.	28d-05h-00m[a]
NYC – San Francisco	31d-05h-00m

[a] Times are based on the most favorable of conflicting arrival or departure times.

Following them came the Army car with Lieutenant Rosenthal and his party and next in line was a car containing Joseph E. G. Ryan of the editorial staff of the *Chicago Inter Ocean* and a party of automobile officials. Following them was the machine carrying the detail from the California Coast Artillery and succeeding them was a number of motor vehicles occupied by civilians.[81]

According to the *San Francisco Call*, Ryan, "dean of the automobile writers in the United States," had traveled with Gilson from Chicago to San Francisco, acting as the Mitchell company's publicity agent.[82]

Adjusting for the time difference between coasts, the Mitchell Ranger's elapsed time for the crossing was exactly 31 days, 5 hours, more than twice as long as the fastest crossing—15 days, 2 hours, 12 minutes—set in 1906. But then the Army had said from the beginning that it was not after a speed record (see Table 2). The Mitchell's running time is difficult to gauge, given the lack of information on the car's daily movements. Press reports also offered little specific information about what sort of mechanical breakdowns the Mitchell may have encountered, apart from the *Examiner*'s rather general statement that "outside of the adjustment of the carburetor to meet the requirements of the various temperatures in the mountainous country very little attention was required by the car."[83] Nor do press accounts mention the car's gas mileage.

Exactly how far the Ranger roamed will be forever in dispute, as was typical of the early transcontinental trips. In stories reporting the trip's finish, the *Nevada State Journal*, *Racine Daily Journal*, and four San Francisco newspapers quoted an unrealistically low mileage of 3,524. Between New York City and Chicago alone—normally a 1,000-mile trip—the Ranger had, for example, traveled 1,600 miles because of various detours, according to a Chicago newspaper. It was most likely the Mitchell company that, even before the car left New York, circulated the widely quoted figure of 3,693 miles. But as *Automobile* noted in reporting the figure, the distance was "probably much more," for these were map miles.[84]

Unfortunately, although it is obviously understated, this is the best figure available. To cover 3,693 miles in just over 31 days, the Ranger would have averaged 4.93 mph and 118 miles per day. Assuming that the crew generally followed its plan to travel 12 hours daily from August 19 to September 19, the car thereby averaged 9.86 mph during its estimated running time of 375 hours.

OFF TO THE RACES

After traveling perhaps 4,000 miles or more in 31 days, across parts of twelve states, through mud, rain, and snow, in the first automobile to carry an official U.S. Army dispatch from New York to San Francisco, the dispatch bearers encountered one final problem. An article that appeared in the *Chronicle* the day after their arrival revealed that "General Weston has been ill for some time and confined to his room at the Presidio Hospital. He was not well enough yesterday to brave the cool winds that blew over the Presidio hills, so the dispatch was delivered to Lieutenant Homer, who transmitted it to Colonel F. H. Crowder, Judge Advocate-General, U.S.A. [U.S. Army], who in turn handed it to Captain M. H. Barnum, aid[e]-de-camp to General Weston, who will make personal delivery of it to the commanding officer." According to the post-run Mitchell booklet, a "Post Adjutant General Wheeler" was also involved in conveying the "sealed packet of dispatches" to Weston (see Fig. 7).[85]

That the car carried one or more messages from Wood to Weston was common knowledge. By accident or design, however, the nature of the message remained a secret. Said the *San Francisco Chronicle*: "The contents of the message are not known, but [it] at least contains some word of greeting from General Wood and allusions to the recent Red and Blue Army maneuvers, of which General Wood was in command."[86] Historians at the Presidio searched for but could find no record of this communiqué,[87] which is perhaps still being passed from hand to hand on its way to General Weston. On November 13, 1909, less than two months after the Ranger's arrival, Weston retired from the military on his 64th birthday.[88]

Fig. 7. Soldiers stand at attention as Parrott, right, passes the military dispatch to an unidentified officer—perhaps Lieutenant W. H. Homer. Zirbes is at the wheel of the Mitchell, and Rosenthal is in the car's back seat. (Motor Age, September 30, 1909)

After delivering its message, the coast-to-coast Mitchell was immediately to be "taken to a race track and given a five-mile run against time without even being touched," one report indicated. According to Gilson, at the invitation of Sonoma County Automobile Club officials, the speed test occurred at Santa Rosa. As he explained it:

> Inasmuch as the machine was mechanically perfect after its strenuous run, the Mitchell people readily gave their consent to have the car featured in a time event. It was . . . driven to the track, and in the presence of a throng of enthusiasts circled the track in a five-mile sprint at almost a mile-a-minute clip. The original Hartford tires that were part of the equipment of the Ranger upon leaving New York were still on the wheels when the exhibition five-mile event was given.[89]

Press accounts unfortunately say nothing about the fate of the car. As for its occupants, Rosenthal planned to leave for home on the Overland Limited passenger train on September 20, the day after the trip ended, while Zirbes and Parrott would stay on in San Francisco for "several days," the *Chronicle* reported.

AUTOS BECOMING A "BIG FACTOR IN WARFARE"

Mechanically, the Mitchell Ranger was undoubtedly less perfect after its long run than Gilson let on. Whether or not the car actually broke its frame in Wyoming, as the *Sacra-*

mento Union asserted, is open to some speculation, if only because the *Union* was the sole newspaper to report such an incident. Regardless, the car evidently proved its worth by speeding around a track at nearly 60 mph after the hard coast-to-coast crossing. The Wisconsin automaker got its name and a photo of its car in many automobile journals and countless newspapers from New York to California. From the perspective of the Mitchell company and its parts suppliers, the trek was therefore very successful indeed (see Figs. 8 and 9).

The press had nothing but praise for the results. The Mitchell's transcontinental journey showed that "automobiles can be utilized successfully in wartime were railroads and other lines of communication to be cut off," declared the *San Francisco Call*, while *Automobile Topics* called the trip "a remarkable demonstration of the capabilities of the automobile for dispatch carrying purposes." In the opinion of the *San Francisco Examiner*: "The success of the trip is expected to have a salutary effect in support of the arguments that will be made before Congress for an appropriation of half a million dollars for automobile equipment for the Signal Corps."[90]

Fig. 8. The Mitchell Ranger made headlines everywhere it stopped.

Gilson, the Mitchell official who had organized the trip, "was well pleased with the performance," *Motor Age* reported, "and army officials who had followed the progress of the car with the greatest interest expressed the belief that such cars undoubtedly would be a big factor in warfare."[91] *Motor World* expounded on usefulness of the automobile:

> Every time a motor car is pressed into such mock-serious service in the way of carrying a missive from one official in the employ of the government to another of similar rank and station, the incident serves to call the attention of such officials directly to the ready response which might be expected of the motor vehicle under any circumstances of real need; it establishes a precedent, so to speak.
>
> This particular trip was the longest ever made on such a quest, and while in point of speed, it could lay claims to no rivalry with the more standard means of rapid communication, its illustration of the possibilities of motor courier service, likely will not be lost sight of by those to whom such service at another time might be a consideration of vital importance.[92]

From Ocean to Ocean

The Military Mitchell car which left New York, Aug. 19 bearing despatch from Gen. Wood to General Weston, of California, arrived in San Francisco, Sept. 19. This car was equipped with a

SPLITDORF MAGNETO

which gave perfect ignition the entire trip—another of the many strenuous demonstrations which prove beyond doubt the Efficiency and Reliability of SPLITDORF Ignition. You should have the same on your car.

Ask for Magneto catalog.

C. F. SPLITDORF WALTON AVENUE AND 138TH STREET BRANCH, 1679 BROADWAY **New York**

Fig. 9. Makers of the Splitdorf magneto capitalized on the Mitchell's high-profile publicity stunt. (Motor Age, October 7, 1909/NAM)

"Considering the inexperience of the driver and crew in this sort of work, the time made for the long trip from coast to coast was very good," *Automobile* allowed. The *Racine Daily Journal*, addressing the military implications of the trip, concluded that "the automobile has shown its adaptability to carry dispatches across prairie, desert and mountain under any and all conditions."[93]

Even though the military did not immediately embrace the automobile following the Mitchell's demonstration, motor vehicles continued to make inroads as an implement of war, replacing horses and mules. But Wood's vision of a fully motorized Army was evidently still unrealized as late as 1915, when he pushed for establishing a citizens' motor corps in times of war. His plan was to create training camps "to which millions of motorists would go with their vehicles and receive instruction from regular army officers," as one newspaper account explained it.[94] The following year, Wood actively supported another coast-to-coast, automobile-borne dispatch mission involving a Marmon that set a transcontinental speed record (see Chapter 7).

The primary driver on the Mitchell Ranger trek, Frank X. Zirbes, was in the spotlight again from February 23 to April 5, 1910, when he drove a Mitchell on a mapping trip over the 2,850-mile route of the upcoming Glidden Tour, the American Automobile Association's annual reliability contest. It was a publicity stunt, made before the official pathfinding auto, a Chalmers 30, set out to trace the same route through thirteen states in the South and Midwest. When Zirbes finished his tour in Chicago, S. M. Butler, chairman of the AAA Contest Board, asked if he would turn over his notes to the official pathfinder, Dai Lewis, and his crew. Zirbes "has made a detailed log of the trip, which Chairman Butler thinks will be of assistance to the official pathfinders," the *New York Times* reported, adding that he had collected "a mass of valuable data concerning inundations, ferries, bridges, blind roads, levee highways, corduroy roads," and the like. Photos suggest that Zirbes made his 1910 trek in a 6-cylinder Model S Mitchell, a bigger, longer car than the Mitchell Model T that he drove across the country in 1909.[95]

While Zirbes was still plying the Glidden route, William Mitchell Lewis, who had recently replaced his father as president of the Mitchell company, decided to give Zirbes "an extended European vacation as a reward for services."[96] His vacation—which consisted of driving Lewis through France, Great Britain, Italy, and Switzerland—nearly killed him. Lewis, his wife, and their two children, along with Joseph E. G. Ryan and René Petard, the automaker's Paris representative, were descending the Alps in a Mitchell auto. As Lewis related it:

> While [we were] creeping around the turns and practically hanging over the edges of terrible precipices . . . a runaway automobile [bore] down upon us, threatening to overtake us at "Death Curve," the fifth turn in the descent of 1,200 feet.
> Zirbes had to think quickly. He pressed on the accelerator, and the big car responded instantly. It was a case of putting on the brakes every moment as we struck the curves. Petard got out on the footboard to help Zirbes, and, seeing the only clay bank we had encountered, gave the driver the order to ditch our car.
> He obeyed, and the runaway limousine dashed past us, to be wrecked fifty yards beyond. Our glass windshield was dashed into bits, but Zirbes was not injured. Our mecanicien was hurled fully twenty feet, but landed on his feet. I crouched in the tonneau and escaped injury. As for Petard, he was hurled a considerable distance, landing on his head.[97]

It seems doubtful that Zirbes was ever persuaded to accept another invitation to join his employers on vacation, but the Mitchell company continued to make automobiles in Racine from 1903 to 1923. Annual production approached 10,000 autos in 1919 but slipped to one-quarter that number during the early 1920s, partly as a result of some unpopular styling changes. Finally, in June 1923, the company filed for bankruptcy.[98]

The first motorist laboriously crossed America for the simple purpose of proving that it could be done. Dr. H. Nelson Jackson's 1903 journey and a variety of other stunts in the following years firmly established the utility of the automobile—a possibility that the U.S. Army had appreciated and experimented with since 1899. Thus it was a decade after its first automotive experiments that the Army took part in the dispatch-bearing Mitchell's 1909 coast-to-coast trip. The journey clearly proved that, even on poor roads and despite sometimes-bad weather, the automobile could replace railroads, the telegraph, and other means of communication in delivering wartime messages—and, by extension, supplies and troops.

In 1919, a decade after the Mitchell crossing, a U.S. Army convoy that included future President Dwight D. Eisenhower, the father of the U.S. Interstate Highway System, crossed the continent. Transportation historians today celebrate the 1919 convoy as something of a breakthrough—an impetus for the development of modern highways and a demonstration of the military value of good roads and reliable motor vehicles.

But the Army had learned these lessons many years earlier, not only from the Mitchell's 1909 trek but also from a host of other transcontinental tests involving cars and trucks, with and without active Army participation. The 1919 Army convoy was important, and generated so much more publicity than did the 1909 Mitchell run, because the postwar America of 1919 was ready, willing, and able to build roads. Wartime demands had badly strained America's railroads, which emphasized the national need for a reliable alternative to rail travel. In addition, there were more cars on the roads than ever before, and Congress had in 1916 voted to allocate federal funds for highway development.

The convoy also reinforced a lesson taught on the muddy battlefields of Europe during World War I: the motor truck was a vital weapon in modern warfare. For all these reasons, the 1919 Army convoy receives nearly unanimous credit for teaching the Army—and Americans in general—lessons that were initially taught before and during the Mitchell's 1909 coast-to-coast trip. Unfortunately, in 1909 relatively few people were ready to listen.

One problem was that even by 1909 standards a 31-day crossing was slow—too slow, at least, for the delivery of a vital military dispatch. Until automobiles could match the speed of locomotives over long distances, motor cars would appear merely as a better-than-nothing substitute for the railroad. In 1910, however, five men in a Reo would narrow the disparity between rail cars and motor cars in the first serious attempt to break the 15-day coast-to-coast speed record that had been set in 1906.

"BEAT IT WHILE THE GOING IS GOOD"

2

I got a bit too ambitious and nearly turned the car over on a sharp slippery curve.
To avoid this danger, I gave her a wide swing which slammed her broadside into a
three-foot ditch.

—Lester L. Whitman, describing a crash
that damaged the rear axle and a wheel

IN THE LATE SUMMER of 1910, Lester L. Whitman and Eugene I. Hammond, who in 1903 had traveled together in the third car to cross the country, teamed up again in hopes of breaking the transcontinental record driving a 4-cylinder Reo automobile. Whitman, the acknowledged dean of transcontinental drivers, knew the route like no one else, with crossings in 1903, 1904, and 1906 to his credit. During his 1906 trip in an air-cooled Franklin, fast running—up to 60 mph down narrow dirt highways—had contributed to two collisions and an arrest for speeding. Older and wiser, Whitman brought a new philosophy to his fourth transcontinental run: slow and steady wins the race. Accordingly, he vowed to break the record without exceeding 35 mph.

Three other drivers joined the men for a nearly nonstop 3,557-mile relay run from New York City to San Francisco. To garner even more publicity, they continued their journey south to Los Angeles. Off-duty drivers took catnaps while riding ahead on the train. The Reo bent an axle and broke a wheel when Whitman slid off a muddy Indiana road at night. The accident necessitated five subsequent repair stops that delayed the racers by 16 hours, making it by far the most serious mishap of the trip. The drivers also struggled through a Nebraska thunderstorm, bounced into 10- and 15-foot-deep washouts in Wyoming and Nevada, and crossed the Sierra Nevada on the steepest grades of the trip. When the dust settled, they had driven from New York to San Francisco in a record 10 days, 18 hours, 12 minutes, cutting more than four days from the existing record.

"We jumped right in and drove like the devil straight west across the middle of the United States until we smelled salt air and found ourselves in the streets of San Francisco," was Whitman's terse explanation for how they had accomplished it. "We went out to drive her night and day and made arrangements accordingly."[1] Preparing for the trip was actually a much more complex operation than his remark suggests. Whitman had planned the route meticulously and timed it carefully to coordinate with railroad schedules.

In 1903, Whitman and Hammond, who were at the time working for a Los Angeles Oldsmobile dealer, drove the third car to cross the continent, a curved-dash Olds that traveled from San Francisco to New York in 72 days, 21 hours, 30 minutes. In two later runs, Whitman and Clayton S. Carris drove Franklin autos across the country in 32 days, 17 hours, 20 minutes, in 1904 and in 15 days, 2 hours, 12 minutes, in 1906. Their 1906 time was still the record in 1910, and "none of the manufacturers appeared to have any ambition to make an effort to cut it down," the *San Francisco Chronicle* wryly observed.[2]

Accompanying Hammond and Whitman was Dave Fassett of Grand Rapids, Michigan, who with Percy Megargel made a double transcontinental drive in 1905–6. Joining them as well were C. E. "John" Griffith of Lansing, Michigan, and Percy J. Haycock of New York, whom the *New York Times* called "mechanicians," while Whitman called them "companions and assistants." In addition, "G. J. Thomas, a mechanical expert from the Reo factory, inspected the car at various points along the line in an unsuccessful effort to find any material trouble," *Motor Age* reported.[3]

CAR CARRIES OVERSIZE GAS TANK

Ransom E. Olds, who had left Oldsmobile to build a car bearing his initials, supplied Hammond and Whitman with a slightly modified 4-cylinder Reo Thirty, a 1911 touring car that sold for $1,250. R. E. Olds and his general sales agent, R. M. Owen & Company, of Lansing, sponsored the trip "to bolster sagging Reo sales that year," according to one retrospective article. Another article, published in *Automobile Quarterly*, indicates that while sales had declined "by just a few units" in 1910, they fell "by many hundreds" in 1911, to 5,278.[4]

Fig. 10. Cover of the post-run booklet that Whitman wrote for the Reo company's publicity efforts. (AACA)

One of the automaker's 1911 models was the "Reo Thirty," although many newspapers called it the "4-30," referring to its 4-cylinder engine and what the automaker claimed was a 30-horsepower rating. In fact, according to the formula used by the Association of Licensed Automobile Manufacturers, the engine produced 25.6 horsepower. Cast in pairs, the cylinders had a bore and stroke of 4 x 4½ inches. The Reo Thirty was available as a Model R or S; they shared a 108-inch wheelbase, but the 2,350-pound Model R outweighed the Model S by 50 pounds. Both had tires measuring 34 x 3½ inches; Whitman's car used Michelin tires. The only account to so identify the 1911 transcontinental Reo called it a Model R. Contrary to the usual practice, the 1911 Reos used left-side steering wheels.[5]

The transcontinental car was in showroom trim except "in place of the tonneau, a thirty-gallon gasoline-tank was mounted on the rear. On the baggage-rack we bolted a five-gallon water-tank for the deserts, and a five-gallon tank for cylinder-oil," Whitman wrote in *Coast to Coast in a Reo*, a 22-page publicity booklet published by R. M. Owen & Company (see Fig. 10).[6] Despite the missing seat, the Reo could still carry passengers in the back: photos show riders sitting on cushions in front of the gas tank and using the tank as a backrest.

The car had at least one ax and shovel—and the men used

both to dig out the stuck auto on several occasions. According to Whitman, the travelers also carried assorted other gear:

> In the body of the car we packed tools, extra parts, inner tubes, mud-hooks, camera, lunch-box and extra clothing. The "extra clothing" consisted of some old leather coats, linen dusters and fisherman's oilskins with "sou'wester" hats for rainy weather. We also had a large rubber boot that would button over the dash and cover us nicely in case of rain. We found this very comfortable to keep out the cold winds at night.
>
> Two leather pockets were fastened on the dash; one contained a compass and maps, the other held several pairs of goggles. In plain sight of the driver was nailed a card saying, "Beat it while the going is good." Besides the regular headlights a swinging searchlight was fastened in reach of the operator.[7]

A SECRET START?

At 12:01 A.M., Monday, August 8, 1910, the president of *Horseless Age* magazine, Fred J. Wagner, gave the signal for the car to start its long journey from New York City. Surviving photos of the start show the car parked beside the New York branch of R. M. Owen & Company, whose showrooms displayed Reo and Premier automobiles (see Fig. 11). Whitman and Hammond posed in the car for photographers, but according to Whitman's account the two men never drove together during the trek to San Francisco. Whitman indicates that he and Haycock drove the first leg to Utica, New York (see Table 3). According to the *New York Tribune* reporter who observed the start:

> They left the New York branch of R. M. Owen & Co., at No. 1759 Broadway, very early Monday morning—at exactly 12:01 in fact—and were reported at Albany at 6:40, after an uneventful run up the [Hudson] river over good roads. They arrived at Utica five hours ahead of their fast schedule.
>
> The "water level" route was then taken through the Mohawk Valley and so west. . . . The present record tryout will be a night and day continuous run, Whitman and Hammond alternating at the wheel. The only stops to be made between New York and San Francisco are to be for taking on gasolene and oil.[8]

"Prior to the start Whitman maintained great secrecy as to the time he would leave New York," *Motor Age* claimed, "but once he left the great eastern metropolis his race against time was bulletined on the windows of every Reo agency in the country. Whitman, however, did not suffer from this, for all the way across the continent he was not molested by the police."[9] On the 1910 Reo trek and other well-publicized coast-to-

Fig. 11. Whitman at
the wheel, flanked by
Hammond, outside the
New York City Reo
agency. Other crew-
men or guides could
ride on the cushion
behind the front seat.
(FLP)

coast journeys made prior to World War I, police officers often permitted drivers to
bend local speed ordinances. Many drivers were nonetheless careful to avoid speeding
on congested roads, fearing that any show of recklessness would undermine their efforts to generate positive publicity for their automobile and its manufacturer.

Similarly, automakers who sponsored transcontinental trips in hopes of setting a
record were careful to conduct these trips in an open, above-board manner—this to
avoid the charges of fraud that followed the nation's first successful coast-to-coast auto
trip, made by Dr. H. Nelson Jackson and Sewall K. Crocker in 1903. Jackson unwit-
tingly invited such charges by refusing to meet with reporters during the first half of
his trip from San Francisco to New York City. Therefore, even seven years later, in

TABLE 3. Drivers on Various Portions of the Reo Trip

Relay	Drivers[a]
New York City–Utica, N.Y.	Whitman–Haycock
Utica–Buffalo, N.Y.	Hammond–Fassett
Buffalo–Cleveland, Ohio	Whitman–Griffith
Cleveland–South Bend, Ind.	Hammond–Haycock[b]
South Bend–Cedar Rapids, Iowa	Whitman–Fassett
Cedar Rapids–Council Bluffs, Iowa	Hammond–Griffith
Council Bluffs–North Platte, Neb.	Whitman–Haycock[b]
North Platte–Laramie, Wyo.	Hammond–Fassett[b]
Laramie–Green River, Wyo.	Whitman–Griffith
Green River–Ogden, Utah	Hammond–Haycock
Ogden–Montello, Nev.	Whitman–Fassett
Montello–Battle Mountain, Nev.	Hammond–Griffith
Battle Mountain–Reno, Nev.	Whitman–Haycock
Reno–Sacramento, Calif.	Hammond–Fassett
Sacramento–San Francisco	Whitman–Griffith

SOURCE: Lester L. Whitman, *Coast to Coast in a Reo: 10 Days, 15 Hours, 13 Minutes.*

[a] The drivers' full names are Dave Fassett, C. E. Griffith, E. I. Hammond, P. J. Haycock, and Lester L. Whitman.

[b] Whitman fails to name the second driver on this leg of the trip, but the pattern was to switch from Haycock to Fassett to Griffith.

1910, the Reo company's general sales agent bristled at the post-run suggestion that the Reo trip was conducted secretively:

> This severe test was made absolutely openly. The starting time (August 8, 12:01 A.M.) was announced in the newspapers ahead of time, so that everybody could see it. The number 69862 was stamped upon the dash, so that the car could be identified all along the line, and at every important point the arrival of the Reo Number 69862 was checked and affidavits made of its arrival and departure under its own power by disinterested men well known in the community. The newspapers were kept informed of the Reo's progress until the finish at San Francisco, on Thursday, August 18.[10]

A Reo ad in the October 1910 *American Magazine* clears up the confusion surrounding the question of secrecy, however, when it says that officials "announced the start in the newspapers on Sunday, August 7, one day ahead."[11]

NO "PHONEY TALK"

As would be the case throughout most of the Reo's trip, the first leg, from New York City to Utica, went reasonably smoothly. "At Yonkers, twenty miles out, a spark-plug blew out and we had to renew it," Whitman said. "This was the first and only occasion during the entire trip of 3557 miles when we had to touch the engine with a wrench. The only other thing we had to do was to put in oil and water, and mighty little water at that. I don't believe the engine used over two gallons in the whole run." But Haycock and Whitman did have to contend with one other mishap en route to Utica, when "before daylight, up by Poughkeepsie, the car ran over a skunk," Whitman recalled. "We had to hold our noses for some time afterwards."[12]

Besides stopping for gas and oil, or perhaps a quick meal, the men also checked in with local officials. "We had records made of the arrival and departure of the car every one to two hundred miles by well-known persons in those communities and affidavits made before notaries or justices-of-the-peace," Whitman wrote. "I don't want to hear any 'phoney talk' about 'shipping the car.'" As Whitman told the *San Francisco Chronicle*, the official check-in points were at Utica and Buffalo, New York; Cleveland; South Bend, Indiana; Cedar Rapids and Council Bluffs, Iowa; North Platte, Nebraska; Laramie and Green River, Wyoming; Ogden, Utah; Montello, Battle Mountain, and Reno, Nevada; and Sacramento and San Francisco, California. "That there might be no question whatever of the authenticity of the record, we checked in unofficially at dozens of other places," he added.[13]

According to the *Los Angeles Times*, the Reo carried a time card that was punched by officials along the route. Whitman declared that he "did not travel more than 100 miles without checking in before a notary, as I had heard that someone was following up to check on my journey, and to see . . . that I did not ship [the car by train], as had been claimed for some continental record breakers." After the 1910 trip, Reo officials told the automobile journals that "sworn affidavits of these checkers may be seen at the executive office of R. M. Owen & Co., 1759 Broadway, New York."[14]

Whitman was perhaps alluding to some rumors that had circulated after Dr. H. Nelson Jackson, an amateur autoist piloting a secondhand Winton, became the first person to drive across the country. Specifically, the Packard Motor Car Company had suggested that Jackson either used two automobiles on his 1903 journey or shipped his car by rail to avoid the worst roads. The Packard factory was vitally interested in discrediting Jackson in order to lay claim to the first crossing themselves. As it stood, a Packard

TABLE 4. The Reo's Route from New
York City to San Francisco and Los
Angeles, 1910

New York City start:
  12:01 A.M., Thursday, August 8, 1910

New York	Nebraska
Yonkers	Columbus
Poughkeepsie	Grand Island
Albany	Kearney
Schenectady	North Platte
Amsterdam	Ogallala
Utica	Sidney
Syracuse	*Colorado*
Geneva	Julesburg[a]
Buffalo	*Wyoming*
Pennsylvania	Cheyenne
Erie	Laramie
Ohio	Medicine Bow
Cleveland	Fort Steele
Fremont	Rawlins
Fostoria	Green River
Bryan	Cumberland
Indiana	Evanston
Kendallville	*Utah*
Ligonier	Ogden
Goshen	*Nevada*
South Bend	Tecoma
Valparaiso	Montello
Illinois	Battle Mountain
Joliet	Golconda
Aurora	Sparks
Geneva	Reno
Iowa	*California*
Clinton	Truckee
Cedar Rapids	Sacramento
Marshalltown	Benicia
Council Bluffs	Pinole
	Oakland

San Francisco finish:
  3:13 P.M., Thursday, August 18, 1910

Los Angeles finish:
  6:40 P.M., Saturday, August 20, 1910

SOURCES: Lester L. Whitman, *Coast to Coast in a Reo:
10 Days, 15 Hours, 13 Minutes*; newspapers and auto
journals.

[a] Although he doesn't mention Julesburg, Colorado,
in *Coast to Coast in a Reo*, Whitman passed through
the city in 1910. Moreover, he claims he traversed
twelve states in 1910, but without Colorado the total
is only eleven.

touring car had become the second automobile to cross the country, reaching New York City on August 21, 1903, just 26 days behind Jackson. The Winton Motor Carriage Company responded
to Packard's suggestions of impropriety by offering a $25,000 re-
ward "to anyone proving that at any time on his journey across
the continent conditions of transportation were other than represented by Dr. Jackson." This challenge quelled the rumors.[15]

In agreeing to travel from east to west, Whitman relin-
quished his personal preference, which was to travel from California to New York. As he explained in a 1906 interview, "the
ascent of the mountains is easier coming that way."[16] Drawing
upon his experience and seeking every advantage, Whitman
plotted the most direct route possible between the coastal cities
(see Table 4). He had traveled 4,225 miles in 1903; 4,500 in 1904,
which included detours to Denver and Detroit; and about 4,150
in 1906. The 3,557-mile route he plotted for his 1910 trek therefore cut 600 miles from his shortest trip to date and nearly 1,000
miles from his longest. The savings came in part from bypassing some large cities—including Toledo, Ohio, and Chicago—
where he had stopped during earlier runs.

On his fourth and final record-setting transcontinental trip,
in 1910, Whitman largely followed the route of the future Lincoln Highway from Indiana through Wyoming. On all four of
his trips, Whitman took nearly identical routes through northern New York state. With the exception of 1903, when he traveled through Canada between Detroit and Buffalo, Whitman's
four runs also followed similar routes in five states: Pennsylvania, Nebraska (where floods forced a detour in 1903), Wyoming
(aside from a detour to Denver, also in 1903), Utah, and Nevada.
On his 1910 trip, however, he traveled farther south of Lake
Erie in Ohio, thereby avoiding Toledo, and shifted his route
slightly through parts of Indiana, Illinois, and Iowa to pass south
of Chicago and north of Des Moines. Whitman speaks of traveling through twelve states. Although he does not say so directly,
the Reo evidently followed the established route across western

Nebraska by dipping south a few miles to pass through Julesburg, Colorado, as Whitman had also done during his 1906 trip. Colorado was thus the twelfth state.

The Reo drivers either took aboard a pilot—a guide familiar with the local roads—or followed a pilot car most, if not all, the time. According to the *Coast to Coast in a Reo* booklet, as well as scattered newspaper references to guides, the drivers employed pilots in at least eight of the twelve states, including all the eastern states.

"WE NEVER ATTEMPTED TO GO FASTER"

Whitman's strategy? He set an 11-day schedule and the drivers never fell behind it. "At one time we were twelve hours ahead of it . . . and finished nine hours ahead," Whitman said, somewhat inaccurately. Adjusted for the time changes en route, the figures in Table 5 show that the car was actually fourteen hours ahead of schedule at Council Bluffs but arrived in San Francisco only six hours early. Indeed, the Reo ran four to seven hours ahead for roughly three-quarters of the trip. In Whitman's opinion, the relatively consistent figures suggest "a steady, reliable performance—and not a victory won by spurts and dashes, followed by hours of repairs and replacing." The schedule called for continuous yet "conservative driving," as Whitman termed it. "We set a consistent pace of from 25 to 35 miles an hour, and we never attempted to go faster. . . . We might have beaten it often, but a little fast driving might have invited disaster and spoiled the whole thing." At night, the car averaged just 15 to 25 mph, "as we never took chances in the dark."[17]

Whitman's caution is understandable, given that speed nearly spoiled the record twice during his 1906 transcontinental trip in a Franklin, although he was not in the car at either time. In a rush, one of the Franklin drivers hit a farm wagon in Iowa, for which the crew was arrested and detained eight hours. Speed evidently contributed as well to a nighttime crash near Conneaut, Ohio, which idled the car 36 hours for repairs. In addition to those two incidents, police in Buffalo, New York, later held the crew for 1½ hours on a speeding charge.

In comparison to four years earlier, as Whitman undoubtedly realized, local police were more likely to be equipped with autos for chasing speeders in 1910. The Reo Motor Car Company may well have imposed the 35 mph speed limit to avoid some of the bad publicity that accrued to the Franklin company during Whitman's 1906 run: his Franklin at times "made a speed of sixty miles an hour," according to a newspaper in

TABLE 5. The Transcontinental Reo's Times at Relay Points, 1910[a]

Relay Point	Approx. Local Arrival time[b]	Scheduled Hours	Actual Hours	Hours Gained	Total Hours
Utica, N.Y.	8/8 noon	16	12	4	12
Buffalo, N.Y.	8/9 1 A.M.	16	13	7	25
Cleveland, Ohio	8/9 8 A.M.	10	7	10	32
(change to Central Time)					
South Bend, Ind.	8/9 9 P.M.	15	14	11	46
Cedar Rapids, Iowa	8/10 4 P.M.	20	19	12	65
Council Bluffs, Iowa	8/11 8 A.M.	18	16	14	81
North Platte, Neb.	8/12 noon	20	28	6	109
(change to Mountain Time)					
Laramie, Wyo.	8/13 6 A.M.	19	19	6	128
Green River, Wyo.	8/14 5 A.M.	22	23	5	151
Ogden, Utah	8/14 8 P.M.	16	15	6	166
(change to Pacific Time)					
Montello, Nev.	8/15 noon	18	17	7	183
Battle Mountain, Nev.	8/16 3 P.M.	25	27	5	210
Reno, Nev.	8/17 5 P.M.	25	26	4	236
Sacramento, Calif.	8/18 7 A.M.	14	14	4	250
San Francisco	8/18 3 P.M.	10	8	6	258
Complete trip		264 (11 days)	258	6	258

SOURCE: "The Reo Record in Detail," table in *Coast to Coast in a Reo*, p. 21.

[a] The original scheduled time adds up to 264 hours, or exactly 11 days—the time Whitman was racing to beat. In this table, three hours have been added to the actual and total times, and three hours subtracted from the "hours gained." This corrects for time changes on the east-to-west run, something R. M. Owen & Company failed to do in the timetable it published in *Coast to Coast in a Reo*.

[b] Local arrival times are based on the actual travel time between relay points as given in the timetable in *Coast to Coast in a Reo*, p. 21; these times frequently conflicted with the times Whitman mentioned in the text of the booklet. Local newspapers often reported slightly different arrival times as well.

Marshalltown, Iowa. "On the trip from Carroll they killed no less than twenty chickens, mortally wounded a pig and had some narrow escapes," the newspaper reported in an article titled "Auto Hits Farmer." Contradicting the headline, the article reveals that the Franklin struck not a farmer but a farmer's wagon.[18]

Not surprisingly, the automaker sought to keep a tight rein on the five men involved in the 1910 trek. At the finish of their trip, the *Los Angeles Times* reported on

the list of instructions issued to the . . . drivers who hurled the car across the continent in less than eleven days. These orders were explicit, to the point and decisive. The man who read them knew what was expected of him and acted accordingly. There was almost a threat [at] the end of the instructions. If the car was damaged or injured in any way the driver who was then in charge would be held personally responsible for his machine.

The man at the wheel was ordered to take no chances. He was to rush the car ahead where smooth road offered, take his time over the sandy and rocky roads, be courteous to teamsters along the way, and must always keep within the bounds of safety. The factory offered every facility possible and then left it to each man's good judgment to get the car through.[19]

ROUNDING CURVES LIKE A BULLET

Still on the first leg of their 1910 run, Whitman and Haycock encountered "splendid" roads from Albany to Utica, arriving in Utica about midday on Monday, August 8. There they turned the car over to Hammond and Fassett, who would drive through northern New York to Buffalo, which they reached 25 hours into the trip, or at roughly 1:00 A.M. Tuesday, Day 2. From Buffalo, Whitman and an unidentified co-driver again took the wheel, following a road that led across the northwestern corner of Pennsylvania to Cleveland. They reached Cleveland at 6:00 A.M., according to *Motor Age*, or at either 7:00 A.M. or 8:00 A.M., according to conflicting information in *Coast to Coast in a Reo*. Throughout the trip, Whitman and the local newspapers frequently quoted slightly different arrival and departure times for the car.

Driving from Cleveland into northwestern Ohio, Hammond and an unnamed assistant passed through Fostoria at 1:50 P.M. and, at 3:02 P.M. on Tuesday, they fell in behind a pilot car at Bryan, Ohio. These times suggest that the Reo covered the approximately seventy-five miles between Fostoria and Bryan in 72 minutes—an average speed of 62.5 mph, well above Whitman's 35 mph limit.[20] About fifteen miles west of Bryan, the two autos crossed the Indiana border. Their route would take them through

Kendallville and Ligonier to Goshen, in north-central Indiana, near South Bend. According to the *Goshen Daily Democrat*, Goshen's Reo agent had sent the pilot car to Bryan the previous evening. "Responding to a hurry-up call, Roy Noel and Shirley Larimer left here yesterday in the Noel Bros. Reo racer for Bryan, O., from where Mr. Noel will pilot the New York car to South Bend. Mr. Noel made a fast trip to Bryan, covering much of the distance at the rate of a mile a minute."[21] Because of muddy roads that forced Hammond to install his car's tire chains, Noel averaged a much slower 25 mph on his return trip while leading the transcontinental car, reaching Goshen at 6:10 P.M. on Tuesday, the *Democrat* said.

According to his *Coast to Coast in a Reo* account, Whitman had taken the train from Cleveland to South Bend, so he was not even in the car when it arrived in Goshen. The Goshen newspaper evidently attributes what must have been Hammond's remarks to "Whiteman," as it calls him:

> The trip from Bryan to Goshen[,] a distance of 78 miles, was covered in exactly three hours and eight minutes and was over rough roads much of the way. "This is my home," said Mr. Noel to Mr. Whiteman as the two automobiles stopped in front of the Noel Bros. garage for gasoline. "I thought you were on your way home," answered Mr. Whiteman, "the way you pulled out of Bryan and kept on going."
>
> A stop of 20 minutes was made in Goshen, Whiteman using a wrench, he said, for the first time since the car left New York Monday morning. . . . Whiteman declared Mr. Noel to be the most fearless as well as the most competent chauffeur that has piloted him since leaving New York. "He sent his machine around a number of curves near Ligonier like a bullet, but with perfect grace," said Mr. Whiteman. The trip from Kendallville to Ligonier was made in a terrific rain storm.
>
> The start was made from Goshen at 6:30[,] both cars stopping in front of the Otis Motor Car Co. in South Bend at 7:15 where supper was served in the garage. The schedule was lowered between Bryan and South Bend [by] one hour and 45 minutes.[22]

CRASH SPLINTERS WHEEL AND BENDS AXLE

Despite the rain, the car was 11 hours ahead of schedule in reaching South Bend, where Whitman and Fassett, rested from their train ride, climbed aboard. They would drive the Reo across northwestern Indiana and through the northern Illinois towns of Joliet, Aurora, and Geneva, to Cedar Rapids, Iowa, bypassing Chicago to avoid twenty-five miles of busy streets. "We should have liked also to cut out the mud but the only thing we could do was to put on the Weed [tire] chains and 'go to it,'" Whitman said.[23] Southeast of Chicago, near Valparaiso, Indiana, Whitman ran into trouble at 11:00 P.M. on Tuesday, as he related in the *Coast to Coast* booklet:

> I got a bit too ambitious and nearly turned the car over on a sharp slippery curve. To avoid this danger, I gave her a wide swing which slammed her broadside into a three-foot ditch, slivered half of the spokes of one rear wheel and bent the axle at the outer bearing. Cranking up, we ran the car into the road and proceeded slowly about a mile into the city, found a garage open, straightened the axle, twisted some wire around the splintered spokes, and were on the road again in about thirty minutes."[24]

The mishap actually "smashed all the spokes but two," Whitman told a reporter upon reaching Los Angeles. "I bound up the others with wire and wrenches and ran clear to Clinton, Iowa, on that wheel."[25] The incident was far from closed, however. Axle problems resulting from this accident plagued the drivers until they made permanent repairs at Ogden, Utah. They lost 13 hours making two stops for temporary repairs in Nebraska, according to newspapers there.

If the Reo resumed its journey at 11:30 P.M. on Tuesday, as Whitman's account suggests, it would have passed south of Chicago sometime after midnight—or at least 49 hours from the start of the trip, adjusting for the one-hour time difference. Two weeks after the Franklin's 1906 transcontinental trip, four crewmen (excluding Whitman) drove the car from Chicago to New York City in a record 56 hours, 58 minutes. Just one year later, another car lowered the New York–Chicago record time to 39 hours, 53 minutes. Yet, in discussing the 1910 trip during a stop in Council Bluffs, Iowa, Hammond claimed that "the time of forty-eight hours between New York and Chicago beats all records between those cities for ordinary touring cars," the *Council Bluffs Daily Nonpareil* reported. (As we just noted, however, the Reo's time to Chicago was at least 49 hours.) Similarly, Whitman later told the *San Francisco Chronicle* that "our fastest running was done between New York and Chicago," although he did not claim to have set a speed record.[26]

Whitman and Fassett passed through Joliet at 2:30 A.M. and then Geneva at 4:30 A.M., before crossing the Mississippi River into Clinton, Iowa, at noon on Wednesday, August 10, Day 3 of the expected 11-day journey. "Making the dust fly over good roads," they reached Cedar Rapids "the same time that the 'Boys' arrived by train through Chicago," Whitman wrote (see Figs. 12 and 13).[27] According to the newspaper in Council Bluffs—the town where the "Boys," Hammond and Griffith, would arrive the next morning, after an all-night drive—Whitman and Fassett reached Cedar Rapids at 3:15 P.M.. Before the Reo left Cedar Rapids, however, crewmen re-

Fig. 12. Haycock poses atop a haystack in the Midwest. (NAHC)

placed the splintered wood-spoked rear wheel that Whitman had patched up following his accident in Indiana some 17 hours earlier, Whitman said in *Coast to Coast in a Reo*, although he told a Los Angeles reporter that the car received the new wheel in Clinton.

REO "MAKING PRETTY GOOD TIME" IN MIDWEST

Hammond was at the wheel when he and Griffith reached the Missouri River at 7:00 A.M. on Thursday, August 11, ending a nearly 16-hour, 316-mile drive across Iowa, the *Council Bluffs Daily Nonpareil* reported.

> The actual distance between the New York city hall and the Atlantic Automobile company's garage in Council Bluffs is 1,575.4 miles. . . . [Hammond] and Griffith will take a train at this point, and meet the car at North Platte, Neb., this afternoon. . . . Driver Ham-

mond states that they have had no accidents and no troubles during the trip with the exception of replacing tires which have been worn out by strenuous use. . . . The car carries all the ordinary equipment and during the greater part of the journey it has carried four men and never less than three.[28]

Hammond and Griffith evidently carried a third person—a local guide—into Council Bluffs with them. They arrived 14 hours ahead of their 11-day transcontinental schedule, the greatest margin attained during the trip. To cover the distance to Council Bluffs in 79 hours, 59 minutes, the transcontinental Reo must have averaged 19.7 mph —only slightly less than the rate of approximately 20.4 mph from New York City to the Chicago vicinity.[29]

On Thursday and halfway into Friday, Whitman and an unidentified companion would travel west to North Platte, Nebraska, along the Platte River route through

Fig. 13. According to Motor Age, Whitman, right, with an unidentified Reo crewman or pilot, at times followed Iowa's smooth River-to-River Road. (NAHC)

Fig. 14. Haycock at the wheel of the coast-to-coast Reo in Nebraska, where the corn was ripening. (NAHC)

Columbus, Grand Island, and Kearney, before turning the car over to Hammond and a co-driver, who would then proceed west through Ogallala and Sidney, Nebraska, and on into Wyoming. Whitman telegraphed ahead to secure a guide, reporting his intention of leaving Council Bluffs at 8:00 A.M. and arriving in North Platte by midnight on Thursday. After crossing the Missouri River to Omaha, "all day long we dashed by more than 200 miles of waving corn and grain and on toward North Platte," he recounted (see Fig. 14).[30] Evidently mistaking Whitman's co-driver and guide for "friends," the *Columbus Telegram* offered this summary:

> From New York to Columbus in three and a half days seems like making pretty good time. L. L. Whitman, driving a Reo "4-30" touring car, left New York City . . . Monday morning and arrived in this city Thursday noon on a trans-continental run, with San Francisco as the objective point. A stop of only a few minutes was made at the Columbus Automobile garage to take on gasoline. . . . With Mr. Whitman in the car were several friends who are making the trip merely for pleasure. They reported the roads in fine condition in the east, and stated that the car had maintained an average speed of over twenty miles per hour.[31]

REPAIRS FORCE A 12-HOUR HALT

Having received the telegram Whitman sent from Council Bluffs, North Platte Reo agent J. S. Davis arranged to meet Whitman at Kearney and ride with him to Ogallala, according to a North Platte newspaper. Unbeknownst to the Grand Island newspapers, however, Whitman made an unscheduled 12-hour stop there, where Davis eventually joined him. Friday's *North Platte Evening Telegraph* related that Whitman

> arrived here about 11 o'clock this morning, twelve hours late. They had expected to arrive here not later than midnight last night. At Grand Island something went wrong with the rear axel [*sic*] and in making repairs matters were made worse. The machine limped into North Platte and was overhauled at the garage of Davis & Chorpenning, where a new axel was substituted.
>
> Mr. Davis met the party at Grand Island and returned with them to this city. Shortly after noon the tourists made a fresh start and are headed for Laramie, Wyo., where they expect to arrive at 3 o'clock tomorrow morning. . . . The trip thus far has been free from mishap except the one at Grand Island and the puncturing of one tire.[32]

According to Whitman's *Coast to Coast in a Reo* account, his schedule allowed 20 hours to cover the 300 miles between Council Bluffs and North Platte. This assumed an average speed of exactly 15 mph—considered an attainable pace despite the rough, meandering dirt roads of 1910. But in fact it took Whitman 28 hours to cover the full distance. Leaving Columbus at noon on Thursday and traveling 15 mph, he should have covered the approximately 205 miles to North Platte by 2:00 A.M. Friday, but he arrived instead at 11:00 A.M. Whitman does not explain what went wrong: he refers in his *Coast to Coast* account to making repairs at North Platte but not at Grand Island. He does imply, however, that bad weather early Friday morning slowed him down:

> At two o'clock in the night, we were hit by a terrific thunder storm but we were prepared for it with our oil skins, "sou'westers," and rubber boot. The water just emptied down, the lightning streaked in long zig-zags to the ground. At one moment everything stood out in the vivid brightness and the next was plunged into inky blackness. You can get a real thunder storm in Nebraska. At North Platte we borrowed an axle, sent ours ahead to Ogden to be thoroughly straightened out and pushed along.[33]

Tall grass growing in the center of the road in both Nebraska and Wyoming (see Fig. 15) "prevented rapid progress for many miles," the *New York Times* reported, suggesting yet another reason why Whitman may have lost time. As to the repairs made in North Platte and the ensuing journey, the *North Platte Semi-Weekly Tribune* reported that "the relay men driving the Reo car through from New York to San Francisco

made fast time west of this city. After placing a new axle and a set of wheels under the car here, they left at noon [on Friday], reached Cheyenne at one o'clock that night, and at eight Saturday morning were in Laramie."[34]

SMOOTH-RUNNING REO SLIPS INTO CHEYENNE

With Hammond and an unnamed partner in charge, the Reo continued west from North Platte on drying roads, which allowed them to remove their tire chains at Sidney, Whitman recalled in *Coast to Coast in a Reo*. From there, they "flew over good roads to Cheyenne, secured a guide and reached Laramie at seven o'clock the next morning," Saturday, August 13.[35] (The car evidently reached Laramie at 7:00 A.M. mountain time, which corresponds to the arrival time of 8:00 A.M. central time reported in the *Semi-Weekly Tribune* of North Platte.)

Hammond wasted no time in Cheyenne, according to the local *Wyoming Tribune*, whose headline revealed that the Reo "Slipped into Cheyenne and Leaves Again by

Night on What Promises to Be a Most Remarkable Automobile Run from New York to San Francisco." The newspaper erroneously reported that it was Whitman, rather than Hammond, who "reached Cheyenne Friday night and went on without a stop, and with few here knowing of his arrival. . . . Out of this city Whitman was piloted to Laramie by Earl Boyle, who rode in the Reo car with the transcontinental speeders. They left this city shortly after midnight and found the roads to Laramie very rough. The run to that city was made in four and one half hours."[36] This would have put them in Laramie at about 4:30 A.M. on Saturday, August 13, although Whitman's account states that they arrived at 7:00 A.M.

It seems likely that they reached Laramie somewhere between those times, roughly at daybreak. "As dawn's first lights were chasing one another" the *Laramie Daily Boomerang*'s reporter spotted three men in an auto streaking into town as if shot from a gun. "They were in a Reo car, which evidently they were advertising. The machine seemed none the worse for the trip so far from New York, and every indication was that it would get to Frisco working like the pendulum of a clock."[37]

Throughout the trip, Whitman chose experienced local guides and sent them telegrams detailing his progress. Guiding him out of Laramie would be Payson W. Spaulding, the lawyer from Evanston, Wyoming, who in 1908 had accompanied the Murdock family—the first family to drive across the country—from Evanston to the East Coast. Spaulding, who had arrived in Laramie Friday night, "will assist the driver in finding the way in the fast run," the *Laramie Republican* reported.[38] From Laramie, Whitman wired to the Sharman Automobile Company of Salt Lake City, informing Sam Sharman—who in 1909 had acted as pilot between Salt Lake City and Reno for Alice Ramsey, the first woman motorist to cross the country[39]—"that everything was running smoothly," according to the *Salt Lake (City) Herald-Republican*. "Mr. Sharman and party left last night [Saturday] to meet the car and accompany it to Ogden and west." Sharman traveled to Green River, Wyoming, to guide the Reo to Ogden. "Another pilot will accompany the transcontinentalists from Ogden to Sparks, Nev.," according to the *Salt Lake (City) Tribune*.[40]

"DIG WE DID"

Whitman and Griffith were assigned to drive from Laramie most of the way across southern Wyoming, through Medicine Bow, Fort Steele, and Rawlins to Green River.

The scheduled 22-hour drive took 23 hours, from about daybreak Saturday to just before daybreak Sunday, according to Whitman's *Coast to Coast* account:

> Out of Laramie we ran over a vast plain of cattle and sheep ranges. For seventy-five miles we did not pass a house or ranch. When we arrived at Medicine Bow a husky maiden was ringing the dinner bell and, record or no record, we sat down at a rough plank table and found a dinner fit for a king. It certainly fitted us—a big, heaping platter of mountain trout, corn cake, mashed brown potatoes, sweet corn on the cob, apple pie and big bumpers of rich milk.[41]

The car stopped in Rawlins for five minutes at 6:00 P.M. on Saturday, where according to the *Rawlins Republican* it received "a new supply of gasoline and oil." During the stop, Whitman recalled, "Griffith ate some of those round cast-iron doughnuts, holes and all, that you find at railroad eating-counters and they went to his head, so that he tried to drive in a circle and we lost some time." In a differing version of the tale, the *Republican* reported that "the car left Cheyenne one night and went fifteen miles out of the way, the pilot losing his road." Nonetheless, the paper claimed, the car was "still more than eleven hours ahead of its schedule and two or three days ahead of the best time heretofore made when it reached Laramie,"[42] although Whitman reported being just six hours ahead of schedule at Laramie.

In both the *Coast to Coast* booklet and newspaper interviews, Whitman described a washed-out stretch of road along southwestern Wyoming's Bitter Creek as among the

Fig. 17. The Reo crosses a muddy spot or stream at an unidentified location, possibly in Wyoming, where Whitman said the car "got stuck in some alkali mud-holes." (Motor World, August 25, 1910/NAM)

journey's most harrowing. From 1:00 A.M. until daylight on Sunday, August 14, the Reo "struck some of the worst roads on the trip" near Rock Springs (see Fig. 16). He went on to say that

> old Bitter Creek had been on the rampage the winter before and made wash-outs all over the country. The trail followed down this, and for thirty miles we found a succession of wash-outs from one to fifteen feet deep across the road. The sides were almost perpendicular. We generally had to stop the car on the brink and look down to see what the prospect was; if it looked passable, we would let the car down carefully on the brakes, and, as the rear axle came down, slip in the low speed and, throwing the throttle wide open, rush up the opposite bank.[43]

As he told the *San Francisco Chronicle* at the end of the run, "it was not so difficult to drop over the side, although we occasionally hung ourselves up by the middle [of the chassis] so that we had to dig the dirt out from under the car. The main trouble was in getting back on the road again when we struck a sheer rise of several feet. The only thing was to get out our shovel and dig. Dig we did—and here we are."[44]

Upon reaching Green River that Sunday morning, Day 7, Whitman and Griffith turned the car over to Hammond and Haycock. On their drive through Cumberland to Evanston, Whitman recalled, "they got stuck in some alkali mud-holes and used the mud-hooks [on the tires] for the first time" (see Fig. 17). The next challenge was to traverse Weber Canyon east of Ogden, where "the team road, the railroad and the Weber

River crowd together," Whitman said. "The driver wants to keep his eyes 'skinned,' for the wheels of the car often run within a foot or two of the edge of perpendicular cliffs, with the rushing river at their base hundreds of feet below."[45]

ALKALI FLATS AND OTHER FREAKS OF NATURE

Reaching Ogden on Sunday at 9:15 p.m., the car went immediately to L. H. Becraft's garage, where "we put back our original axle, which had been sent ahead and straightened out," Whitman recalled.[46] The repairs took two hours, agreed the *Ogden Daily Standard* and the *Tribune* and *Evening Telegram* of Salt Lake City. According to Monday's *Daily Standard*:

> The record-eclipsing Reo car which is attempting to make the run from New York to San Francisco in ten [*sic*] days stopped in Ogden for two hours last evening for the purpose of having the working parts of the machine overhauled at the Becraft garage.
>
> The car was in excellent condition notwithstanding the excessive strain to which it has been subjected during the wonderful flight across 2,700 miles of variable roads between Ogden and the Atlantic coast.
>
> This is the most spectacular run as regards continuous travel ever attempted in the United States and the fact that only six and a half days have elapsed since the start from New York was made is evidence of the terrific speed which has been made night and day to this point.[47]

The next three relays into Reno, Nevada, represented "some six hundred miles of the worst part of our journey," said Whitman. Late Sunday night, he and Fassett resumed the westward journey from Ogden, bound for Montello, Nevada. They drove on into Monday, August 15, Day 8. The area "is totally uninhabited and is one vast desert of sagebrush, sand, and alkali flats, with a sprinkling of barren hills. The only oases are the [Southern Pacific] railway stations and we drove from one to the other like a mariner who guides his ship from one friendly port to another," Whitman wrote. "Here the road is simply a case of 'Take it or leave it and drive where you please,' and we often were 'pleased' to drive somewhere else to avoid the high centres, rocks and sagebrush [clumps] that made the road absolutely impossible; in fact, we often got hung up by our axles and had to dig ourselves out with an axe and shovel."[48]

After reaching Montello at about midday Monday, Fassett and Whitman climbed aboard the train to Battle Mountain, Nevada, while Hammond and Griffith set out in the Reo for an all-night drive. The drivers arrived late to Battle Mountain, pulling into

Fig. 18. Less than two days away from San Francisco, Haycock and the Reo reach the railroad depot at Golconda, Nevada, on August 16, 1910. (DBG)

town on Tuesday, August 16, Day 9, at about 3:30 P.M., according to *Motor Age*. Although it took them 27 hours to make the scheduled 25-hour drive, they still brought the car into north-central Nevada at a pace five hours ahead of Whitman's 11-day transcontinental schedule. Hammond "reported that he had met the worst roads he had ever seen or heard of"—the result of a cloudburst months earlier, according to Whitman. "Sand, rocks, and boulders filled the roads for miles and, in some places, the road was washed out ten feet deep. Through this somehow they forced the car, finding their way with a lantern and rolling boulders aside."[49]

Haycock and Whitman drove on overnight from Battle Mountain into Day 10, Wednesday, August 17. "Anyone who hasn't motored all night at an altitude of 6000 to 9000 feet doesn't know how intense the cold becomes," Whitman later exclaimed. "The cold just gets to the marrow in your bones and your blood seems to clog. The brilliant starlight gives you a horizon that seems only a few hundred feet away. Beyond that is clouds and you feel as if you were riding off the rim of the earth and are so cold and miserable that you don't care much if you do."[50]

Between Battle Mountain and Reno, Whitman and Haycock passed through Golconda, Winnemucca, and Lovelock (see Fig. 18). About 50 miles northeast of Reno, "we struck a strange freak of nature," Whitman wrote. "Scattered clumps of sage-brush had caught the sand blown from miles away. The brush had grown taller, the sand had drifted higher, the whirlwinds of alkali had helped cement the whole and the result was hummocks ten to twenty feet high. . . . These hummocks were so near to-gether that the Reo had barely room to pass and the trail was filled with drifted sand; so we had to pick our way, dodging around for miles."[51]

PARADE GREETS RECORD BREAKERS

Whitman and Haycock arrived in Reno at 3:00 P.M. Wednesday and "left by train to take the wheel at Sacramento," while "Fassett and Thomas" left at 4:00 P.M. for the drive to Sacramento, Reno's *Nevada State Journal* reported. In his *Coast to Coast in a Reo* account, however, Whitman, lists Fassett and Hammond as the drivers from Reno to Sacramento. Thomas is identified in press reports as G. J. Thomas, the factory me-chanic who periodically inspected the automobile en route, although Thomas may have joined Fassett and Hammond for the trip to Sacramento. Whether they were two or three, however, "the men and the machine were in splendid condition when they left here," the *State Journal* commented. "They stopped at Col. Lundy's salesrooms in Commercial row during their stay."[52]

Hammond and Fassett drove over the Sierra Nevada north of Lake Tahoe, through Truckee, California, and into Sacramento. It was "the steepest and longest climb on the trip," Whitman recalled. "At one place the road rises 1200 to 1500 feet in one mile. . . . The Reo made it all right, and long before midnight was on the summit among the [railroad] snow sheds."[53] The two drivers traveled all night, arriving in Sacramento early Thursday, August 18, their eleventh calendar-day of travel. "The Reo car reached Sacramento after a run from Reno at about 6 o'clock [Thursday] morning," the *San Francisco Chronicle* reported. "A stop of more than two hours was made in the capital city—it is reported that the dusty Whitman and his companions took time for a luxurious bath."

Griffith and Whitman were at the wheel for the final run to San Francisco through Benicia, Pinole, and Oakland, where they would take a ferry across San Francisco Bay.[54] The Reo "was met at Pinole by a crowd of local enthusiasts and escorted through Oak-land and brought over to San Francisco on the 3 o'clock boat," according to *Motor Age*. "It was a race of seconds to catch the boat," since the men had planned to cross the bay on the next ferry, noted the *San Francisco Call*.[55] Their ferryboat landed at the foot of Market Street, where reporters checked the car in at—accounts differ—3:12 or 3:13 P.M. "At the ferry landing the Reo was met with a brass band in a sight-seeing motor car and a large crowd of motorists. A procession was formed and the winning Reo was escorted through the main streets of the city, up to the headquarters of the local Reo representatives, where more music and congratulations were indulged in" (see Figs. 19 and 20). The crowd contained "a thousand automobile enthusiasts," Whitman estimated.[56] As the *Chronicle* recorded the finish:

> At Pinole the car was met by Captain F. W. Cole of the Pacific Motor Car Company and the press representatives, acting as the official checkers for the finishing time of the run. In the car also was R. C. Ruecshaw, sales manager of the R. M. Owen Company, who has made the trip out by train to be in at the finish. The car was escorted through Oakland and brought over to the city on the 3 o'clock boat. It was the center of a big crowd at the ferry building, and then there was a parade of honor up Market street and Van Ness and Golden Gate avenues.
>
> The car presented the cleanest and most "fit" appearance of any record-breaker that has ever come into this city. There did not seem to be even a nut or bolt loose, and Whitman and his companions were in equally fine shape, having taken the car along in continuous relays, so that each secured a sufficient amount of rest.[57]

Fig. 19. Although Griffith and Whitman drove the last leg of the trip, this photo of the Reo at the ferry landing in San Francisco shows Whitman, right, congratulating Hammond. The graphic superimposed on this photo in the Reo publicity booklet indicates "255 hours," but the coast-to-coast run actually consumed 258 hours. (Coast to Coast in a Reo / AACA)

But the autoists were wearier and the car dirtier than the *Chronicle* let on, at least according to Whitman. They had enjoyed the parade, he said, "although physically we felt more like a shave, bath, and bed than a parade. With all the Reo's crew on board, we attracted as much attention as a cage of wild animals. All had beards of an unknown growth. Grif looked like a gorilla. Our clothes were begrimed with the dirt and dust of twelve States, but what did we care?" Likewise, "dust and mud hung from every projection" on the car.[58]

Fig. 20. The five-man crew celebrates at the San Francisco Reo agency. Hammond is on the running board, Whitman is on the hood, and Haycock is second from right in the back row. The figure standing on the far right in the back row appears to be Fassett, which means the man next to Whitman must be Griffith. The Reo company, however, failed to provide enough information to allow all five men to be conclusively identified. (Motor Age, August 25, 1910)

"Absence of trouble made us the record," declared Whitman, who also reported little improvement in the roads since he set his 1906 Franklin record. "Anyone who attempts to lower this time will know they have been in a race. The roads are bad and the least bit of trouble would stall them. The fact that I was familiar with the country helped us in making such good time, as we seldom were forced to stop on account of not knowing the roads." But his familiarity with the trail offered only a limited advantage, for "a whole lot of it is through mighty bad country, where rains change the whole face of the country from one year to another, especially between Green River and Medicine Bow," in Wyoming.[59]

NO "CHEAP AFFAIR"

The Reo's coast-to-coast trip shaved 21 days, 23 hours, 28 minutes from the 1904 speed record, and exactly 4 days, 8 hours from the Franklin's 1906 record (see Table 6). But the trip "wasn't made just for the fun of beating a six-cylinder car that cost $4000," Reo advertised, referring to the Franklin. "This record clears away at one stroke all the imaginary disadvantages of a well designed and well-built light car, and leaves the advantages standing out clear and strong." When the Reo left New York City, "not one in a hundred believed the record of the Franklin would be smashed," the *Los Angeles Times* noted, adding that "in this city a wager of ten to one that the car would fail was made."[60] The Reo mark would stand until Cannon Ball Baker lowered the record in 1916, driving a V-8 Cadillac (see Chapter 6).

The Reo Motor Car Company's general sales agent, R. M. Owen & Company, was quick to see the implications of the transcontinental record:

> This highly successful test solves all questions and answers all possible doubts about the strength and get-there-and-back ability of the Reo. No car could keep going continuously at that rate over the various kinds of bad roads in that 3557 miles, unless it had several times the strength necessary to meet the emergencies of ordinary motoring. It is also a perfect illustration of how the Reo construction permits full use of power on rough roads, without injury to mechanism or discomfort to passengers. By the way, the car that made the previous record was four thousand dollars. The Reo is only $1250.[61]

The Reo company did not say how it arrived at the figure of 3,557 miles, and in fact the Reo's New York–San Francisco mileage was a matter of guesswork. "I don't know just what the exact distance traveled is," Whitman conceded, "because our speedometer got overworked at Winnemucca, Nev., and quit on us after we had scored up 3200 and some odd miles."[62]

According to Stuart Gayness, the *San Francisco Examiner*'s automobile writer, "the tour from New York to this city . . . in less than eleven days is considered remarkable, especially when the size of the car and the horsepower are considered. Besides being

TABLE 6. Relative Travel Times of Whitman's 1904, 1906, and 1910 Trips

	Franklin, 1904	Franklin, 1906	Reo, 1910
New York City–Cleveland	4d-02h-05m	3d-05h-12m	1d-05h-59m[a]
New York City–Chicago	approx. 8d	4d-00h-12m[a]	2d-00h-59m
New York City–Omaha, Neb.	approx. 10d	5d-19h-12m	3d-07h-59m[b]
New York City–Ogden, Utah	at least 23d	11d-05h-07m[a]	6d-22h-59m[a]
New York City–Reno, Nev.	—	13d-20h-12m	9d-16h-59m
New York City–San Francisco	32d-17h-20m	15d-02h-12m	10d-18h-12m

SOURCES: Local newspapers and national auto journals.

[a] Travel time is based on the most favorable of conflicting arrival or departure times.

[b] The 1910 travel time is from New York City to Council Bluffs, Iowa, just across the Missouri River from Omaha.

one of the medium-priced cars, the record-breaking car is also one of the lowest-powered, and the showing demonstrates the point of efficiency reached by American makers."[63] To F. W. Cole, who only days earlier had taken over the San Francisco Reo agency, the record run likewise proved the utility of lower-priced autos. "There are lots of people who think that the low-priced car is a cheap affair, not to be called upon for really hard work. This is entirely an erroneous idea. . . . Of course, in many details they have not the beauty and extravagance of finish that is lavished upon the more expensive cars, but in the motor and in the other important details nothing is shirked. The American public has just been given the best possible demonstration of this in the performance of the transcontinental Reo."[64]

Eleven months earlier, the *San Francisco Call* had covered the arrival of the Mitchell Ranger, the first auto to carry a military dispatch from coast to coast (see Chapter 1). On Friday, one day after the Reo's arrival, the *Call* remarked on the military implications of the Reo's journey:

> This is a wonderful performance when one stops and soberly considers the distance traveled, the road conditions and the elements that must have been met in such a journey. The fact that the human mind can devise machinery that will withstand such a trying ordeal has been proved in this Reo car.
>
> But there is another factor in all such great contests and that is the master hand of physical endurance as displayed by Whitman and his co-workers, who made this magnificent run across the continent. In these, the budding days of aerial navigation, the public is wont to pass up the motor car, yet a lesson was taught yesterday that even with the destruction of railroads it would be possible for the government to handle its troops with the assistance of the motor car.[65]

DEAD FOR SLEEP

A sign painter had been summoned to paint the record-breaking elapsed time on the side of the Reo during the car's brief stay in the Bay City (see Fig. 21). Less than 11 hours after reaching San Francisco, the Reo left the office of the Pacific Motor Car Company at 2:00 A.M. on Friday, August 19, bound for Los Angeles. "Its object is to establish a mark between New York and the southern metropolis, which has never before been done, and at the same time to demonstrate in the most forceful manner the entire fitness of the car after its test of endurance," the *San Francisco Chronicle* explained. "The sturdy little Reo is not attempting to establish any speed record between

San Francisco and Los Angeles, but only to jog along at its consistent pace of from twenty-five to thirty miles an hour without let-up" (see Fig. 22).[66]

Whether the Reo truly maintained such a sensible pace throughout its cross-country trek is a matter of some doubt, given the apparent number of roadkills. In his *Ocean to Ocean* account Whitman wrote of hitting and killing a skunk early in the trip; later, while making no mention of the skunk, he insisted to the *Los Angeles Examiner* that "we didn't kill anything but two pigs on the trip": "I got one in Iowa and Hammond killed his in Nebraska." The *Los Angeles Times*, however, reported a higher body count: "The Reo killed two pigs, twelve chickens, a dog and a skunk."[67]

The *Times* went on to assure its readers that the car "did not frighten a horse, cause a runaway of any kind or injure a person during the 4000 miles of rapid running," thus contradicting Whitman's assertion that the men would drive no faster than 35 mph. "At times the car made fifty miles an hour," the paper commented. "Over good roads Whitman observed the motto printed on the front of the car which reads: 'Beat it while the going is good.'" Whitman was apparently doing just that as he neared his destination, the *Times* reported: "Just outside of Hollywood the record run was almost ended. While the car was making forty miles an hour a front and rear tire exploded with loud

Fig. 21. Hammond (standing) hands a wrench to an unidentified crewman—perhaps Griffith—sometime after the Reo received its new sign in San Francisco. (MSU)

reports. Whitman held the car on the pavement and shut off his power. This occasioned a delay of thirty minutes."[68]

Leon T. Shettler, a Los Angeles Reo and Apperson agent who had known Whitman at least since 1903, when both Whitman and Hammond worked as mechanics at Shettler's Oldsmobile agency in Los Angeles, was planning to meet up with the car and escort it into town. According to the *Los Angeles Times*, Shettler "tried his best to get some trace of the Reo car," but without notable success. "Agents along the way were asked to flag Whitman. The Reo driver saw the signals in Paso Robles and in San Luis Obispo, but supposed he was about to be arrested and tore away at a terrific clip."[69] Shettler eventually met up with the Reo north of Los Angeles at 6:40 P.M. on Saturday, August 20, the *Los Angeles Times* reported. The paper also gave the car's total trip mileage as 4,118. Given a 6:40 arrival, the car's time from New York City to Los Angeles was 12 days, 21 hours, 39 minutes. Despite the Reo's coast-to-coast record, its San Francisco–Los Angeles time of 40 hours, 40 minutes, was a full day slower than the intercity record, which in 1910 stood at 14 hours, 49 minutes, for the approximately 500-mile route.[70]

Whitman was driving with Hammond as his passenger, reported Monday's *Los Angeles Examiner*:

Both men were numb from the terrible tension of driving the Reo car from New York to San Francisco, clipping five days off the old record there, and then dashing on to Los Angeles without rest. Whitman, the chauffeur, could scarcely stand as he crawled from behind the steering wheel. His companion was equally wearied. . . . When they reached the Shettler agency of the Reo car here they were so dead for sleep that they disappeared immediately to "the feathers" and slept straight through to last night.[71]

DELAYS IDLE "NONSTOP" AUTO FOR 24 HOURS

Although the company's sales agent boasted about the Reo "going continuously," this does not necessarily imply "nonstop," for the transcontinental Reo actually sat idle for many hours. In the *Coast to Coast in a Reo* booklet, Whitman fails to account for this down time. He told the *San Francisco Chronicle* that his crash near Valparaiso, Indiana, was the biggest setback of the trip: "This hour's delay with another of less than an hour later, were really the only times that the motor was quiet for any reason except our meals."[72] In the *Coast to Coast* booklet, however, Whitman talks of spending just 30 minutes temporarily repairing a rear wheel and axle at Valparaiso. Replacing the wheel in Cedar Rapids thus evidently took another 30 minutes.

More revealing than Whitman, local newspapers account for over 18 hours of lost time:

- *20 minutes* in Goshen, Indiana, for unspecified repairs (*Goshen Daily Democrat*, Aug. 10, 1910)

- *12 hours* in Grand Island, Nebraska, repairing the rear axle. (*North Platte [Neb.] Telegraph*, Aug. 18, 1910)

- *1 hour* in North Platte, Nebraska, installing another rear axle and replacing the wheels (*North Platte Semi-Weekly Tribune*, Aug. 16, 1910, and *North Platte Telegraph*, Aug. 18, 1910)

- *2 hours* in Ogden, Utah, installing the original rear axle after it was straightened (*Ogden Daily Standard*, Aug. 15, 1910, and two Salt Lake City newspapers)

- *1 hour* in Reno, Nevada, for unspecified reasons (*Nevada State Journal* [Reno], Aug. 18, 1910)

- *2 hours* in Sacramento, California, where the men bathed (*San Francisco Chronicle*, Aug. 19, 1910)

Whitman unfortunately failed to catalog routine repairs or other maintenance to the car. But in addition to the delays listed above, the drivers lost an undetermined amount of time eating meals, getting gasoline and oil, changing tires, stopping at 14 official and what Whitman called "dozens" of unofficial check-in points, installing and removing tire chains, and digging the car out when it repeatedly got stuck in the sand and mud and in gullies between central Wyoming and Reno. The transcontinental, day-and-night Reo thus evidently sat idle for a minimum of 24 hours, or 9.3 percent of the elapsed time—and perhaps much longer. This, however, was far better than Whitman's record in 1906, when his Franklin, also supposedly traveling night and day, sat idle for nearly 4½ days, or at least 30 percent of its elapsed time of 15 days, 2 hours, 12 minutes.

Confusion exists today about the Reo's exact coast-to-coast time. Most accounts agree the car started its trip at 12:01 A.M. August 8 and ended at either 3:12 or 3:13 P.M. on August 18. Even before the Reo left San Francisco for Los Angeles, the Reo Motor Car Company painted a sign on the side of the car, proclaiming its record time to be "10 Days/15 Hours/12 Min's." Some later Reo advertising, however, added one minute, giving the time as 10 days, 15 hours, 13 minutes.

Both times are wrong, however, for one simple reason: the automaker's calculations failed to recognize that an auto traveling east to west would gain three hours by the clock. (In the *San Francisco Chronicle* afterward, the local Reo agent advertised the incorrect time. A Reo supplier, the Michelin Tire Company, used the correct time in its own ad on the next page.) Correcting the error yields a transcontinental time of 10 days, 18 hours, 11 minutes, if 3:12 P.M. is taken as the finish time. The automaker seemed to prefer an ending time of 3:13 P.M., making the Reo's true elapsed time 10 days, 18 hours, 12 minutes, or 258.2 hours.

REO AVERAGES 331 MILES DAILY

To cover 3,557 miles in 258.2 hours, the 4-cylinder Reo averaged 13.78 mph. If the Reo sat idle for 24 hours—the best estimate of its down time—the automobile averaged at least 15.19 mph for its running time. The Reo drivers covered a great deal more ground per day in 1910, averaging nearly 331 miles, in comparison to the record-setting Franklin's 1906 average of just under 275 miles per day. Interesting though the information would have been, Whitman's *Coast to Coast* account says nothing about the cost of the trip or the car's gasoline and oil consumption.

For about a month after the trip, Reo officials displayed the auto on the West Coast, and possibly they entered the car in races, too. The *San Francisco Call* reported that after the Reo reached Los Angeles, "it is to be sent all along the coast, the object being to try out this 1911 Reo not only as to its racing qualities, but to see if there are any defects brought on by going through the severest tests." A photo in the September 27, 1910, *San Francisco Call* showed "the transcontinental record breaking Reo taking the train at the Western Pacific sheds for the trip to the Denver [auto] show. The picture [of the car climbing a set of stairs] is interesting from the fact that it shows the flexibility of this popular auto."[73] The fate of the record-setting Reo is unknown.

With the 1910 trip, Hammond and Whitman ended their days of setting cross-country records. Fassett and Griffith, however, took part in at least one later transcontinental trip, in 1924, when the two men and one other Reo employee drove a 21-passenger Reo Sedan Bus on a meandering 9,306-mile trip from New York City to San Francisco and back. Leaving New York on July 23, 1924, the 6-cylinder bus averaged 175 miles daily—303 miles on its best day—and carried a total of 636 people for various distances, the factory boasted. The bus arrived in San Francisco on August 25, 1924. Predicting that the event would "herald a new mode of transcontinental travel," the *San Francisco Chronicle* also pointed out that "their trip takes on added importance to San Franciscans, in that there is a possibility of this city being made the Western terminus for a New York to San Francisco passenger bus line in the near future."[74]

Fassett had worked for the Reo factory or its branches since 1905, a Reo official told the press in 1924, while Griffith was a 15-year Reo employee. "Both Fassett and Griffith are members of the engineering division of the company."[75] Hammond died on November 20, 1948, in Riverside, California. According to a book about his 1903 Oldsmobile crossing, Whitman, who retired from transcontinental racing to assume "the rather prosaic life of a Pasadena residential builder," died in Pasadena, California, on February 12, 1932.[76] But neither the *Pasadena Post* nor the *Pasadena Star-News* carry a Whitman obituary from that period. A search of various biographical indexes and sources likewise failed to uncover an obituary for Whitman. In truth, the evidence suggests that he died in the late 1920s, for although his name appears in the 1928 Pasadena city directory, the 1929 directory lists his wife as the "widow" of L. L. Whitman.

SWIFT AND STEADY (CAREFUL, TOO)

Aside from Whitman's wreck in Indiana, the 1910 Reo trip serves as an ideal example of what all modern driving manuals advise: steady, consistent (and considerate) driving is more productive—as well as easier on cars and their operators—than is hard, fast driving. It is also easier on a manufacturer's reputation. The evidence suggests that Whitman and his drivers often exceeded their 35 mph speed limit. Yet they were careful. "One of Whitman's strong points is his courtesy to all drivers along the road," the *Los Angeles Times* observed—praise enough to warm the hearts of Reo agents everywhere. "This has made him the most popular record breaker who ever handled a car. He is never abusive. He realizes, he says, that others have a right to the road as well as he. Therefore he is particularly careful to avoid annoying anybody."[77]

As usual, Whitman also planned the trek in great detail, lining up reliable pilots and synchronizing the Reo's pace with train schedules. Experience gained on his three earlier coast-to-coast trips gave him an edge as well. Characteristically, Whitman was for the most part very careful to document the trip. Organizers of at least one later transcontinental trip—Bobby Hammond's, in 1916—neglected to take such pains, and consequently had their claim of a record time discredited.[78] Although self-serving, Whitman's praise of the Reo in post-run interviews and his condemnation of the roads together suggest that automobiles were improving faster than the highways they plied.

The stellar performance of Fassett, Griffith, Hammond, Haycock, and Whitman changed the nature of transcontinental record setting for the next half a decade. In addition, their publicity stunt gave the Reo Motor Car Company bragging rights for six long years to the fastest New York–San Francisco auto trip ever. The number of coast-to-coast pleasure trips increased dramatically between 1910 and 1915, especially after the 1913 creation of the Lincoln Highway between New York City and San Francisco. But so low was the 1910 Reo mark that it was not until 1915 that another driver, Cannon Ball Baker, even attempted to challenge it. Baker fell short in 1915 but broke the Reo record in 1916 (see Chapters 5 and 6), setting off a new speed craze that was cut short only by America's entry into World War I. In the interim, however, transcontinental drivers would focus on breaking other records.

MILLIONAIRE AUTO PARTY LEADS DRIVE FOR TRANSCONTINENTAL HIGHWAY

3

Every owner of an automobile has a latent desire to make the ocean to ocean trip,
and I am confident that if the real conditions were known there would be
hundreds [who] attempt it for every one who starts now.

—John Guy Monihan, a tour organizer

PERPLEXED BY THE SIGHT, vacationers strolling along the boardwalk in Atlantic City, New Jersey, early one June morning turned and gaped in wonder as a dozen automobiles backed down the beach and into the frothy, surging surf. The motorists, beginning a trip reminiscent of the wagon trains of pioneer days, planned to travel as a group until they wet their front wheels in the Pacific Ocean at Los Angeles. It was the first time an auto caravan and group of amateur drivers crossed the country. The organizers believed that transcontinental racers had glorified their conquests by making the roads sound more treacherous than they actually were. More than 40 travelers, including 12 women and 3 boys—the youngest 12 years old—proved their point by making the trip in relative luxury.

The members of the caravan, whose combined worth was estimated at $100 million, sought to encourage other wealthy motorists to spend their time and money seeing the United States rather than touring abroad. Better highways could help to bring this about. In addition to federal aid, the motorists contended, "the only requirement now necessary to bring the national highway to a state of perfection is the hearty cooperation of state executives."[1] Besides meeting with President William Howard Taft, members of the caravan visited personally with at least five governors and carried good-roads messages to the chief executives of all fourteen states they traversed.

From the start on June 26, 1911, the travelers coaxed their twelve Indianapolis-made Premier automobiles along a meandering route from Atlantic City to San Francisco, none of the cars needing more than minor repairs. They continued to Los Angeles, traveling the 4,617 miles from Atlantic City in a running time of 35 days and an elapsed time of 45 days, 9 hours. The travelers could have reached California in 20 to 25 days, one of the organizers said afterward; what slowed the group was its frequent mingling with governors, mayors, lesser dignitaries, and motoring enthusiasts. In nearly every big city along the route, auto clubs and government officials sponsored banquets and other entertainment, which reduced the caravan's daily progress to as little as 45 miles. On its best day, the group traveled 236 miles.

Ordinary Americans who followed the Premier trip doubtless understood that if these tourists could cross the country without too much suffering, so could they. The trip thus inspired hundreds, and then thousands, of ordinary families to make the cross-country journey by automobile. The tour also became a test case, whereby lawmakers could determine whether Americans wanted a transcontinental highway. Many East Coast automobile owners had already begun lobbying for a good cross-country route so they could drive to San Francisco's Panama-Pacific International Exposition, scheduled to open in 1915. As a *New York Times* editorial about a proposed national highway put it: "For that reason the entire automobile world has its eyes on the daring Premier amateur owner-drivers who with their families and friends are now in the great Western plains, camping out at night and cooking their own meals, in an attempt to demonstrate to the world, and the United States Congress in particular, the absolute necessity of this strip of road."[2]

Fig. 23. Monihan (far right) stands beside Ray F. McNamara, who drove at the head of the caravan. The other two men are unidentified. Monihan's wife is seated in the car behind him; the boy is presumably their son, John G. Monihan Jr. (NAHC)

ANY GOOD CAR CAN DO IT

A group of Premier owners conceived the tour idea in May or early June 1911. "Some of our wealthy owners in and around Philadelphia became tired of ordinary touring," said John Guy Monihan, the recently hired advertising manager for the Premier Motor Manufacturing Company (see Fig. 23). "Several of us were lolling about the club wondering how we would spend [our] vacation, when the ocean to ocean trip was suggested." Organizing themselves as the Philadelphia Motor Tourists and duly electing officers, the men pledged $10,000 toward the cost of the trip. "They aspired to cross the continent and so I mapped out a scheme for them, to which they agreed," said Monihan, who was also secretary of the new group. Throughout the trip, he wrote nightly telegrams to the Premier factory, signed "Motor Tourists, J. G. Monihan, Sec."[3]

All told, 10 of the 30 automobile owners who received invitations decided to join the caravan. The Premier company eagerly lent its support, in part by reserving a spot

Fig. 24. Ray F. McNamara, driver of the Premier caravan's pilot car. (FLP)

in the caravan for Monihan, who sent regular dispatches to newspapers and automobile trade journals, in addition to his telegrams. Factory driver Ray F. McNamara, fresh from a 1910 transcontinental mapping trip in a Premier car, would drive a "pilot car"—the eleventh Premier—at the head of the caravan (see Fig. 24), as well as spread confetti to mark the route and plant warning flags at dangerous points in the road. The factory also supplied the caravan's twelfth vehicle, a Premier baggage car fitted with a curved canvas back so as to resemble a Conestoga wagon. It carried 3,000 pounds in parts and supplies.

"Single cars had made the trip so frequently across the continent that no special credit resulted from a simple journey from Atlantic to Pacific. Any good car at this stage of automobile development can do it with ease," Monihan asserted.[4] Driving twelve cars an average of 4,617 miles apiece—a total of 55,000 miles—with mechanical troubles amounting to, reportedly, just four broken springs was a sensational feat in 1911, however, and one the Premier company was quick to exploit.

"LUXURY-LOVING PEOPLE" ON BOARD

Who made the trip? In a three-part chronicle of their adventures written for *Automobile*, Monihan calls them "amateur motorists from Philadelphia, New York, Washington [D.C.], and Newark." They were "bankers, professional men, men of society, manufacturers and merchants, all wealthy Premier owners," according to a Premier ad. Besides Monihan and McNamara, the travelers included a physician, a judge, two tobacco brokers, an unspecified number of lawyers, and, generally, "some of the most prominent business men of New York and Philadelphia," *Motor Age* asserted.[5]

Table 7, compiled from names given in auto journals and local newspapers, lists 43 tourists: 28 men, 12 women, and 3 boys. Conflicting accounts make it hard to pin down the exact number, however. Even Monihan's own figures differ. "There are thirty-eight of us—eight women," he told the *Chicago Daily News*. In an article for *Automobile*, however, Monihan gave a total of 39: 26 men, 10 women, and 3 boys (who, newspapers agreed, were 12 to 14 years old).[6] In a telegram from Los Angeles, Monihan

TABLE 7. Passengers on the 1911 Premier Tour[a]

George C. Allen (driver),[b] *wife*,[c] and son, *John*
> President of the Republic Trust Company, Philadelphia, and treasurer of the Philadelphia Motor Tourists, the group that organized the cross-country tour.

P. W. Baker (driver), *wife*, and son, *Carl*
> A "prosperous tobacco grower" of Landisville, Pennsylvania.

Harry O. Bechtel
> A Schuylkill County Court judge, Pottsville, Pennsylvania.

J. C. Bell
> Photographer with the William Rau studio, Philadelphia.

C. E. Brown and *wife*
> Residents of New York City.

Dr. Hugh F. Cook (driver) and *wife*
> A surgeon from Newark, New Jersey.

Countess de Calatrava
> The sister of John J. Murphy (see below), "the widow of a Spanish nobleman, who after her husband died, returned to her native city of New York to live."

Harry Davis
> Resident of New York City; a representative of the United States Tire Company, the maker of the tires used on the transcontinental Premiers.

Dr. Edward Dennis
> Resident of Erie, Pennsylvania.

G. E. Horton and *wife*
> Resident of New York City.

C. Francis Jenkins (driver) and *wife*
> Resident of Washington, D.C.; an inventor of the motion-picture camera, Jenkins also shot movies documenting the trip.

Charles E. Lex Jr. (driver)
> Resident of Philadelphia.

F. Hazzard Lippincott (driver)
> Publisher, "of the famous Lippincott family" of Philadelphia, and president of the Philadelphia Motor Tourists.

C. G. A. Loder (driver)
> "A prominent druggist of Philadelphia" who won a lawsuit against the National Wholesale Drug Association, reportedly the first legal test of the Sherman Anti-Trust Act.

John Matthews[d]
> Resident of New York City.

Ray F. McNamara (driver)
> Resident of Indianapolis; an employee of the Premier Motor Manufacturing Company, McNamara—"the only professional driver in the party"—served as the pathfinder for the caravan.

(cont'd)

F. A. Moller (driver)
> "Son of a retired banker of New York City."

L. J. Moller
> Resident of New York City.

John Guy Monihan (driver), *wife*, and son, *John Jr.*
> Advertising manager of the Premier Motor Manufacturing Company, Indianapolis, secretary of the Philadelphia Motor Tourists, and spokesman for the coast-to-coast tour group.

John J. Murphy (driver) and *wife*
> Tenement House Commissioner of New York City.

George A. Parker
> Publisher, of Philadelphia.

Samuel M. Root (driver) and *wife*
> A "prosperous tobacco grower" of Landisville, Pennsylvania.

W. Sherman Rose[e]
> Resident of New York City.

Ellsworth Sprague (driver) and *wife*
> Resident of Long Island, New York; "known throughout the East as the 'Oyster King' by virtue of his ownership of practically every oyster bed on Long Island Sound."

Herbert Swarr
> Residents of Landisville, Pennsylvania.

Frank E. Trout[f] and *Miss Barbara Trout*
> Residents of Landisville, Pennsylvania.

F. L. Howard Weatherly
> Resident of Philadelphia.

Harry D. Weller (driver)
> Resident of Indianapolis; driver of the Premier prairie schooner.

A. J. Wolf
> Resident of Indianapolis.

SOURCES: Auto journals and local and national newspapers; city directories from Erie, Pa., Indianapolis, Landisville, Pa., New York City, Newark, N.J., Philadelphia, and Washington, D.C.; various other records, including obituaries.

[a] Local newspapers often listed the Premier tourists by name, and, in a dozen instances, a new name popped up briefly. These people—perhaps local Premier agents, guides, or motorists who traveled a short distance with the caravan—have been excluded here.

[b] Private owners drove ten Premier autos, according to the automaker, while McNamara drove the pilot car and Weller the truck. Instead of naming the ten drivers, however, press accounts named the twelve Premier owners who belonged to the Philadelphia Motor Tourists. Since no further information is available, the present list thus contains, in addition to McNamara and Weller, twelve drivers for ten cars—two too many.

[c] Premier press releases did not provide the names of wives.

[d] Appears as "Matthew" nearly as often as "Matthews."

[e] Also frequently spelled W. "Herman" Rose.

[f] Some newspapers rendered the surname "Trout" as "Trant," "Traut," or "Trent."

announced the safe arrival of the ten privately owned Premiers "with the same forty occupants" who started the trip.[7]

Heralding the trip in a 52-page advertising booklet, *Ocean to Ocean Tour of the Premierites Told by Wire and Photo*, the Premier company refers to "over forty luxury-loving people," including 10 women. Drawing on press releases and hotel registries, in addition to their own observations, most newspapers along the caravan's route quoted figures ranging from 33 to 42 persons, including some 8 to 12 women. A photo of the San Francisco Premier agency, however, shows a banner proclaiming: "10 Premier Cars Bringing 60 Tourists [To] Be Here Aug. 3rd."[8] One might be tempted to attribute this unusually high figure to a confused agent or a mix-up at the printer's, but the *San Francisco Call*, *San Francisco Chronicle*, and the *Los Angeles Examiner* also quote the 60-person figure.

A group photo taken near a Kearney, Nebraska, landmark shows 40 people, including 9 women and 5 boys, although the group probably does not include the photographer, J. C. Bell. Another group photo—again, most likely excluding the photographer—at the Colorado-Wyoming border shows 39 people, including 10 women and 3 boys.[9] In later accounts, both *Motor Age* and the *New York Times* refer to "forty-odd" participants.

INVENTOR SHOOTS MOTION PICTURES

Among the participants was C. Francis Jenkins, who developed a prototype motion-picture projector in the mid-1890s and later contributed to the birth of television. One biography also credited Jenkins with designing, in 1901, the "first motor sight-seeing bus," and, in 1911, an early automobile self-starter. At the time of the transcontinental trip, Jenkins had patents on some thirty inventions, including "automatic box making devices," and held some four hundred patents at his death in 1934.[10] Even though he lost money by selling some patents, "Mr. Jenkins is not a subject for the poor house," as he proved by buying a new car—his sixth—especially for the transcontinental trip. "You see," he told the *Salt Lake (City) Herald-Republican*, "I didn't happen to own a Premier in my collection and as every other car in the party was a Premier, I didn't want to spoil the uniformity with a different brand."[11]

On the trip, Jenkins "equipped his personal car with one of his 'movies' and made the entire journey," reported the *New York Times*. "Mr. Jenkins is making moving pictures of the entire trip to give to members of the party on their return home," said another newspaper, echoing similar accounts elsewhere. What became of his movies of the trip is unknown. Photographer J. C. Bell of Philadelphia also shot what the *New York Times* called "hundreds of intensely interesting scenes" using two still cameras, "one of them being a huge 'circuit' or 'panorama' type."[12] Some of Bell's images survive in the Premier photo files at the Detroit Public Library's National Automotive History Collection.

STARTING FROM THE OCEAN'S EDGE

A *New York Times* dispatch from Atlantic City sent on Monday, June 26, 1911, describes the festive start of the cross-country trek:

> Cheered by hundreds of spectators and carrying pennants bearing the inscription, "Ocean to Ocean," twelve automobiles backed into the waters of the ocean at the beach end of Ohio Avenue this morning, and then started away on the first pleasure transcontinental motor run in the history of the motor car industry. . . .
>
> Early morning promenaders along the Boardwalk cheered the motorists as each of the machines was splashed by the salt sea spray and the motors whirred as the big cars leaped across the strand on the start of the long transcontinental trip.[13]

The Premier company later estimated that not "hundreds" but 10,000 onlookers witnessed the 8:00 A.M. start (see Fig. 25). "There was quite a crowd on the Boardwalk," the *Atlantic City Daily Press* ventured, but it stopped short of guessing the size of the crowd. Unfortunately for the automaker, photographs of the start support the *New York Times*'s estimate. Before departing, the wealthy tourists attended a reception at the Marlborough Blenheim Hotel, "at which the state flags of Pennsylvania and New York were presented by United States Senators Penrose and O'Gorman, to be carried across the continent," a newspaper reported. Some of the travelers "filled bottles with water from the Atlantic ocean," *Motor Age* recounted. "This liquid will be emptied into the Pacific main."[14]

The start was even more suspenseful than *Motor Age* and the *New York Times* suggested. Drivers traveled down the beach on "a runway [that] has been built over the soft sand to the water's edge."[15] As Monihan revealed to a Denver newspaper:

> The only real trouble we have had with the roads was at the beginning of the trip. It looked for a time as if some of the machines would not be able to leave Atlantic City. De-

termined to start from the very brink of the ocean, we drove down on the beach. The beach is a most deceptive place for an automobile driver and some of our amateur drivers went out below high-tide mark and sunk to their hubs in the sand. [See Fig. 26.] Escaping from this predicament we have been coming along without any serious difficulty.[16]

Before repeating the dipping ceremony seven weeks later at the Pacific Ocean, the Premier caravan would travel through New Jersey, Pennsylvania, Maryland, West Virginia, Ohio, Indiana, Illinois, Iowa, Nebraska, Colorado, Wyoming, Utah, Nevada, and California (see Fig. 27). The cars crossed the Appalachian, Rocky, and Sierra Nevada mountain ranges, traveling on highways that to East Coast residents were steeped in mystery.

"From Denver to the West the road conditions were absolutely unknown, although diligent efforts had been made by the secretary of the tourists to get reliable

Fig. 25. Sightseers line the boardwalk before the turreted Marlborough Blenheim Hotel as the Premier autoists prepare to start on their trip from the Atlantic City beach. (NAHC)

road information," said Monihan, the secretary.[17] In fact, anyone making a truly diligent effort would have discovered that at least seven record-setting transcontinental trips had passed through Denver, including three of the first four cars to cross America—Tom Fetch with Marius C. Krarup, and Lester L. Whitman with Eugene I. Hammond, both in 1903, and Whitman and Clayton S. Carris in 1904. But Monihan clearly feared the worst: "When the tour was first proposed the belief was unanimous that it would have some of the roughest kind of going and that in some places it would be practically impossible to get through," he wrote. "It was with this in view and the possibility of injury to the tourists that arrangements were made with the Union Pacific trains to signal or flag trains at any time or place while running parallel with the railroad. This was done so that in the event the running became too strenuous for the ladies, they could get relief and comfort in the railroad trains, while the men of the party continued on the road."[18] No trains were signaled.

Fig. 26. Although not yet sunk to its hubs, this Premier is evidently stuck in the soft sand. Friends help the driver by cranking his stalled engine back to life. (NAHC)

COAST TO COAST BY AUTOMOBILE

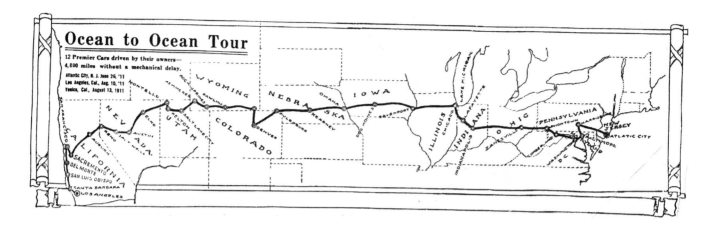

PRESIDENT TAFT GREETS THE TOURISTS

Near Philadelphia, on Day 1, the tourists were met by "an escort of the city's mounted police and motorists in their cars, this escort feature being observed in all the large cities included in the itinerary."[19] During a one-hour luncheon at the Hotel Walton, Philadelphia's mayor presented the tourists with a flag of the city. They concluded their 168-mile first day at the Columbus Hotel in Harrisburg.

On Tuesday, June 27, members of the so-called millionaire auto party parked their autos at the Pennsylvania Capitol Building to meet with Governor John Kinley Tener— "a good roads enthusiast"—before leaving town at 11:00 A.M., the *Harrisburg Patriot* said.[20] On their 117-mile detour south to Baltimore, the tourists narrowly avoided a disaster (see Fig. 28). As a telegram sent by one of the drivers, John J. Murphy, described it:

> Run from Harrisburg to Baltimore . . . strenuous one on account of heavy rains and muddy roads. The entire touring party arrived at Baltimore on schedule time, without tire or mechanical trouble, despite cloudburst, washout, and hurricane encountered. Mc-Namara's car narrowly escaped falling tree, uprooted by wind as car passed. Clever driving and brake efficiency saved occupants' lives.[21]

According to Murphy's telegraphed account, the Premier tourists arrived in Washington at 1:40 P.M. the following day—late for their scheduled noon appointment with President Taft. They had traveled just 45 miles, making it the shortest one-day run of the trip (see Fig. 29). "Escorted into capital by a large delegation of autoists and police, twenty miles from Washington," Murphy wired. "Received by President Taft at 2:30, when he presented American flag to tourists to carry across continent."[22]

Arriving at the White House, the motor tourists "were met by President Taft, who

Fig. 27. While on the whole correct, this map depicts the tourists' zigzag route through Pennsylvania and Maryland somewhat inaccurately and mistakenly includes Cheyenne, Wyoming, on the route. It also places Montello in Utah instead of Nevada. (Ocean to Ocean Tour booklet / FLP)

Fig. 28. A falling tree nearly hit one of the autos on the drive to Baltimore. (Ocean to Ocean Tour booklet / FLP)

shook hands with the party and wished them good luck on their long journey to the Pacific coast," the *Washington Post* reported. "The President, who is an enthusiastic automobilist himself, inquired as to the route and the length of time which the party expected to take in crossing the country. He presented them with another flag."[23] So genuine was Taft's enthusiasm that by a telegraph hookup in 1909 he had started the five entrants in a New York–Seattle automobile race.[24]

The caravan had already received a Philadelphia city flag and the state flags of New York and Pennsylvania, and according to news reports, green "Ocean to Ocean" banners bedecked every car. Photos reveal that during the rest of the journey various autos—including the baggage truck and McNamara's pilot car—carried Taft's gift of a silk flag, "the handle of which is appropriately engraved," observed the *Indianapolis News*.[25] When they bid farewell to Taft, the transcontinental tourists were also "carrying a message from him to the mayor of San Francisco," reported the *Indianapolis Star*, without elaborating. Although Monihan had expressed hopes of leaving Washington that afternoon, "it was evening before the banquet was over," another newspaper reported.[26] Thus the travelers stayed overnight at the Hotel Willard.

A HOOSIER WELCOME

Covering 383 miles during a leisurely three-day drive through Maryland, Pennsylvania, and the northern tip of West Virginia (see Figs. 30 and 31), the Premier caravan lumbered up to the Clarendon Hotel in Zanesville, Ohio, at 8:00 P.M. Saturday, July 1, according to the *Zanesville Signal*. All the way across Pennsylvania, shallow ditches known as "thank-you-ma'ams" or water breakers, frequently ran across the roads. "Between the rough roads, the notorious Pennsylvania water breakers and the steep grades the tourists had some of the worst going of the entire trip," Monihan said. "The arrival in Zanesville was a matter of much joy to the Premier tourists because it marked the end of the water breakers."[27] Sunday's trip was the longest of the journey—236.4 miles into Indianapolis through Columbus, Ohio, and Richmond, Indiana.

To make the day even longer, the caravan ran afoul of the law west of Richmond, the Indianapolis newspapers reported. At Nolan's Fork, a stream between Centerville and Germantown, Indiana, the cars pulled up "at the east end of a wagon bridge, which was blocked by a long-eared mule, hitched to an ancient buggy," as the *Indi-*

Fig. 30. Just west of Philadelphia at Coatesville, Pennsylvania, the tourists stop in front of a hardware store that advertises "Oils and Greases." (NAHC)

anapolis News told it. A "tall individual, swinging a long stick, stepped into the middle of the old National road . . . and cried 'Halt!' in a commanding manner." The wealthy motorists "were informed that they had violated the law of Indiana by not showing license tags and were further informed that it would take the sum of $25 from each car to settle the grievance."[28] "There were strenuous protestations and evidences of a real panic," said the *Indianapolis Star*, taking up the narrative. "All manner of suggestions were offered to escape the predicament, some of the autoists showing a willingness to pay the $25 a car demanded by the 'constable.' George A. Weidely, vice president of the Premier company, who had headed a reception committee, interceded for the tourists without result, and the situation began to look serious."[29]

Acting the role of a "constable," the *Indianapolis News* said, "Bernard Randall, of the Murat Theater Stock Company, was ideally made up for the part—dilapidated slouch hat, high top boots, short chin whiskers and all, and he carried out the part in an extremely deceptive manner. After the visitors had been held over the fire half an hour the plot was exposed when the following letter of welcome from Governor Thomas R. Marshall was read:

> To the ocean-to-ocean tourists, greeting:
>
> The word "Hoosier" is, in reality, "Who's here?" Indiana always inquires at the state line, "Who's here?" Whenever she finds any one knocking at her doors who simply wants to stay with her or pass through her boundaries, she is always glad to welcome him. But she is more pleased when, in a marvelous age, any one performs a marvelous feat, whether of skill or endurance. She is glad to know that your effort in the line of skill and endurance, unexampled in the history of motoring, has brought you within her boundaries. She bids you welcome.[30]

According to the *News*, the message prompted "loud laughter and hilarity all around, and the run into Indianapolis was continued." Seven days and 949 miles from the East Coast, the Premier tourists "attracted much attention Sunday night at 10:30, when they filed into the city on East Washington street and went to their headquarters at the Claypool hotel," the *Indianapolis Sun* observed (see Fig. 32).[31]

Fig. 31. At Brownsville, in southwestern Pennsylvania, the caravan crossed the Monongahela River on a ferry. (Ocean to Ocean Tour booklet/FLP)

Fig. 32. In Indianapolis, the tourists posed with their Indianapolis-made autos outside the local Premier agency. (Ocean to Ocean Tour booklet / FLP)

"The first 1,000 miles of the long journey, from Atlantic City to Indianapolis, were accomplished with no more wear or tear or mishaps than are generally encountered," *Automobile* wrote. On Monday, July 3, Harold O. Smith, president of the Indianapolis-based Premier company, treated the motorists to "a clam bake and picnic, lasting all day, at beautiful Broad Ripple, where boating and swimming are chief diversions." Also invited to the clam bake were "scores of Premier owners," according to the *Indianapolis Star*. Tuesday's program included "a visit to the Indianapolis Motor Speedway, which the majority of the visitors have not yet seen," the *Star* said. "Several impromptu races have been arranged among the amateur drivers," while many others "went to the Country club and played golf."[32]

MCNAMARA'S SECOND COAST-TO-COAST TRIP

All manufactured in Indianapolis, one 1909, five 1910, and six 1911 Premiers made up the fleet of twelve autos. Ten Premiers had 4-cylinder engines of either 30 or 40 horsepower, and two had 60-horsepower, 6-cylinder engines. The circulating oil pumps featured on the six 1911 Premiers had replaced the mechanical oilers and splash oiling systems of the older engines. Eleven of the cars, which had been on the road from three to thirty-six months, had traveled 20,000 or fewer miles, but McNamara's pilot car, still wearing the "1" assigned to it for the 1910 Glidden Tour, already had 57,820 miles on its odometer from that contest and others, according to Monihan.[33]

McNamara, who hailed from Indianapolis, was well qualified to pilot the caravan. He had almost won the Glidden Trophy in the American Automobile Association's 2,850-mile reliability tour of 1910—the so-called Glidden Tour, which penalized contestants for making repairs or arriving late at check-in stations. McNamara's winning Premier lost a total of only 93 points in the contest. A Chalmers placed second with 116 points, followed by a Maxwell (208 points), another Premier (806), a Glide (2,247) and a Cino (2,414), according to *Automobile*.

McNamara, who was among just five of the twenty-six starters who always arrived on time, earned the best road score by losing only nine points, "for taking on water and repairing and replacing fan belts." At the end of the race, his Premier lost 64 points in a brake test, 5 points in an axle inspection, and 15 points in a post-run technical examination. Ultimately, however, the AAA's Contest Board ruled that an oil tank and hand pump on McNamara's auto constituted an illegal modification. The Premier company, whose autos had finished with perfect scores in the 1907, 1908, and 1909 Glidden tours,[34] argued that it had, in 1910, produced 74 cars with such an oiler. But to no avail: the AAA belatedly awarded its 1910 Glidden Trophy to the second-place Chalmers.[35]

Later in 1910, McNamara drove A. L. Westgard of the Touring Club of America on a 49-day, 4,203.5-mile transcontinental trip. Their goal was not to break speed records; rather, their purpose was "arousing enthusiasm for the improvement of bad stretches on the route," according to Westgard. His other interest was "supplying the material for the beginning of a continuous coast-to-coast highway," Westgard wrote in *Collier's* magazine.[36] Leaving New York City on October 11, 1910, McNamara drove a

Fig. 33. Harry D. Weller, left, and an unnamed companion pose in the Premier prairie schooner before it acquired headlights. (NAHC)

1911 Premier 4-40 westward, generally following the traditional central route as far as Omaha. There, he turned south to Kansas City, Missouri, traveled the Santa Fe Trail through Kansas and Colorado to Santa Fe, New Mexico, and crossed Arizona and southern California to reach Los Angeles on November 29, 1910.[37]

"PRAIRIE SCHOONER" JOINS CARAVAN

McNamara's pilot car was one of two "official" cars to join the ten privately owned Premiers on the journey. The second was a 4-cylinder, 40-horsepower Premier that the automaker had turned into a baggage truck (see Fig. 33), which, the *Indianapolis Star* contended, joined the caravan at Indianapolis.[38] The *Star* appears to have been correct. News reports of the start in Atlantic City make no mention of the baggage truck; furthermore, the first photo of the truck in the Premier company's *Ocean to Ocean* advertising booklet shows it in Indianapolis. Despite the "Ocean to Ocean Tourists" sign on its canvas sides, the truck evidently did not make a full coast-to-coast trip.

"The first automobile 'prairie schooner' ever built, patterned after the old-time prairie schooners of the plains, attracted much attention in Indianapolis," the *Indianapolis News* reported. The oft-nicknamed "repair car," "grub wagon," or "commissary truck" carried such things as luggage, spare parts, cooking equipment, and food. Traveling at the rear of the caravan, the truck "renders aid to any of the cars that break down or have any trouble."[39]

Only the baggage truck had electric lights; the rest of the autos used acetylene-burning headlamps. By all accounts the cars were ordinary Premiers in every detail except for oversize tires—larger in diameter than the originals to improve the cars' ground clearance and wider, too, so they could carry heavier loads. Although McNamara, driving the pilot car, threw out confetti to mark the trail, the drivers behind him more often than not followed the distinctive track of his car's United States brand "nobby tread tires," which were "of the greatest possible value in showing direction," the Premier company claimed.[40] In reporting on the trip, some local newspapers overlooked McNamara's car and the baggage truck, referring only to the 10 autos driven by their owners. Other newspapers, evidently mistaking escorting autos as part of the caravan, noted the arrival of 13, 15, or even 18 Premiers.

CHICAGO WELCOMES CARAVAN

After spending two days idle, the ocean-to-ocean caravan left Indianapolis at noon on Wednesday, July 5, heading northwest on an easy 75-mile drive to Lafayette, Indiana, which was already bracing itself for the tourists' arrival. "The Hotel Lahr received word this morning to have eleven rooms with baths ready for the tourists and to have a special dinner prepared at the Bohemia," reported Wednesday's *Lafayette Daily Courier*. "The travelers will eat breakfast in the Bohemia to-morrow morning and will then leave on another stage of the journey."[41] The *Chicago Daily News* recorded the travelers' reception following their 146-mile drive into the Windy City on Thursday, July 6 (see Fig. 34):

> Some little distance outside of Chicago, down near Hammond [Indiana], the tourists were met by the Chicago escort, sent out by W. E. Stalmaker, and made up mostly of local Premier owners, who are interested in the undertaking and were only too glad to extend a welcome to the easterners. With pennants flying and in orderly array, the procession found its way along the south side boulevards to the Congress hotel. All along motor row the visitors were given the glad hand, and at the Premier store the pace slackened a bit while the tourists saluted the place.[42]

Fig. 34. Motorcycle police joined auto enthusiasts who greeted the Premier tourists at the Indiana state line and escorted them into Chicago. (NAHC)

On Friday, city officials escorted the reluctant sightseers "through parkways and boulevards of Chicago," the *Chicago Inter Ocean* reported.[43] Monihan later confessed to the *Denver Times* that, rather than spending the day in Chicago, he had wanted to drive to Davenport, Iowa, on Friday, to make up for losing a day in Washington, D.C. "We lost the second day in Chicago," he explained to the paper. "When we arrived Mayor Carter Harrison had one of the city officials in each of our cars and gave us a personally conducted trip over the city. We did not think it was courteous to jump out at once and so decided to stay in Chicago over night."[44]

So it was on Saturday, July 8, Day 13 of the trip, that the caravan rolled westward from Chicago, "escorted out of town by a squad of Chicago motorcycle police," according to Saturday's *Chicago Daily News*. Law officers from Atlantic City to Los Angeles treated the wealthy motorists kindly, according to Monihan. "Our way has been made easy by letters which the chief of police of Philadelphia has sent to the police superintendents in every town through which we go. In consequence of this we are shown every courtesy and in several cities police escorts have been sent out to meet us."[45]

MISHAPS AND MUD IN IOWA

The transcontinental tourists had planned to cross the Mississippi River into Iowa at Clinton, but "due to the activity of the Greater Davenport committee were induced to change their course and travel through Davenport over the River-to-River road," said the *Davenport Democrat and Leader*. The Premier tourists would subsequently follow the River-to-River Road across Iowa. During the caravan's 178-mile journey to Davenport, the Countess de Calatrava "narrowly escaped a serious accident" when the car in which she was riding blew a tire 100 miles west of Chicago at about noon Saturday (see Fig. 35). It "skidded across the road and missed overturning by [a] fraction of an inch," the newspaper said.[46] At the time of the accident, she was presumably still riding in the Premier touring car that her brother, John J. Murphy, drove from New York City.

Reaching Davenport early Saturday evening, the tourists "stopped for the night at

Fig. 35. John J. Murphy drives a Premier occupied by his sister, the Countess de Calatrava (back seat, left), and his wife (back seat, right). John Matthews flanks Murphy in the front. (NAHC)

the Kimball hotel, where they also had supper and breakfast," said the *Davenport Daily Times*. "As no word was received from them in advance, they were not met out of the city by local automobilists who expected to meet them and escort them into the city."[47] After leaving Davenport, the travelers, who missed their 7:00 A.M. Sunday departure time by upwards of an hour, had originally planned to drive through Iowa City, Newton, and Colfax to spend Sunday night at the Chamberlain Hotel in Des Moines. But they changed their plans even before encountering "rain and sticky gumbo roads between the [Mississippi] river and Colfax," reported the *Des Moines Evening Tribune*.[48] The Premier tourists instead spent the night at the Hotel Colfax, 20 miles east of Des Moines.

The more than 40 miles of wet Iowa roads were far worse than the *Evening Tribune* hinted. "At South Amana the ideal of gumbo roads, fast, elastic and smooth riding, because of the downpour of rain changed into one of the worst roads of the trip, slippery beyond imagination, and the cars held to the road and stayed out of the ditches only with the greatest difficulty," Monihan related. "From a road upon which one could run as fast as desired in comfort, it became impossible to go faster than 12 miles an hour," until the roads dried up near Newton.[49]

Reaching the Hotel Chamberlain in Des Moines at 10:00 A.M. Monday, July 10, "the members of the party took time to wash and inquire for mail and were off again for Omaha," Monday's *Des Moines Capital* reported (see Fig. 36). They also purchased lunch during their short stay, during which Premier driver F. Hazzard Lippincott gave the *Capital* his opinion—in sharp contrast to Monihan's—of the River-to-River Road: "Except for one mud hole, which we struck just out of Homestead, we have found the road to be in the best possible condition. Paved streets alone can surpass that road."[50]

According to the *Capital*, "Vere Reynolds at the wheel of John M. Robbins' big Welch touring car, piloted the ocean-to-ocean party out of Des Moines at 10:30 o'clock this morning and several miles along the River-to-River road to Omaha, where the party will stop over night." The *Des Moines Register and Leader* reported that the group took on a supply of oil during their stop in the city and that the baggage truck "was running one-half hour behind the other cars when they went through Des Moines." Murphy was running even farther behind, however. Perhaps the blowout that nearly wrecked his auto between Chicago and Davenport Saturday had caused more damage than Monihan let on. Murphy's car arrived behind the others in Colfax "late Sunday night, because of a mishap," and did not join the others for the run into Des Moines on Monday morning, reported Tuesday's *Register and Leader*. All the same, Murphy and his passengers "expect to join the other tourists at Omaha this morning," the paper added.[51]

PREPARING TO CAMP IN STYLE

Three Omaha cars—a Premier, driven by local agent Al Cahn, and two Velies, one occupied by Henshaw Hotel proprietor Tom O'Brien and the second carrying several reporters—crossed the Missouri River to meet the Premier caravan at Underwood, Iowa. So escorted, the transcontinental autoists ended a 190-mile day. They arrived in Omaha Monday evening "in twelve dust begrimed cars and were simply bubbling over with good nature, despite the heat of the day," the *Omaha World-Herald* declared. "They were scarcely more beautiful than the cars when they arrived, but a bit of soap and water made them highly presentable and after a dinner at Tom O'Brien's New Henshaw cafe they began to feel themselves again."[52]

Remaining in Omaha on Tuesday, July 11, Day 16 of the trip, the voyagers—uncertain about finding sufficient food and amenities farther west—loaded the baggage truck and their cars with camping equipment and other supplies (see Fig. 37). The motorized pioneers "will establish a tented village with their fifteen 7 x 7 tents and five 14 x 14 tents of the regular United States army equipment," the *Indianapolis Star* had earlier reported. "In lieu of the crude wood fire, however, the tourists will resort to the

Fig. 36. The "Baths" sign visible above the third car in line suggests that this Des Moines photo was taken at the Hotel Chamberlain. (NAHC)

more modern gasoline stove, and Prest-O-Lite tanks [of compressed acetylene gas]
will take the place of candles used in days gone by." The cooking equipment also included "bake-ovens, stew pans and a great lot of other stuff," Monihan explained.[53]
What's more, the "pleasure bent" travelers would have their cooking done for them.
"Tom O'Brien of the Henshaw [café] furnished the party with a Bohemian chef and
two experienced cooks, as well as two waiters, who they will take into the mountains
with them," the *Omaha World-Herald* said. In Monihan's version, however, the tourists
"hired the chef of one of the largest clubs in Philadelphia," who, accompanied by an assistant, met the caravan in Omaha.[54]

Adding cots, tents, blankets, dishes, extra tires, and other supplies in Omaha
nearly overloaded the cars, some of which were also carrying a full load of passengers.
The 3,000-pound Premier 4-40s weighed 4,800 pounds loaded, while the 3,600-pound
Premier 6-60s tipped the scales at 5,300 pounds loaded. "It was shown to be impossible
to avoid carrying a load of less than 1,600 pounds, and this must be carried whether the
small, light car is used or a car of medium weight, like those used" by the members of
the caravan, Monihan said.[55]

Each car already carried its regular tool kit, valve-grinding tool and tire-repair kit, five pounds of rags, a roll of adhesive tape, a short-handled shovel, twenty feet of three-quarter-inch rope, a tire pump, a jack, and a roll of copper wire. Afterward, Monihan advised anyone crossing the country by car to buy a $1.50 five-gallon African water bag, made of canvas. His bag, which hung from his car's windshield post, "permitted of sufficient sweating to keep the water cool. It was the rule to fill these bags from water which was free from bacteria and alkali. This made it unnecessary to drink from the water supplies found along the road, and unquestionably saved the party from much illness."[56]

The travelers left Omaha on Wednesday, July 12, for an easy 88-mile drive to Columbus, arriving at 6:00 P.M. "after a beautiful run over magnificent roads," Monihan wired to the Premier Motor Manufacturing Company that night. "Cars have now assumed business like air with camping outfits on running boards," but the forty tourists nevertheless spent their night in Columbus at the Thurston Hotel. They left the next day for a 160-mile drive to Lexington. That afternoon, five miles west of Kearney, the tourists passed a sign marking "the geographical center of the United States," where they staged a group photo (see Fig. 38). "As the crow flies, it was 1,733 miles east to Boston and west to San Francisco," *Automobile* reported.[57]

Fig. 38. The Premier motorists pose at the midway marker in Kearney, Nebraska. (Ocean to Ocean Tour booklet/FLP)

A $2,000 BLUNDER

Reaching Lexington at 6:30 P.M. Thursday, the tourists made their first camp of the trip five miles outside of town, Monihan said. Two generations earlier, Conestoga wagon trains that crossed the Plains formed a circle at night for protection. The Premier tourists, however, lined up their cars for convenience. "The best way to lay camp is to alternate the cars and tents, using the spokes of the wheels instead of pegs," said Monihan, who telegraphed from Denver that "tourists will camp in Rockies during remainder of trip."[58]

According to an itinerary printed in the July 16, 1911, *Denver Republican*, the tourists planned to camp eleven times between Denver and San Francisco. This was a fantasy. Their Lexington stop was the only occasion on which the small army of tourists actually erected a "tented village." Unscheduled stops west of Denver twice forced the men to sleep in barns or their automobiles, however, and the tourists evi-

Fig. 39. In what appears to be western Nebraska, the caravan encounters roads that must have been wet and sloppy a short time earlier. (NAHC)

COAST TO COAST BY AUTOMOBILE

dently cooked some of their own noon meals and perhaps some evening meals west of Denver. Otherwise, though, they were generally able to find a hotel large enough to feed and house them at each night's stop. "The carrying of an expensive cook, camping outfit, chef, assistant chef and all the other non-essentials are most beautiful to contemplate, but, as a matter of fact, are entirely unnecessary," Monihan concluded. Thus the tourists wasted nearly $2,000 on preparations that "were absolutely unnecessary for we found adequate hotel accommodations practically all the way across the continent."[59]

On Friday, July 14, Day 19, the Premier caravan passed North Platte, Nebraska (see Fig. 39), and crossed the state line during a 173-mile jaunt into Julesburg, "a most hospitable town." Despite its small size, the northeastern Colorado town of 1,200 persons "received the Ocean to Ocean tourists with a brass band and a committee composed of suffragettes, the mayor and leading citizens in automobiles that formed an escort of twenty cars," an obviously impressed Monihan telegraphed the Indianapolis factory (see Fig. 40). "The right of line was held by a band of cowboys."[60]

Fig. 40. Residents line the street and a uniformed brass band serenades the Premier tourists as they arrive in Julesburg, Colorado. (NAHC)

After their night of roughing it in tents, the travelers settled into Julesburg's Brown's Hotel. Even if they had wanted to, they would not have been able to camp again until they reached southeastern Wyoming, for "the general commissary [truck] was shipped [by rail] from North Platte to Rawlins to wait for the party," reported the *Rocky Mountain News* of Denver, for reasons the paper did not explain.[61] Evidently the truck wasn't shipped quite as far as Rawlins. Its familiar white canvas top, missing from photos taken in Julesburg and Denver, actually reappears in what the Premier company's *Ocean to Ocean* booklet identifies as a street scene in Laramie, 120 miles east of Rawlins.

TALES OF BAD ROADS "PURE BUNCOMBE"

Refreshed for the 213-mile run ahead of them, the autoists left Julesburg at 7:00 A.M. on Saturday, July 15. They reached the Brown Palace Hotel in Denver at 7:30 P.M. or a little after, where they would spend Sunday and Monday in Denver, the local newspapers reported. The Easterners, who had now traveled some 2,351 miles from Atlantic City, would also visit Pikes Peak, Monihan wired to the Premier factory. "We found fine roads from Omaha to Julesburg and from Julesburg into Denver it was like a pavement," an ebullient Monihan told the *Rocky Mountain News*.[62] Neglecting to mention the stretch of deep Iowa mud in his comments to the *Denver Republican*'s reporter, he seemed equally enthusiastic in his further comments about roads:

> Our party, unlike previous transcontinental trips, is advertising no make of automobiles, and we have no object in exaggerating the conditions of the roads. When an advertising tour is made the object is, of course, to show how bad the roads are. Hence the pictures of the machines in deep mud holes, fording rapidly running streams and climbing precipitous hills, all to show the wonderful endurance of one make of cars or another.
>
> All this is pure buncombe. We have found the roads generally good, some of them, the road through Iowa for example, in splendid condition. Every owner of an automobile has a latent desire to make the ocean to ocean trip, and I am confident that if the real conditions were known there would be hundreds [who] attempt it for every one who starts now.[63]

Despite his avowals, Monihan—who was, after all, Premier's advertising manager—broadcast the Premier name far and wide and freely exaggerated road conditions. In a collection of 125 contemporary articles about the Premier trip, more than half identify the autos as Premiers, a testament to Monihan's golden touch. The Premier company's ads afterward capitalized on the trek (see Fig. 41), and the automaker

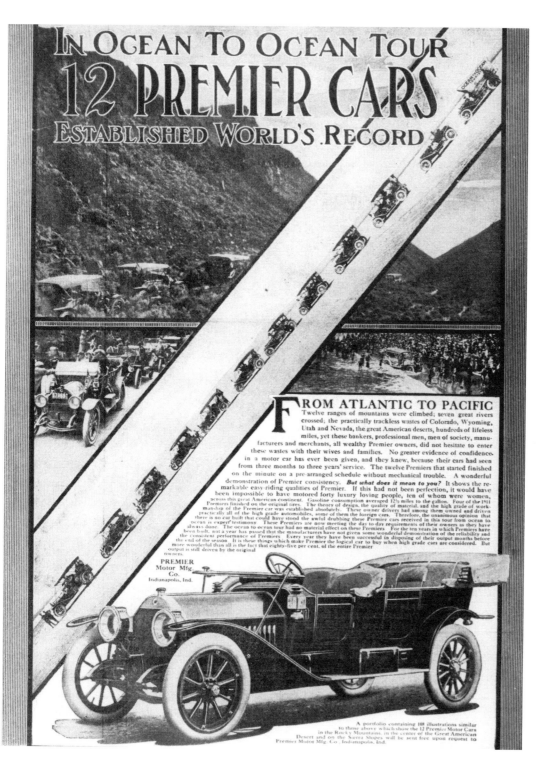

Fig. 41. A Premier ad in the December 28, 1911, issue of Automobile.

also published a booklet showing its machines mired in deep mud holes and climbing precipitous hills (although not, alas, fording any rapidly running streams). No doubt, then, the journey was at least partly an advertising gimmick.

The presence of a Spanish countess and the inventor of the motion-picture camera among the party of travelers only added to the trip's publicity value. But the crossing would have attracted attention anyway because it ultimately shattered so many myths about travel in the West—myths that Monihan at times used to his own advantage. Upon reaching Denver, for instance, the Premier tourists "were assured by those in the automobile business that it was impossible to proceed further, and that not a car had successfully traveled through from the East to the West or from the West to the East between Denver and the Pacific Ocean," Monihan wrote in a 1912 summary of the trip.[64] Pure buncombe! At least seven record-setting transcontinental trips had come through Denver, as Monihan, the route planner, and any alert Denver automobile agent should have known. The Premier group was thus able to proceed along an established route from Denver through Wyoming, Utah, and Nevada to Los Angeles—on roads that Monihan would describe as occasionally "marvelous" and frequently better than those in the East. But, he eventually conceded, "it is no exaggeration to say that the worst conditions in the roads were found in Pennsylvania."[65]

NO BEDS FOR THE WEARY

Originally scheduled to travel north to Cheyenne, Wyoming, the autoists headed northwest from Denver at about 7:00 A.M. on Tuesday, July 18, bound for Laramie. But "a very heavy rain and washouts" stopped the travelers at Forks, Colorado, nearly 90 miles from Denver and 50 miles shy of Laramie, according to the *Laramie Daily Boomerang*.[66]

Although on occasion the women undoubtedly endured some improvised sleeping arrangements, Monihan manages to confuse the record on whether the women were actually forced to sleep in barns at Forks and, later, during a similarly unscheduled overnight stay at Lucin, Utah. The regular dispatches Monihan wrote for *Motor Age* and his telegrams published in the Premier company's *Ocean to Ocean* promotional booklet state that the women did sleep in barns at both locations. But in a three-part trip summary he wrote for *Automobile* Monihan says that the Forks Hotel had just enough room for the women, while the men slept in a barn "on alfalfa beds," and in the autos.[67] He also noted that "it will be a source of comfort to all women who are contemplating a transcontinental tour to know that the complexion of none of the ladies of the party was injured," since the cars generally traveled with their folding tops up to shade the passengers. With the top and the snap-on side curtains in place, he added, "a very comfortable emergency sleeping place is at hand."[68]

Leaving Forks at 7:30 A.M. on Wednesday, July 19, Day 24, the tourists climbed ever higher into the Rocky Mountains. Over muddy roads (see Fig. 42), they reached the literal high point of their trip—approximately 8,000 feet—at Tie Siding, Wyoming, departing from there at 12:35 P.M.[69] According to the *Laramie Daily Boomerang*, it was 1:10 P.M. when the travelers reached that city (see Fig. 43). In the paper's account:

> Members of the party stated that they are a day and a half behind their schedule, the delay being caused by heavy roads. There has been no serious accident upon the trip whatever, only a moderate amount of tire troubles and a few broken springs. . . .
>
> The tourists were met between here and Tie Siding by a number of automobiles from this city and exchanged very cordial greetings with the occupants. A dinner of fresh trout was prepared for the party by the Chamber of Commerce at the Anderson cafe. . . .
>
> The intention of the party was to proceed to Medicine Bow for the night, but reports of the bad condition of the roads, consequent upon the heavy rains, caused them to change their minds and decide to remain in Laramie. After considerable difficulty rooms sufficient were found at the various hotels.

Fig. 42. Standing water softened the road at this unidentified location in Colorado. (NAHC)

Fig. 43. A young cow-
boy joins other Laramie
residents in inspecting
the Easterners. (NAHC)

A large number of the tourists seized the opportunity to spend the afternoon witnessing the ball game at the fair grounds between the Cowboys and the Indians. Others went
shopping and sightseeing.[70]

Some of the ocean-to-ocean tourists, however, spent a large part of the afternoon
trying to secure rooms for the forty people, the *Daily Boomerang* recounted. Arriving
in Laramie without hotel reservations, the travelers found the Union Pacific Hotel so
full "it was necessary for the ten ladies to sleep in two rooms, while the gentlemen in
the party secured accommodation in groups of seven and eight," according to the automaker's *Ocean to Ocean* booklet.[71] Crowding also forced the three boys to sleep in one
bed. As the caravan's unexpected arrival demonstrated, Laramie's hotels tended to fill
up "whenever there is a little more than the ordinary demand," Thursday's *Daily
Boomerang* editorialized, further pointing out that

> a prominent business man of the city is authority for the statement that five traveling men,
> who arrived on one of the late trains, could get absolutely no accommodations in the town
> last night, and spent the night playing cards and "cussing" their luck. One of these men
> did secure a bed at 5 o'clock in the morning, after the room had been vacated by another
> man who had to take an early train.[72]

THE "CONSTANT MENACE" OF PRAIRIE DOGS

The caravan drove 157 miles from Laramie to Rawlins on Thursday, July 20, passing through Medicine Bow and Fort Steele. Eight miles west of Medicine Bow, "where the road runs apparently smooth, there is a rock with a drop of over 18 inches," Monihan wrote (see Fig. 44). "Three cars which had preceded the party came to grief at this point, the cars dropping on the rock, breaking crankcases, and in one instance driving the connecting-rods through the cylinders." The advantage of the Premier auto's generous road clearance became apparent on other sections of the road immediately west of Medicine Bow as well, Monihan indicated. "The cars showed 11 inches, which was sufficient to run in the trails [ruts] at a speed of from 20 to 22 miles an hour, whereas 1 inch less would have required straddling the trail at a speed not to exceed 10 or 12 miles."[73]

At Fort Steele, "the natives said that the bridge was down and that it would be necessary to travel along the railroad ties and use the railroad bridge," Monihan recalled. But "when the tour arrived it was found that a modern up-to-date steel bridge was in place"—an incident that, in Monihan's view, illustrated "how unreliable is the

Fig. 44. A flag marks a dangerous spot in the road west of Medicine Bow, Wyoming. (Ocean to Ocean Tour booklet / FLP)

roadside information."[74] Through central Wyoming's Bitter Creek district, "a rate of 6 miles an hour was great speed," he wrote. "Some of the washouts here were 50 feet deep. The cars in front disappeared completely on the slide down the east side, and first speed was necessary to climb up the west side." According to Monihan, however, burrowing animals posed the greatest threat the travelers faced on western roads. "It must be realized that the prairie dog, gopher and badger holes are a constant menace, as these animals will dig a hole in the center of the road over night. . . . These holes are the spring breakers, axle twisters and frame wreckers."[75]

At least one of the travelers, however, remained undaunted by these threats. Upon reaching Los Angeles, Countess de Calatrava, the "Spanish noblewoman" of New York City, reported that she had enjoyed these and other hardships. "Transcontinental touring is wonderful and I never expect to have another experience so enjoyable. . . . I hope to make another ocean-to-ocean motor car trip before long under greatly improved road conditions," she exclaimed. Others evidently shared her view. In fact, Monihan, presuming to speak for all forty travelers, sent a July 21 telegram from Rock Springs, Wyoming, telling the Premier factory that the tourists had reported "not one minute of monotony" to that point (see Fig. 45).[76]

Fig. 45. One of many telegrams Monihan sent back to the Premier factory in Indianapolis. (Ocean to Ocean Tour booklet / FLP)

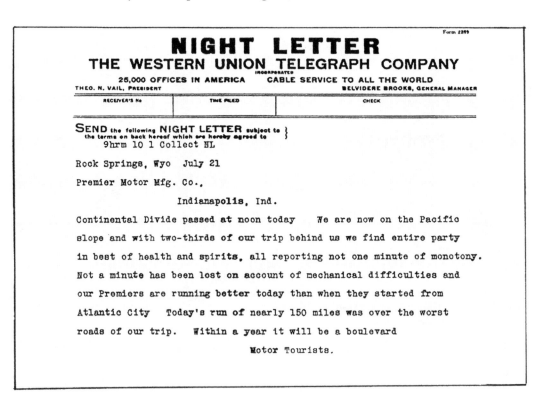

COAST TO COAST BY AUTOMOBILE

Fig. 46. A coast-to-coast Premier crests a steep hill at an undisclosed point in Wyoming. (NAHC)

The autoists reached Rock Springs after a 129-mile drive on Friday, Kemmerer after a 100-mile drive on Saturday, and Salt Lake City after a 145-mile drive through Evanston, Wyoming, on Sunday, July 23, Day 28 of the trip (see Figs. 46 and 47). "For no other reason than the crankiness of a ranchman," Monihan reported, the trail near Evanston "has been fenced off with wire fencing, making it necessary to swing far to the north and south and up occasionally steep grades." He added that "in some places here it was necessary to blaze the trail."[77] Fortunately, some unexpected pleasures tempered such trying experiences in Wyoming. "From Salt Wells to Rock Springs proved to be pretty good going," Monihan wrote. "When 10 miles from this city the tourists were met by its chief executives with a tonneau full of quart bottles of Budweiser in ice. This, perhaps, was the most unexpected courtesy of the trip."[78]

Temperatures ranged from 40 to 110 degrees during the coast-to-coast trip, according to Monihan. In the untamed West, much to their surprise, the tourists were able to find enough gasoline—they needed 150 gallons or more at a time—and oil for their fleet of twelve cars. "Gasoline was quite as common as sage brush and was available practically every day of the Ocean-to-Ocean tour.... Experience in getting lubricating oils was about parallel with that of gasoline. Undoubtedly the reason for this is that practically every ranch of any size in the great West now uses the gas engine in its daily routine," Monihan explained.[79] Gas prices, though, reflected the cost of shipping five-gallon cans hundreds of miles in some cases. Accustomed to paying about 8 cents a gallon for gas, the group of Easterners—"the combined wealth of which is estimated at $100,000,000"[80]—surrendered up to 50 cents a gallon in the West.

Fig. 47. While following a railroad's abandoned roadbed somewhere in Wyoming, the Premiers suddenly came upon a field of flowers. "It seems that a smashed carload of seeds, covering an eighth of a mile, took root and grew," reads the caption on the back of this trip photo. (NAHC)

SALT LAKE OFFERS AN "ABUNDANCE OF PLEASURE"

Mayor John S. Bransford, Police Chief S. M. Barlow, a city councilman, and other members of a welcoming committee drove out almost as far as Kemmerer on Sunday to escort the caravan into Salt Lake City. "Yesterday they prepared dinner a few miles east of Evanston," Monday's *Salt Lake Herald-Republican* recounted. The Premier group would hardly resort to pork and beans, however. "That the camp life is not so rough as one might expect is evidenced in the first exclamation of Mayor Bransford, as he reached Salt Lake, when he turned to a friend and said: 'What do you think? Porterhouse steak and mushrooms out on those prairies.'"[81]

The autos, "dust-stained and loaded with baggage,"[82] reached the Hotel Utah in Salt Lake City at 8:15 P.M. Sunday, according to two local dailies. As Monday's *Herald-Republican* described the arrival:

The Philadelphia motor tourists presented a novel spectacle as the party drove up to the south entrance of the hotel. Twelve machines, each bearing its share of the passengers and luggage necessary for the trip, pulled up to the entrance in a line headed by the mayor's party. This the motorists consider an excellent record for cross country traveling, as last night's count showed every machine that made the start was still in sound condition and ready to continue the journey. . . .

The motor truck, driven by Harry D. Weller of Indianapolis, Ind., a university graduate and professor of numerous degrees, was left a few miles behind and did not arrive until several hours later. All the machines of the party were taken in charge by the members of the Salt Lake piloting party and housed in the yards at the city jail for the night.[83]

The United States Tire Company had sent Harry Davis of New York City along with the tourists to observe how the Premiers' tires held up on the expected 4,000-mile trip. In 1911 tires generally lasted just a few thousand miles even on the best of roads. Regardless, Davis "has made a table of tire records, and at Salt Lake City, it is stated, the original air was in thirty-eight of the fifty-two tires," *the San Francisco Chronicle* reported. "The only blowout up to that time was caused by hitting a horseshoe."[84] How Davis arrived at 52 tires is a mystery: the twelve cars traveled on 48 tires and, assuming that each auto had one spare, carried 60 tires in all. Davis may have been counting the 48 road wheels plus four new tires purchased along the way.

Arriving in Salt Lake City, Monihan told reporters: "We are two days behind schedule but it is the entertainment accorded us that is responsible for this. We have been treated very cordially in every city we have stopped [in] and it has been hard to break away on time and continue the journey,"[85] although, he said, the tourists hoped to make up the lost time and reach the West Coast on schedule. In addition, Monihan noted that their journey contained an important lesson:

If these motorists can make the trip, suffer no inconvenience and find an abundance of pleasure, then it is evident that the roads of America offer the same inducements to the amateur motorist as the foreign roads. This would result in the keeping of millions of dollars at home and a development of the western country, for every dollar spent in a certain locality means development to that section.[86]

The Easterners went sightseeing on the morning of Monday, July 24, the first of two days spent idle in the city of the Mormons. The *Herald-Republican* summarized other Monday activities:

Following the organ recital at the Tabernacle at noon and luncheon, the automobilists went to Saltair at 3:30 for a dip in the lake. After bathing, the visitors witnessed the bull fight [part of the lakeside resort's Spanish Festival] and returned to the city for dinner at the Hotel Utah.

After dinner the visitors were taken out to Wandamere in automobiles. . . . After witnessing the motorcycle races, the various attractions at Wandamere were taken in. . . . The visitors rode the miniature railway, roller coaster, launch, shoot the chutes, [and] tried their eyes at the shooting gallery and the Japanese games; in fact, took in every attraction at Wandamere as guests of the management.[87]

JENKINS FILMS A "SPECTACULAR" DEPARTURE

After spending a similarly entertaining Tuesday, the tourists left Salt Lake City on Wednesday, July 26, for a 61-mile drive north to greet Ogden officials. The tourists had asked Salt Lake City Mayor John S. Bransford "to send them out of town in a spectacular manner, because they wanted a moving picture of their departure," the *Deseret Evening News* reported. Just before 11:00 A.M., with C. Francis Jenkins filming near the Brigham Young Monument, Bransford sent the fire and police departments' vehicles out in a high-speed parade. "The picture shows William H. Glore, fire chief, in his runabout, passing the Hotel Utah at full speed," the *Herald-Republican* said.[88] Next behind Glore, according to the *Deseret Evening News*, came

the auto-engine snorting blue smoke; the aerial truck; the chemical engine; hose Nos. 1 and 2 and ladder and truck companies No. 2. Following the fire wagons came the auto-patrol driven by Chauffeur George Moore.

The run had been so timed that the automobiles of the tourists fell in behind. These were led by the Greyhound driven by Chauffeur Walter Griffen and occupied by Chief of Police Barlow and Heber J. Grant, who will accompany the tourists as far as Ogden. Mayor J. S. Bransford, in his electric, will have a prominent part in the picture. . . . The tourists were particularly pleased with the "thriller," which was well timed and went off without an accident.[89]

Trailing local officials who rode in escorting autos, the Premier tourists arrived in Ogden about 2:00 P.M. on Wednesday, the *Ogden Morning Examiner* reported:

Upon their arrival here the large party went direct to Glenwood park, where a basket lunch was served. Following this an hour was spent in listening to the Chautauqua lectures and entertainment. Shortly after 4 o'clock they again entered the waiting autos and were driven about the city. After spending a brief period at the hotel the visitors left for the Hermitage.

The banquet in the canyon was the chief feature of the program prepared for the transcontinental tourists. An elaborate chicken and trout dinner was served at 6:30 o'clock, and about 60 persons, including a number of Salt Lake people and the Weber club committee, were seated about the tables.[90]

The travelers, who retired to their Reed Hotel rooms at 9:30 P.M., left Ogden early Thursday, July 27, hoping to drive north around Utah's Great Salt Lake along sandy roads leading into northeastern Nevada. They traveled 25 miles to reach Brigham City at 8:45 A.M., one newspaper reported. "They were met soon after their arrival by citizens and a crowd of curious people had soon gathered around the automobiles as they were lined up on Main street. Seven cars were somewhat delayed, and arrived only a few minutes before the party departed for the west. . . . The visitors were given a goodly supply of peaches, apricots and other fruits in this city." The scheduled night stop Thursday—"and practically the only stopping place after leaving this city"—was Montello, Nevada, according to a wire story from Brigham City. "We are a little behind schedule," Monihan explained, "but we just couldn't break away from Salt Lake."[91]

OF PREMIERS AND PREVARICATING PLUNGERS

The cars had to bounce up and over exposed rails at many unimproved railroad crossings in Utah between Ogden and Lucin, Monihan said. "It was necessary at every place for one of the occupants of the car to get out to see whether or not the flywheels were clear." The caravan spent the night at Lucin, a tiny settlement 152 miles from Ogden, only because of "misinformation on the part of the natives, who said that the run [to Montello] was 40 miles shorter than it really was," Monihan complained.[92] Hence the travelers were still on the road at nightfall.

The uncomfortable night spent in Lucin reinforced what the travelers had learned at Fort Steele, Wyoming: asking for directions can lead to trouble. "Our men are sleeping in cars and our women in a barn," read Monihan's telegram to the Premier factory that night. But the text of the Premier company's *Ocean to Ocean* booklet, which reprinted Monihan's telegram, contradicts him about the fate of the women. The booklet pictures "the famous Belview Hotel at the western terminus of the Lucin cut-off of the Southern Pacific Railroad, over the great Salt Lake," where "there was only room to accommodate the ladies of the party in beds." How comfortable those beds actually were is open to some doubt: their posts "were set in tomato cans filled with water for obvious reasons"—those evidently being to deter scorpions and bedbugs (see Fig. 48).[93]

After leaving Lucin, the ocean-to-ocean autoists traveled 149 miles to reach Elko, Nevada, at 7:00 P.M. on Friday, July 28, 1911. Utah shared with Wyoming the honor of having the worst roads to that point, one unidentified weary traveler told the *Elko Daily*

Fig. 48. The tourists' cars occupy more space than does their hotel in Lucin, Utah. (Ocean to Ocean Tour booklet/FLP)

Free Press. But the roads had improved enough to make Friday "one of the best days of the trip," Monihan telegraphed from Elko. "We had been warned of Nevada roads but so far they have been ideal. Cars running fine, people feeling fine, everything fine."[94]

Evidently, however, Monihan sent his telegram early in the evening. Later on Friday night local law officers burst in on "a number of men who were indulging in the forbidden pastime of gambling in the club rooms in the rear of the Commercial hotel," the *Free Press* reported. Among the nine men arrested for betting on roulette and faro were four "strangers" with the Premier tour, who gave the fictitious names of R. J. Bonmar, Frank Maloney, George Monroe, and Walter Smith. "Not only did we catch the men gambling, but after they were placed under arrest, the dealers paid the players money for the chips, which was indisputable evidence that they were playing for money and not pastime," District Attorney James Dysart told the newspaper. "This case will be prosecuted and no partiality shown to anyone."

The unfortunate hotel owner paid $250 apiece to bail out the tourists and guarantee their appearance in court Saturday morning, where they won a continuance to August 2, citing a need to hire lawyers. "The four strangers left at ten o'clock with the automobile party, of which they were members, going south to Eureka and expecting to spend the night in Austin, and will continue on tomorrow to Reno," Saturday's *Free Press* reported. "It is to be regretted that the raid caught the four strangers, who were merely passing through the state on a sightseeing tour, as the main object of the law is to convict the principals."[95]

MILLIONAIRES IN NEED OF BATHS

The Premier tourists made it only as far as Eureka Saturday night but traveled 132 miles to Eastgate on Sunday and 128 miles to Reno on Monday, July 31. "Eight millionaires, a countess and thirty-three other people" reached Reno's Riverside Hotel at 8:00 P.M. "The party was met outside the city limits by about 20 machines carrying Mayor Turrittin, President Sadleir of the local automobile organization and numerous enthusiasts," the *Nevada State Journal* said.[96] The tourists—forty-two of them by the paper's count—included "famous surgeons or leaders of the bar," reported the *Reno Evening Gazette*:

> Others lead cotillions, but none of them look like it. Even the Countess de Catalavara [*sic*] needed a bath when the cars were parked in front of the Riverside and rooms were assigned the party. But she smiled . . . and a witty remark by another member of the party caused a tear of laughter to leave a pearly white wake as it coursed down her dingy cheek. . . .
>
> The entry into Reno was a triumphal one, the autos white with dust, were also glad with flags, the most prominent of which being the banner presented by President Taft. It adorned the car of J. G. Monihan, the leader of the party.
>
> Mr. Monihan said, after he had registered the guests at the Riverside: "We have accomplished one thing, and that is to prove that there is a national highway across the continent that can be negotiated in ease and comfort."[97]

The garage of Reno's agency for the Dorris brand of automobile "was about packed to its capacity on Monday night when the 'Ocean to Ocean' party stored their machines

Fig. 49. Four cars sank in the mud where a ruptured irrigation ditch had flooded the road east of Reno, Nevada. (NAHC)

there. J. E. Threlkel, the owner of the garage, met the party about ten miles out of Reno and escorted them into town. They were headed for the Dorris garage and there their machines were carefully attended, replenished with gasoline and oil and cleaned up somewhat," the *Reno Evening Gazette* said.[98]

"Your Nevada roads are not bad," Monihan told the Reno newspapers. "They are infinitely superior to those in Wyoming and far better than many we passed over in the east." In his trip summary for *Automobile*, however, Monihan told a different story. To reach Reno, the transcontinental autos wound through deep sand north of Fallon, he recalled, after which the road became a "regular boulevard" to the town of Hazen, "excepting for a water hole, caused by a break in an irrigation ditch flooding a considerable area. . . . Four of the cars at one time were hub deep in this mire, which was apparently without bottom. With the assistance of mud hooks, chains and a considerable amount of sage brush, which was cut and thrown in front of the wheels, the party was able to extricate the cars. This was the only point on the entire transcontinental tour where mud hooks were resorted to" (see Fig. 49).[99] It was also the only time that some of the Premier drivers bumped along a nearby railroad track rather than take their chances on the road.

Tuesday's *Nevada State Journal*, however, seems to have agreed with Monihan's initial assessment of the roads. "The party has met with no untoward incident in all its four weeks of travel so far as traveling mishaps go, the most disagreeable feature being the arrest of four of their members at Elko for gambling," the paper reported. "The members at the hotel last night were reluctant to shed any light on the identity of those who were caught in the raid at Elko last Friday night. Several of them, however, declared that they considered the raid a frame-up and commented on the fact that the necessity of enforcing the law did not occur to the peace officers until a party of strangers happened to come to town. . . . The time for the preliminary [hearing] was set for tomorrow but it does not appear likely that the four will be present."[100]

THE PREMIER PARTY PAUSES AT THE PACIFIC

Threlkel guided the tourists for ten miles after they left Reno late Tuesday morning for a 50-mile climb into the Sierra Nevada to Tahoe Tavern, California, on the northwestern shore of Lake Tahoe, near Truckee (see Figs. 50 and 51). On Wednesday, Au-

Fig. 50. By climbing the Sierras west of Truckee, California, the tourists earned a breathtaking view of Donner Lake, visible just above the car's top. (Ocean to Ocean Tour booklet / FLP)

Fig. 51. The cars forded this narrow, fairly deep creek while traveling in the Sierra Nevada. (NAHC)

gust 2, the tourists traveled 134 miles to Sacramento, where they presented Taft's silk U.S. flag, along with a letter from the president, to California Governor Hiram Johnson. A 142-mile drive then brought the party to San Francisco on Thursday, only a day behind schedule. According to Friday's *San Francisco Call*:

> Some eight or 10 local owners of Premier cars, headed by E. C. Collins, local Premier representative, went to Livermore yesterday afternoon to greet the visitors and pilot them to the city. The tourists were expected to reach Livermore at 2 o'clock, but a late start from Sacramento caused a delay of some three hours and it was 5 o'clock before pacemaker Ray McNamara, who has two transcontinental trips to his record, came in sight closely followed by the rest of the party. There was a tooting of horns and a general informal greeting enjoyed for a few minutes before the trip was resumed to this city by way of Sunol, Mission, San Jose, Niles, Hayward and Oakland.[101]

"Somewhat dusty but in the brightest of spirits, the sixty [*sic*] eastern tourists who crossed the continent in ten Premier cars reached this city at 8:30 last evening, and

112   COAST TO COAST BY AUTOMOBILE

were escorted to the St. Francis Hotel by a crowd of motor car enthusiasts headed by Mayor [Patrick H.] McCarthy and a big brass band," the *Call* reported. There, the travelers presumably delivered President Taft's message to the San Francisco mayor. According to the *San Francisco Chronicle*, the wealthy tourists were not "strong on the brass band idea, and all signs were stripped off the band truck before the parade up Market Street was begun."[102]

The city's newspapers do not reveal the contents of President Taft's message to Mayor McCarthy. But, as the *Salt Lake (City) Herald-Republican* had reported, the three boys in the tour, "all ardent supporters of the Boy Scouts . . . carry a letter from George D. Porter, Boy Scout commissioner of the east, to the Boy Scouts of the west. A big reception is planned for the Boy Scouts of San Francisco, the party planning a big 'joy ride,' in which fifty machines will be used for the San Francisco Scouts." The Premier tourists also had "many messages to deliver to California officials received from various officials and dignitaries they have visited en route," the *New York Times* earlier noted.[103]

The travelers had covered 4,075.5 miles between Atlantic City and San Francisco in a running time of 31 days and an elapsed time of 38 days, 15 hours, 30 minutes. Idle in San Francisco on both Friday and Saturday, the tourists traveled 143 miles south to Del Monte on Sunday, August 6, Day 42. They spent a day in Del Monte before traveling 162 miles to San Luis Obispo on Tuesday, 126 miles to Santa Barbara on Wednesday, and 100 miles to reach Los Angeles at 2:00 P.M. Thursday, August 10, where some three hundred autos met the caravan twelve miles from the city limits, Monihan claimed. The *Los Angeles Times* likewise mentioned three hundred cars in the escort, but reporters for the *Los Angeles Examiner* and *Los Angeles Herald* counted only one hundred autos.

The slow-moving Premier prairie schooner, which left Santa Barbara at 5:00 A.M. Thursday to arrive in Los Angeles with the others, was actually the first to arrive at the mouth of Laurel Canyon, the *Examiner* reported. The baggage truck

came down the winding mountain road and drew up in front of Bungalow Inn, in Laurel Canyon, where 2000 Angelenos had assembled to welcome the tourists. . . . Then followed in rapid succession the other cars, with the exception of two which met with tire punctures shortly before the Inn was reached. . . . They were escorted to the grounds in front of the Bungalow where a luncheon was served consisting of fruit, sandwiches and coffee. . . .

Shortly after 3 o'clock a start was made for the city, a handsomely decked little roadster leading the procession. . . . Down the canyon the procession moved with horns and sirens blowing. The autos then passed through Hollywood, where the streets were lined with cheering people.

At Third and Figueroa the party was met by the mounted police and a band. From this point the parade moved down Figueroa to Seventh, to Broadway, to First, to Spring and then to the Alexandria Hotel, where rooms for the entire party had been reserved. . . . As the procession moved through the downtown streets the visitors were cheered again and again by the crowds which lined the curb on each side.[104]

In their coverage of the Premier caravan's arrival, two Los Angeles dailies ran photos showing Harry D. Weller, driver of the baggage truck, holding up "'Utah Mike,' the coyote captured in the desert after its mother had killed the Premier caravan's yellow dog."[105] The pup would be placed in a zoo, according to the *Los Angeles Times*. At a banquet Thursday night, Lewis Schwaebe, the Premier distributor for Southern California, awarded to Dr. Hugh F. Cook, one of the Premier drivers,

> a handsome prize . . . for having the best score across the continent. It is doubtful that any man has ever carried an automobile across the country in better shape and time than did Dr. Cook. He has the original New York air in three of his tires and has had no mechanical trouble whatever. Members of the party state that the doctor has assisted other cars several times when it was not necessary that he linger behind the parade.[106]

On Friday and Saturday, the Eastern travelers relaxed and went sightseeing in and around Los Angeles. The Premier caravan left the Alexandria Hotel at noon Sunday, August 13, bound for the seashore at Venice, where the cars would touch salt water again. "Ellsworth Sprague drove at a swift clip over the roads and showed no fear of the speed cops," the *Los Angeles Times* reported. "When a Pope-Hartford driver tried to pass Sprague the 'Oyster King' refused to take a back seat but drove like Barney Oldfield and kept his place in the line."[107]

At exactly 2:00 P.M. Sunday, as high tide neared at the City of Venice Park near Los Angeles, "thousands of motoring enthusiasts witnessed the immersion, and cheered themselves hoarse when the brass bands were not engaged in making music," according to the *New York Times* account of the journey's end (see Fig. 52). "The cars were run into the ocean under their own power, and by their own amateur-owner drivers, on a plank chute that was built from the cement walk into the surf. More than 2,000 motor cars were parked in the open-air garage in full view of the ceremony, and thousands occupied places of vantage on the pier and Ship Hotel, which is situated . . . about one thousand feet from the shore."[108]

The Premier company, prone to overestimate crowds, said 50,000 people watched the Premier drivers end their run. The *Los Angeles Times* quoted the same number, although it was the highest estimate given by the three Los Angeles dailies that covered

the event. The *Los Angeles Herald* put the turnout at 10,000 people, while the *Los Angeles Examiner* said that 10,000 people crowded the beach "and twice 10,000 persons lined the streets and avenues of the seaside city to participate in the rousing welcome."[109] Whatever their number, the spectators were densely packed, the *Los Angeles Times* observed. "It was necessary to call the lifeguards to keep back the over-zealous welcomers who were too anxious to extend a western greeting of their own making," the paper said. "When F. K. McCarver, president of the Chamber of Commerce of Venice, arranged the unique ceremony he had no idea the crowd would be so large. The police had difficulty clearing a path for the cars."[110]

The first car in the surf was Ray McNamara's pilot Premier, whose passengers included John Guy Monihan, his wife, and their son. McNamara's car "dropped from the specially constructed runway at exactly 2 o'clock, ran about fifty feet through the surf and returned to the street by another runway," the *Los Angeles Examiner* reported. Added the *Los Angeles Herald*: "As the big Premier splashed into the brin[e], throwing

Fig. 52. One of the Premier autos splashes through the Pacific surf at Venice, California, the ceremonial end of the trail for the first ocean-to-ocean automobile caravan. (Ocean to Ocean Tour booklet/FLP)

spray over its occupants, a tremendous cheer went up from thousands of throats. Hats were thrown into the air and handkerchiefs were frantically waved."[111]

McNamara had some trouble as he pulled out of the waves, however, as "the chute built to the water proved difficult to steer into," noted the *Los Angeles Times*. "As Ray McNamara drove the six-cylinder Premier into the waves and then whirled about to make the return run, the front wheels missed the boards and the big car plowed into the soft sand. In spite of this the car yanked itself out and reached the shore and was driven back to the speedway." Likewise, "the second car, containing the Jenkins party, was turned too short and struck the deep beach sand, delaying the ceremony a few minutes. The tide was coming in and the occupants in the last five machines were splashed with the waves." Weller in the Premier prairie schooner "had difficulty in keeping his pet coyote in the machine during the run through the waves, as that desert animal was exceedingly frightened." *Automobile Topics*, in a later review of movies that Jenkins shot at the Venice beach, noted that "hundreds of the spectators are in bathing suits and the occupants of the last car are showered with water."[112]

Afterward, several Easterners further distinguished themselves during a tour of the resort city, followed by a "feast" at the Ship Cafe. Dr. Hugh F. Cook "watched the sea nymphs sporting in the waves and then donned a bathing suit and showed his Apollo-like form," reported Monday's *Los Angeles Times*. George C. Allen "covered himself with glory yesterday by taking in everything there is that is worth taking in. Until a late hour last night he was still seeing the sights."[113]

And then, the group that had been together for nearly 50 days began to break up. "A number of them will return to their Eastern homes by the Southern route," according to the *San Francisco Chronicle*, but many more accounts suggested that the tourists actually shipped their cars home by rail.[114]

COST PER PERSON: $6.99 A DAY

Except for the baggage truck, which started in Indianapolis and was reportedly shipped by rail from western Nebraska to southeastern Wyoming, the autos traveled 4,617.6 miles apiece from Atlantic City to Los Angeles.[115] Hence they averaged 131.93 miles per day for their running time of 35 calendar days, or 101.77 miles per day for their elapsed time to Los Angeles of 45 days, 9 hours, which included 11 days spent idle (see Table 8). It was a reasonably impressive feat: as late as 1924, one road guide called

TABLE 8. Itinerary of the Premier Caravan, 1911.

Day/Date	City to City	Daily Mileage[a]	Cumulative Mileage
1/June 26 Mon	Atlantic City, N.J.–Harrisburg, Pa.	168.1	168.1
2/June 27 Tue	Harrisburg, Pa.–Baltimore	117.1	285.2
3/June 28 Wed	Baltimore–Washington, D.C.	45.0	330.2
4/June 29 Thu	Washington, D.C.–Bedford Springs, Pa.	150.2	480.4
5/June 30 Fri	Bedford Springs, Pa.–Summit, Pa.	85.0	565.4
6/July 1 Sat	Summit, Pa.–Zanesville, Ohio	147.3	712.7
7/July 2 Sun	Zanesville, Ohio–Indianapolis	236.4	949.1
8/July 3 Mon	*idle day in Indianapolis*	0	949.1
9/July 4 Tue	*idle day in Indianapolis*	0	949.1
10/July 5 Wed	Indianapolis–Lafayette, Ind.	75.2	1,024.3
11/July 6 Thu	Lafayette, Ind.–Chicago	145.6	1,169.9
12/July 7 Fri	*idle day in Chicago*	0	1,169.9
13/July 8 Sat	Chicago–Davenport, Iowa	178.2	1,348.1
14/July 9 Sun	Davenport, Iowa–Colfax, Iowa	178.6	1,526.7
15/July 10 Mon	Colfax, Iowa–Omaha, Neb.	190.2	1,716.9
16/July 11 Tue	*idle day in Omaha*	0	1,716.9
17/July 12 Wed	Omaha, Neb.–Columbus, Neb.	88.2	1,805.1
18/July 13 Thu	Columbus, Neb.–Lexington, Neb.	160.4	1,965.5
19/July 14 Fri	Lexington, Neb.–Julesburg, Colo.	172.8	2,138.3
20/July 15 Sat	Julesburg, Colo.–Denver	212.6	2,350.9
21/July 16 Sun	*idle day in Denver*	0	2,350.9
22/July 17 Mon	*idle day in Denver*	0	2,350.9
23/July 18 Tue	Denver–Forks, Colo.	88.4	2,439.3
24/July 19 Wed	Forks, Colo.–Laramie, Wyo.	50.2	2,489.5
25/July 20 Thu	Laramie, Wyo.–Rawlins, Wyo.	157.3	2,646.8
26/July 21 Fri	Rawlins, Wyo.–Rock Springs, Wyo.	129.1	2,775.9
27/July 22 Sat	Rock Springs, Wyo.–Kemmerer, Wyo.	100.3	2,876.2
28/July 23 Sun	Kemmerer, Wyo.–Salt Lake City	145.4	3,021.6
29/July 24 Mon	*idle day in Salt Lake City*	0	3,021.6
30/July 25 Tue	*idle day in Salt Lake City*	0	3,021.6
31/July 26 Wed	Salt Lake City–Ogden, Utah	60.6	3,082.2

(cont'd)

32 / July 27 Thu	Ogden, Utah–Lucin, Utah	152.4	3,234.6
33 / July 28 Fri	Lucin, Utah–Elko, Nev.	148.8	3,383.4
34 / July 29 Sat	Elko, Nev.–Eureka, Nev.	106.2	3,489.6
35 / July 30 Sun	Eureka, Nev.–Eastgate, Nev.	132.4	3,622.0
36 / July 31 Mon	Eastgate, Nev.–Reno, Nev.	127.6	3,749.6
37 / Aug. 1 Tue	Reno, Nev.–Tahoe Tavern, Calif.	50.1	3,799.7
38 / Aug. 2 Wed	Tahoe Tavern, Calif.–Sacramento, Calif.	134.2	3,933.9
39 / Aug. 3 Thu	Sacramento, Calif.–San Francisco	141.6	4,075.5
40 / Aug. 4 Fri	*idle day in San Francisco*	0	4,075.5
41 / Aug. 5 Sat	*idle day in San Francisco*	0	4,075.5
42 / Aug. 6 Sun	San Francisco–Del Monte, Calif.	143.2	4,218.7
43 / Aug. 7 Mon	*idle day in Del Monte*	0	4,218.7
44 / Aug. 8 Tue	Del Monte, Calif.–San Luis Obispo, Calif.	162.4	4,381.1
45 / Aug. 9 Wed	San Luis Obispo, Calif.–Santa Barbara, Calif.	126.1	4,507.2
46 / Aug. 10 Thu	Santa Barbara, Calif.–Los Angeles	100.4	4,617.6[b]
47 / Aug. 11 Fri	*idle day in Los Angeles*	0	4,617.6[b]
48 / Aug. 12 Sat	*idle day in Los Angeles*	0	4,617.6[b]
49 / Aug. 13 Sun	*dipping ceremony in Venice, Calif., ends trip*	n/a	4,617.6[b]

SOURCE: Premier Motor Manufacturing Company, *Ocean to Ocean Tour of the Premierites Told by Wire and Photo.*

[a] Distances are from the *Ocean to Ocean Tour* booklet, p. 2.

[b] Adding the daily distances for the points between San Francisco and Los Angeles yields a cumulative trip mileage of 4,607.6—10 miles less than the total given in the *Ocean to Ocean Tour* booklet. This table assumes that the total mileage given in the booklet is accurate and that the Premier company erred in recording one of the daily distances.

a 100-mile run "a moderate day's drive" for a transcontinental motorist.[116] The Premiers averaged 4.24 mph for their elapsed time between Atlantic City and Los Angeles, which compares favorably to the 1.23 mph average achieved by a three-wheeled Motorette that also crossed the country in 1911. (The Reo that set a transcontinental speed record in 1910 averaged 13.78 mph.) The dozen Premiers averaged 12.5 miles per gallon of gas, Monihan said, which means that the convoy consumed about 4,350 gallons.

Despite the large number of cars and inexperienced drivers on mile after mile of unfamiliar roads and trails, the caravan experienced little trouble aside from wornout tires and broken springs, the Premier company claimed at the time, although a member of the Premier caravan later reported that more serious breakdowns did occur.

Writing to *Scientific American* in 1912 to urge the establishment of a national highway, C. Francis Jenkins advised motorists to make long-distance trips in groups for safety, noting that "a broken side-frame in the Allegheny Mountains, and a broken crankshaft on the plains, during our trip, were rendered innocuous . . . by reason of the attendance of the other cars." The 1911 trip was also hard on car springs: four broke on the trail. In an age when a set of tires lasted 5,000 miles with good care, "four of the 1911 cars went through on their original shoes," Monihan said—an impressive record. "On the 1910 cars the average was two [new] shoes to a car."[117]

Crossing the country by Conestoga wagon five or six decades earlier was a perilous affair; many pioneers died of malnutrition and disease brought on by fatigue. Quite the opposite was true for the Premier transcontinentalists, whose byword was luxury. "There was no illness en route and the physical condition of the whole party was even better at the end than at the beginning," Monihan claimed. Because the Premiers had long wheelbases—140 inches for the big 6-cylinder models—and comfortable suspensions, "at no time was exceptional fatigue shown by any of the tourists." The travelers also stopped at the "best hotels" along the route, he told *Motor Age*.[118]

The trip probably cost more than the $10,000 subscription that the organizers initially pledged. Because of the group's size, "we get convention rates and it looks now as if the cost will not amount to more than $250 per person," Monihan had said in Chicago. "Our trip will demonstrate the economy of traveling in a large party like this," he predicted.[119] But the tourists seldom camped out west of Omaha, so they probably spent considerably more at hotels than Monihan had originally planned. Contending that the tourists gave Monihan the nickname "Money," the *Los Angeles Times* said at the end of the trek that "the $10,000, which was appropriated by the men of the party for tour expenses, is gone and now 'Money' is hustling more money. One of the familiar sights is to see the Premier man with a bunch of bills in his hand ready to assess the party and from Count Loder to Dr. Hugh Cook the men dig down deep in their pockets and 'pay the piper.'"[120]

In truth, the travelers exceeded their $10,000 budget by more than 50 percent, as "ten thousand dollars have been spent by the Easterners for hotel accommodations alone," the *Los Angeles Examiner* reported. The travelers spent an extra $2,000 on tires and accessories, $2,000 for gasoline, oil, and "incidental expenses," and $1,800 on the seldom-used camping outfit.[121] The wealthy tourists received many free meals along the way, however, which trimmed their food expenses, at least. Even so, at a final cost of $15,800, the trip cost each of the forty travelers $395—well above Monihan's estimate of $250 per person. That works out to $8.70 per day per person. Excluding the $2,000 cost of tires and accessories, however, the daily rate per capita drops to $6.99.

Either way, the motor tourists overpaid for their outing. The "millionaire auto party" traveled the route of the future Lincoln Highway through Illinois, Nebraska, Wyoming, Utah, Nevada, and California. And, as the *Complete Official Road Guide of the Lincoln Highway* advised transcontinental tourists in 1924: "The entire expense of a car and four passengers from New York to San Francisco, a distance of 3,140 miles, via the Lincoln Highway, should not at any time exceed $5.00 a day per passenger under normal conditions." The figure included gasoline, oil, "and all provisions," but excluded repairs and tire expenses. The Premier tourists could, however, have cut their daily rate much further, Monihan acknowledged in a 1912 *Harper's Weekly* article: "By taking camping equipment and camping out throughout the entire journey the trip can be made approximately at an expense of one dollar a day for each member of the party. The sum of two dollars a day ought to provide for every item, including gasoline, oil, etc. The Motor Tourists carried a camping outfit, but they used it on only one occasion."[122]

THE CENTRAL OR THE SOUTHERN ROUTE?

According to Premier pilot Ray McNamara, "the trip can be made in from 20 to 25 days easily, taking a direct route from New York, or in 30 days, taking time out to visit several of the great cities requiring detours from the direct route." The Premier caravan's central route was faster than the southern route that McNamara had taken on his 1910 transcontinental trip, he advised. Commenting that the central route's steepest grades, in the Sierra Nevada, "are easy to negotiate, so there is nothing to fear on this route except the Summer rains in Iowa," he nonetheless advised tourists to use the central route only until mid-October, when heavy snowstorms typically closed the Sierra Nevada passes. Moreover, McNamara pointed out, even though the southern route is open at any season, it has few hotels west of Albuquerque. As he further remarked:

> Then again it is necessary to roll boulders and build roads in spots on the Santa Fe trail, while the central route can be traveled without block and tackle, shovel, or any road building. . . . The Santa Fe trail might be classed as the scenic route and the central as the more practical route. It would not cost a great deal of money to put both routes in fine shape. The land consists of material better than macadam for road surface, and it would only be necessary to grade trails and put in a few bridges and sign boards.[123]

Although it was Monihan's view that even on the central route, "the going is rough in places," he agreed that "they are the exceptions rather than the rule, and while a sturdy car is necessary, and in some places a quick eye and steady nerve are essential, any driver of reasonable experience can get through in happiness, comfort and safety."[124]

All in all, McNamara concluded, the Premier trip proved what the average driver could accomplish:

> I believe the tour to be the best showing ever made by the automobile. It demonstrated that the modern car can be capably handled by the amateur driver over all sorts of road conditions without serious mishap.... I think that within the next few years as a result of this trip many motorists will make the ocean to ocean run, and by the time that the Panama-Pacific exposition is opened [in 1915] it is a certainty that many motorists will come to the coast in their own machines.[125]

ADVICE TO TRAVELERS

Monihan cautioned that a successful crossing required "four great essentials": a slow pace, a reliable car, a cheerful disposition, and a group of travelers, as opposed to an individual.[126] He might also have mentioned the importance of planning the trip. Although the Premier tourists were at one point two days behind schedule, they reached Los Angeles at what the Premier company claimed was the hour designated during a planning meeting held in Denver, 2,250 miles to the east.

"Limit, by all means, the number of passengers to four," Monihan urged would-be travelers. "If this is done transcontinental touring will be a comfort, and if moderate speed is insisted upon no fatigue will result. The crowded car means discomfort, added baggage, greater load and is altogether undesirable." Advising against the even greater discomfort of breaking down in the desert, Monihan cautioned that "the one danger of the ocean-to-ocean run lies in going alone." In that regard, perhaps earlier coast-to-coast drivers had not exaggerated the perils of the journey as much as Monihan often contended they had. Because these earlier drivers traveled in single automobiles rather than in a caravan, a breakdown in the desert could have meant dying from lack of food, water and shelter—hazards that remained real for solo travelers for many years to come. Even though "not less than" 25,000 transcontinental autos drove the central route in 1923, its desert stretches were still dangerous. "Don't allow the car to be without food of some sort at any time west of Salt Lake City," the Lincoln Highway

Association warned in 1924. "You might break down late in the day and have to wait a number of hours until the next tourist comes along."[127]

Such hazards notwithstanding, the Premier company clearly appreciated the trip's potential as advertising fodder. It quickly published an advertising booklet "containing 108 illustrations and telling in detail the story of the transcontinental tour of 12 Premier cars."[128] The story is told primarily through photos and Monihan's telegrams from along the route. At its annual fall auto display, the Premier Sales Company of Indianapolis also created a desert scene in which "sand, cactus and sage brush were used, surrounding the tents of the campers and two of their cars, the pilot and the prairie schooner." A photograph shows a third car in the background. The campsite was, of course, pure fiction: while crossing the arid West, the ocean-to-ocean tourists had stayed in hotels.[129]

The automaker claimed a generous share of credit for the trip's success, asserting that the feat "shows the remarkable easy-riding qualities of Premier. If this had not been perfection, it would have been impossible to have motored forty luxury loving people, ten of whom were women, across this great American continent." In short, the trek was the "Greatest Achievement in the History of Motoring," the factory declared, one that "gives Premier the world's amateur touring record and makes Premier America's greatest touring car and the safe car for you to buy."[130]

MOVIES AND A NEW MODEL

Jenkins's motion pictures were shown informally at the Venice Auditorium after the dipping ceremony on August 13. A more polished screening occurred in December 1911, four months after the Pacific Ocean wheel-dipping ceremony, in Indianapolis, home of the Premier company. The automaker was still showing the motion picture years later, according to a photo that ran in the April 16, 1914, issue of *Automobile* (see Fig. 53). "The pictures prove that much fun is to be derived from a trans-continental motor trip," *Automobile Topics* observed in a review of the new movie, noting that "one scene shows many of the men of the party playing a game of baseball in the heart of the Great American desert, in Nevada, the contest closing with the mobbing of the umpire." As the review also pointed out:

> The pictures show the great strain to which trans-continental cars are put, it being possible to see the twisting and jolting of the machines on some of the roads. . . . In addition to the

moving pictures some of the most striking of the hundreds of [still] photographs of scenes on the tour are thrown on the screen.

As soon as the Indianapolis engagement is filled the pictures will be sent to all the principal cities of the country to be used in furtherance of the movement for good roads and "seeing" America first.[131]

Also in December 1911, the automaker introduced "the tangible outcome of the expedition"—a new model designed especially for long-distance touring, *Automobile Topics* reported. The "touring Premier de luxe" converted easily from an open car to a landaulet—an auto having an enclosed rear compartment with a driver's seat that is roofed but otherwise open to the elements. The design of the new touring Premier de luxe could be "attributed directly to needs observed under the peculiarly favorable circumstances which the tour brought forth," the magazine said. "To convert the body into its open touring guise it is necessary merely to lower the sashes, drop the uprights into pockets in the doors and lower the screen behind the driver's seat into a similar place of concealment. If desired, the top also may be folded in the regular way."[132]

A NEW EPOCH IN MOTORING

The press reaction was as favorable as the automaker's own, if slightly less effusive: "The completion of the ocean to ocean tour . . . will mark a new epoch in the annals of motoring," the *New York Times* said as the caravan neared the West Coast. "For the first time a party of amateur-owner drivers, accompanied by families and friends, including eight women, will have crossed the American Continent in motor cars. For the first time more than one car will have made the trip, and for the first time more than one car containing pleasure tourists." Thus transcontinental touring, "not long since a hazardous undertaking, is fast becoming very much in the nature of a safe and pleasurable experience."[133]

During his visit to the West Coast in November 1911, Premier President Harold O. Smith expressed confidence "that the tourist traffic now going to Europe can be diverted to Southern California," according to the *Los Angeles Times*. "He sees a great future for cross-continent touring and says he has had at least 3000 requests from automobile owners for information concerning the route across the country. Of this number Smith believes about 300 will make the trip across the continent this coming year."[134] Other newspapers saw additional implications in the Premier crossing. "The great impetus that their efforts will give to good roads construction will place them in the annals of this new mode of interstate communication as the pioneers," the *Los Angeles Herald* predicted. "An ocean-to-ocean boulevard is not a dream, but a possibility," the *Los Angeles Times* agreed. "The tour of the . . . Premier cars from the Atlantic to the Pacific has proved that a highway across the United States would mean the sale of thousands more automobiles."[135]

A half-century earlier, railroads, in serving their own interests, also served the public good by laying steel rails that truly united the United States. Likewise, auto manufacturers—including the Premier company—helped create a stronger demand for their own products by promoting a greater social good: better roads. Despite all the publicity surrounding their tour and despite personal meetings with the governors of Pennsylvania, Indiana, Nebraska, Utah, and California, however, the Philadelphia Motor Tourists failed to inspire an immediate federal road-building effort. But even without the federal government's involvement, the 1911 Premier stunt, for all its occasional glitz, fueled the push for highways both to free farmers from their rural isolation and generally to improve commerce.

Several automobile and touring clubs—including the Touring Club of America, which in 1910 had sent A.L. Westgard across the country in a Premier auto driven by Ray McNamara—had already plotted various routes for the transcontinental highway. Yet until shortly after the Premier trek, no one had aggressively promoted a specific plan to build such a road. Then, in September 1912, Indianapolis Motor Speedway promoter Carl G. Fisher announced his "transcontinental stone road project," an idea he had hatched in late 1911, according to *Automobile*. Fisher asserted that "the highways of America are built chiefly of politics, whereas the proper material is crushed rock, or concrete."[136] His inspiration undoubtedly came in part from the Premier tourists, who not only traveled through Fisher's hometown of Indianapolis but also drove automobiles that had been manufactured there.

Fisher sought to raise $10 million from automakers and accessory manufacturers, who would pledge one-third of 1 percent of gross sales to improve the existing road linking New York and San Francisco. Named in honor of Abraham Lincoln, the Lincoln Highway would become "the first road in the United States to be definitely laid out and its improvement urged by a national body," the organizers claimed.[137] But it was not until July 11, 1916, when President Woodrow Wilson signed the Federal Aid Road Act of 1916, that the federal government began regularly financing road construction. Even with federal aid, moreover, transcontinental highways were slow to improve: by 1924, the 3,143-mile-long Lincoln Highway had only 837 miles of concrete, brick, or other permanent surfacing.[138]

One automobile journal in 1913 praised Monihan as "largely responsible [for] the development of across country automobile literature and the tremendously increasing number of private motor car owners who see the great vacation possibilities of the now famous trail to the sunset."[139] The successful Premier crossing forever changed the way Americans viewed transcontinental motoring, another journal declared:

> There is a general feeling that the Pacific and Atlantic coasts have been brought closer together and transcontinental touring by pleasure parties is now expected to become common since the first tour of this kind has been such an unqualified success. It has been proven that there are no unsurmountable difficulties in the way and when anticipated improvements have been made on the transcontinental motoring highway the trip is expected to be one of unusual pleasure.[140]

To capitalize on these new possibilities, later in 1911 the American Automobile Association teamed up with a touring company to sponsor the first public transcontinental automobile tour, a profit-making venture.

PARDON ME, BOY— IS THAT THE AUTOMOBILE CHOO-CHOO?

4

I do wish I had seen more rosy cheeks.

—Auto tourist Sarah Legg, bemoaning the
pale complexion of the "Western girl"

IN 1911, eight weeks after the Premier caravan crossed the country, well-to-do East-erners were given the opportunity, for $875 per person, to see America from the first "transcontinental automobile train." Unlike the Premier excursion, this was a profit-making venture, sponsored by a New York City touring agency, the Raymond and Whitcomb Company. The company "has been running a series of New England tours this summer in which Garford cars were used exclusively with great success," according to *Motor Age*.[1] Aspiring to even greater success, the agency hoped to persuade fifty people to pay a total of $43,750 to travel the "Trail to Sunset" route across the country by auto.

Raymond and Whitcomb had a dozen Garford touring cars ready for its grandest tour of the season—the first transcontinental tour "where each day's mileage and each night's stop have been definitely fixed in advance." As the company assured prospective travelers, "it is expected that this schedule can be followed throughout, enabling friends to reach passengers by wire or mail on specified dates." (Properly speaking, the Raymond and Whitcomb tour could not claim this breakthrough, for the Premier tourists had also followed a schedule.) If the Garford trip succeeded, predicted one Midwestern newspaper, "it is expected to be made an annual event."[2]

The tourists would travel about 100 miles a day—the longest day was 155 miles, the shortest 24—except on Sundays, to reach Los Angeles by Thanksgiving. On a 52-day, 4,000-mile schedule as precise as any railroad's, the Garford motor train would travel through thirteen states, following a route "carefully and deliberately chosen, from a strictly touring standpoint, offering the most varied scenery and numerous points of historic interest."[3] Tour organizers also planned to map the route for other motorists and, by reporting road conditions to the U.S. government, to push for a transcontinental highway.

Although intended as a sight-seeing excursion, the Garford trip was not without its adventures. Sand, snow, and mud posed the greatest obstacles to the tour's progress. The entire caravan bogged down along a muddy stretch of prairie road in Kansas, forcing the drivers to dig their cars out with shovels. A blizzard briefly stranded the pilot car and baggage truck in the Colorado Rockies, and the cars sank in quicksand along a New Mexican river. In Arizona, the temperature plummeted shortly after the automobiles stalled in deep mud, which froze and held the cars fast for 12 hours. To escape, the travelers had to cut down trees and build a log road.

THE AAA PREPARES A MAP

The American Automobile Association's Touring Bureau had received so many requests for maps and transcontinental touring information that the association had decided to cooperate with the Raymond and Whitcomb tour, according to the *New York Times*:

> Many have been deterred by the lack of complete running directions and specific mileages, experienced pilotage, and other elements of uncertainty—particularly gasoline, oil supplies, and hotel accommodations—inevitable in such an undertaking at this time. Therefore the American Automobile Association stepped into the breach and found a means for ridding tourists of the incidental hardships mentioned above.[4]

The AAA was preparing a map of the route "and the booklet covering same will be available to others making the whole or any part of the trip after Oct. 1." Thus the expedition "will eventually establish a well marked transcontinental automobile highway from coast to coast," the *Trinidad (Colo.) Chronicle-News* predicted. What's more, the paper reported, "the A.A.A. contemplates the passage of a bill in Congress which will provide for a transcontinental highway."[5]

The association lent to the tour its prominent mapper, Anthon L. Westgard, 46, a native of Norway who acted as tour guide or "pilot" in the automobile train's lead auto. Twice within the previous year, Westgard had traversed the "Trail to Sunset" route that the caravan would follow. Most notably, on October 11, 1910, with Ray F. McNamara at the wheel of a Premier auto, Westgard had left New York on a 49-day, 4,203.5-mile trip to Los Angeles that followed the Santa Fe Trail in the Southwest. During his second trip, which began early in 1911, Westgard rode in a Saurer truck that became the first truck to cross the continent. Before joining AAA, Westgard had laid out routes for the Automobile Club of America and the Touring Club of America.

Prior to leaving on the Garford trip in October 1911, Westgard had been "engaged in making 64 strip maps that contain all the details from Chicago to Los Angeles," *Automobile Topics* reported in its September 23 issue. "These maps show the detail going through towns, and give all information essential for making the trip with [the] most comfort and safety."[6] The result was the 128-page AAA booklet, *Strip Maps of the "Trail to Sunset" Transcontinental Automobile Route: Chicago–Los Angeles Via Santa Fe Trail*. Printed on tan paper, "which will relieve as much as possible any strain upon the eyes in reading in the sunlight, the booklet appeared right around the time the Garford auto train departed."[7]

Acting as "special good road representative of the United States government,"[8] Westgard would report on road conditions to the Department of Agriculture's Office of Public Roads, as he had after his 1910 Premier and 1911 Saurer crossings. Although Westgard was to guide the tour, it would be "personally conducted" by H. D. Ashton, manager of Raymond and Whitcomb's automobile touring department.

THE AUTO AS A "COMMON CARRIER"

Was the automobile becoming a competitive threat to railroads and steamship companies? One newspaper believed so. In the opinion of the *New York Times*, the Raymond and Whitcomb tour would attract passengers "who have no interest in the machines, but who have paid their fare for the journey in exactly the same way as they would buy a railroad or a steam ship ticket." As the *Times* put it:

> While it is true that coast to coast journeys have been made before this, it is also true that they were private enterprises. But the coming tour is a public thing. It is conducted by a touring agency, and the participants will neither be chosen by invitation nor will they go to earn their salary. The project marks the gasoline car as a common carrier of inter-State traffic, and is for that reason most significant.[9]

Unfortunately for the organizers, just eight pleasure seekers signed up to tour the country by auto, according to Chicago newspaper reporter Victor Eubank, who wrote an article titled "Log of an Auto Prairie Schooner" for *Sunset: The Pacific Monthly*. Eubank, 28, traveled with the Garford autos as the press agent for the Raymond and Whitcomb Company. A Missourian who would join Associated Press in 1913 as editor of its Chicago bureau, Eubank started writing for the *Kansas City Star* in 1903 but joined the *Chicago Inter Ocean* in 1904 and had since worked for four other Chicago dailies. According to several press accounts, however, Eubank was working for the *Inter Ocean* while covering the transcontinental tour.[10]

According to Eubank, the eight paying customers "were absolutely pioneers; they formed the advance guard of what is to be a mighty procession crossing the American continent, east and west, from ocean to ocean. They were personally conducted tourists, traveling for pleasure, in a train of automobiles, running on schedule time, from New York to California, and they had paid their fare."[11] Eubank's calculations indicate that helpers and various others brought the total number of tourists to eighteen, although some newspapers reported sixteen, fourteen, or even as few as twelve travelers. The eighteen included Eubank, the eight paying customers, six professional drivers, Westgard and his wife, and H. D. Ashton, of Raymond and Whitcomb, who took photos for the *Sunset* article. Table 9, a list of passengers compiled from newspapers and auto journals, includes the names of twenty travelers, however.

The wealthy passengers had earned their money primarily through manufacturing and finance. "Three of this party are traveling for their health, one of them a woman just up after an operation in a hospital," Eubank wrote. She apparently gained twenty-five pounds while recuperating on the trip, and the three who started off in ill health also improved under the regimen of constant fresh air and exercise. "Enforced and beneficial exercise was shared by even the ladies of the party," Eubank pointed out, "for they were drafted into service when an extra eight or ten pounds' pressure was needed in a slippery place on a steep grade."[12] The women in the party numbered three. Bachelors filled one car, nicknamed the "Blind Pig."

FOUR CARS AND ONE TRUCK

In New York City at the start of the trip, each car was assigned a number, displayed on a cloth sign. At the conclusion of the trip, the *Los Angeles Times* identified the driver of the Garford pilot car as Edward Grabow and the other drivers as Horace Horne, Mike Ryan, and J. T. "Fred" Springer, in autos 2, 3, and 4, respectively. Other press accounts identify a fifth driver as George H. Reye, who presumably drove the baggage truck. Press accounts made no mention of relief drivers, yet Eubank—who unfortunately did not name them—claimed there were six hired drivers on the tour.

TABLE 9. Passengers Aboard the Garford "Automobile Train," 1911[a]

H. D. Ashton
Resident of New York City, manager of the Raymond and Whitcomb Company's automobile touring department, and "conductor" of the automobile train.

Frederick Bierschank[b]
Variously reported as from New York City or Northport, Long Island.

Victor Eubank
A *Chicago Inter Ocean* reporter who acted as press agent for the caravan.

George Foote
An administrator at Cornell University, and *wife*,[c] of Ithaca, New York.

Richard L. Fox
Resident of Philadelphia, a broker and "globe trotter."

Sydney B. Gladding
Superintendent of the waterworks, Newport, Rhode Island.

Edward Grabow (driver)
Resident of New York City.

W. F. Harris
A "manufacturer," of South Orange, New Jersey.

Horace Horne (driver)
Resident of New York City.

John Legg
President of the Worcester Woolen Mill Company, wife *Sarah*,[d] and son *Howard*, of Worcester, Massachusetts.

Leonard Ormerod[e]
    Resident of Chicago, "nicknamed Ramrod, the publicity man of the tour."

George H. Reye (driver)
    Resident of Elyria, Ohio.

Mike Ryan (driver)
    Resident of New York City.

J. T. "Fred" Springer (driver)
    Resident of New York City.

W. J. Studwell
    "A financier," from Brooklyn, New York.

A. L. Westgard
    "Official pathfinder for the American Automobile Association" and pilot for the Garford auto train, and wife *Helen*, of New York City.

SOURCES: Auto journals and local and national newspapers; biographies; obituaries.

[a] Trek organizers claimed that there were eight paying customers (but failed to name them) and eighteen travelers overall. Compiled from various press accounts, this list contains twenty names.

[b] Bierschank's name also appears as "P. B. Biershenk."

[c] According to the Oct. 15, 1911, *Chicago Inter Ocean*, Mrs. Foote would join the tour in Chicago. Note that press accounts did not provide the names of wives, though some could be located by other means.

[d] According to the Oct. 11, 1911, *Cleveland Leader*, Sarah Legg would join the tour in Chicago.

[e] The name is also spelled "Omerod" and "Ormrod."

Four Garford autos and one Garford truck were scheduled to leave New York City from the Raymond and Whitcomb offices, 225 Fifth Avenue, at 10:30 A.M. on Monday, October 2. The cars had arrived in the city only that morning, after concluding a trip from North Conway, New Hampshire, in the White Mountains, "where they have been in continuous service for the last three months," Tuesday's *New York Herald* reported. According to the *Herald*: "The train really started in two sections, one consisting of four cars and the 'baggage coach' leaving this city, the fifth car starting from Boston to Albany, where the two sections will join. At Cleveland a second truck will be added to the train, making seven cars in all."[13] Before leaving New York City, the tourists posed for pictures at Grant's Tomb, overlooking the Hudson River (see Figs. 54 and 55). The photos show not four but five cars lined up in front of the tomb for the "start of the most recent transcontinental party,"[14] the four autos behind the pilot car bearing the numbers 2, 3, 4 and 5. The *New York Herald, New York Times, Automobile,* and *Motor Age* all state that just four Garford cars and one truck started from New York City. But a second surviving photo also shows five Garford cars—and no truck—at the curb in front of the Raymond and Whitcomb headquarters in New

Fig. 54. A photographer (far right) snaps a picture of the five Garford autos in front of Grant's Tomb. (NAHC)

York City (see Fig. 56). The touring company probably used the fifth Garford auto to haul baggage until the truck joined the caravan, apparently at the Garford factory in Elyria, Ohio. The truck later carried the number "5" sign that the extra auto displayed in New York City.

"Mrs. Pauline Stein," who would start from Boston and drive a carload of passengers, apparently planned to join the auto train later. According to the *New York Times*, she would be "making the trip independently and driving her own car," which would have added a fifth auto (although there was no word on whether she drove a Garford or another make).[15] Later news accounts, however, fail to mention Pauline Stein, who evidently did not make the trip after all. All the same, for the remainder of the journey some newspapers continued to report that the train consisted of five cars, although Eubank's account and the surviving photos make it clear that the correct number (except at the start) was four cars and one truck. The report that a second truck would join the caravan at Cleveland also proved to be false.

The truck was "equipped with spare parts, extra tires, tubes, etc., in charge of an expert mechanician," according to the *Elyria (Ohio) Evening Telegram*, located in the Garford factory's hometown, just west of Cleveland. "The truck which will be high-

Fig. 55. One source
names the driver of car
No. 2 as Horace Horne.
The other men are
unidentified. (NAHC)

geared and capable of good speed will carry part of the hand baggage so as not to over-crowd the cars with luggage," the *Telegram* continued. "Through New Mexico and Arizona a commissary and camping outfit will also be carried for the occasions where hotels are lacking, a part of the tour which will be particularly fascinating." Even the reluctant campers among the tourists would be able to sleep comfortably on the two occasions when the Garford tourists planned to camp: "It has also been arranged to have Pullman sleeping cars sidetracked at certain of the night controls in the South-west so that those who prefer may sleep indoors," *Motor Age* reported.[16]

Loaded, the Garford truck weighed nearly 7,000 pounds, Eubank said. "It is un-like the usual truck in that it has been built on a public chassis such as is used by fire, ambulance and police patrols," instead of an automobile chassis, said one report.[17] The truck's canvas covering, similar to a prairie schooner's—and obviously a copy of the earlier Premier caravan's motorized prairie schooner—sported a sign:

The Raymond-Whitcomb Trail to Sunset
New York to Los Angeles
Garford Cars
Co-operation of American Automobile Association

Fig. 56. The five-car transcontinental automobile train prepares to depart from the Raymond and Whitcomb headquarters. A. L. Westgard—sporting a goatee and holding a cigar—sits at the far right in the back of the lead auto. The woman in the back seat is quite likely Westgard's wife, Helen. (OHS)

PENNANTS FLYING, THE GARFORDS REACH THEIR HOMETOWN

After leaving New York and stopping for lunch at the Nikko Inn, the travelers spent their first night out in Poughkeepsie, the *New York Herald* reported.[18] The second night would find them in Albany, the third in Utica, and the fourth in Syracuse. In fact, the tourists lingered a week in New York State and from Buffalo even crossed the Canadian border to visit Niagara Falls. "The idea seems to be a variation from the general run of transcontinental tours in that comfort and a route of unusual interest have been considered above speed," commented the *Elyria Evening Telegram*. From New York State, the automobile train would travel to Erie, Pennsylvania, and Cleveland, and then on to Chicago, following "the conventional paths, affording mostly macadam and good gravel roads," Westgard told the Elyria newspaper (see Table 10).[19]

TABLE 10. Itinerary of the Garford Automobile Train, 1911.

Day/Date	City to City	Daily Mileage	Cumulative Mileage
1/Oct. 2 Mon	New York City–Poughkeepsie, N.Y.	75.0	75.0
2/Oct. 3 Tue	Poughkeepsie, N.Y.–Albany, N.Y.	75.0	150.0
3/Oct. 4 Wed	Albany, N.Y.–Utica, N.Y.	95.3	245.3
4/Oct. 5 Thu	Utica, N.Y.–Syracuse, N.Y.	49.9	295.2
5/Oct. 6 Fri	Syracuse, N.Y.–Rochester, N.Y.	100.7	395.9
6/Oct. 7 Sat	Rochester, N.Y.–Buffalo, N.Y.	76.7	472.6
7/Oct. 8 Sun	*visit to Niagara Falls, Canada*	0	472.6
8/Oct. 9 Mon	Buffalo, N.Y.–Erie, Pa.	93.3	565.9
9/Oct. 10 Tue	Erie, Pa.–Cleveland	100.0	665.9
10/Oct. 11 Wed	Cleveland–Fremont, Ohio	86.0	751.9
11/Oct. 12 Thu	Fremont, Ohio–Bryan, Ohio	86.7	838.6
12/Oct. 13 Fri	Bryan, Ohio–South Bend, Ind.	99.3	937.9
13/Oct. 14 Sat	South Bend, Ind.–Chicago	101.4	1,039.3
14/Oct. 15 Sun	*idle day in Chicago*	0	1,039.3
15/Oct. 16 Mon	Chicago–Ottawa, Ill.	86.6	1,125.9
16/Oct. 17 Tue	Ottawa, Ill.–Davenport, Iowa	113.4	1,239.3
17/Oct. 18 Wed	Davenport, Iowa–Marengo, Iowa	100.0	1,339.3
18/Oct. 19 Thu	Marengo, Iowa–Des Moines, Iowa	100.0	1,439.3
19/Oct. 20 Fri	Des Moines, Iowa–Guthrie Center, Iowa	76.0	1,515.3
20/Oct. 21 Sat	Guthrie Center, Iowa–Omaha, Neb.	91.2	1,606.5
21/Oct. 22 Sun	*idle day in Omaha*	0	1,606.5
22/Oct. 23 Mon	Omaha, Neb.–Auburn, Neb.	92.1	1,698.6
23/Oct. 24 Tue	Auburn, Neb.–Kansas City, Mo.	155.3	1,853.9
24/Oct. 25 Wed	*idle day in Kansas City*	0	1,853.9
25/Oct. 26 Thu	Kansas City, Mo.–Emporia, Kan.	139.7	1,993.6
26/Oct. 27 Fri	Emporia, Kan.–Hutchinson, Kan.	131.9	2,125.5
27/Oct. 28 Sat	Hutchinson, Kan.–Dodge City, Kan.	153.8	2,279.3
28/Oct. 29 Sun	*idle day in Dodge City*	0	2,279.3
29/Oct. 30 Mon	Dodge City, Kan.–Syracuse, Kan.	109.5	2,388.8
30/Oct. 31 Tue	Syracuse, Kan.–La Junta, Colo.	110.2	2,499.0
31/Nov. 1 Wed	La Junta, Colo.–Trinidad, Colo.	104.5	2,603.5

(cont'd)

32/Nov. 2 Thu	Trinidad, Colo.–Raton, N.M.	24.2	2,627.7
33/Nov. 3 Fri	Raton, N.M.–Las Vegas, N.M.	120.3	2,748.0
34/Nov. 4 Sat	Las Vegas, N.M.–Santa Fe, N.M.	70.1	2,818.1
35/Nov. 5 Sun	Santa Fe, N.M.–Albuquerque, N.M.	66.0	2,884.1
36/Nov. 6 Mon	*idle day in Albuquerque*	0	2,884.1
37/Nov. 7 Tue	Albuquerque, N.M.–Laguna, N.M.	65.0	2,949.1
38/Nov. 8 Wed	Laguna, N.M.–campsite	—	—
39/Nov. 9 Thu	campsite–Nation's Ranch, N.M.	107.0	3,056.1[a]
40/Nov. 10 Fri	Nation's Ranch, N.M.–stuck in Arizona bog	—	—
41/Nov. 11 Sat	stuck in Arizona bog–Cooley's Ranch, Ariz.[b]	100.0	3,156.1[a]
42/Nov. 12 Sun	Cooley's Ranch, Ariz.–campsite	—	—
43/Nov. 13 Mon	campsite–Globe, Ariz.	118.0	3,274.1[a]
44/Nov. 14 Tue	Globe, Ariz.–Phoenix, Ariz.	112.0	3,386.1
45/Nov. 15 Wed	*visit to Grand Canyon*	0	3,386.1
46/Nov. 16 Thu	*visit to Grand Canyon*	0	3,386.1
47/Nov. 17 Fri	*visit to Grand Canyon*	0	3,386.1
48/Nov. 18 Sat	Phoenix, Ariz.–	—[c]	—
49/Nov. 19 Sun	–Yuma, Ariz.[d]	—	—
50/Nov. 20 Mon	Yuma, Ariz.–Brawley, Calif.	—	—
51/Nov. 21 Tue	Brawley, Calif.–San Diego	—	—
52/Nov. 22 Wed	*idle day in San Diego*	0	—
53/Nov. 23 Thu	San Diego–Los Angeles	—	4,025.6

SOURCES: Article and map in the February 1912 issue of *Sunset*; auto journals; national and local newspapers.

[a] Here, the daily trip mileage is the distance traveled during the past two days.

[b] Cooley's Ranch was at or near Show Low, Arizona.

[c] The map accompanying Victor Eubank's article in the February 1912 issue of *Sunset* does not indicate the distance traveled on Days 48–51 and Day 53.

[d] The caravan traveled most of the night to arrive in Yuma on Sunday morning, November 19, according to the *Yuma Daily Examiner*.

The Garford auto train drove 93 miles from Buffalo to reach Erie on Monday, October 9, 1911, Day 8 of the trip, Tuesday's *Erie Dispatch* noted. "Snorting like ponderous racing cars with pennants flying and spattered with mud a train of automobiles, four in number, wended its way down State street, shortly before 4 o'clock yesterday afternoon and discharged a party of twelve tourists at the Reed House, for a stay in this city over night." Curiously, the *Dispatch* also reported that the drivers would leave the four cars at the Garford Company's factory "and four new ones will be substituted." Other reports fail to confirm this information.[20]

The cars traveled 100 miles to reach Cleveland at 4:00 P.M. on Tuesday, October 10, for an overnight stop, according to the *Cleveland Leader*. The auto train "arrived in Elyria Wednesday forenoon in time to lunch with President Arthur L. Garford, at the restaurant of the Garford Automobile company," the *Elyria Evening Telegram* reported (see Fig. 57).[21] The travelers spent several hours in Elyria before departing at 3:00 P.M. for their overnight stop in Fremont, Ohio. According to the Elyria newspaper:

> Before the company departed, Mr. Garford informed the chauffeurs that after the safety and comfort of the passengers, the Garford Company was interested in the careful opera-

Fig. 57. The transcontinental autos and baggage truck at the Garford factory in Elyria, Ohio. (LCHS)

tion and maintenance of the equipment. To the driver who made the best showing day by day in this respect, he promised to give one hundred dollars at the end of the trip as a premium for efficiency. . . .

Mr. Garford complimented the passengers on their courage in undertaking the trip and the management for the courage and enterprise in promoting it, introducing in this connection H. D. Gibson, vice president and general manager of the Raymond Whitcomb Company.

Mr. Gibson told something of the difficulties encountered in organizing the expedition but already out of the inquiries of those whose courage failed this time he has made a number of bookings for next year. . . . At the conclusion of the informal program the party were conducted through the factory and given an opportunity to see how the cars which have been carrying them are made.[22]

A GARFORD PRODUCT FROM START TO FINISH

For years the Garford Company had made automobile chassis for various cars, including the Cleveland, Rainier, Royal, and Studebaker models. Having acquired new facilities for making its own chassis, in 1910 Studebaker stopped buying from Garford, which then began producing its own complete cars, including a Garford G-8 model for 1911. Although the auto train left late in the summer of 1911, when some automakers were introducing their 1912 cars, press accounts indicate that the transcontinental caravan was using 1911 models. "It is [a] Garford product from start to finish, all parts of the motor, clutch, gearset, and rear axle being made in the company's factory," the December 22, 1910, *Motor Age* said. The Garford's performance apparently pleased the AAA, which chose a Garford for its president, R. H. Hooper, to drive in the 1911 Glidden Tour, the association's annual endurance event. "A predominating feature is the fact that the president's car is not a new Garford, but one which President Hooper has personally used this year and has already seen hard service, having covered several thousand miles since Spring," the *New York Times* reported.[23]

The G-8 used a 4-cylinder engine with a T-head valve-in-block arrangement, a bore and stroke of 4¾ x 5¼ inches, and a 4-speed amidships transmission. It developed 36.1 horsepower, according to the ALAM (Association of Licensed Automobile Manufacturers) formula, though most press accounts refer to the transcontinental tourists as riding in 40-horsepower Garfords. Its unusual low-tension ignition system used magnetic spark plugs, each of which contained a coil winding, a soft iron core, and two points—parts that other makers bolted to the block, *Motor Age* explained. As current

Fig. 58. While driving to South Bend on October 13, 1911, the Garfords encountered soft roads near Kendallville, Indiana. A crewman adjusts tire chains on the car at the right. (MoToR, December 1911)

passed through it, the spark-plug winding became a magnet that "attracts a steel hammer which is rocked to it. The moment this is done the circuit is broken in the coil and the two points in the plug are separated," thus firing the plug. Mounted on a 118-inch wheelbase with Goodyear tires 36 X 4 inches front and 36 X 4½ inches rear, the 3,600-pound car cost $3,500.[24]

Four autos and a truck passed through Mishawaka, Indiana, during a 99-mile drive from Bryan, Ohio, to South Bend, Indiana, on Friday, October 13, the *South Bend Times* reported (see Fig. 58). According to Eubank, the tour had covered 938 miles from New York City to South Bend. "The members who are making the trip stopped at the Oliver last night and will make the trip to Chicago this morning," the *South Bend Times* reported on Saturday. "They will spend Sunday in the Windy city, after which they will resume the run."[25]

ROADS AHEAD HOLD QUICKSAND "TERROR"

When the Garfords steamed into Chicago on Saturday, October 14, their odometers registered 1,039 miles for the trip to that point. As the Sunday *Chicago Inter Ocean* reported it:

> After a trip from New York, over all sorts and conditions of roads, the first public "pay-as-you-enter" transcontinental automobile train reached Chicago yesterday afternoon and the sixteen passengers aboard were unanimous in expressing their enthusiasm over the journey thus far.

The party, which is officially known as the Raymond & Whitcomb "Trail to Sunset" tour, left South Bend, Ind., yesterday morning and entered the city through South Chicago and over Michigan boulevard. The five seven passenger Garford touring cars and the big baggage truck, covered with dust, attracted considerable attention as they made their way leisurely down the avenue. . . .

The women passengers declare that the journey from New York to Chicago far exceeded their expectations. They say they have been subjected to no discomfort at any time and see no reason why women should not make the transcontinental trip every year, if they so desire.[26]

From Chicago, the trail "crosses Illinois on good gravel road to the Mississippi River, crossing same into Davenport, Iowa. From this point to Omaha [Nebraska] it traverses the now famous River-to-River Road, graded and marked throughout its entire length," the *New York Times* recounted. "From Omaha the route swings southward in the valley of the Missouri River to Kansas City, at which point it enters the historic Santa Fe Trail, which is followed across the entire length of Kansas."[27]

Despite the assurances of a comfortable tour offered by Raymond and Whitcomb, Westgard was well aware of the difficulties of transcontinental motoring. According to a 1909 AAA *Club Journal* article in which Westgard discussed the coast-to-coast journeys made from 1903 to 1906:

One thing learned by the trips already made is the real nature of the country west of Chicago—a land of probable flood at any season of the year, of sandy deserts and sage brush plains, and deep prairie roads. The vast stretch of country between the Rocky Mountains and the Sierra Nevadas is a country with stiff climbs and steep descents in succession. . . . Quicksand is one of the terrors of the route.[28]

Westgard evidently conveyed his concerns to the paying passengers, who dressed accordingly west of Chicago, one newspaper revealed: "While most of the tourists wore their business suits on the two weeks' trip between New York and Chicago, they laid aside these garments . . . and entered the Mississippi Valley clad in all the informality of canvas coats, puttees and soft collars."[29]

WESTGARD AND THE "PIONEER FREIGHTER"

The bad roads began immediately west of Chicago, Eubank laconically observed, as "the campaign for good roads seems not to have struck the Illinois River valley very hard." He likened the 1911 auto tourists to pioneers who streamed westward along America's overland trails beginning in the 1840s. On the generally good roads of the

East, "the Raymond-Whitcomb tourists were lulled by easy-running Garfords into forgetfulness that they had started out to conquer the wilderness with gasoline and rubber," Eubank wrote. "Any old kind of an automobile can get from New York to Chicago, and tourists have nice hotels to stop at and everything is lovely. But west of Chicago the real trip commences. We were motorists as far west as Chicago. Then we became pioneers."[30] Eubank's point was more poetic than factual, however, considering pilot A. L. Westgard's later praise of the roads in Iowa and farther west.

Westgard well knew the state of America's highways. In early March 1911, he and other adventurers left Denver in the first truck to cross the continent. Some reports say Westgard actually drove the 5-ton Swiss-made Saurer truck; others call him the "pilot," or guide—his more likely role. From Denver, the westbound "Pioneer Freighter" largely followed the same route along the Santa Fe Trail that Ray F. McNamara and Westgard had mapped in autumn 1910. The truck hauled a 3-ton load of camping equipment and timbers, which the crew used to build and reinforce bridges. South of Algodones, New Mexico, "it was necessary to strengthen seventeen small bridges over irrigation ditches," *Motor Age* reported. "At one place the truck broke through one of these bridges, although the bridge was newly constructed and appeared strong." Fitted with Goodrich solid tires, the truck also carried "a powerful winch, operated by the regular motor, with which it hauled itself out of some of the bad spots."[31]

The 132 miles between Magdalena, New Mexico, and Springerville, Arizona, represented the worst conditions the group had encountered since leaving Denver. "Combined with the poorest possible apology for a road, there has been every other obstacle previously met with—weak bridges, arroyos, sand and rocks without end," wrote Westgard, who afterward planned to file a road report with the U.S. Department of Agriculture's Office of Public Roads. The roads got worse, if possible, west of Springerville. Grinding through "bottomless mud" in the White Mountains on April 12, 1911, the men struggled for eight and a half hours to advance a mere 2.5 miles, according to Westgard's logbook as printed in *Automobile*. "We do not measure stretches between towns by distance any longer, but by time," an exasperated Westgard told *Motor Age*.[32]

The Saurer truck reached Los Angeles on May 8 and continued to San Francisco, from whence the crew shipped the truck by rail to Pueblo, Colorado. On June 12, "in charge of A. C. Thompson and George McLean," the Swiss truck started eastward, passing through Kansas City, Chicago, and Detroit to reach New York City and complete its two-stage transcontinental journey on August 2.[33] Just three weeks later, on August 24, a 3-ton Packard truck that left New York City on July 8 reached San Fran-

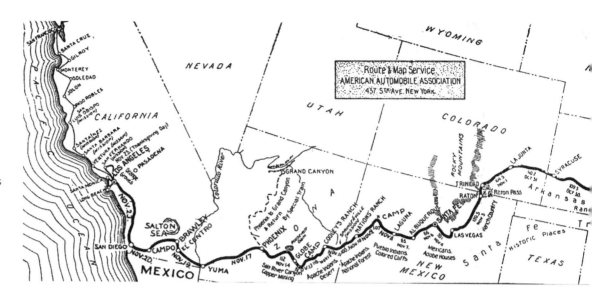

Fig. 59. The Garford caravan's 1911 "Trail to Sunset" route. The dates and overnight stops shown on the map between Phoenix, Arizona, and Los Angeles are incorrect. Furthermore, the route north of San Diego was primarily along the oceanfront, not inland as depicted. (Sunset, February 1912)

cisco, completing the first uninterrupted coast-to-coast run by a truck. In 1912, Westgard would cross the country three times to map auto routes that would connect New York City with Los Angeles (the Midland Trail), Seattle (the Northwest Trail), and San Francisco (the Overland Trail).[34]

TOURISTS REACH THE HALFWAY POINT

In contrast to his journey by Saurer truck, Westgard's trip over Iowa's River-to-River Road as part of the Garford expedition left him with nothing but admiration for the all-dirt highway. The road—which linked Davenport, a Mississippi River port, and Council Bluffs, on the east bank of the Missouri River opposite Omaha—was "one of the best I have ever seen," Westgard told the *Omaha World-Herald*. "When the national highway is established, I do not believe there is any doubt but what it will pass through Omaha."[35]

To reach Omaha on Saturday, October 21, the auto train made four overnight stops in Iowa, beginning at Davenport on Tuesday, October 17. "Woodworth Clum, secretary, Decker French, president[,] and several members of the Davenport Automobile club will meet the party in Illinois and escort them to the Kimball hotel, A.A.A. headquarters," forecast the *Davenport Daily Times*. (The Premier tourists who traveled as a group from Atlantic City, New Jersey, to the West Coast had stayed at the Kimball Hotel three months earlier.) Crossing Iowa at a leisurely pace, the Garford tourists stayed overnight at Marengo on Wednesday, Des Moines on Thursday, and Guthrie Center

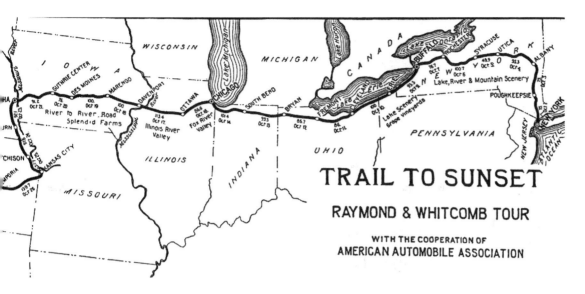

TRAIL TO SUNSET

RAYMOND & WHITCOMB TOUR

WITH THE COOPERATION OF
AMERICAN AUTOMOBILE ASSOCIATION

on Friday, October 20. Between Marengo and Des Moines, the travelers stopped in Grinnell at noon Thursday to tour the Morrison-Ricker Manufacturing Company, maker of Grinnell brand of leather driving gloves, according to the *Grinnell Herald*.[36]

The tourists crossed the Missouri River into Omaha at 4:45 P.M. Saturday, the *Omaha World-Herald* reported, and would spend Saturday and Sunday nights at the Henshaw Hotel, where the Premier tourists had stayed before them. The four Garford cars and one truck "have all made the trip so far in perfect condition," *Automobile* reported in an Omaha dispatch, possibly written by Eubank. "Next Sunday's stop will be at Dodge City, Kan. As towns of any size and consequently hotels of the better class are far apart in that part of the country the longest single day's run of the whole tour will be made next Saturday. This will be from Hutchinson to Dodge City, a distance of approximately 154 miles, the stop for lunch probably being made at Larned."[37]

From Omaha, the caravan traveled 92 miles south to Auburn, Nebraska, on Monday, October 23, Day 22 of the trip (see Fig. 59). On Tuesday, the travelers were scheduled to cover 98 miles to Atchison, Kansas, and, on Wednesday, the auto train would chug into Kansas City after a short 58-mile drive. The travelers made good time en route to Atchison, arriving there at 2:00 P.M. on Tuesday. Consequently, "the cars did not remain in Atchison over night, but proceeded after a half hour's stop, for Kansas City," reported the *Atchison Daily Globe*. "There is a young man with the party [Eubank] who works newspapers. He fairly gushes information, and all he asks is that mention be made of Garford cars and their Goodyear tires."[38]

Although the upcoming Hutchinson–Dodge City leg had been scheduled as the longest day's drive of the trip, Tuesday's trek from Auburn to Kansas City—155.3 miles—exceeded it by nearly two miles. Because the long drive on Tuesday put the caravan one day ahead of schedule, the tourists were able to spend Wednesday idle in Kansas City, Missouri, which was the approximate halfway point of the tour. The Garford autoists stayed at the Hotel Baltimore, where at least some of the contestants in the 1909 New York–Seattle auto race had also put up.

"The country hotels are among the nicest things about the trip, so far," passenger Sydney B. Gladding of Newport, Rhode Island, told the *Kansas City Star*. "We stopped for dinner in one town in Iowa and they don't put better food on the table anywhere than we got in that little country hotel. Of course, the service isn't much, but the food is excellent."[39] One tourist, however, voiced a complaint, although not about the food. According to Sarah (Mrs. John) Legg of Worcester, Massachusetts:

> There has been just one disappointment to me, and that is in the Western girl. You know, I heard so much about the beauty of her complexion, its rosiness and all, that when I came out here and saw so many pale-faced girls I was really disappointed. The trouble is that they do not get enough outside exercise. They are actually so busy with society way out here in the West that they don't have time enough to become healthy. I do wish I had seen more rosy cheeks.[40]

For his part, Westgard registered just one "objection" to Kansas City: "The streets are not marked. A stranger cannot find his way through them. At no place downtown have I been able to find a street sign. It's the only fault I can find."[41]

KANSAS A "MASS OF GUMBO MUD"

The old Santa Fe Trail across Kansas, "over which the early pioneers toiled and died, is supposed to be a good one for automobiles. And it is, in dry weather," Eubank wrote. But when the tour reached Emporia, Kansas, the caravan's first night control—nighttime stopping point—west of Kansas City, "snow and rain came down upon the land, and in the morning the roads were a mass of gumbo mud. . . . Out of Emporia, the big Garfords exerted their forty horse-power mostly on first and second speeds. Time and time again the drivers were compelled to stop and dig the gumbo out of the wheels." Rather than wait a day or two for the roads to dry, as the Kansas natives advised, tour manager H. D. Ashton "declared he was running that automobile train on schedule time and he was going to make his schedule or 'bust.'"[42]

On Friday, October 27, a 132-mile drive would take the tourists from Emporia to Hutchinson through Florence, Peabody, Walton, and Newton, Kansas. In addition to the mud, a washout in the road near Florence, some fifty miles southwest of Emporia, delayed the tourists, who had expected to eat lunch in Newton. Instead, they stopped only briefly in Newton at 9:00 P.M. Traveling the eight miles between Walton and Newton had taken them nearly an hour, according to the *Newton Evening Kansan-Republican*. "We do not want to get behind our schedule," Ashton told the newspaper. "If we get behind we will have difficulty in catching up and, although our schedule is not fast, we want to keep up to the schedule all the way through and I expect we will be able to do so. This little delay on account of the weather will amount to nothing."[43]

The caravan pulled up to Hutchinson's Bisonte Hotel about five hours late, reported the *Hutchinson Daily Gazette*. Their arrival early Saturday morning came "after a fight, all day and half the night[,] with slick, slimy, Kansas mud," observed Saturday's *Hutchinson News*:

> Manager Maguire of the Bisonte did a very unusual thing and an act that proved how courteous the Harvey system and Mr. Maguire can be, when he served a hot meal for the travelers, in the big dining room. This was between one and two o'clock this morning, but it was appreciated. After the long ride it was fine to be able to have such a dinner awaiting one and the thoughtfulness of Mr. Maguire will make these long-distance riders, and the thousands of others they will meet, talk of the excellence of the Harvey plan of doing things for the traveler's comfort. . . .
>
> A few of the members of the party, because of the severity of the weather, came by train from Peabody, arriving earlier at the hotel. But two ladies, Mrs. [Helen] Westgard and Mrs. Foote, with their husbands, and nearly all the men, came through. "I am ready to go to Dodge City tonight, if the others could be induced," said Mrs. Foote, after dinner was over.[44]

The Garford train ran over the finest roads of the trip between Kansas City and Emporia, said Westgard, after devouring a plate of fried chicken. "And," he added graciously, "we could see that they were even better this side of Emporia [westward to Hutchinson], if possible, but for the rain and snow. The roads are formed well for drainage and they show much care through dragging."[45]

Leaving Hutchinson at 9:45 A.M. on Saturday for the 154-mile drive to Dodge City, the Garford train followed a pilot car to Lyons, where the tourists hoped to visit a salt mine, reported the *Hutchinson News*. "Pilots are arranged for a good share of the way to the state line, wherever they are desired."[46] Another pilot, E. J. Oliphant of the Santa Fe Trail Garage in Dodge City, traveled 37 miles northeast to Kinsley and escorted the tourists to Dodge City's Harvey House, where they arrived at midnight Saturday.

Containing the "Barons of the East," the four Garford autos "were so heavily loaded with mud that they looked much like moving hillocks," the *Dodge City Globe* reported. "The party found soft, muddy roads from the time it left Emporia until Dodge City was reached, and there was little prospect of better roads from here on." The travelers stayed in Dodge City on Sunday, October 29, and left in their four autos on Monday. But "the large motor truck which carries the baggage for the party was late in arriving here," the *Globe* commented. "It did not reach Dodge until after the tourists had left on Monday."[47] But the newspaper offered no explanation for the delay.

WINTRY BLAST SLOWS THE AUTO TRAIN

After a nine-and-a-half-hour drive, the caravan reached Syracuse, Kansas, for the night at 7:00 P.M. on Monday, October 30, according to the *Syracuse Journal*. Crossing the Colorado border 15 miles west of Syracuse, the tourists would pass through La Junta and Trinidad in southeastern Colorado, cross Raton Pass into New Mexico, and follow the Atchison, Topeka, and Santa Fe railroad tracks most of the way to Santa Fe, New Mexico. The route "traverses large cattle ranches" and "passes by Mexican adobe houses and Indian pueblos," according to one newspaper's description. "From Santa Fe to Albuquerque the route passes Indian settlements, and from this interesting town it again swings west to the Indian pueblo of Laguna. At that point the tourist will leave the railroad and not see it again for several hundred miles, entering a country little known, but affording the most magnificent scenery to be found anywhere in the United States."[48]

The following day—Tuesday, October 31, Day 30 of the trip—the caravan left Syracuse at 9:00 A.M. and lumbered into La Junta at 5:30 P.M. after a 110-mile drive. "The passengers are enthusiastic over this part of the country and declare the trip has been even more pleasurable than anticipated," the *La Junta Tribune* declared. "They were guests of the Harvey House while in La Junta."[49]

On a 105-mile southwesterly drive from La Junta to Trinidad on Wednesday, November 1, the tourists bounced over "a rough prairie trail" dotted with arroyos so deep that the Garford truck lagged hours behind the paying tourists in reaching Trinidad. According to Thursday's *Trinidad Chronicle-News*:

> Buffeted by a chilling wintry blast that swept across the eighty miles of prairie, in the face of a driving blizzard, the Raymond-Whitcomb transcontinental automobile tourists completed another leg of their ocean to ocean journey when the four big Garford cars reached

Trinidad last evening. Two cars reached the city a few minutes before seven o'clock, a third car entered the city half an hour later, and pilot A. L. Westgard[,] who remained behind a few miles out to help the big truck out of a bad place, reached Trinidad about 10:30 last night. The party consisting of eighteen people put up at the Cardenas hotel for the night. . . .

Arriving here last night the tourists were cold and hungry and in need of warmth and refreshments more than entertainment. Arrangements had been made by joint committees of the chamber of commerce and the local motor club to receive the tourists at an informal smoker at the Trinidad club, but instead the R. and W. party sat around the lobby of the Harvey house and spent a social evening with the chamber of commerce directors.

The start was made from La Junta yesterday morning about 9:30. The ride from that city to Trinidad gave the tourists a glimpse of real desolation. Members of the party declared that the road was about the worst they have encountered since leaving New York. . . . When the tourists left La Junta yesterday morning a storm was brewing and it broke upon them before they had gone very far. The heaviest snowfall of the year detained the party in Trinidad.[50]

The pilot car, containing Westgard and apparently also Eubank, "remained behind to persuade the prairie-schooner to negotiate the bad places" (see Fig. 60), Eubank wrote in his trip summary for *Sunset*:

> To make matters worse, heavy snow began to fall and obliterated the trail left by the other cars. Out on the stark prairie, with no fences, no railroad, no trees, nothing to look to as guideposts, the affair looked serious. The only way out of the difficulty was to get out and feel for the tracks. This was done for a number of miles until the snow became lighter and the trail was visible. The pilot car brought the prairie-schooner into Trinidad three hours after the other cars had reached there.[51]

Fig. 60. Between La Junta and Trinidad, Colorado, Westgard's pilot car lingered to assist the baggage truck over a rough, snowy prairie trail. (Sunset, February 1912)

FROM SNOW INTO QUICKSAND

The Raymond and Whitcomb tour covered 2,603.5 miles from New York City to Trinidad, according to trip records. Though the snow failed to derail the auto train, it did cause Ashton to revise his plans for Thursday. The automobile train's itinerary called for a short 24-mile drive into New Mexico, but Ashton announced his intention of changing these plans—perhaps to outrun any additional snow. He proposed having the caravan scale the Rocky Mountains through the Raton Pass via the town of Raton—the "Gate City"—and then head south for Las Vegas, New Mexico, Thursday's *Trinidad Chronicle-News* reported. But Ashton was forced to change plans yet again:

> When the party arrived last night the arrangement was to start away about eight o'clock this morning, whistle in Raton and continue on to Las Vegas for the night stop. But old Jup Pluv [a reference to Jupiter, the Roman god who controlled the weather] interposed in behalf of the gate city, and when the manager of the tour looked out this morning upon a snow covered landscape he decided to keep the party here until after the lunch hour and buck the snow over the hill this afternoon and accept the hospitality which the Gate city boosters will provide. . . .
>
> Reports state the road over the hill to be in bad shape as the result of the snow and the tourists contemplate some trouble in crossing the divide. The tourist party was accompanied by E. C. Sperry and C. W. Coppers, John H. English, Edgar P. Sherman and Miss Sarah Robson as far as Gate City.

The party set out along the "scenic highway" to Raton at 1:00 P.M. Thursday, the *Chronicle-News* reported. "The tourists left with words of praise for Trinidad and its people," the paper said, "and before departing were given souvenir booklets of Trinidad views by the Chronicle-News."[52]

The travelers spent Friday night, November 3, in Las Vegas, according to the *New Mexican* of Santa Fe:

> Captain A. L. Westgard and his party of "Seeing America First" tourists arrived here per autos Saturday night from Las Vegas and declared that the road . . . to the capital is superb and "one of the best ever." The party spent the night at the Montezuma hotel and then motored to Albuquerque, leaving right after breakfast Sunday.
>
> It was unfortunate that the weather was so bad, as the tourists wished to enjoy the sunshine and fine climate of Santa Fe. . . . Their powerful machines . . . literally ploughed through the mud and showed that no trains are to take their cars in tow between here and California.[53]

Arriving in Albuquerque Sunday evening, November 5, the paying tourists spent Monday idle. The Raymond and Whitcomb employees, however, were busy all day, reported Tuesday's *Albuquerque Morning Journal*:

> The impending trip over the desert where there are no accommodations for a large party necessitated increasing the number of attaches by one. A chef, Henry Henderson, who is well known in Albuquerque as a first-class culinary artist, was engaged and will leave with the tour this morning.
>
> All day yesterday Manager Ashton was busily engaged in obtaining supplies to last for the trip to Globe [Arizona]. . . . In the meantime the chauffeurs were also busily engaged in taking down the machines, which were placed in a local garage, and giving them a thorough overhauling.
>
> While the officials of the party were yesterday engaged in getting ready for the next move, the travelers were enjoying themselves looking over the city. They all appear jubilant over the fact that the trip was made to Albuquerque without mishap and that they arrived here one day ahead of the schedule.[54]

On Tuesday, November 7, the cars struggled through deep sand (see Fig. 61) from Albuquerque, New Mexico, west to the Rio Puerco, a stream that "in ordinary fall sea-

Fig. 61. According to the Los Angeles Times, this scene shows the pilot car negotiating an arroyo near Albuquerque, New Mexico. (LCHS)

Fig. 62. The paying passengers help winch a stranded automobile out of the Rio Puerco west of Albuquerque, New Mexico. The caravan has swelled to five cars. The fifth auto is perhaps temporarily acting as the baggage truck, which is missing for reasons Eubank's account neglects to mention. (Sunset, February 1912)

son is dry and easily forded," Eubank related. "But this fall there was about a foot of water in the river bed. Certain treacherous quicksand was neatly covered. The cars stuck fast in this sand and four hours were spent in extricating them from that peril" (see Fig. 62). Quicksand notwithstanding, "the weather was shining and delightful, and all the passengers got out and worked and looked upon the incident as a lark."[55]

MOTOR "PIONEERS" CAMP IN LUXURY

As scheduled, the tourists spent the night at Laguna, New Mexico, and left the next morning, Wednesday, November 8, Day 38, bound for Nation's Ranch. From New York City to west-central New Mexico, the auto train had run on time, Eubank noted in his article for *Sunset*. "But the roads laughed at man-made schedules and night found the train halted in the mountains, in one of the wild picturesque spots that only the traveler who goes by automobile will ever find." They pitched their tents in the glare of automobile headlights but otherwise suffered little. "The pioneers killed their food wild," reads the caption under a photo in Eubank's article. "We brought ours with a chef from Albuquerque and camped in luxury when camping was a necessity" (see Fig. 63).[56] The chef traveled with the tourists as far as Globe, Arizona, on a stretch of road devoid of hotels.

On Thursday, November 9, the tourists spent the night at Nation's Ranch, near the Arizona border in west-central New Mexico, which early in 1912 would become the nation's forty-seventh state. "At this ranch," one of the biggest in New Mexico territory, "the automobilist is always welcome," Eubank wrote. "We experienced the best sort of western hospitality. The fatted calf—or rather sheep—was killed for us and we met the real cowpuncher in his native element and all that evening we of the 'effete East' listened to his tales of life in the open. Not one cent could we pay for any of this, not even for the thirty-two gallons of gasoline that we got from the owners." The free gasoline came at the right moment, for soon thereafter, at the White River Indian Agency, the tourists paid the highest price of the trip—Eubank omits the figure—for gas, "although at other places it had had to be carted twice as far and under greater difficulties."[57]

Through western New Mexico, the tourists would cross the Mal Pais Lava Beds and skirt the Laguna Salina de Zuni, the Zuni Salt Lake, "so penetrated with salt that it is said no one can sink in it," the *New York Times* informed its readers. The tourists would then enter Springerville, Arizona, a Mormon settlement, and cross the White Mountain National Forest. "On this portion of the tour the plateau of the White Mountain is crossed; this is above timber line, 10,400 feet above sea level. It passes through the

Fig. 63. The Garford tourists take a roadside lunch break at an unrecorded location. Eubank's narrative, however, suggests that the photo was taken somewhere west of Albuquerque. (Sunset, February 1912)

Fig. 64. With passengers walking to lighten the load, the transcontinental Garfords bounce along the dry Black River southwest of Springerville, Arizona. (Sunset, February 1912)

Apache Indian Reservation," the *Times* said. "A visit is made to Fort Apache, a cavalry post of the United States Army," following which the tour would proceed through San Carlos to Globe. There, the governor of Arizona, Richard E. Sloan, and "District Attorney George Bullard, who is the leading A.A.A. official in Arizona, with a distinguished party, will meet the tourists and escort them over the magnificent Government road leading via Roosevelt Dam and down the gorgeous Salt River Canyon, dotted with giant cactus, to Phoenix. . . . From Phoenix a special train will take the tourists for a visit to the Grand Canyon, thus affording the mechanics a couple of days to look over the cars."[58]

CUT LOGS BEAT BOG

At 9,300 feet in the White Mountains west of Springerville, where seven months earlier Westgard and his Saurer truck had battled deep mud, "the automobile train ran into a bog," Eubank recounted. "Did you ever hear of a bog on the top of a mountain? Well, this was a real one, all bog and eight miles wide. The cars sank in over their hubs, and, when they were snugly in, the mercury sank also, down to zero. We spent just twelve hours getting those cars out." The travelers cut trees from a wooded area two miles away, "jacked up the cars and placed the logs under the wheels for mile after mile until we got out."[59]

In the same vicinity but farther south, the autoists drove for a distance along the rocky dry channel of the Black River (see Fig. 64). Later, the cars crawled along a narrow shelf road in the Salt River Canyon near Roosevelt Lake, the culmination of a 1906–11 irrigation project to dam the Salt River in south-central Arizona (see Fig. 65).

No doubt a welcome change, excellent roads took the tourists over the Apache Mountains to Globe, and on Tuesday, November 14, 1911, they followed the "wonderful government road" to Phoenix through Roosevelt and Mesa, Arizona. "Here is one of the great automobile rides of the world," Eubank raved. "Brave any desert with

Fig. 65. The Garford caravan wends its way through Arizona's rugged Salt River Canyon. (Sunset, February 1912)

your car to reach this stretch; it's worth it." After lunch at Roosevelt Dam, "we tackled Fish creek grade, the stiffest on the transcontinental route; it rises a thousand feet in less than a mile. Up we went as easily as though for the past few weeks we had been taking the cars merely through a metropolitan park system."[60]

Their Tuesday arrival in Phoenix—just 640 miles short of their goal—put the tourists two days behind schedule. According to a wire story from Phoenix, reporting on the auto train's arrival:

> The tourists and their escort formed a most important array, for among the score of cars that met them at the Roosevelt Dam, seventy-five miles east of here, was that of Gov. Sloan of Arizona, in which was the Chief Executive himself. Some of the members of the Phoenix Automobile Club toured to Globe....
>
> As was expected, the week just finished was the most trying one, both on the tourists and machines, but the tourists declare they have had the time of their lives, and the four Garford touring cars have stood the test perfectly and met every demand made on them. It had been anticipated that the rough roads would necessitate frequent tire changes, but the extra supply of Goodyear tires carried was not necessary, and these tires have given excellent service throughout the entire trip.[61]

After reaching Phoenix on Tuesday, the tourists took a train to visit the Grand Canyon. This excursion evidently consumed three days, for they resumed their journey through Agua Caliente to Yuma on Saturday, November 18, Day 48 of the trip. For this leg of the trip, they followed a pilot car—a Flanders auto driven by Bill La Casse, "the well known race driver." Beset by unspecified "tire problems," the tourists "arrived in Yuma Sunday morning instead of Saturday evening as expected," according to Monday's *Yuma Daily Examiner*. As a result, "the banquet which was to have been given them Saturday night at the Stag Cafe was postponed" until Sunday evening, the *Arizona Sentinel* reported.[62]

As part of their sight-seeing in Yuma, the tourists were shown the Yuma Irrigation Project. Completed in 1909 with the construction of Laguna Dam on the Colorado River 14 miles northeast of the city, the project had transformed Yuma from a freighting center to an agricultural oasis. According to the *Sentinel*:

> On account of being up practically all night, few of the visitors got up much before noon yesterday, but at 2:00 P.M. the local citizens with all the available autos met them at the Gandolfo and showed them over the orange grove, down in the valley and back up to the reclamation grounds, where Project Engineer Sellew kindly allowed the visitors and citizens to go down in the great siphon under the river and inspect the work. This proved an interesting treat for the visitors.
>
> At 7:30 last night there was an impromptu reception to the visitors at the parlors of the

Hotel Gandolfo, and at 8:30 all adjourned to the Stag Cafe where the delayed banquet was tendered the visitors, and also the crowd from Brawley and El Centro [California] which journeyed to Yuma to escort the visitors to the Imperial valley and to bid them welcome.[63]

ASHTON "RUN OVER BY HIS CAR"

As the *Yuma Daily Examiner* reported, the Garford train left Yuma on Monday morning, November 20, on a trip that would take the travelers through California's Imperial Valley to San Diego. According to Westgard, "the citizens of Brawley came to Yuma to meet us and interest us in making an official preliminary survey of the route entirely in American territory connecting Yuma with Imperial Valley." All the same, Eubank later wrote, "we took care to slip over the line into Mexico, that we might look back to our hour at Niagara Falls, in Canada, and realize that we had made an international run while we were about it."[64]

According to *Automobile Topics*, the tourists had originally planned to travel some sixty miles north of the Mexican border, passing through Blythe, Mecca, and Riverside, California, and then on to Los Angeles. They changed their route, however, on the advice of George Bullard, the Phoenix district attorney and AAA official, who was also the founder of "the celebrated Los Angeles–Phoenix automobile road race," the *San Diego Union* revealed. "Mr. Bullard pointed out that the route through Imperial valley and San Diego was the best one to the coast and the autoists taking his advice are headed this way."[65]

On Tuesday, November 21, the caravan drove from Brawley to San Diego, following a route that took them through Campo and Dulzura. Owing to two mishaps, however, the cars separated along the way, the first auto reaching San Diego's U.S. Grant Hotel at 7:00 P.M. and the last at about 10:30 P.M., Wednesday's *San Diego Union* reported. According to the *Union*:

> The last lap of the trip into San Diego was filled with almost as much excitement as the entire remainder of the journey. Out of Phoenix, H. Ashton had his right foot fractured as a result of being run over by his car. Again when he neared Dulzura yesterday afternoon his car broke down. One of the other cars containing representatives of the *San Diego Union* who met the travelers, lost the road, journeyed to Alpine, and lost nearly forty miles, arriving here at 10:30 last night.

Ashton "was taking some photographs near Phoenix last week when one of the rear wheels of his automobile passed over his right foot, fracturing the bones and disabling him," the *Union* added. "He pluckily continued the journey, however, and intends to remain with the party until Los Angeles is reached."[66]

Arriving in San Diego, Westgard took the opportunity to promote his favorite cause:

> What we need is a national highway. The only practical way has now been thoroughly demonstrated, and that is by the southern route, through to San Diego. If the people will get busy now Congress will make the appropriation necessary for the work and the national highway can be completed in time to allow eastern automobile men to visit the Panama-California exposition in San Diego in 1915 and the Panama-Pacific exposition which is to be held in San Francisco in the same year.
>
> Generally speaking the roads east of the Missouri river are in good condition. With few exceptions the roads west of the Missouri are also good, but much work is necessary. This is especially true of New Mexico, where the grades are steep and the sands deep and heavy. There is a bad stretch of road from Phoenix to Campo, but from Campo into San Diego the traveling was fine.

Admitting that "the bad roads we encountered for the most part were only in small stretches," Westgard concluded that, despite the problem posed by New Mexico (which was not yet a state), "if the United States would agree to build twenty miles of road and bridges just at the places where they are needed, it would insure us a good road all the way across the continent."[67]

CHEERING THOUSANDS GREET AUTO TRAIN

The four Garford cars and the prairie schooner left San Diego early on Thanksgiving morning, Thursday, November 23, for the drive north to Los Angeles (see Fig. 66). Arthur L. Garford, who maintained a winter residence in Pasadena, met the tourists just a few miles southeast of their destination. "He was the first to grasp each driver by the hand as the transcontinental party rolled into Whittier," according to the *Los Angeles Evening Herald*. Garford, who had offered a $100 prize to "the driver making the most perfect score," later examined the record of each auto. According to the *Los Angeles Times*, "there was so little difference that each man drew a prize"—a gold watch.[68]

The auto train pulled up to the office of the *Los Angeles Times* at 6:00 P.M., arriving, the paper said, "after one of the most strenuous automobile runs on record. With eighteen tired, but happy, tourists the cars rolled down Spring street to the finish of the

transcontinental tour, with thousands of spectators cheering plucky women and the men who have crossed the continent together." As Friday's *Times* described it:

> The last day's run proved one of the hardest of the entire trip. The 4000-mile tour was severe, but the autoists were so tired yesterday that it was almost impossible to get the drivers to hustle. As a result the pilot car was forced to wait from time to time as the other machines plugged on to the finish. The cars reached this city, however, almost to the minute on schedule time.
>
> It was dusk when the cars reached Whittier, and A. L. Garford, the man who designed and built the machines, was there to greet the ocean-to-ocean tourists. Garford glanced quickly at the dust-covered cars and then smiled. It was enough. He had seen them at their best. The same cars that had been delivered from the Garford factory had crossed the hardest route in the United States.[69]

The autos, whose elapsed time for the coast-to-coast trip was 52 days, 10 hours, 30 minutes, had thoroughly lived up to his expectations, Garford told the *Los Angeles Times*. "They have finished the run to my entire satisfaction, without mechanical trouble, and now we can rest assured that a tour across the continent has no terrors for the autoist. . . . We do not wish to say the Garford cars are the only cars that can cross the continent. All I wish to do is to point to the record of the cars on the long and fierce run. That record is clean."[70]

Garford spoke gingerly, aware that 12 Indianapolis-made Premier autos carrying

Fig. 66. Wrote Eubank of this photo: "We found fine roads along the edge of the blue Pacific, starting northward from San Diego, and realized that we had made an ocean-to-ocean run." (Sunset, February 1912)

TABLE 11. Relative Performance of the Premier and Garford Caravans, 1911

	Premier	Garford
Distance (miles)	4,075.5	4,025.6
Elapsed time[a]	38 days	52 days
Running time[b]	31 days	43 days
Average speed	4.39 mph	3.21 mph
Miles per day	105	77

[a] Rounded down to the nearest day for the Premier's trip from Atlantic City, New Jersey, to San Francisco and the Garford's trip from New York City to Los Angeles.

[b] In calendar days.

forty passengers had reached San Francisco four months earlier, concluding a 38-day trip, their journey stretching to 45 days as the group continued on to Los Angeles. Altogether, the dozen Premiers had traveled 55,000 miles, compared to about 20,000 miles for the four Garford autos and their baggage truck. But the automaker did not make any comparisons to that earlier, larger, coast-to-coast caravan. Tactfully, neither did the Los Angeles newspapers. Neither expedition had sought a speed record, but on its central route from New York City to San Francisco, the Premier caravan easily outperformed the Garford auto train, which took the southern route from New York City to Los Angeles (see Table 11).

The Goodyear tires on one of the four transcontinental Garfords held "clear to San Diego, after rubbing along over four thousand miles of fierce roads," Eubank said. He put their total New York–Los Angeles distance at 4,025.6 miles, covered in an "actual running time of 33 days, 9 hours and 20 minutes."[71] But Eubank was mistaken. The Garfords in fact consumed 53 calendar days traveling between New York City and Los Angeles, and they were idle on 10 of those days. Thus, the correct running time is 43 days.

"HONORED AND TOASTED"

Thursday evening, the Garford tourists attended a banquet at the Hotel Alexandria in Los Angeles before driving on to spend the night in Pasadena. During the banquet, "the autoists were honored and toasted by business men and prominent autoists of this city who are interested in motor touring across the United States," the *Los Angeles Times* reported. The speakers included Garford, Westgard, and Walter Raymond of the Whitcomb and Raymond Company. At least two other Whitcomb and Raymond officers—H. D. Gibson, vice president and general manager, and M. B. Johnson, "a leading official of the big concern"—were on hand to greet the tourists.[72]

At the banquet, Garford "boosted hard" for the creation of a coast-to-coast highway along the Santa Fe Trail, the *Times* related. "He declared it will be better to spend $30,000,000 on an ocean-to-ocean boulevard than to expend the same amount to build three battleships. He pointed out the advantages of such a highway and showed how it will be possible to create a great desire for travel by automobile, provided a road is built from the Atlantic to the Pacific."[73] Road signs were a rarity in 1911, prompting Westgard to praise the Automobile Club of Southern California for marking the route between San Diego and Los Angeles so clearly. "The Garford pilot said it would not have been necessary for him to guide the Garford cars into this city because of the signs posted at every important turn along the coast route," according to the *Los Angeles Times*. "Those signs show the route perfectly," Westgard agreed.[74]

According to the *Pasadena Star*, Raymond "declared that the company of which he was the founder has been the pioneer in different lines of travel and will doubtless be the pioneer in bringing the first air train across the continent. In the more immediate future, however, it is their ambition to make Southern California and Pasadena the center of the nation's automobile travel." Although he neglected to explain what an "air train" might be, Raymond also announced that the touring company planned to begin regularly offering "personally conducted transcontinental tours."[75] But this service never evolved.

From the Los Angeles banquet, the "four very ordinary looking big touring cars with the dust of many roads on them" proceeded to the Hotel Maryland in Pasadena, arriving shortly before midnight, the *Pasadena Star* reported (see Fig. 67).[76] Leading the automobile procession from Los Angeles to Pasadena, the *Pasadena Daily News* noted, was Calbraith P. Rodgers, who, a few weeks earlier, had become the first person ever to fly across the country. From September 17 to November 5, with frequent stops and several crash landings, Rodgers had flown 3,220 miles from New York City to Los Angeles in a special Wright biplane.[77] His trip of seven weeks, just three days shorter than that of the Garford automobile train, took nearly five times longer than the fastest automobile crossing of 10 days, 18 hours, 12 minutes, set by a Reo in 1910 (see Chapter 2).

Fig. 67. Participants in the first public coast-to-coast auto tour conclude their 52-day trek by posing for photos beside Pasadena's Hotel Maryland. The baggage truck is inexplicably absent. (OHS)

DISPROVING THE HARDSHIP THEORY

The *New York Times*, *Elyria (Ohio) Evening Telegram*, and *Motor Age* all carried an identical wire story from Los Angeles, heralding the finish:

> While heretofore the trip by automobile across the continent was considered one to try the stoutest heart, the expedition just ended, is declared to disprove the "hardship" theory and in the future all sorts of transcontinental automobile excursions are expected to be in vogue. The three women in the party were especially enthusiastic over their trip.
>
> "It was good fun all the way across," says Mrs. Foote, "and [one] of these days I intend to make it all over again. The idea that a woman should not make a transcontinental automobile trip is foolish. I think it is the only way to see America. I did not suffer any discomfort or inconvenience during the journey and I think other women who can should make the trip."
>
> Most of the passengers had been to the coast before. In fact, all of them are "globe trotters," and have visited many parts of the world. They all declare that the scenery of the Alps doesn't begin to compare with the mountain vistas to be seen from an automobile crossing the continent.

Their transcontinental journey complete, the party would shortly undertake "a series of excursions up and down the coast," lasting to the end of the month. The wire story also indicated that "most of the passengers will not return east until spring, several going to Hawaii and the Orient."[78]

Earlier in the year, forty passengers had spent a total of $15,800 to finance the Premier caravan, a private tour. This figure was the actual cost of repairs, tires, accessories, gasoline, oil, hotels, and camping supplies—although it apparently excluded meals. It amounted to $8.70 per passenger per day. The eight riders aboard the Garford auto train—a for-profit excursion, open to anyone—paid the Raymond and Whitcomb Company $875 apiece, $7,000 in all, to ride to the coast. Their fare was thus $16.73 per passenger per day, or twice what the Premier riders paid.

In truth, however, the Premier trip cost its passengers more than it might initially appear. Unlike the tourists in the Garford auto train, the Premier owners drove their own autos, but the Premier tour's daily per-passenger rate of $8.70 failed to reflect the depreciation due to wear and tear on the vehicles. Including that hidden charge would have inflated the actual cost of the Premier trek to well beyond the daily rate of $8.70 per person. To earn a profit, the Raymond and Whitcomb Company accordingly needed to recoup not only the tour's out-of-pocket expenses but the depreciation on its five Garfords as well. "The low cost per mile of the tour is remarkable," insisted the *Los Angeles Times*, paraphrasing A. L. Garford.[79] The Raymond and Whitcomb Company also found the cost remarkable—remarkably high. Apparently little profit remained even at a daily fare of $16.73 per passenger, for the touring company never again sponsored a coast-to-coast auto train.

AN "EPOCH IN TRANSPORTATION"

Raymond and Whitcomb's representative, H. D. Ashton, would remain in California to conduct automobile tours during the winter, before returning to New York in the spring over the same route with another group of tourists, the newspapers predicted. But no articles appeared in *Automobile* or *Motor Age* in 1912 (or later) to indicate that Raymond and Whitcomb repeated the crossing. With its touring headquarters set up at Pasadena's Hotel Maryland, the company advertised early in 1912 that it was "conducting regular automobile tours in southern California and between Los Angeles and San Francisco." The tours ranged from a one-day viewing of Southern California beaches to a nine-day tour from Pasadena to San Francisco. For these tours, Raymond and Whitcomb used the same 7-passenger Garford autos that had been driven out from New York City.[80] According to Eubank, however, at least one of the transcontinental Garfords—Westgard's mud-covered pilot car—would be shipped back to New York and displayed, unwashed, at an upcoming automobile show.

The Garford touring cars set no new speed records between New York and Los Angeles. Nor does any proof exist to indicate that Raymond and Whitcomb even turned a profit by sponsoring the first public coast-to-coast auto tour. The trip's greatest contributions were, perhaps, in reinforcing the need for better highways and fueling the demand for them, which simultaneously increased the demand for automobiles. Building better roads and more cars and trucks to ply them would reduce travel time and shipping costs for farmers and manufacturers. It represented an economic boost all the way around.

The Garford trek also inspired other drivers to make long-distance tours, in part because it illustrated the relative freedom of vacationing by auto instead of by train. It also demonstrated that the automobile possessed a unique ability to transport riches to remote places—in the form of tourist dollars spent on gasoline, food, lodging, repairs, and trinkets. The *New York Times* hailed the tour for establishing "the gasoline car as a common carrier of inter-State traffic."[81] The trip did, in fact, foreshadow the rise of the automobile bus (early buses were merely elongated autos), which competed with the railroads for passenger traffic.

While in California, Westgard wrote an article for the *Los Angeles Times* in which he argued that the southern route was the logical choice for a transcontinental highway. The Santa Fe Trail boasted a better road and climate than did the Oregon Trail, and it passed through a more populated region, Westgard maintained. Building the highway "will take money but will also take energy on the part of prominent business men," he wrote in the *Times*. "We have both and if we get right down to business, work can be commenced on an ocean-to-ocean turnpike, over the Trail to Sunset, inside of three years."[82] Who would pay for the highway? Westgard predicted that the U.S. Department of Agriculture's Office of Public Roads would furnish engineering assistance, but, he admitted, "I am not prepared to say that [the] United States government will undertake to finance this project." Earlier, a reporter for the *Larned (Kan.) Chronoscope* had asked Westgard about federal aid for the highway: "Mr. Westgard shook his head dubiously and said there was so much trading among the congressmen and such rivalry existed that it was uncertain whether anything could be gotten through the next session."[83] He hoped that the project could instead rely upon assistance from state and local governments.

Three years later, in 1914, as vice president of the National Highways Association, Westgard was still actively promoting federal support for highway construction. He mapped routes all over the United States for the National Highways Association, which identified 50,000 miles of highway that it believed the federal government should develop.[84] But it was not until 1916 that Congress approved the idea of regularly using federal money to build roads.

Other groups eventually followed the lead of the Raymond and Whitcomb Company by sponsoring other coast-to-coast tours. "Of the organized tours to move across the country from the Atlantic seaboard the first will start from New York City June 15," *Motor West* reported in its June 1915 issue. "This is the initial transcontinental tour conducted by the National Highways Association, which during this summer will promote several such trips. All will be to California. On the first tour A. L. Westgard, veteran pathfinder, will be at the head of the party, which will tour the entire State, that the motorists may see both expositions and all the points of interest."[85]

In 1915, as thousands of autoists planned to drive to expositions in San Diego and San Francisco, Westgard also offered touring advice in articles he wrote for *MoToR* and *Motor Print*. Driving across America just five years earlier "required a courage and ingenuity not surpassed by that evidenced by the hunters and explorers of nearly a hundred years ago," Westgard acknowledged. But he advised the 1915 motorist to "remove from his heart all fear of danger, insurmountable obstacles or serious discomforts. They no longer exist."[86] In addition to such encouragements, his illustrated articles offered a variety of practical advice (see Fig. 68).

Westgard later rejoined AAA, "mainly as a consulting authority in his special field, preparing a camping manual and doing occasional writing for *American Motorist* and other publications." In 1920 he published a book of memoirs, *Tales of a Pathfinder*. He died in San Diego the following year, on April 3, 1921, when he was only 55 years old. Eubank, who retired from the Associated Press in 1948, died in New York City on December 11, 1955, aged 72.[87]

Fig. 68. A cartoon illustrating West-gard's advice in an article titled "Preparing the Transcontinentalist." (Motor Print, March 1915)

"This trip marks an epoch in transportation," Eubank declared after reaching California by auto. "It foreshadows the building of a great national highway from ocean to ocean, entirely free from the hardships we encountered." According to Eubank, three other events—all of which occurred while the automobile train was in motion—underscored the changes to come. "The first wireless [radio] message had leapt across the country from Point Loma, near San Diego, to Norfolk, Va.," he pointed out. Second, "for the first time a man had taken up the receiver of a telephone in Los Angeles and heard the voice of another man, answering him in New York City—speech itself had performed the transcontinental journey."[88] And, third, despite several crack-ups, Cal Rodgers had become the first person to fly across the country.

Members of the automobile train, however, reported no crack-ups, although the *San Diego Union* revealed that Ashton's Garford had suffered an unspecified breakdown near San Diego. According to Eubank, though, the only real threat to a member of the Garford party came "when an impressionable occupant of the stag car called the 'Blind Pig' gazed too deeply into the dark eyes of a Mexican senorita and it looked for a while as if the old days of scalp-taking were to be revived."[89]

In comparison to the trials of immigrants sixty years earlier, there was nothing heroic in the Garford automobile crossing, even though the "Trail to Sunset" was "by no means a path of roses," Eubank wrote. "There are roads and roads, some good, some bad, and others horrible." Overall, however, "instead of a weary trek across the wilderness, burdened by hardship, scourged by disease and danger," the group enjoyed what he called "a luxurious pleasure jaunt." Yet, as Eubank astutely recognized, "the time is coming when we shall seem, to the travelers of the day along the Trail to Sunset, much as the pioneers appear to us."[90]

The next record-setting ocean-to-ocean auto trip involved just one driver, Cannon Ball Baker. Like the Garford tourists, Baker, in his Stutz Bearcat roadster, followed a southern route. His goal was not to prove that the trip could be made: the 1911 Premier and Garford tours had convincingly shown that men, women, and children could cross the country by automobile comfortably and safely. Instead, Baker intended to show how fast a single driver could travel across America.

CANNON BALL BAKER SMASHES SINGLE-DRIVER RECORD

5

The car thundered down Chestnut street at such a rate that some of the spectators thought he might get to New York this afternoon, or at the very latest tomorrow morning.

—*Dodge City (Kan.) Daily Globe*

ON MAY 7, 1915, at midnight, police strained to control the crowd that had gathered to see Erwin G. "Cannon Ball" Baker, holder of the coast-to-coast motorcycle record, leave San Diego in a modified 4-cylinder Stutz Bearcat. Accompanied by *Indianapolis News* reporter William F. Sturm, official "observer" and unofficial assistant to the driver, Baker in just two days reeled off the 1,001 miles to El Paso, Texas, "over roads that are pronounced the worst in history."[1]

Bound for New York City on a southern route, Baker was attempting to set a new transcontinental speed record for a single driver. On the way, he and Sturm would race a train across southern New Mexico, find themselves lost in the desert and low on gas, crash through a barbed-wire fence at 40 mph, and battle the twin road hazards of mud and mules. Bewhiskered and barely recognizable—for they had traveled from San Diego without shaving—Baker and Sturm pulled into New York on May 18 to end their 3,728.4-mile run. They had traversed the country in 11 days, 7 hours, 15 minutes. In 1908 it had taken the previous record holder, Jacob M. Murdock, nearly three times as long. The only crossing time faster than Baker's—10 days, 18 hours, 12 minutes—had been set in 1910, but by relay team of five drivers (see Chapter 2).

The Stutz Motor Car Company of Indianapolis had hired Baker, the hometown hero, "to do with an auto what he did with a motorcycle, that is, set a one-man drive record from coast to coast," observed the *Advocate* of Greenville, Illinois—a town through which Baker had zoomed on his motorcycle in 1914 and would again in the Stutz a year later.[2] The Stutz company's president, Harry C. Stutz, backed Baker's record-setting attempt for the same reason he sponsored a Stutz racing team—to promote the power and dependability of the car he began building for the 1912 model year.

CRAZY ON FOUR WHEELS

Talking with automotive writer Russ Catlin, Baker recalled that Harry Stutz met with him in late 1914 to ask, "Bake, could you be as crazy on four wheels as you are on two? I want the transcontinental record for Stutz with Cannon Ball Baker driving." Baker replied by asking, "And just what is the transcontinental record for an automobile, Mister Stutz?" To which the automaker responded: "Whatever the last claim was, my Bearcat can beat it. I'll furnish the car and set the conditions. You drive it, break the record, and the car is yours!"[3]

To break the record, Baker would clearly have to drive at what were then considered to be high speeds—40 or 50 mph or faster—over clear roads (where he could find them) so as to make up for the inevitable slowdowns due to mud, deep sand, and the necessity of fording many rivers. That such high speeds could pose a danger to pedestrians and horse-drawn vehicles went without saying. But, curiously, few if any observers expressed concerns about Baker's high-speed dash over public highways. This, perhaps, is an indication of his reputation as a skillful driver. Furthermore, as we will see in the following chapter, Baker was known to be especially respectful of the rights of others with whom he shared the roads. The issue of high speeds over public roads arose just five years earlier, in 1910, during Lester L. Whitman's coast-to-coast dash in a Reo (see Chapter 2). But Whitman himself raised the issue, and it was because high speed had contributed to two collisions and an arrest for speeding during a record-setting transcontinental trip he had organized in 1906. Those mishaps prompted Whitman to announce that he would slow down for safety and adopt a new philosophy for his 1910 Reo trip: slow but steady wins the record.

At the conclusion of Baker's 1915 trip, Harry Stutz became the first automaker on record to submit his transcontinental car to independent testing. It was a calculated risk. The Automobile Club of America's technical committee did, in fact, expose a few warts—extreme wear to the car's transmission, wheel bearings, and some of the engine bearings, for instance. But its conclusion that "the car as a whole was in very good condition, especially in view of the hard usage which it must have received," was welcome advertising fodder for the Stutz company.[4]

Stutz's choice as driver, Baker was born on March 12, 1882, in a four-room log house on a farm near Lawrenceburg, Indiana. At the age of twelve, Baker moved to Indianapolis, where he apprenticed as a machinist and subsequently pursued his trade for eight years. In the meantime, he had also become "an expert at fancy bag-punching," according to a 1953 feature in the *Indianapolis Star*. At the age of about twenty, Baker joined a local drill team and left home to travel the vaudeville circuit for a year. Quitting the team, he and a partner performed on their own for the next two years. "His was a punching-bag act," syndicated columnist Ernie Pyle wrote of Baker in 1940. "He was so good he could keep 11 bags going at once."[5]

"I NEVER SAW SUCH A RACE"

Although historians disagree about the specific year, Baker entered his first motorcycle race in about 1906.[6] His reputation as a daredevil soon spread. On July 3, 1911, at an Indianapolis dirt track, Baker won all four of the motorcycle races he entered. Charging through the five-mile race on his Indian motorcycle, he shaved 32 seconds off a 1908 track record for the event and then lowered his own mark the next day in a close finish with another racer. According to the *Indianapolis News*, President William Howard Taft "personally congratulated Erwin G. Baker and John Sink after their match race, which was only decided at the tape, Baker winning by a foot." The president "received the startling finish with a perceptible thrill of excitement," the *Indianapolis Star* observed. "Mr. Baker, I congratulate you upon winning a great race," Taft said. "I never saw such a race before."[7]

Three years later, in May 1914, Baker drove a 2-cylinder, 7-horsepower Indian motorcycle some 3,400 miles between San Diego and New York City in 11 days, 12 hours, 10 minutes.[8] According to the *New York Times*, this broke the previous motorcycle record of 20 days, 9 hours, 1 minute.[9] "To my way of thinking, I really achieved the feat four months before," Baker later remarked. First, he explained, he had carefully laid out his route. Then,

> I enlisted the co-operation of a weather expert and together we examined weather conditions over my chosen territory for ten years. Analysis showed that, contrary to general opinion, May was the best month for me to undertake a coast-to-coast ride on a motorcycle. So, relying on the weather's past performances, I determined to start in May, leaving San Diego on the 3d. The weather ran true to form and I did not hit rain until after I had gotten east of the Mississippi valley, at which point I struck gravelly roads, which absorbed moisture readily and gave me minimum trouble.[10]

If the weather cooperated, so did the law. In his native Indiana, "the authorities raised the speed limit for one day so that I could do my best," he later recalled.[11] As part of his preparations, Baker also arranged to have gasoline waiting for him at remote points along the way.

KEEN EYES AND AN UNCOMMON MEMORY

Baker, who disavowed drinking and smoking, slept for just 46 hours during the long motorcycle trek—about four hours per day. He did the same thing on his automobile treks. "On a long road grind, if I get too sleepy, I sometimes stop the car and lie down beside the road for twenty minutes. I can go to sleep instantly and wake up on the dot."[12]

Aside from his stamina, he drew upon two other physical traits in setting his many records: keen eyesight and an uncommon memory. Baker told an interviewer in 1923 that, during a recent eye exam, "the 'Doc' stuck up the usual lettered card on the opposite wall—and I rattled off all the letters, including the small lines at the bottom. 'Good heavens, man,' he said, 'if I had your vision I wouldn't even speak to an oculist, to say nothing about paying him a professional call!'" Vision was at the core of his driving philosophy as well, he explained:

> People often ask me how I can drive so fast. Well, part of it's due to developing the knack of far-sightedness. It's just like drawing a long bead with a rifle; you spot a "target" a good

ways distant and ride like the very deuce for it—yet all the time remaining conscious of every bend and bump in the road just beyond. The farther ahead you can see, the quicker you can cover the distance between where you are and where you want to be; and I reckon that this thing holds as good in the rest of life as it does in racing.[13]

As Baker described it, his apparently photographic memory was an extension of his keen vision:

> On my road races I go over the route once or twice before the real grind and chalk every twist and turn of it down in my memory. I seem to be able to remember these things indefinitely. Even the long stretches across the continent are just as fresh in my mind as if they were my own back yard.
>
> It's a funny thing, but I always prefer to study a route backward. For instance, if I were going to race from Detroit to Chicago, I'd make a trial spin over the road from Chicago to Detroit. Later, when I took the actual run, everything I'd seen would unwind itself before me just like the reel of a motion picture.[14]

FROM A DEMON TO A CANNON BALL

Over the next two decades, Baker would become the most famous of the transcontinental racers. "Oddly enough," the *New York Times* commented when Baker reached New York in the Stutz, "he had not had much previous experience in driving a car, his total mileage in a four-wheeled machine being 9,000 before this record trip." *Automobile* likewise mentioned that Baker was "new in transcontinental motoring," while also noting that he "has had considerable experience in transcontinental traveling with a motorcycle"—a reference to his May 1914 trip on an Indian cycle.[15]

Erwin George Baker accumulated many nicknames early on, according to syndicated columnist Ernie Pyle, who interviewed the driver in 1940:

> As his records grew, he acquired such names as Demon, Warhorse, Daredevil and The Fox. But it was when he rode into New York in 1914, at the end of a new transcontinental, that he got the name of Cannon Ball. A reporter on the *Tribune* named George Sherman gave it to him. The reporter is dead now. And so is the "E. G." part of the Baker signature. He's in the Indianapolis phone book as Cannon Ball Baker. But Mrs. Baker calls him Erwin, and friends call him Bake.[16]

Aside, however, from a May 17, 1914, story reporting that Baker would arrive "within the next twelve hours," the *New York Tribune* wrote nothing about him in the wake of his trip. It therefore seems unlikely that the *Tribune* reporter gave Baker his nickname. Nor, apparently, did Baker's friend Bill Sturm know him as "Cannon Ball" when they made their Stutz Bearcat trip. Neither in Sturm's 1915 *Indianapolis News* dispatches nor in a twenty-page booklet he wrote afterward for Stutz did the famous nickname appear. Moreover, a collection of forty articles about the 1915 trip contains only two that mention the name.

Baker himself was loath to use his new nickname. In a letter of endorsement written for the Hartford Suspension Company, in which Baker claims that his 1915 Stutz record "would not have been possible without Hartford Shock Absorbers," he signed himself "E. G. Baker."[17] Eventually, however, the nickname caught on, sometimes written as one word, sometimes as two. Baker preferred "Cannon Ball."

"SIMPLY TAKING NOTES"

Accompanying Baker on the Stutz trek was William F. "Bill" Sturm, 31, who covered auto racing for the *Indianapolis News* and had managed Baker's career since about 1907 (see Fig. 69). Sturm "was exceedingly handy with his 'dukes' in those days and a worthy contestant in the boxing ring," the *Indianapolis News* later recalled. "His stamina as a boxer served him well in the gruelling drives across country."[18]

Whether Sturm ever took the wheel of the Bearcat during the 1915 trip is an open question. "He does none of the driving, simply taking notes on the trip," said one Midwestern newspaper, although this grossly understates the reporter's contributions. Likewise, "he was in no sense a mechanic, being unacquainted with automobile work. He can not drive an automobile," the Stutz company claimed in an editor's note to Sturm's summary of the trip, which the automaker published as *Stutz: 11 Days 7 Hours 15 Minutes—A Story*.[19] A number of contemporary and retrospective articles, however, suggest that Sturm did drive the car on occasion. One such source—a long, detailed obituary, obviously written by a close colleague at the *Indianapolis News*, where Sturm worked from 1903 until his death in 1937—contends that "when weariness overcame Baker he was relieved at the wheel by Sturm."

Perhaps—although not according to Sturm himself. "I do not drive a car even on asphalt streets," he confessed in a summary of the trip he wrote for *American Chauffeur*. "Baker did the driving. I kept an accurate log of the trip."[20] Sturm's log was in part photographic. As he explained in *American Chauffeur*:

> It was my business to take pictures without stopping the progress of the trip. We stopped ten and fifteen minutes to eat. Occasionally we had to make a second's stop along the road

for various things. It was during these "hesitations" that I had to get my pictures. I got six dozen of them. This will show about how busy I was with my camera, not to mention the thousand and one other details. I mention these things lest any of my readers will imagine that my job was that of a passenger pure and simple.[21]

Fig. 69. Sturm (foreground) with Baker at the wheel of the Stutz in San Diego before the trip east. (FLP)

A number of Sturm's photos survive in Stutz photo files at the Detroit Public Library's National Automotive History Collection. Information scrawled on the back of the original small snapshots—they measure 2¾ x 4½ inches—may be in Sturm's own hand. Most, if not all, of the photos in the collection were taken in Arizona, New Mexico, and Texas.

"More or less athletically inclined" at 151 pounds, Sturm spent weeks helping Baker plan the trip. But when the Stutz was "hurtling across the country at a speed of from 25 to 60 miles an hour," Sturm spent most of his time clinging to a foot brace and a handhold, he wrote. Responsible for sending some ten to fifteen telegrams each night during the run, Sturm got even less sleep than Baker. "Long after Baker was in the hay," he recalled, "every night of the trip I was still busy writing wires or working carefully on my log of the trip."[22]

In the daily dispatches that he telegraphed to the *Indianapolis News*, Sturm revealed that he had many other responsibilities, one of which was to feed Baker while he drove. So well did Sturm carry out his responsibilities that he rode again with Baker on a 1916 transcontinental trip in a Cadillac, and the same year assisted in an effort by speed demon Ralph Mulford to drive a Hudson to a coast-to-coast round-trip record (see Chapters 6 and 8). Of greater interest to the press in 1915, however, was Sturm's role as the "official observer." According to *Automobile*, it was Sturm "who had the car officially checked out at San Diego, by A.A.A. [American Automobile Association] officials, checked at the night stops with official signatures and seals, and checked at the finish by an A.A.A. representative."[23]

MIDNIGHT START LAUNCHES STUTZ

Baker and Sturm arrived in San Diego on Wednesday, May 5, 1915. According to Sturm, the factory had shipped the Bearcat by rail to Los Angeles, whence the two men drove to San Diego, evidently so that Baker could get a feel for the car. They intended "to establish an automobile record of less than fifteen days," said an unsigned article in the *Indianapolis News* that was probably written by Sturm. At 11:55 P.M. on Thursday, May 6, in front of the *San Diego Union* office, Baker started the 4-cylinder Stutz. The car "responded with a bark that brought a smile to the crowd."[24]

As midnight approached, according to Sturm, the two men pulled on racing hoods, goggles, and one-piece "monkey suits," which in photos appear to be made of heavy cloth—perhaps cotton or wool. Sturm, who wore a wool army shirt underneath his monkey suit, pulled a rubber slicker over the top. "I felt for my kodak case to be sure it was still on the strap around my neck; then I carefully went over my eight pockets in the suit and those in my shirt to be sure that the flaps were all buttoned securely and that my scanty wardrobe and my films were safe."[25] So many spectators assembled that they blocked traffic, according to a wire story from San Diego that appeared in the next day's *Indianapolis News*:

> As the hour of midnight drew near, Bill Mountain, an old New York newspaper man, and secretary of the fair [the Panama-California Exposition] here, fingered an envelope, which he was to give Baker to carry to Frank X. Mudd, of the A.A.A. touring bureau in New York. A. F. Guellow, city editor of the *Union*, held the watch, and J. H. Fletcher, a motorcycle racer of note, acted as judge. . . .
>
> With but five minutes left before the start the crowd became so great that the police experienced difficulty in handling it. Promptly at 12, after shaking hands with Baker, Mountain gave the word and the car shot forward on its long trip.[26]

BEARCAT MODIFIED FOR TREK

Produced since 1912, the Stutz Bearcat that Baker drove on his 1915 record-setting trip was already a legendary automobile. "Mention the word Stutz and the Pavlovian-like response invariably is Bearcat," automotive historian Beverly Rae Kimes has written. "Seldom has a car become so indelibly etched in memory via a single model."[27]

According to *Automobile* and the company's own booklet, the 1915 Bearcat's standard parts included Goodyear tires of 35 x 5 inches mounted on Houk wire wheels, including two spares strapped on back, Hartford shock absorbers, a Stewart horn, and a Bosch two-spark magneto that fired eight AC spark plugs, one over each valve in the T-head Wisconsin engine of 4¾ x 5½ bore and stroke.[28] A 1915 specifications table says the Bearcat developed 36.1 horsepower according to the formula used by the Society of Automotive Engineers.[29] The SAE horsepower rating is typically far lower than the brake horsepower of an engine, which is derived by actually testing the engine on a special machine known as an engine brake. With a Stromberg H-3 carburetor, the Stutz company claimed, the engine actually developed more than 60 horsepower at 1,500 rpm.

Though most American automakers switched to left-hand drive with their 1913 models, Stutz produced only right-hand drive cars until 1922. The 1915 Stutz was also unusual for having its transmission mounted on the rear axle, a style that many automakers had abandoned in favor of placing the transmission amidships or bolting it directly to the engine. Baker's car had a 120-inch wheelbase and sold new for $2,000 (see Fig. 70).[30]

Baker's Bearcat Model F roadster, serial no. 2746, differed in five ways from a stock model, according to Harry C. Stutz's sworn statement to the Automobile Club of America:

1. As was typical in racing engines, the piston-to-cylinder wall clearance "was slightly more than that allowed in stock cars."

2. The car "was fitted with two sets of Hartford shock absorbers in the front and two sets in the rear, whereas only one set in the rear are furnished on stock models."

3. "The fenders regularly supplied on stock cars were not carried."

4. "The rubber bumpers used under the front springs are not regularly furnished with stock cars."

Fig. 70. Harry C. Stutz (standing, hand on seat) poses with Baker (driving) and Sturm in the unfinished racer. Before starting on the trip, the car received new headlamps, cowl lamps, tires, and license plates. A sign painter would shorten the faintly visible name stenciled on the hood—"Erwin G. Baker"—to "E. G. Baker." (FLP)

5. Even though regular Stutz cars had adopted an electric lighting and starting system, Baker's car carried kerosene side and tail lamps and a Prest-O-Lite tank of compressed acetylene, which operated a pair of acetylene headlamps. Aware that early electric lighting and starting systems were heavy and fickle, Baker presumably chose acetylene for its reliability and light weight. In lieu of an electric starter, he cranked the engine manually using the handle attached to the front of the car.[31]

According to *Horseless Age*, "an interesting feature of the car is that it is equipped with a motor which was turned in by a New York Stutz owner who complained that it was 'no good.'" Likewise, *Automobile Topics* stated that "the motor used in the car was taken from a customer who complained that it wasn't right. He was satisfied with another motor, the first one tested by dynamometer at the Stutz plant in Indianapolis, mounted on a chassis and then sent West for the start of Baker's trip."[32] The Stutz company, however, made no such claim. Why would the automaker risk its reputation, not to mention a considerable cash outlay, by using a possibly faulty engine? If the engine was a used one, logic suggests that Stutz mechanics had carefully rebuilt it to achieve the larger-than-normal piston clearances that Harry Stutz specified.

According to *Automobile*, the Stutz carried a wire radiator screen and had its springs taped, presumably to keep sand and mud from working between the spring leaves. Notwithstanding the Lincoln Highway emblem attached to its radiator screen, the Stutz traveled that transcontinental route only in Pennsylvania and perhaps New Jersey. Sturm spoke of the engine's "bark," and he also mentioned that the starter "shouted" the question, "Everything ready?" as he shook hands with them moments before the midnight start. In all likelihood, then, the car was either mufflerless or had been fitted with a muffler bypass, or else it was simply very loud.[33]

To get traction on slick roads, Baker used Easyon tire chains, which "can be applied in a moment even when stuck in the mud," its maker advertised.[34] The car carried other special equipment or extra items as well, Sturm noted in his account:

> On each side of the car, hanging from the oil lamps, was a two-and-a-half gallon desert water bag. Slung on the steering column was a big 44 Colt revolver. . . . Between the gas tank immediately behind the seat was strapped an axe. All oil was carried in the crank case, with an extra gallon under the hood in a tin container. On the driver's side of the car, extending alongside the box which housed the tools, hung a shovel. Fastened to two iron standards on the front of the car were banners of the Hoosier Motor Club of Indianapolis, Ind. On a four-foot staff directly behind the seats fluttered Old Glory. Thus the car stood, ready to start a battle that was to end on the other side of the continent.[35]

SPECTATORS WARN OF DANGERS

From the *San Diego Union* office, Baker, 33, launched the Stutz into the hills outside San Diego, muddy from recent rains. But despite the mud, Baker piled up his best daily mileage on Days 1 and 2 of the 11-day journey. The travelers had planned to take the Santa Fe Trail from New Mexico through Kansas, as Baker had done during his 1914 motorcycle trip. But ten feet of snow clogged the mountain passes on the old overland trail. Baker and Sturm instead opted for a more southerly route that would take them through extreme southern California, Arizona, New Mexico, the Texas and Oklahoma panhandles, Kansas, Missouri, Illinois, Indiana, Ohio, West Virginia, Pennsylvania, New Jersey, and New York (see Table 12).

TABLE 12. City-by-City Itinerary of the Stutz Bearcat, 1915

Day/Date	City to City	Daily Mileage	Cumulative Mileage
1/May 7 Fri	San Diego to Campo, Calif. Coyote Wells, Calif. El Centro, Calif. Holtville, Calif. Yuma, Ariz. Dome, Ariz. Agua Caliente, Ariz. Phoenix, Ariz.	409.1	409.1
2/May 8 Sat	Phoenix, Ariz., to Florence, Ariz. Tucson, Ariz. Tombstone, Ariz. Bisbee, Ariz. Douglas, Ariz. Lordsburg, N.M. Deming, N.M. El Paso, Texas	592.0	1,001.1
3/May 9 Sun	El Paso, Texas, to Alamogordo, N.M. Roswell, N.M.	244.4	1,245.5
4/May 10 Mon	Roswell, N.M., to Plains, Texas Lubbock, Texas Plainview, Texas	264.4	1,509.9
5/May 11 Tue	Plainview, Texas, to Amarillo, Texas Stratford, Texas[a] Liberal, Kan. Plains, Kan.	374.0	1,883.9
6/May 12 Wed	Plains, Kan., to Dodge City, Kan. Emporia, Kan.	335.2	2,219.1
7/May 13 Thu	Emporia, Kan., to Kansas City, Mo. Lexington, Mo.	182.2	2,401.3

8/May 14 Fri	Lexington, Mo., to Boonville, Mo. Columbia, Mo. St. Louis, Mo. Greenville, Ill.	323.2	2,724.5
9/May 15 Sat	Greenville, Ill., to Vandalia, Ill. Indianapolis Dayton, Ohio	322.1	3,046.6
10/May 16 Sun	Dayton, Ohio, to Springfield, Ohio Columbus, Ohio Zanesville, Ohio[b] Donora, Pa. Greensburg, Pa.	303.0	3,349.6
11/May 17 Mon	Greensburg, Pa., to Stoystown, Pa. Gettysburg, Pa. Lancaster, Pa. Philadelphia	275.8	3,625.4
12/May 18 Tue	Philadelphia to Trenton, N.J. New York City	103.0	3,728.4

SOURCES: W. F. Sturm's *Indianapolis News* dispatches for May 1915; W. F. Sturm, *Stutz: 11 Days 7 Hours 15 Minutes—A Story*; national auto journals; and local newspapers.

[a] Baker passed through the Oklahoma panhandle between Stratford, Texas, and Liberal, Kan.

[b] Baker crossed the northern tip of West Virginia between Zanesville, Ohio, and Donora, Pa., but trip chronicler W. F. Sturm makes no mention of the cities along this route.

From San Diego, the pair followed the Mexican border and struck Campo, California, 55 miles out, at 2:07 A.M., and El Centro, 87 miles out, at 3:20 A.M. Friday. Between the two cities lay Devil's Canyon, through which the men traveled in the dark. As Sturm wrote in his dispatch from Phoenix, Arizona, the next day:

Part of the trip last night lay through the famous Devils [sic] canyon, over a cliff road cut out of the face of the mountain, with a sheer drop of hundreds of feet. Baker's popularity was in evidence all along the route as autoists and motorcyclists greeted him and warned him of the treacherous places. Time and again the Prest-O-Lite brought up a dangerous curve.[36]

At sunrise Friday, they ran into Holtville, California, "and the beginning of the deep sand," Sturm reported. "Baker plowed through at 26 miles an hour. We were continually drenched with sand, if one may use that word in describing anything except water. Between spells of holding on and being jerked half out of the seat I kept my eyes on the motometer [a thermometer on the radiator cap], but never once did the red fluid get dangerously near the top." They paused for fifteen minutes on the sands while Sturm photographed Baker in the Stutz roadster. The Stutz followed a six-mile plank road across sand dunes on this stretch, Sturm said.[37]

According to news reports, this leg of the trip took the car over some of the worst roads in the country. "During the night," said the *Indianapolis News*, "they covered one stretch of fifty miles of sand and much muddy road."[38] Such hazards notwithstanding, at 7:25 A.M., the Stutz pulled into Yuma, Arizona, 185 miles from San Diego, where Baker made a short stop to "snatch a light breakfast." While they were there, L. W. Alexander of the Yuma County Commercial Club signed Sturm's record book, Sturm recalled.

"WE WERE MAKING SPEED"

The manager of a Yuma garage had arranged it so the ferry was waiting for them to cross the Gila River at Dome, 23 miles east. "We got on the ferry at 8:25 [A.M.], and six Indians, who remembered Baker from the year before, poled us across the treacherous stream." They then headed east and slightly north toward Phoenix, over the Castle Dome Mountains and "through a desert country with deep washes that made cautious driving and good brakes an absolute necessity," Sturm wrote.[39] After pausing in Agua Caliente, Arizona, for lunch with Postmaster John Modesti, "again we sought the rough road to Phoenix, the car being subjected to constant strain as we drove in and out of the ruts. It is impossible to make speed in this section without punishing the car severely—and we were making speed."[40] To help soften the road shocks, Baker and Sturm sat on doughnut-shaped cushions, as one of Sturm's photos reveals (see Fig. 71).

As the last 40 miles "offered no barrier to high speed," the duo sped into Phoenix at 5:40 P.M. Mountain Time to conclude their first day of driving, Sturm reported to the *Indianapolis News*.[41] The elapsed time of 16 hours, 40 minutes, from San Diego "is considered exceptionally fast for the rough going," he observed. Baker drove 409.1 miles to average nearly 25 mph for his elapsed time and better than 27 mph for his running time of 15 hours to Phoenix over roads of mud, sand, and deep ruts.

"A royal welcome was given to the two men here, John Hohl and French Jacks,

former Indianians, having everything ready. The car was put into a garage and Hugh Miller, winner of the El Paso to Phoenix desert auto race last year, kept a watch all night," according to *Automobile Topics*.[42] "Here we got a hot bath and a rubdown, which I certainly needed, for we had hit a concealed bump just out of Phoenix and I hit the sharp edge of the seat in coming down with my right ribs, landing all sprawled out over the gas tank and the tool box," Sturm wrote. A "certain newspaper man in Los Angeles" had predicted that their one-day drive to Phoenix would take two days; at the end of two days, however, Baker was hoping to be in El Paso, Texas, some 1,000 miles from San Diego, Sturm also noted.[43]

Following a nine-hour stop, which included five hours of sleep, Baker and Sturm left Phoenix at 3:00 A.M. Saturday, May 8, Day 2 of their trip. "I like it best from three to four in the morning, when there is almost no other traffic," Baker said. Their route across southern Arizona would take them through Florence, Tucson, Tombstone, Bisbee, and Douglas. "Baker is in his usual good condition, a huge Porterhouse steak this morning making him fit for a long grind," Sturm reported from Phoenix on Saturday. "When we got into Tucson, at 7:25 [A.M.], 135 miles away, we stopped long enough to get some oranges and a kodak, as mine had been put out of commission the day before."[44]

Fig. 72. A stop for gas in Tombstone, Arizona. Sturm has his back to the car while Baker leans over the left rear wheel. (NAHC)

FASTER THAN A SPEEDING LOCOMOTIVE

On the Borderland Trail now, they climbed into the hills east of Tucson, made a short stop for gas and oil at Tombstone (see Fig. 72), and reached Bisbee, 5,300 feet above sea level, at 1:00 P.M. "The first person we shook hands with in Bisbee was Joseph Gray, secretary of the State Auto Association, and the first thing he did was to sign the route book to show that we had not skipped his town," Sturm wrote. "The roads around

Bisbee are of the finest," which contributed to Baker's best one-day romp of the trip—592 miles from Phoenix to El Paso (see Figs. 73, 74, and 75).

To cover such distances, Baker said in a 1923 interview, "you've got to tear off better than a mile a minute to make up for the hills and curves that force you to slow up and change your gears. At times I've speeded up to eighty-five miles an hour—which is about all you can coax out of any stock car."[45] East of Bisbee, Baker and Sturm crossed into New Mexico, their third state of the trip, stopping at Lordsburg "only long enough to run into the Southern Pacific depot and get a signature from the operator," Sturm recalled. "We challenged the Southern Pacific passenger train for Deming, 65 miles away, to a duel—and drove into the latter place five minutes before it arrived."

But Baker got lost in the desert beyond Deming. "Round and round we rode in the darkness in an endeavor to find the trail. Our gasoline was getting low. We even considered going back to Deming, but our slogan was 'El Paso or bust,'" Sturm wrote. "Finally I approached a Mexican house and by dint of much grunting and shouting of 'El

Fig. 73. Baker pauses at a marker along the Continental Divide near Bisbee, Arizona. (NAHC)

Fig. 74. Baker and the
Stutz on a smooth but
meandering mountain
road near Bisbee.
(NAHC)

Paso!' we were directed to go in a direction which we felt sure was wrong, but went, and soon arrived at El Paso."[46] Their arrival at 1:15 A.M. Sunday, May 9, was 3¼ hours later than they had hoped. The car's odometer showed they had driven 1,001.1 miles from San Diego in an elapsed time of 2 days, 1 hour, 15 minutes, Sturm said.[47]

After eating—"for Baker ate every time he got a chance"[48]—the two men slept three hours, until 6:00 A.M., when they started northeast on the Borderland Trail out of El Paso (see Figs. 76 and 77), aiming to reach Alamogordo, New Mexico, by noon Sunday, Sturm said. Mountain ranges lay before them as they turned eastward toward Roswell.

> We can not forget those mountains. I waded into a little torrent, the Ruidoso, to find a safe ford, and the water was icy. The next ford we came to looked bad and a young man with a couple of horses volunteered to take us across for a consideration. We knew we could not get across under power, for an engine won't run under water. We got in the middle of the stream behind those horses and there we stuck. Forward motion ceased and vertical motion began, which I knew would land the car in China if it continued long enough.[49]

Automobile called it quicksand. Whatever it was, it immobilized the Stutz for five hours, Sturm said. The young man rounded up two more horses as Sturm took photos showing the river water running over the car's floorboards (see Fig. 78). But even with four horses pulling away at it, the car would not budge. "By this time Baker was a raving maniac," according to Sturm. "He called on high heaven to witness that those four horses could not pull as much as the billy goat he owned when a kid."[50] Scared by the yells of a half-dozen onlookers and helpers, the horses strained harder and finally pulled the Stutz out of the sand and up onto the bank.

The motorists got help shortly afterward in crossing another ford without incident—this time, it took merely an hour to cross—and then drove 80 miles in wet clothes to Roswell, New Mexico, where they spent the night. Hiring horses had cost them $20, and the delays held them to 244.4 miles on Day 3 of the trip. The good news, Sturm added, was "so far, we have certainly outrun the puncture jinx, for he has not been in evidence once during the entire distance of 1,245 miles."[51]

"A HUGE PIECE OF MUD"

They were off again in the Stutz Bearcat on Monday morning, May 10, crossing the border into Plains, Texas, in time for lunch (see Figs. 79 and 80). "I shall always remember Plains because the postmaster refused to put his official stamp in my book because he did not consider it official business," Sturm recounted. "He compromised by

Fig. 75. Baker rounds a blind curve near Bisbee. (NAHC)

Fig. 76. On the prairie north of the city, a soldier from El Paso's Fort Bliss snapped a photo showing Sturm seated in the Stutz and Baker checking the water level in the radiator. (NAHC)

writing his name, however. It was at Plains, too, that the man in the sombrero insisted on Baker going into the garage office with him. Baker came out feeling mighty pert, but I leave it to the reader to form his own conclusions."[52]

The two used their shovel for the first time between Plains and Lubbock, Texas. "We were meandering over the prairie about 50 miles per when without warning our starboard wheels dropped into a soft spot and left us marooned high and dry in the center. With the center cut down so the wheels could get a little traction we were soon on our way," Sturm wrote.[53] At nightfall, the Stutz pulled into Lubbock, where the men got a fresh Prest-O-Lite tank and decided to continue driving for 50 more miles. "With the Stutz Bearcat resembling a huge piece of mud we rolled into Plainview, Tex.," Sturm wrote in the *Indianapolis News*. There, they concluded a 264.4-mile day of slow traveling over mostly muddy, unfamiliar trails. According to Sturm:

It seemed as if all the mud in that section of the country had been saved up for days and piled in the path of the Stutz. Time and time again the body scraped, but we experienced no difficulty in getting through although any attempt at making time was impossible. Our entire route lay through the ranch lands of New Mexico and Texas and we traversed practically all new roads as we were forced to change our original route which lay to the north, on account of snow covered and impassable roads in the White mountains.
    Our unfamiliarity with the roads made Baker cautious. . . . We passed scores of old-

fashioned prairie schooners wending their way slowly but steadily over the immense stretches of cattle country. We were forced to pick our way through thousands of cattle and opened no less than fifty-two ranch gates. Baker took every advantage of the few comparatively good stretches of road, or rather ranch lands[,] in an endeavor to make up for the slow time through the mud. . . .

We were forced to ask questions concerning distances in order to verify our calculations, but the answers we received were misleading. An old man hauling a bale of cotton told us that Plainview was "'bout thirty miles"; just a little farther on we spied an old prairie schooner drawn by a white horse and a mule, and the driver told us that Plainview was sixteen miles, but the third inquiry addressed to the girl wearing a sombrero brought forth the information that it was only seven miles, and this proved to be correct.[54]

The 337-mile detour off the Santa Fe Trail, Baker recalled in a 1923 interview, "was the toughest ride I ever took on any trip"—except, he said, for a later motorcycle ride in Hawaii.[55]

BAKER BATTLES BARBED WIRE

In his dispatch from Plainview, Sturm reflected that "four days of riding has made a veteran out of me, as I was a novice when I started. I have become so proficient that I

Fig. 77. Like a mariner on a sea of sand, a begoggled Baker pilots the Stutz along a two-rut trail northeast of El Paso. "There were 125 miles of this," proclaims a scrawled note on this original trip photo. (NAHC)

Fig. 78. When four
horses failed to free
the Stutz from the
icy grip of the Rio
Ruidoso west of
Roswell, New Mexico,
Baker—still calm
enough in this photo
—became a "raving
maniac." (NAHC)

can lather Baker's sunburned nose with cold cream and feed him an orange while traveling forty miles an hour over rough roads, at the same time hanging on with my toes." Actually, Baker protested, he generally took care to avoid overeating. "All my life, except when I was racing, I ate only two meals a day. When I raced I ate continuously to keep up my energy."[56] Tales about Baker's hearty appetite grew nearly as tall as the racer's 6-foot-2-inch frame. As columnist Ernie Pyle wrote in 1940:

> Baker is a tremendous eater. He is tall and weighs 225 pounds, and thinks that if God has one special piece of work it is a big thick steak. He's the steak-eatingest man I ever heard of. Sometimes eats four a day. And, boy, I mean big ones!
>
> On these devastating coast-to-coast runs, where he drove on and on with no sleep or rest, he existed solely on steaks, hash-browned potatoes and black coffee.
>
> On one trip he wired ahead to a restaurant friend in Santa Fe, N.M., to have the biggest steak in town ready for him. It was ready, and a yard long. Baker downed it with relish. And then his restaurant friend told him it was horse meat. Baker hadn't known the difference.[57]

Baker was considerably trimmer in 1915 than he was in 1940, Sturm revealed— around 190 pounds. Before breakfast on Tuesday morning, May 11, Baker drove some 90 miles from Plainview to Amarillo in the Texas panhandle. Besides mile after mile of buffalo grass, Sturm said, "we passed scores of empty skins and piles of bleaching bones which marked the last stand of sick cattle. Water is sometimes hard to find and many cattle die of thirst." Along this section of the road, Texas ranchers had adopted grated cattle guards, which meant that the Stutz team could dash through an opening in a barbed-wire fence without stopping for a gate. As Sturm recalled in the Stutz publicity booklet:

> We were 'beating it' over the prairie and saw what we supposed was an auto opening. When within fifteen feet of it we saw there was no passageway. The highest strand of wire did not come above our radiator and we tore through [at] 40 miles an hour, since it was impossible to stop. Then we went back and repaired the fence. It is a crime in Texas to leave gates open or fences down.
>
> At another time we came to a fence that had been built across the trail to prevent vehicles taking a short cut. We had gone forty miles and did not propose doubling back. The

Fig. 79. Baker (left) and Sturm make a "Gas Oil" stop in Plains, Texas, population 100. (NAHC)

Fig. 80. Baker poses in the car alongside a burro-drawn wagon on a muddy road near Plains, Texas. (NAHC)

fence was rather loose, so I put all my weight on it and bore it to the ground. Baker drove over it while I lay prostrate; I got up, the fence flew back into position, and we were off.[58]

He and Baker ate lunch at Stratford in northern Texas, and then "we crossed over the narrow strip of Oklahoma which lay in our way and got into Kansas. Incidentally, it may be remarked that Oklahoma held us as long as she could. We hit a small bunch of mud there which I hopped out and succeeded in recording with the camera. When we put up at Plains, Kan., that night we had covered 374 miles."[59]

GOIN' TO KANSAS CITY

The car was holding up well, Sturm wrote in his daily *Indianapolis News* dispatch. "Outside of a little magneto and carbureter trouble we have experienced no difficulties and have been unusually fortunate with tires, as they still retain the California air from San Diego."[60] If not for the mud, he added, the travelers would have reached Dodge City, Kansas, that night:

Mud at many points along the route made the going very slow, although we covered 110 miles more than we did the day before through Texas and New Mexico. We were enabled to make some very good time over comparatively few good stretches and our casualties today were two gophers, one snake, two black birds and two rabbits. Missouri mud is still ahead of us, but as Baker has been over a part of this country several times, we do not anticipate any serious difficulties.[61]

Baker started the Stutz early Wednesday morning, May 12, Day 6, and in 2 hours, 10 minutes, drove the 69 miles to Dodge City over a road that was a "trifle rough" in spots, Sturm said. They arrived in the city at 7:00 A.M., the *Dodge City Kansas Journal* reported.[62] "Since we had resolved not to shave until we reached New York, we didn't present a dining-room appearance." The transcontinental travelers consequently asked F. J. Kihm of the Harvey House, who had breakfast waiting, to serve them in the kitchen, "which he absolutely refused to do." *Automobile Topics* reported that Kihm, "an old friend of Baker's, had the town tuned up, and he gave the car crew the best meal it had had and insisted on making the bill 'on the house.'"[63]

Wednesday's *Dodge City Daily Globe* also reported that Baker, "who is driving a Stutz Bearcat car in a wild ride across the United States, was in Dodge City this morning for an hour and took breakfast at the Harvey House."

> His first inquiry when he reached town was "How are things coming on for the world's motorcycle race in Dodge on July 3?"
>
> When he was assured that everything would be in better shape for the big race this year than last, he said:
>
> "Well, they can count on me. I intend to be here and ride in that race again this year. Last year I had some hard luck with my machine and couldn't finish, but things will be different this year. If I ever get to New York with this motor car, I intend to get busy at once getting a motorcycle in shape for the Dodge City race, and I think I'll be among those present at the finish, too."
>
> Those who saw him leave the Harvey House to continue his trip eastward did not doubt for a minute that he would reach New York all right. The car thundered down Chestnut street at such a rate that some of the spectators thought he might get to New York this afternoon, or at the very latest tomorrow morning. However, Baker planned to go only as far as Emporia today.[64]

The *Daily Globe*'s coverage of the 300-mile motorcycle race on July 4 of the previous year revealed that Baker's Indian motorcycle was in fifth place at the 240-mile mark. But the newspaper didn't specify what "hard luck" befell him before the finish line. Despite his vow to do so, Baker did not enter the 1915 Dodge City race, according to the *Globe*'s 1915 race coverage. When Baker arrived during his 1916 coast-to-coast

Cadillac dash, however, the *Globe* insisted that Baker "is well known to Dodge City folks through his participation in the motorcycle races here for the last two years." The *Globe* stood alone in describing the transcontinental Stutz as "a powerful roadster which Baker bought from Barney Oldfield."[65]

Better roads east of Dodge City allowed Baker to cover 65 miles in 80 minutes at an average pace of 48.75 miles per hour. "Although we had some stretches of mud," Sturm wrote in his daily *Indianapolis News* dispatch, "the going was comparatively easy, and, with the exception of several delays on account of nail punctures, we made good time."[66] The "puncture jinx" had indeed caught up with them: four punctures—all to the rear tires—reportedly occurred in Kansas. All the same, the men ended a 335.2-mile day Wednesday at Emporia, Kansas, to average 370 miles per day in covering the 2,219 miles from San Diego.

Their daily average took a beating on Thursday afternoon, May 13, Day 7, when the men lingered from noon until after 5:00 P.M. in Kansas City, Missouri. "Baker looked the car over thoroughly and we both rested up for the final grind," Sturm explained, although *Automobile Topics* blamed the five-hour delay on "broken shock absorbers." Baker's face was "burned a deep brown from exposure to the sun and wind," observed the *Kansas City Post*.[67] In the end, Sturm and Baker traveled only 182.2 miles, between Emporia and Lexington, Missouri, on Thursday, the worst one-day progress of the trip.

The Kansas City Stutz agent got quite a scare early Thursday, Sturm also reported:

We wired P. D. Karshner that we were coming via the trail, meaning the Santa Fe trail. The [telegraph] operator made it read "train," and Karshner thought the attempt had failed. Karshner was agreeably surprised to see us roll in with the car purring just as it did when we left San Diego, and he gave us a royal welcome.

People all along the route come out in force, as Baker's several trips through this part of the country have made his good-natured smile and determined look familiar to the majority of them, and we are continually greeted with wishes for the success of the trip.[68]

"NO TIME TO GET SHAVED"

Friday, May 14, saw the Stutz crew travel 323.2 miles east from Lexington through Boonville, Columbia, and St. Louis, Missouri, to Greenville, Illinois. "Greenville was out in force," Sturm wrote for his newspaper audience, "as they remembered Baker's motorcycle trip when he stopped there for the night." Mules and constables were the primary roadblocks on Friday, Sturm recounted:

We found Missouri roads dry and rough, but even this was better than the mud we had anticipated, for conditions in Kansas presaged heavy rains in Missouri, and Missouri mud is sticky enough to put the quietus on any moving vehicle, although nothing has delayed us more than a few minutes except nails. We passed any number of the slow-going Missouri mules, and there would have been only one way to make time, and that would be to run over them. Calmly they watched us approach and leisurely they allowed us about one-third of the road. Some of them never saw an auto, and numerous times I was forced to hold them while Baker drove by.

We were just coming out of a restaurant in a small town in Missouri, and spied the constable eyeing the place on the rear of our car where the license should have been. He was intent on making some easy change, and we were just as intent on getting away without further delay, as we were endeavoring to make up some lost time. We had lost the rear plate back in Kansas, so we told the constable that Indiana laws required the license on the front of the machine only. He apologized for causing us any trouble (can you imagine it), and we rolled away.[69]

"The boys," who stayed overnight in Greenville's Thomas House, "left for Indianapolis Saturday where a big reception in their home town awaits them from friends and the Stutz people," the *Greenville Advocate* reported. Despite churning through mud near Vandalia, Illinois, early in the day, the Stutz team managed to travel through parts of three states during their ninth day. The Stutz rolled up to the *Indianapolis News* office at 4:00 P.M. for a one-hour stop in the city. "If friends can't recognize us, they'll know the car," Sturm had warned from Greenville. "We have not had time to get shaved."[70]

The men "got a royal welcome from the Stutz forces in Indianapolis, and Baker deserved it all," Sturm observed. "Harry Stutz and his official family came out to meet us with an auto parade headed by the chief of police. Treading the roads of our own bailiwick made us ambitious, and we steered a course for Dayton, which we reached in a driving rain. We called it a day and turned in."[71] Saturday's 322.1 miles raised the trip total to 3,046.6.

LIGHTNING FLASHES, THUNDER BELLOWS

Baker and Sturm began Sunday, May 16, Day 10 of the trip, with a drive from Dayton into Springfield, Ohio, for breakfast, "and then rode all the rest of the way through puddles of water. We were drenched by every hole that we hit, and it was impossible to miss any."[72] As they traveled east into the Allegheny Mountains of Pennsylvania, Sturm explained in his daily *Indianapolis News* dispatch, they discovered that the National road is all torn up and being paved with brick in this section. We had to ride over broken stones big as a man's head for miles. We got to Donora, Pa., at dusk and, as we wished to go on to Greensburg, Bert Blinn, auto enthusiast[,] offered to show us a short cut and so we came into Greensburg slipping and sliding endwise and crossways in a rain coming down in torrents. To make matters worse two autos had collided in the dark and we had to wait while the wreck was cleared.[73]

In the Stutz booklet, Sturm refers to their guide as "Ben Binns," the same spelling used in the *Donora American*'s account:

Ben Binns, the local banker and auto enthusiast, met the tourists on the Ginger Hill road and after a talk volunteered to pilot them to Greensburg. He piled in with them at the Donora Webster bridge and the trip to the Westmoreland county seat was made in record time.

Both of the tourists were attired in the regulation automobile racing outfit and their clothes and machine told plainly the condition of the roads in many parts of the country. They were covered with mud, but the machine showed no bad effects of the long trip.[74]

"I hope never again to have to go through such a wild ride," Sturm said, elaborating upon the perilous nighttime drive. "Several times I thought we were due for the ditch, but Baker's masterful hand steadied the car in time, and thus slipping and sliding and clawing, and with lightning flashing and the thunder bellowing, we came into Greensburg."[75]

During their eleventh day on the road, Monday, May 17, the Stutz left Greensburg and continued through raw and rainy weather east across Pennsylvania. Through Stoystown, Gettysburg, and Lancaster they passed on a 275.8-mile trip to Philadelphia. There, at the Vendig Hotel, Sturm and Baker ate a steak dinner with one of Baker's motorcycle friends, Bob Robertson, who guided them into New York City the next day.

They reached Trenton, New Jersey, "Tuesday morning," at a time the *Trenton Evening Times* failed to specify, and "were entertained while in this city by Horace E. Fine, local consul for the Lincoln Highway Association." As the paper also noted, "Baker attained a cross-country record on a motorcycle a year ago, when he covered the same route in 11 days, 12 hours and 10 minutes. He expects to break his own record on this trip."[76]

Baker did so by reaching 42nd and Broadway at 10:15 A.M. after a fast 103-mile trip from Philadelphia (see Fig. 81), thereby smashing two records. His one-man coast-to-coast crossing time of 11 days, 7 hours, 15 minutes, was roughly five hours shorter than his time by motorcycle the previous year. It also far surpassed the one-man mark of 32 days, 3 hours, 7 minutes, set in 1908 by Jacob M. Murdock, the first person to

drive his family across the country. In addition, Baker's 1915 crossing became the second-fastest transcontinental auto dash yet recorded. He was just 13 hours, 3 minutes, shy of the transcontinental record set by five relay drivers who in 1910 had driven from New York City to San Francisco in 10 days, 18 hours, 12 minutes (see Chapter 2).

Fig. 81. In their very dirty Stutz, Baker and Sturm, who is obscured behind the steering wheel, pose beside the Maine Memorial at Columbus Circle, 59th and Broadway. Large chunks of sidewall rubber have peeled off the right front tire. (FLP)

GRIMY STUTZ REACHES NEW YORK

An AAA official, James A. Hemstreet, checked the car in at 42nd and Broadway. The run, however, "was not made under the sanction of the American Automobile Association, for the reason that the A.A.A. will not sanction a trial of this nature where speed on public highways is a factor," reported the *New York Herald*.[77] As the *Indianapolis News* added:

From there Baker drove the car to the Automobile Club of America, where it was taken in charge by Herbert Chase, engineer of the A.C. of A., who is now giving the car a thorough inspection, and who will make a detailed report on its condition. Harry Stutz insisted on the car's going directly to the laboratory of the Automobile Club of America, in order that the report on its condition might be strictly official and not hearsay.

Stutz made [an] affidavit that the car was strictly a stock Bearcat and Baker made [an] affidavit that he had made no repairs to the car and that he had driven every inch of the way himself. The affidavit also included the mileage, amount of gasoline, etc.[78]

According to Baker's sworn statements, the car logged 3,728.4 miles over the southern route from San Diego. Further, it consumed "approximately" 352 gallons of gasoline to average 10.6 mpg, and averaged 440 miles per gallon of oil. Baker drove 13.75 mph or 327 miles per day, on average, for his elapsed time, which included time off the road for sleeping and eating. For his actual running time of "approximately" 148 hours—or 6 days, 4 hours—Baker averaged 25.2 mph. Thanks to rain, mud, rough or unfamiliar roads, punctures, and other mishaps, Baker's cumulative daily average mileage fell steadily from the second-day high of 500.6 miles (see Table 13). Other than in cities, Baker recalled in a 1940 interview, he encountered just four miles of paved road on his first transcontinental auto trip—near Marshall, Illinois.[79]

As Wednesday's *New York Times* described the finish:

Covered with the mud and grime of its terrific drive, an automobile pulled up at the Automobile Club of America yesterday morning with the distinction of having broken transcontinental records and come from San Diego to New York in eleven days, seven hours and fifteen minutes. The most remarkable part of the performance was that there was no relay driving, as E. G. Baker of Indianapolis, holder of the coast-to-coast motor cycle record, drove for the entire distance. The car, a stock model Stutz "Bearcat," came through the test without repair. The San Diego air is still in the two front tires, and the rear casings are intact, two new tubes having been used in each of them.[80]

To celebrate the finish, Harry Stutz, New York Stutz agent William Parkinson, Baker, and Sturm "were guests at a newspaper men's dinner at the Automobile Club of America, and the two tourists related some of their interesting experiences," according to the *Indianapolis News*. From Springfield, Massachusetts, the makers of the Indian motorcycle, on which Baker set a transcontinental motorcycle record in 1914, telegraphed congratulations. Baker reportedly sent the Stutz factory a telegram reading: "Stutz safe and sound in New York purring just as smoothly as when we left. No mechanical trouble and absence of tire trouble, with the exception of a few nail punctures, has made this record possible."[81]

TABLE 13. Average Daily Mileage of the Stutz Bearcat, 1915

Day/Date	City to City	Cumulative Daily Average Mileage	Sources of Delay
1/May 7 Fri	San Diego–Phoenix, Ariz.	409.1	Mud, rain, ruts in road
2/May 8 Sat	Phoenix, Ariz.–El Paso, Texas	500.6	Lost in desert
3/May 9 Sun	El Paso, Texas–Roswell, N.M.	415.2	Stuck in Rio Ruidoso
4/May 10 Mon	Roswell, N.M.–Plainview, Texas	377.5	Mud, unfamiliar road
5/May 11 Tue	Plainview, Texas–Plains, Kan.	376.8	Mud, fences
6/May 12 Wed	Plains, Kan.–Emporia, Kan.	369.9	Mud, punctures
7/May 13 Thu	Emporia, Kan.–Lexington, Mo.	343.0	Suspension repairs
8/May 14 Fri	Lexington, Mo.–Greenville, Ill.	340.6	Rough roads, mules
9/May 15 Sat	Greenville, Ill.–Dayton, Ohio	338.5	Rain, mud
10/May 16 Sun	Dayton, Ohio–Greensburg, Pa.	335.0	Rain, mud, potholes
11/May 17 Mon	Greensburg, Pa.–Philadelphia	329.6	Rain, mud
12/May 18 Tue	Philadelphia–New York City	327.3	None

SOURCE: Daily distances as given in W. F. Sturm, *Stutz: 11 Days 7 Hours 15 Minutes—A Story.*

CAR'S CONDITION: GENERALLY GOOD

In the past, automakers had tended to conceal the beatings their cars suffered during transcontinental trips. The Automobile Club of America's report on Baker's Stutz would cast doubt on such posturing. The Bearcat's "purring" had a knock in it, for instance. And contrary to the *Times*'s report that the car "came through the test without repair," Baker had in fact made minor repairs and two adjustments. As the ACA test lab reported in its clipped prose: "The only accessories or parts thereof that were replaced were brackets for set of front shock absorbers, one bracket for Prest-O-Lite tank, one tail lamp, and four tubes in rear tires." Twice, Baker had to adjust the brake rod to take up slack in the car's mechanical-brake linkage.[82]

Although overall it was "in excellent running condition," the Wisconsin engine had loose wrist pins—the pins that fasten the connecting rods to the pistons. The pins were "still in good serviceable condition except for the one in piston No. Three, which showed the most wear and was sufficiently loose to cause a distinct knock when the motor was running. The side of No. Two cylinder wall toward the front of the motor was worn at the bottom of the ring slide. The main [crankshaft] bearings showed no sign of being loose, but the large end connecting rod bearings showed more end play than is desirable. All the cylinders and the piston heads showed a considerable deposit of hard carbon," the ACA report said.

Mechanics then removed the engine for further tests but first had to adjust the carburetor. "It was found that the motor did not run steadily at speeds below 800 R.P.M. —the conditions indicating some leakage by the inlet valves which appeared to interfere with proper carburetion at the lower speeds," the report noted. Run on a test stand for an hour at 1,235 rpm, the engine nonetheless developed an average 47.8 brake horsepower.[83]

The Houk wire-spoke wheels were tight and still ran true, "but the wheel bearings showed considerable wear," as did the ball bearings on the transmission countershaft. The transmission gears themselves were in good condition, however. The rough roads had given a pounding to the front suspension of the transcontinental Stutz: the car arrived in New York with two broken leaves in its left front spring. All four Goodyear tires "were badly worn at the sides, those in front being in poor condition." But all other parts, "including in particular the steering gear and axles, were in uniformly good condition," the ACA concluded. It was perhaps no coincidence—in view of the report's assessment of the front suspension—that the new 1916 Stutz would use springs "made of alloy-steel instead of carbon-steel in order to obtain greater strength and longer life," as *Automobile* reported in autumn 1915.[84]

THE POWER OF PUBLICITY

Given the ACA report, New York City's Stutz dealer stretched the truth to the breaking point by claiming that Baker's modified car ended the run "as fit as when it started —not a part broken nor worn unduly. . . . The car is an exact duplicate of Stutz 'Bearcats' on our salesroom floor."[85] Various Stutz suppliers also hastened to cash in on the transcontinental record. The Wisconsin Motor Manufacturing Company, which made engines for Stutz, touted the Bearcat's gas and oil mileage as remarkably good under the circumstances. In other ads, the motor maker used the Stutz stunt to sell, of all things, truck engines, claiming that "the same endurance, reliability and consistency are found in all Wisconsin Consistent Motors."[86]

Makers of the "New Stromberg Carburetor" reproduced a telegram from Harry Stutz stating that Baker made no carburetor adjustments on the trip. (Never mind that Sturm had written about having "a little magneto and carbureter trouble.") "Write us now for remarkable new facts about Carburetors," the Stromberg company advised motorists. "Learn how to increase the power, the speed, acceleration and flexibility of your car, whether new or old."[87]

The makers of the Stutz's Hartford shock absorbers likewise produced ads touting Baker's transcontinental record (see Fig. 82). The Houk Manufacturing Company reproduced Baker's testimonial letter, written on Stutz stationery, praising Houk wheels: "No doubt some of the roads and paths traversed called for greater stand-up qualities than has ever been asked of wire wheels, especially in view of the fact that we maintained a consistently high rate of speed regardless of road conditions. . . . I would never attempt to duplicate my latest achievement unless I could be assured of 'Houk' wheel equipment."[88]

Fig. 82. The Hartford Suspension Company plugged its shock absorbers by printing Baker's testimonial letter and a photo of the Stutz and crew. (Automobile, June 24, 1915)

Although the transcontinental Stutz Bearcat, serial no. 2746, became Baker's as part of his deal with Harry Stutz, he didn't retain ownership long. "I sure wish I had kept that car," Baker lamented in an interview after he had retired from road racing.[89] Its fate is unknown.

No doubt in response to the favorable publicity Baker's 1915 trip had generated, Stutz planned to try to lower the transcontinental record in 1916. According to a March 25, 1916, letter from the Lincoln Highway Association to its officers and directors:

> It has been suggested by the Stutz Motor Car Co. of Indianapolis, that a transcontinental run over the Lincoln Highway be conducted this year by their company with a Lincoln Highway pilot, the idea being to indicate the state of the transcontinental road by showing the minimum time in which a trip from New York to San Francisco can be made. With favorable weather conditions it is assumed that the entire journey would consume not over ten days. It is likely that some plan of this character will be carried out.[90]

Such a plan was never carried out, however. In 1916, shortly after Stutz began selling stock publicly, a Wall Street speculator gained control of the company. Harry Stutz left to build the H.C.S. auto in Indianapolis, which he would do from 1920 to 1925. From a high of about 5,000 cars in 1926, Stutz production fell to 2,320 in 1929. "In 1934 just six Stutzes left the factory," according to one account. The Great Depression had claimed another victim.[91]

STARS SELL CARS

In launching his career as a transcontinental auto racer in 1915, Cannon Ball Baker changed the nature of such publicity stunts forever. Previous coast-to-coast runs advertised the capabilities of a particular make of automobile—and, by extension, the automobile in general. The cars were the stars. Now, because of Baker's colorful personality and equally colorful nickname, the stars sold the cars. There were exceptions, however: throughout the 1920s and later, factory employees and sometimes an automobile's designer would occasionally take the wheel.

Solo drivers became the norm as better roads and faster autos cut the transcontinental time to under a week. Following World War I and on into the mid-1930s, when coast-to-coast speed runs died out, Baker and a handful of other stars would dominate the scene. Those who would make virtual careers out of coast-to-coast driving included Ab Jenkins, Bob McKenzie, and Louis B. Miller. Transcontinental speed runs remained popular, but after World War I an increasing number of automakers stressed gas and oil economy, rather than speed, on such trips.

Sadly, Harry Stutz's idea of sending a transcontinental auto from the finish line directly to an independent testing lab never caught on. Instead, automakers and their suppliers would continue to broadcast a wealth of vague or unsubstantiated claims as transcontinental records fell. Thus, potential car buyers could not with any confidence compare the performance of the various record-breaking cars. All the same, the era of the coast-to-coast solo driver enticed ordinary motorists to attempt long-distance tours. Baker's record, *Motor West* observed, "furnished convincing proof in the East that touring to California can be accomplished without hardships. Although a motor tourist would not care to go as fast as Driver Baker did, the time he made . . . shows that New York City is not so far from the Pacific Coast by automobile after all. The Stutz stunt undoubtedly will still further encourage motor car travel, already heavy, from the East to California."[92]

Other over-the-road speed records fell in 1915, including those set between New York and Chicago and between San Francisco and Los Angeles, *MoToR* reported, noting the implications. Baker's record and the "new city-to-city records created this year are valuable to the motor industry in that they point out to the buying public the absolute dependability of the modern automobile which now devours distance with an ease and speed that rivals even the railroad train," the journal concluded. "They have demonstrated most forcibly that it is possible to travel hundreds of miles over give-and-take roads at railroad speed and without mechanical mishaps of any sort."[93]

The following year would see no less than six record-setting transcontinental runs, one of them made by Baker himself. Besides Baker's, the two most significant trips of 1916 saw a Marmon automobile set a speed record in the course of delivering a military dispatch. Soon afterward, a Hudson Super-Six set three records while completing a double transcontinental dash.

ACROSS THE CONTINENT FROM MONDAY TO MONDAY

6

A good many cops, if they are "regular fellers," will meet me at the outskirts and tell me that the speed limit is off for the time being.

—Cannon Ball Baker

ONE YEAR AND A DAY after starting east from California to New York on his record-setting transcontinental trip in a Stutz Bearcat, Erwin G. "Cannon Ball" Baker set out to cross the country nearly four days faster, driving a 1916 Cadillac V-8 roadster. A virtual one-man relay team, Baker slept less than three hours a night on the week-long trip. This time, he left at 12:01 A.M. on Monday, May 8, 1916, from Los Angeles, rather than San Diego. Baker was again joined by William F. Sturm, the *Indianapolis News* reporter who had acted as observer and recorder for the Stutz trip. Intent on breaking the 1915 record, the two men had planned a more direct route to the East Coast. "'Lose no time' was our motto," Sturm said. "I fed the driver oranges as we rode, and we took pictures while doing fifty miles an hour." As before, Baker would do all the driving, but this time he would attempt "to cross the continent in eight days and thereby establish a new record . . . and incidentally hang up new records for low consumption of gasoline," as one news account put it.[1]

Baker practiced for the trip by traversing much, if not all, of the route by motorcycle about a month beforehand. Under the Cadillac's electric lights, he averaged nearly 70 mph during the first hour out of Los Angeles. By contrast, at times Baker coaxed no more than 10 mph from the roadster through the mud in Missouri, where the car overturned in a ditch—the only serious delay of the trip. A stroke of good luck prevented another long delay when their car ran out of oil in California's Mojave Desert. In the course of the trip, Baker also grappled with an oil leak, swampy roads in Missouri and Illinois, an arrest for speeding, and a total of thirteen tire changes. Arriving in New York on May 15, Baker had set a new transcontinental speed record of 7 days, 11 hours, 52 minutes, thereby cutting his previous record by 3 days, 6 hours, 20 minutes.

BAKER EMBRACES LUCKY 13

As newspapers revealed, "everything was done to prevent the loss of time."[2] The *Daily News* of Dayton, Ohio, which mistakenly assumed that both men drove, indicated that Cadillac agents in particular aided the effort: "All along the entire route across the United States these drivers were helped as much as possible by the dealers in each section of the country. Roads were cleared wherever possible and the bad spots were made known to the drivers as they came into the territory." In addition, the paper reported, "the coast to coast trip was kept quiet and only a few people in the towns through which the trip was made knew about it."[3]

No reason was given for the secrecy. By 1916, however, anyone who broke the transcontinental speed record also broke the law. At the time, the rural speed limit in states east of the Mississippi River along Baker's route was 25 mph, with the exception of Pennsylvania (24 mph) and Ohio (20 mph). Cities and towns often imposed speed limits of 6 or 8 mph. In later years, Baker kept his plans under wraps because "we started getting county cops on our tail who wanted to be publicized as the cop who got Cannon Ball Baker."[4] For two reasons, though, police posed less of a problem during his early speed runs, Baker said in a 1923 interview:

One is that a good many cops, if they are "regular fellers," will meet me at the outskirts and tell me that the speed limit is off for the time being. The second reason is that you have to catch a speeder *in the act*. Lots of constables who have chased me never saw anything but a puff of smoke and a cloud of dust. I try to be mighty careful, though, in going through places where there are many people. It's all right to take chances on your own life—but I don't believe in putting other folks in danger.[5]

"Old Man Trouble doesn't run on schedule, and he doesn't set out any red lanterns for you," Baker said in discussing his driving philosophy. "You've got always to be expecting the unexpected. I figure that the success of a speed boy is one-third nerve, one-third common sense, and one-third caution."[6] Baker shook his head when an interviewer asked if he had any superstitions:

Not so's you'd notice 'em! I've seen racers who'd look all the morning for a four-leaf clover to stick in their shoes, and others who shied at the number 13 like a scared colt. Why, 13's *my* favorite number!

On my way to Los Angeles for my record transcontinental auto run in 1916, I had berth 13 in the sleeping-car from Detroit to Trinidad, Colorado. At Trinidad—which is 1300 miles from Los Angeles—I decided to get off and make the balance of the journey by motor-cycle, so that I could look over the route again.

On the run to the coast I had to change my tires thirteen times. The company that made the car I drove had been in business just thirteen years—and even a Missouri cloudburst that flooded my route on the thirteenth day of May didn't hold me as long as a deluge of that kind usually does.[7]

"EQUIPPED AS YOUR CADILLAC WOULD BE"

On his earlier trip in 1915, a snow-clogged Santa Fe Trail had forced Baker to steer his Stutz Bearcat along the Mexican border into Arizona, then northeast into Phoenix, through southern New Mexico, and across the Texas and Oklahoma panhandles into southern Kansas. In the end, the Stutz logged 3,728 miles in 11 days, 7 hours, 15 minutes. In 1916, Baker and Sturm hoped to save 350 miles by taking the Santa Fe Trail's more northerly route—from Los Angeles, through northern Arizona and New Mexico, across southern Colorado, and into southwestern Kansas. Then, beyond Dodge City, Kansas, they would travel virtually the same route as they had a year earlier.

Like most other transcontinental autos, Baker's 1915 Stutz differed from a stock model in having a slightly modified engine and suspension, as well as other minor changes that the Stutz company—with a candor rare among auto manufacturers—

publicly detailed. The Cadillac Motor Car Company, which introduced its V-8 engine in 1915 models, was typically less candid—at least in its advertising—about the modifications, if any, to its coast-to-coast auto (see Fig. 83). As the company claimed following the trip:

> The Cadillac which "conquered the continent" was just such a Cadillac as you might buy and drive yourself. It was equipped as your Cadillac would be equipped, with no special preparations other than those which would ordinarily be made for a long-distance tour. The trans-continental Cadillac was not a specially built car "stripped for action"—but a fully equipped standard Roadster; and, granting that you possessed the stamina of its single driver, the journey was one which you yourself might take if you were so inclined.[8]

Some manufacturers modified their transcontinental automobiles by adding stiffer springs and shock absorbers, auxiliary gas tanks, oversize tires, and larger radiators. Yet in reporting on the Cadillac's coast-to-coast trip neither the automaker nor the press explained the factory's claim that its special preparations were "those which would ordinarily be made for a long-distance tour." Thus the only modification we know about is the minor one revealed in one news account: "A small hand hold was fixed on the back of the seat, by which the passenger could hold himself in place and not interfere with the handling of the car."[9]

Using a flathead (valve-in-block) V-8 engine that displaced 314 cubic inches with a 3⅛ x 5⅛-inch bore and stroke, Cadillac's Type 53 roadster, which retailed for $2,080, developed up to 77 brake horsepower. Cadillac advertised its horsepower at more than

Fig. 83. For a publicity pose, Cannon Ball Baker takes the wheel of the V-8 Cadillac roadster in which he set a coast-to-coast speed record. By his side is William F. Sturm. (Motor Age, May 18, 1916)

60, although the SAE formula yields an estimate of 31.25 horsepower. Standard equipment on Baker's car included United States tires—smooth tread on the front, "Nobby Treads" on the rear—a Delco electric starting and lighting system, Stewart-Warner speedometer, AC "Titan" spark plugs, and Kelsey wood-spoke wheels accommodating tires of 36 X 4½ inches. The car had a 122-inch wheelbase.[10]

TIRES BLOW, OIL FLOWS

Baker drove away from the Los Angeles Court House at 12:01 A.M. on Monday, May 8 (see Fig. 84). According to Baker, his Cadillac roadster hit its fastest clip of the trip, 68 mph, during the 63-mile night drive between Los Angeles and San Bernardino. The *San Francisco Examiner*, however, reported that Baker maintained an *average* speed of 68 mph on this stretch, which means that at times he traveled even faster.[11]

   Baker had to deal with one mechanical repair just hours after starting, and he had

Fig. 84. In Los Angeles, Sturm (left) and Baker await the starter's signal. (MoToR, September 1916)

frequent tire trouble while crossing southern California's Mohave Desert on a 120-degree day. "We had to make five tire changes in that run, two in the first eighty miles. It looked as if the heat would fairly melt the rubber, and I had to reduce the usual pressure fifteen pounds." On the desert between Barstow and Needles, California, "an oil pipe became detached and we lost our entire stock of lubricant," Baker said. "I left Mr. Sturm in the car, and walked three miles to a station and obtained a gallon from a passing tourist, which was great luck." The *Dodge City (Kan.) Daily Globe* offered a somewhat different version of the tale, however, which more than doubled the distance Baker hiked:

> The road ran alongside the Santa Fe tracks and the travelers attempted to stop a handcar which came by and use it to go for more oil. But the occupants of the handcar evidently feared a holdup, so they speeded by and it was necessary for Baker to walk eight miles to a little town and come back to his stranded car on a freight train.[12]

Even though the oil loss delayed him for 2½ hours, Baker drove 553.5 miles from Los Angeles to Williams, Arizona, during the first day, *Automobile* reported (see Table 14).[13]

The next day, Tuesday, May 9, Baker drove 555 miles farther east, from central Arizona across the New Mexico line and through Albuquerque to Santa Fe in the north-central part of that state. According to *Automobile*, "the roads in Arizona were so bad that most of the running was done in intermediate gear," Baker driving 84 miles in second gear on one stretch alone. During the trip, "a great deal of the running was also through mountains, where an altitude of 6500 ft. was reached at one time."[14]

On the third day out, Wednesday, May 10, Baker piled up 567.2 miles, his best single day of the trip. Accompanied by Sturm, Baker drove the Cadillac from Santa Fe east and north through Las Vegas and Raton, New Mexico, and then to Trinidad, La Junta, and Holly, Colorado, before finishing the day at Dodge City in southwestern Kansas, 1,675.7 miles from Los Angeles. Early on Wednesday afternoon the Cadillac reached Trinidad, a town Baker had driven through on motorcycle about a month earlier when he was "taking an advance survey of the route over which he was to make an endurance run," the local *Chronicle-News* reported.

> Baker stopped only a few minutes at the Bennett [&] Dale garage to take on gas and oil. He was on his way again almost before the group of local motor enthusiasts had a chance to speak to him. . . . He has sat at the wheel almost continuously since Monday, and asserts he will be able to "stick it out," to New York. . . .
> Baker was escorted several miles on the road to La Junta by a party from the Bennett & Dale garage, who upon their return announced they did not care to make another such trip in the wake of Mr. Baker.[15]

TABLE 14. Cannon Ball Baker's City-by-City Itinerary, 1916

Day/Date	City to City	Daily Mileage	Cumulative Mileage
1/May 8 Mon	Los Angeles to San Bernardino, Calif. Barstow, Calif. Needles, Calif. Kingman, Ariz. Williams, Ariz.	553.5	553.5
2/May 9 Tue	Williams, Ariz., to Flagstaff, Ariz. Albuquerque, N.M. Santa Fe, N.M.	555.0	1,108.5
3/May 10 Wed	Santa Fe, N.M., to Las Vegas, N.M. Raton, N.M. Trinidad, Colo. La Junta, Colo. Holly, Colo. Syracuse, Kan. Dodge City, Kan.	567.2	1,675.7
4/May 11 Thu	Dodge City, Kan., to Hutchinson, Kan. Newton, Kan. Florence, Kan. Emporia, Kan. Kansas City, Mo.	401.0	2,076.7
5/May 12 Fri	Kansas City, Mo., to Columbus, Mo. Boonville, Mo. Columbia, Mo. High Hill, Mo.	216.0	2,292.7
6/May 13 Sat	High Hill, Mo., to St. Louis, Mo. Collinsville, Ill. Greenville, Ill. Greenup, Ill.	210.0	2,502.7
7/May 14 Sun	Greenup, Ill., to Indianapolis Richmond, Ind. Dayton, Ohio Springfield, Ohio		

	Summerford, Ohio		
	Columbus, Ohio		
	Zanesville, Ohio		
	Cambridge, Ohio		
	Wheeling, W.V.		
	Pittsburgh	493.0	2,995.7
8 / May 15 Mon	Pittsburgh to		
	Greensburg, Pa.		
	Coatesville, Pa.		
	Philadelphia		
	Trenton, N.J.		
	Jersey City, N.J.		
	Weehawken, N.J.		
	New York City	385.0	3,380.7

SOURCES: Auto journals; local and national newspapers. Distances are from "A Transcontinental Record," *Automobile*, May 18, 1916, p. 909.

Baker and Sturm reached La Junta at 2:41 P.M., the *La Junta Tribune* reported. "They stopped in La Junta nine minutes, and this is about the limit of any stop made since they left San Francisco [*sic*]. While here they were served with hot coffee and a *light* lunch, which was already [*sic*] for them as soon as they arrived[,] and they will keep up this manner of living on the entire trip." The Cadillac covered the 85 miles from Trinidad to La Junta in 2 hours, 34 minutes, averaging just over 33 mph—"even better than the fastest time of a passenger train on the Santa Fe," the *Tribune* noted.[16] The same day, just east of Holly, five miles from the western Kansas border, an accident damaged the Cadillac, according to the *Dodge City (Kan.) Daily Globe*. "Baker drove off the end of a culvert in passing a farm wagon. The running board and fender caught on the culvert and were torn almost off."[17] The newspaper provided no further details.

INTO A TEN-FOOT DITCH

By this time, they were moving faster than the U.S. mail, Baker exclaimed at the end of his trip. "Six hours before we left Los Angeles a letter was mailed to me at Dodge City, Kansas. We arrived in Dodge City Wednesday two hours in advance of the letter."[18] "Baker Is Going Some," read a front-page headline in Thursday's *Dodge City Daily Globe*:

Fig. 85. As in many other locales, residents of this unidentified city gape in wonder as Baker's Cadillac dashes through, flags fluttering. The unnamed man on the running board is perhaps directing Baker to a local gas stop. (Horseless Age, June 1, 1916)

Baker tore into Dodge City at 11:45 o'clock last night. In the 72 hours since he left Los Angeles he has had but six hours and twenty-five minutes of sleep. . . . He stopped at the Santa Fe Trail garage while in Dodge City. "Red" Alexander, of Alexander & Black, the agents for the Indian motorcycle which Baker rides in the [Dodge City motorcycle] races, supplied Baker with oil.

In spite of his fatigue Baker was feeling well this morning and was confident he would set up a new transcontinental record if no accidents interfered with his schedule. . . . He plans to reach Kansas City tonight. A car which came out from Hutchinson yesterday met Baker at Holly and will accompany him to Hutchinson. "Red" Alexander left this morning with Baker to ride as far as Kansas City.[19]

On Thursday, May 11, Baker pushed the Cadillac across the Kansas plains and Flint Hills, through Hutchinson, Newton, Florence, and Emporia (see Fig. 85) to reach Kansas City, Missouri, for the night stop. Thursday morning, Baker "only lingered a few minutes in Hutchinson, at a local garage, and then darted on eastward," said the *Hutchinson News*. "He left Hutchinson going east over the Santa Fe trail at 10:10 A.M.," added the *Hutchinson Daily Gazette*. According to the *News*, Baker traveled the 36 miles of dirt roads between Hutchinson and Newton in 40 minutes, thus averaging 54 mph on the stretch.[20]

Ending a 401-mile day, Baker and Sturm reached a rainy Kansas City, Missouri, at

7:30 P.M. on Thursday, Day 4 of the trip. He was lucky to travel half that far—216 miles—on Friday, in crossing most of Missouri to reach High Hill, near St. Louis. "Our speed in Missouri figures less than ten miles an hour," Sturm said. "Missouri roads were bottomless for over one hundred miles, due to excessive rains."[21]

The 300-mile drive between Kansas City and St. Louis took so long because "it was rain and mud all the way," as Baker described it. According to the *Indianapolis News*, Baker and Sturm

> reported the roads in Missouri and Illinois as being in the worst possible state, as eighteen hours of continuous rain had made them so slippery and heavy that the going was extremely slow. At a point near Columbus, Mo., they passed five automobiles that were hopelessly mired and, although time was precious to the transcontinentalists, they played the good Samaritan and pulled the fifth automobile, a big touring car, to safety. . . .
>
> Meager telegraph information . . . stated that their Cadillac had met with an accident and emerged with two broken wheels. This was an error, however. Near Columbus, Mo., in what Baker styled "the worst mudhole in the world," Baker was endeavoring to find a footing on a razor back road. They were crawling along about ten miles an hour when they skidded off the road into a big ditch and the Cadillac turned gently over on its side.
>
> Sturm was not hurt and Baker received only a slight scratch. They lost six hours righting the car and getting it out of the ditch, but once on the road again the "eight" barked joyfully and they started out in an endeavor to make up lost time to St. Louis.[22]

The car actually went into the 10-foot-deep ditch near Boonville, Missouri, and "it took a block and tackle to get it out," Sturm later recounted.[23]

YOU'RE UNDER ARREST

Facing similar conditions on the sixth day, Saturday, May 13, Baker managed to drive 210 miles from High Hill, Missouri, and through Collinsville and Greenville to Greenup, Illinois. Crossing the Mississippi River at St. Louis, Baker ran into trouble just 12 miles into Illinois at Collinsville, Sturm related:

> We were breezing along about ten miles an hour I thought when a motorcycle cop told us to stop and consider ourselves under arrest. He led us around the corner to the courthouse and into the august presence of the police chief. There we were told we had been doing thirty-two.
>
> As we expressed a wish to be spared the torture of a long-drawn-out trial the arresting officer called in the judge, who happened to be conveniently near. Meantime about twenty of the citizens had dropped into the room as witnesses to our terrific speed.

Baker pleaded guilty to the charge and asked what he owed. I held my breath as the judge said the fine ranged from $5 to $100. "With the court costs of $3.60, the total amount to be assessed against you," said the judge—and I held my breath—"will be $8.60."

Think of it, $8.60! Baker dug a ten-spot from his clothes while I went out to fill the radiator and the arresting officer said he hoped we would have better luck the rest of the way. Twenty minutes from the time the arm of the law had stuck his hand out as a signal for us to halt we were on our way toward Indianapolis. Who says that justice is slow?[24]

The 493 miles he covered on Sunday, May 14, indicates that Baker found drier roads on Day 7 of the trip, as he traveled from southeastern Illinois, through Indiana, Ohio, the northern tip of West Virginia, and eastern Pennsylvania to Pittsburgh—some 2,995.7 miles from Los Angeles by the Cadillac's odometer. Stopping at the *Indianapolis News* office at 4:25 A.M. Sunday, Baker and Sturm "obtained the signatures of Joe Dawson and Dr. Arthur E. Guedel," the newspaper reported. "They left Indianapolis after getting the signatures and a light breakfast, at 5:05 bound for Columbus, O., which they reached in four and a half hours. Before leaving they were thoroughly examined by Dr. Guedel, who pronounced them in perfect physical shape in spite of the terrific strain under which they have labored in the past six days."[25]

The Cadillac headed eastward, traveling rapidly over Indiana roads. In Baker's record-setting trip, "Indiana played a prominent part with traffic rules suspended and the whole Cadillac corps of several states in this section of the country on the qui vive [alert]," the *Indianapolis News* observed.[26] Beyond Richmond, Indiana, Baker crossed the Ohio border and headed through Dayton, Springfield, Summerford, Columbus, Zanesville, and Cambridge. According to the *Dayton Daily News*:

G. W. Shroyer & Co. picked the team up at Richmond, Ind., at 6:45 Sunday morning. They drove with the tourists to Springfield, Ohio, where they had the right of way through the town, and where the citizens were wondering and awe struck at the sight of three cars dashing through their city at a speed of 60 miles an hour.

The time from Richmond to Springfield was one hour and eighteen minutes and they had to stop for a blowout on a rear tire. The distance is 58 miles. Some going.

The Dayton company conveyed the party to Summerford, the extreme border of their territory, and from there to Zanesville they were taken care of by the Columbus agent.

Cliff Shroyer says they pointed out to the drivers what they supposed were bad spots in the road. But these bad spots were not looked upon as bad in any way as the speed of about sixty miles an hour was not slackened at any place along the route.[27]

The Cadillac zoomed into Columbus at 9:30 A.M. Sunday and would stop only for gas and oil during the rest of the trip into New York City, the *Columbus Evening Dispatch* reported. "To prevent Baker from falling out of the automobile during his long trip Strum [*sic*] strapped him to his seat. Baker kept awake by sheer will power and by the use of strong coffee." The car arrived in Pittsburgh Sunday night, "having made a continuous drive from St. Louis, Mo., a distance of over 700 miles," said the *Indianapolis News*.[28]

From Pittsburgh, Baker drove through Greensburg and Coatesville, Pennsylvania, on Monday. "The coast-to-coast car arrived just outside of Coatesville at 10:45 yesterday morning and was met by a representative of the Automobile Sales Corporation, the Philadelphia agency for the Cadillac automobiles," Tuesday's *Philadelphia Inquirer* told its readers. "From Coatesville the Philadelphia representative piloted the car to this city. It entered along the Lancaster pike and the City line and made its way out by the way of Broad street, the Northeast Boulevard and Castor road. The machine arrived at Trenton shortly after noon, and from there to New York the trip was uneventful."[29]

CHEERING NEW YORKERS SALUTE BAKER

Beyond Trenton, Baker drove through Jersey City and Weehawken, New Jersey. There, related the *New York Tribune*, "a special ferryboat waited . . . for the flying car, and a cordon of motor patrolmen gave it a clear track in its final dash through Forty-second Street to Broadway, where the exhausted driver grinned through his mask of mud at the cheering crowd and tooted his horn in answer to the bedlam of motor salutes."[30] The ferryboat crossed from Weehawken to West 42nd Street "in close to three minutes," according to the *New York Times*. "Three traffic policemen on motor cycles cleared the way along Forty-second Street. The dust-covered car with its two travel-stained passengers riveted the eyes of pedestrians, and a crowd cheered the wind-up at *The Times* Building."[31]

At 2:53 P.M. on Monday, May 15, Baker pulled up at Times Square, 42nd and Broadway. He had driven 385 miles on the final day, traveling the 100 miles from Philadelphia in 2 hours and 50 minutes, better than 35 mph on average. In racing 1,028 miles from St. Louis to New York City in 37 hours, 17 minutes, according to *Automobile*'s account, Baker had averaged nearly 28 mph—well above his average for the coast-to-coast run as a whole. As *MoToR* reported the finish:

> Drooping with weariness, their eyelids puffy with lack of sleep, their faces deep-lined with the strain of ceaseless battling with the elements, two mud-grimed motorists in a battered Cadillac roadster, drew up in Times Square, New York City, on the afternoon of

NEW YORK

LOS ANGELES

Across the Continent from Monday to Monday

Cadillac in thrilling dash from Pacific to Atlantic shows incomparable stability and sustained speed

Los Angeles to New York in 7 days, 11 hours, 52 minutes

Fig. 86. Cadillac heralded Baker's trip as a dash "Across the Continent from Monday to Monday," as this ad detail reveals. (Saturday Evening Post, June 17, 1916)

May 15, 1916. For the moment they forgot their abysmal weariness and the blackened areas of their faces cracked stiffly into smiles as they listened to the cheers of the inevitable New York crowd, the clicking of the movie cameras and the congratulations of those who had gathered to welcome them.[32]

Adjusting for the three-hour time difference between Los Angeles and New York, Baker's 3,380.7-mile trip from one Monday to the next had taken 7 days, 11 hours, 52 minutes (see Fig. 86). Baker, "with eyes red from loss of sleep and the dust of the road," had thus cut 3 days, 6 hours, 20 minutes, from the standing transcontinental record, which a relay team of five drivers had set in 1910. Baker also broke the single-driver record he had set the year before by 3 days, 19 hours, 23 minutes. His own 1915 record "was broken so badly that all the pieces were little more than powder," the *Indianapolis News* chortled.[33]

On the basis of railroad schedules, Baker said, he had calculated that a relay of twenty-two locomotives could pull the fastest train over a shorter, 3,240-mile route between Los Angeles and New York in about 90 hours, or 3 days, 18 hours. Baker's trip was within eight minutes of taking twice that long. But "the train runs over smooth tracks, and as we had to contend with deserts, mountains, and boggy roads, we think the auto did pretty well against the locomotive," he told reporters at the finish.[34] And as *Automobile* pointed out, even though Baker was forced to drive in lower gears through parts of Arizona and Missouri, "the car managed to make from 9 to 10 miles per gallon of gasoline and from 320 to 350 miles per gallon of oil." Under the circumstances, this was a respectable performance, although it failed to "hang up new records for low consumption of gasoline," as one news account had predicted.[35]

If Baker couldn't outrun a speeding locomotive, he could and did outrun the U.S. mail a second time. As he talked with reporters at 42nd and Broadway, someone handed him a postcard. "We beat it here," was Baker's reaction. "That postal was mailed to me just after we passed through Emporia, Kan. We beat it by nearly an hour." Baker had actually mailed postcards to himself at different points on his route, and "most of them are still on the way," the *New York Tribune* remarked.[36]

"WE DID NOT WASTE MUCH TIME"

"Don't look at the figures of the total run and the average of 450 miles a day and think it was easy going," Sturm warned reporters at the finish. Baker's secret? As he revealed in response to a reporter's question, he slept an average of 2½ hours nightly on his week-long trip. "Nineteen hours, all told," Baker replied, counting it up on his fingers. "I can't tell yet what our actual running time was. I'll have to figure it out after I get some sleep, but we did not waste much time by the way. About all we did was to give the car 'gas' and oil and drive it to the limit."[37] Baker would have figured out that for his elapsed time, including stops, he had averaged 18.80 mph in the Cadillac, compared to 13.75 mph in the Stutz a year earlier.

In earlier times, transcontinental autos either lacked odometers or regularly managed to break them, leaving their exact mileage open to speculation. The Cadillac's odometer evidently performed flawlessly; yet the 1916 mileage is still uncertain. The flurry of news reports following Baker's May 15 finish in New York City nearly all put the distance at 3,471 miles (see Fig. 87). But this figure, "as given out by the Cadillac company"—which also advertised the distance as 3,371 miles—was an error, asserted *Automobile*.[38] The auto journal printed a chart showing distances between the "evening stopping stations," which total 3,380.7 miles. On the same page, however, *Automobile* confuses the issue by printing another chart that notes the distances between

Fig. 87. Baker and Sturm dashed across the country leaving dust and headlines in their wake.

two dozen cities on Baker's route. These figures are supposed to add up to 3,380.7 miles as well but actually total 3,312.4. Sturm, however, maintained that the car averaged 450 miles per day, which would suggest that the figure of 3,380.7 miles is closest to the mark.

Based on that distance and his elapsed time of 7 days, 11 hours, 52 minutes, Baker actually averaged a fraction over 451 miles per day. "We would have averaged over 500 miles a day if it hadn't been for the bad roads we struck in Missouri, from Kansas City to St. Louis," Baker said after arriving in New York.[39] For his self-professed running time of 5½ days, he averaged nearly 615 miles per day and 25.6 mph. His average speed was just a bit slower, 25.2 mph, for his 1915 Stutz running time.

"WORLD'S CHAMPION ROAD CAR"

The Cadillac "traveled its distance without so much attention to its motor as the cleaning of a spark plug," Cadillac boasted, calling its Type 53 auto the "World's Champion Road Car."[40] Taking it a step further, *Automobile* contended that "the hood of the car was not lifted during the trip."[41] How Baker repaired a loose oil line in the Mohave Desert and poured a gallon of oil into the engine without lifting the hood would remain as much a mystery as the car's condition upon reaching New York, were it not for a September 1916 *MoToR* ad for Exide batteries. The ad solves the mystery by quoting Baker as saying: "We never lifted the hood, except for oil, and once to adjust the carburetor."[42]

A year earlier, at the finish of Baker's transcontinental trip, Harry Stutz turned his car over to an independent testing lab. The lab reported extreme wear to the Stutz Bearcat's transmission, wheel bearings, and some of the engine bearings but overall found the car in good condition. Like the majority of automakers before and after, Cadillac preferred not to follow Harry Stutz's example. Thus Cadillac could claim that its transcontinental car "was subjected to a more severe trial of stamina and endurance than the average car undergoes in ten years of service; yet it emerged from the ordeal virtually as good a car as when it started" (see Fig. 88).[43] The fate of the virtually new Cadillac Baker drove is unknown.

On Tuesday night, May 16, the day after their arrival, Baker and Sturm "were the guests of eastern Cadillac dealers at a banquet given at the Astor hotel, New York," Thursday's *Indianapolis News* reported. "Both Baker and Sturm are in Detroit today and will return to Indianapolis Sunday, according to a wire from Sturm."[44] They actually returned on Saturday, however, according to that day's paper:

> E. G. Baker and W. F. Sturm, the coast-to-coast record smashers, dropped off the Detroit train this morning and looked like they were glad to tread the paths of their own bailiwick again. Sturm says that they have been royally entertained both at New York and at Detroit by the Cadillac company. They stayed in New York for a day or two and have spent a couple of days at the Michigan city, as guests of the Cadillac company.
>
> Asked if they could lower their record of 7 days, 11 hours and 52 minutes, Baker hesitated a moment and said merely that Missouri mud had caused them to lose a day and that with different conditions the story would have been different.
>
> "One thing [is] sure," said Baker, "this trip has cured me of a hallucination I have always had about eight cylinder cars. I thought Sturm had slipped a cog when he told me he had signed with an eight. Its marvelous getaway saved us several hours."[45]

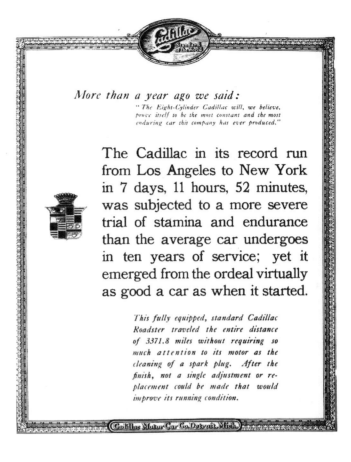

Fig. 88. A Cadillac ad in the August 1916 issue of MoToR.

OF TIME, TIRES, AND TRAINING

Dr. H. Nelson Jackson, the first person to drive across America, made the trip in 63½ days in 1903. During his 1916 Cadillac run, Baker crossed the country in nearly one-tenth that time. Obviously, both the automobiles and the roads over which they traveled had improved dramatically since 1903. So, it seems likely, had a knowledge of those roads: Jackson traveled some 5,000 or 6,000 miles between coasts, Baker less than 3,400.

Tires were still a weak link, however. In 1903, Jackson replaced about a half-dozen tires on his cross-country trip. During his May 1915 Stutz run, Baker had replaced four inner tubes but finished with the same Goodyear tires he started with. In part because the Mohave Desert burned up five of the Cadillac's United States tires, however, the Cadillac required thirteen tire changes.[46]

The two men responded quickly to every blowout, Sturm explained:

> The minute the "pop" told us we had blown a tire, Baker stopped the car. Before the car had stopped I had the jack on the ground. Baker grabbed the jack and elevated the car, while I was loosening the rim nuts and took the spare tire off the rear. While Baker finished putting on the tire, I strapped the old one on and away we flew.[47]

For all of Baker's brawn, he used scientific methods in planning the trip and in controlling all the variables over which he had any power. Prior to his 1914 transcontinental motorcycle trip, for instance, he consulted a weather expert who used records to determine that May was the driest month in which to attempt a coast-to-coast trip along a southern route. Thus, in both 1915 and 1916, Baker started out in early May. In addition, he drove the route in advance of the actual speed run. Clearly, the unpracticed, unstudied driver could not hope to jump in a car and zip across the country at half the pace of a locomotive. No, it required a "speed boy," as Baker phrased it, as well as practice runs, day-and-night driving, and constant speeding—often at three times the legal limit.

RACING ON AND ON

According to an oft-quoted figure, Baker traveled 5.5 million miles on motorcycles and in automobiles in the process of setting various over-the-road records from 1914 until sometime in the 1940s. According to automotive historian Russ Catlin, "at least three nationally known writers gave up trying to compose a book on the life of the 'Record Man.'" As one of these writers put it: "He did so much over such a long period of time it would take a writer a lifetime to document and prove it all, and, even if you did, no one today would believe it."[48]

In the years following World War I, Baker continued setting innumerable records for speed, which included a series of record-breaking transcontinental trips for which he drove a Templar auto (in 1920), a Gardner (1924), a Rickenbacker (1925), a high-gear Ford (1926), a Falcon-Knight (1928), two Franklins (1928 and 1929), another Stutz (1930), and a Graham (1933). In 1927 he also set a coast-to-coast record at the wheel of a General Motors truck. Gradually, however, Baker switched from setting speed records to focusing on fuel-economy records, because "autos have become so perfect that all of them can go too fast," the syndicated columnist Ernie Pyle explained in a 1940 interview with Baker. His last "publicized" transcontinental crossing came in 1941 at the age of 59, when Baker drove across the country on a rotary-engine motorcycle of his own design.[49]

By 1940 Baker had crossed the United States a total of 118 times, the *Indianapolis Times* reported. In a 1953 interview with the *Indianapolis Star*, Baker numbered his transcontinental crossings at 143, although various other retrospective articles put the number at 126 or 128 crossings. On May 10, 1960, Baker, 78, died of a heart attack in Indianapolis. As the *Indianapolis News* said in eulogizing the speed king, "Cannonball Baker's courage and daring did a great deal toward keeping the young automobile industry in the spotlight of public attention."[50]

Back in May 1916, however, the spotlight of public attention soon shifted away from Baker and his Cadillac roadster to two later, equally daring, transcontinental trips. In the first, which took place on the eve of America's entry into World War I, five relay drivers drove across the country in a car of the future—the lightweight Marmon 34. The second trip ended the prewar era of coast-to-coast automobile travel with a large exclamation point: a trip across the country and back made by a cadre of relay drivers in a Hudson Super-Six touring car.

PUSHING THE RAILROADS IN THE MATTER OF TIME

7

The mere establishing of a new transcontinental record and thereby being hailed all over the world as a speed maniac would not of itself have appealed to me at my age.
—Samuel B. Stevens, 42

IN JULY 1916, a relay team of five men, driving day and night, crossed the country in a Marmon Type 34 automobile to deliver a military message from New York City to San Francisco. Simulating the top speed of an armored car, the drivers never exceeded 50 mph on their 3,476-mile crossing, claimed the organizers of the trip. The Marmon company, the Union Pacific Railroad, Western Union, Lincoln Highway representatives, and a host of volunteers helped speed the car on its way. The drivers wrestled with muddy roads in three western states, got lost in the Great Salt Lake Desert, broke through a bridge in Nevada, and made at least two stops for repairs. One of the repair stops followed a head-on crash with another car that sheered off one of

218

the Marmon's wheels, forcing a pit stop of six or seven hours in Salt Lake City—the longest single delay of the trip.

Despite such misadventures, the men drove coast to coast in a record 5 days, 18 hours, 30 minutes—slightly behind their schedule but still nearly two days faster than the single-driver record that Cannon Ball Baker had set two months earlier at the wheel of a Cadillac. Their time rivaled that of some coast-to-coast passenger trains, newspapers marveled, and to some observers proved the need for both a National Motor Reserve and a "great national highway" to serve as a wartime military supply route.

The new transcontinental record did wonders for the popularity of the innovative Marmon, which pioneered the use of weight-saving aluminum. Attracting the participation of two high-ranking Army officers, one of whom furnished the military message that the Marmon would deliver, the trip afforded an officially sanctioned demonstration of the military utility of the automobile.

"AMATEUR" STEVENS A WELL-KNOWN RACER

The Nordyke & Marmon Company of Indianapolis, established in 1851 as a manufacturer of milling equipment and an automaker since 1905, tried to pass off the five relay drivers—"Mr. Stevens and other amateurs"—as inexperienced motorists.[1] Technically speaking, they may have been amateurs. But according to *Automobile*, Samuel B. Stevens, of Rome, New York, was "well known in racing circles around New York." The four other drivers—"friends of Mr. Stevens, amateur automobilists," as the *Rome (N.Y.) Daily Sentinel* observed—could likely claim similar qualifications. They were Fred Barbour of "New York," Walter Bieling and William Binz, both of Chicago, and Robert Creighton, hometown unknown.[2]

Stevens drove four of the nine relays for a total of 1,563 miles, traveling ahead by train each time he turned over the wheel. Stevens thus drove 44 percent of the time— nearly 59 of the 138½ hours. Barbour drove two relays totaling 872 miles; the other relief drivers drove one relay apiece (see Table 15). At least one of the four—Binz, 22— worked for a Marmon agency. Neither the newspapers and auto journals covering the run nor the Marmon company itself provided much information about the four relief drivers. But the automaker did indicate that the trip's organizers had opted for a driver relay—rather than a single driver—because they did not wish "to make a human endurance test out of the trip."[3]

TABLE 15. Performance of the Drivers on the Marmon Transcontinental Trip, 1916

Driver	Mileage (% of total)[a]	Total Driving Time	Average Speed[b]
S. B. Stevens	1,563 (44%)	2d-10h-54m	26.5 mph
Fred Barbour	872 (24%)	1d-01h-45m	33.9 mph
Walter Bieling	451 (13%)	20h-25m	22.1 mph
Robert Creighton	350 (10%)	22h-36m	15.5 mph
William Binz	330 (9%)	10h-50m	30.5 mph
	3,566 (100%)	5d-18h-30m	25.7 mph

SOURCE: Table in the September 1916 issue of *Marmon News*, repr. in Charles L. Betts Jr., "The Marmon Transcontinental Record," *Antique Automobile*, May–June 1966, p. 30.

[a] Mileages given here are from the table printed in the *Marmon News*, but the figures yield a total of 3,566 miles, which is incorrect. The automaker elsewhere cites the correct and widely reported figure of 3,476 miles. Of necessity, however, the proportions given in this column are based on the 3,566-mile figure.

[b] A driver's average speed depended more on the weather and the road conditions than on the driver's ability.

Stevens, a "millionaire auto enthusiast" who had crossed the country in his own cars "several times," was eminently qualified for the trip.[4] In fact, "enthusiast" is an understatement. Stevens bought his first car—a National electric runabout—in February 1901 and within weeks had added two Waverley electrics. That spring, he bought his first gasoline model—a Gasmobile stanhope. "Shortly after buying the Gasmobile I made a trip to Buffalo and return, and I suppose this journey was the most enjoyable motor run I will ever take, as it was all so new and novel," Stevens wrote in a 1904 *MoToR* article. "The sense of freedom as I traveled along I will never forget."[5]

By mid-1904, Stevens was personally maintaining a fleet of eleven American and imported autos in his own large repair shop. Complete with gas and oil tanks, two metal-turning lathes, power hacksaw, forge, and nearly $1,500 worth of hand tools, the shop was "as thorough as any private garage in the land," he boasted. Stevens also began competitive driving: in the annual Glidden Tour reliability contests, in speed trials on the smooth sands of Daytona Beach, Florida, in hill climbs and on race tracks "in practically every section of the country." Stevens "has a bewildering array of trophies won at different automobile races," the *Rome Daily Sentinel* reported in early 1906.[6]

That year, Stevens became president of the upstart New York Motor Club, which the *New York Herald* called "a formidable rival of the Automobile Club of America as an aspirant for national honors." By 1909 Stevens had made his mark as "a well known amateur driver and referee at prominent Eastern contests," the *Chicago Inter Ocean* observed.[7]

In his hometown of Rome, New York, Stevens the "industrialist" was vice president of the Rome Merchant Iron Mills and a director of a local bank, as well as "one of the largest stockholders of the Baldwin Locomotive Works" of Philadelphia.[8] Further, he was a director of the Fiat Automobile Company that from 1910 until 1918 built the American Fiat in Poughkeepsie, New York, under license from its Italian counterpart. Stevens, a Harvard-trained engineer, also "engaged in experimental work in machinery and contributed much to the success of the forging of aluminum and the use of aluminum in pistons and piston rods" in autos.[9]

By 1916, Stevens had become chairman of the Motor Reserve Division of the American Defense Society, a group whose members included former President Theodore "Teddy" Roosevelt and two former secretaries of the Navy. The ADS lobbied Congress for a stronger military, solicited pledges of support from congressional candidates, asked foreign-born citizens to sign "America First" loyalty pledges, formed rifle clubs —"the first need of a country in time of war is men who know how to shoot"—and sponsored lectures, exhibits, and demonstrations.[10]

In his ADS capacity, Stevens arranged and financed the 1916 transcontinental trip. He also solicited from Major General Leonard Wood, commander of the Army's Eastern Department, the military missive that the Marmon would carry, newspapers reported. Wood, stationed at Governors Island in New York Bay, "addressed a letter to the commander of the Western Department, which was carried in the car the entire way and delivered by Stevens in San Francisco," the automaker reported in its September 1916 house organ, the *Marmon News*.[11] Wood's counterpart in the West was Major General James Franklin Bell.

ARMY OFFICERS DEFY PRESIDENT WILSON

As the war in Europe threatened to draw other countries into combat, a political skirmish broke out in the United States. President Woodrow Wilson, backed by his secretary of state, William Jennings Bryan, adopted what some critics termed a peace-at-any-price strategy. But Major General Wood led the charge for peacetime preparedness—the idea being that the United States should begin rearming and training a large citizen army in preparation for entering the war, if it came to that. In fact, Wood sought and won the post of commander of the Eastern Department in 1914 "because he wanted to exploit the mass media of the populous Northeast."[12] Wood came to fame in 1898, during the Spanish-American War, when he and Teddy Roosevelt led the volunteer Rough Riders in a charge up San Juan Hill in Cuba. In the same Rough Rider spirit, Wood backed Stevens's transcontinental trip as a highly visible demonstration of how a well-prepared citizenry could aid a country at war.

Wood, however, paid dearly for his part in the Marmon run and for otherwise opposing the views of his commander in chief. President Wilson viewed Wood as a threat, for newspapers in mid-1916 had already begun reporting on Wood's political ambitions. "Public clashes between an obstinate president and equally stubborn subordinate led Wood to the brink of insubordination and a civil-military crisis," according to the *Dictionary of American Military Biography*. "The administration, in turn, found Wood a difficult problem because he was too politically powerful to be disciplined and not insubordinate enough to be court-martialed. It finally settled on keeping him out of the war in Europe." After World War I, Wood entered the presidential race in January 1920 and soon became the front-runner. Delegates to the Republican convention, however, nominated Warren G. Harding over Wood on the 10th ballot.[13]

Major General Bell, who commanded the Western Department from 1915 to 1917, likewise "took a prominent role in the preparedness movement, thereby incurring the enmity of Woodrow Wilson." Like Wood, Bell was a progressive officer who also supported the Marmon run because he appreciated the military value of the automobile. Bell had been among the first to embrace other emerging technologies: "He played a major role in the adoption in 1906 of the machine gun as a standard part of the armament of all line regiments, and three years later he chaired the board that purchased the first Army plane." While commanding the Philippines Division from 1911 to 1914, "he and John Joseph Pershing conspired to motorize an infantry regiment on Mindanao [Island] out of surplus quartermaster funds."[14]

WHOSE IDEA WAS THIS?

Sources disagree about who first had the idea for the Marmon's coast-to-coast trip. The *Marmon News* claimed that Stevens "was the father of the big idea of making the trip," and the July 31, 1916, *Rome Daily Sentinel* agreed:

It was nearly a month ago that the idea of an ocean-to-ocean run occurred to [Stevens]. He felt that the country ought to be awakened to the need of a great national highway which should connect the Atlantic with the Pacific and should serve as a military road in case of war.

He communicated with Stuart Lake of New York, son of Harry G. Lake, 507 N. Madison street [in Rome]. Mr. Lake is publicity manager of the American Defense Society, and Mr. Stevens told him what he had in mind. Mr. Lake was heartily enthusiastic, seeing in this trip a wonderful opportunity of spreading preparedness intelligence throughout the country. He was glad to co-operate with Mr. Stevens and did a great deal to help.[15]

Stuart N. Lake went on to write books and screenplays—published primarily in the 1930s and 1940s—about the Old West. According to the *San Francisco Examiner*, it was Lake who conceived the idea of sending the Marmon from New York City into the Old West. Originally, said the *Examiner*, Lake had planned

to have an armored motor car cross the continent at a rapid rate of speed, and knowing that Stevens was an experienced motorist, having crossed the continent in his own car on several different occasions, came to him for advice. Stevens went into the subject with Lake exhaustively. Finally it was decided to send an official dispatch car in as brief a time as possible.[16]

Apart from Stevens and Lake, Major General Wood may himself have conceived the 1916 trip as a repeat of a similar crossing he had inspired seven years earlier, in which a Mitchell "Ranger" carried a military message from New York City to San Francisco. The 1909 trip was "the outcome of Major Gen. Wood's desire to see the establishment of an automobile service in connection with the regular and volunteer forces," the *New York Times* said at the time (see Chapter 1).[17]

More recently, the U.S. War Department had sanctioned a July 1915 day-and-night motorcycle relay to deliver a message from Washington, D.C., to the Panama-Pacific International Exposition in San Francisco. "One of the primary ideas back of the relay is to demonstrate to the United States War Department the real worth of the motorcycle in dispatch service," said *Motorcycling & Bicycling* magazine. President Wilson "has promised that he will hand the message in person to the dispatch bearer who rides the first relay out of Washington"—which suggests that this trip had no ties to the preparedness movement that Wilson opposed. In organizing the run, the Federation of American Motorcyclists chose Cannon Ball Baker to ride three of the more than forty relays. Because of Midwestern storms, however, the message arrived nearly five days late.[18]

MILITARY ROADS AND A "MOTOR RESERVE"

Regardless of who conceived the 1916 Marmon trek, Stevens "figured out the entire trip himself, cutting from the schedule minutes, even seconds, until he was able to cover almost the entire distance in the time which he planned," the *Rome Daily Sentinel* observed. The schedule "was laid out like that of a railroad timetable," as *Motor Age* put it. Whereas in 1909 the drivers of the Mitchell Ranger had consumed 31 days, 5 hours, in delivering their military dispatch, Stevens was proposing to make his delivery in five days. He must be "attempting to beat the time of the fastest trans-continental trains from coast to coast," ventured an Iowa newspaper.[19] Actually, Stevens's goals were "to demonstrate the value of the automobile in time of mobilization and to arouse interest in the building of military roads by army engineers, a plan long advocated by General Wood," his hometown paper observed, further explaining:

> Mr. Stevens holds that good military roads and a large motor reserve, with relief drivers along the way, would make the government independent of the railroads and would enable the War Department to mobilize troops in any part of the country at short notice.
>
> He proves his argument by the fact that Paris was saved from German capture because troops were rushed to the front in automobiles. In an effort to arouse the country to the need of this practical form of preparedness, Mr. Stevens arranged and financed this trip.[20]

Besides meticulously plotting a route that would largely follow the Lincoln Highway from Indiana westward, Stevens prepared for the trek by consulting with the U.S. Weather Bureau. But since "he did not expect to be bothered with rain in the mountains or the desert region," he got reports of weather conditions only for the Midwest—a mistake, as it turned out.[21]

Stevens had plenty of help in planning and making the run, however. According to automotive historian Charles Betts, the car was "directed" throughout the trip from the Marmon company's home base in Indianapolis. "During the day the headquarters were at the Marmon factory and at night at the Washington Hotel."[22] How did the automaker assist the drivers? "It was arranged with the headquarters in Indianapolis to have the dealers throughout the entire trip ready to give whatever aid was necessary, so that everything went off smoothly like clockwork." In addition, the *Rome Daily Sentinel* explained, "local pilots met the car at the cities where detours had to be made and conducted it to the main road." But others assisted in the attempt, according to the automaker: "Lincoln Highway officials, members of the Defense Society, and friends of Stevens and the Marmon car, made arrangements along the way and provided pilots where they were needed."[23]

A "REALLY SCIENTIFIC" MARMON

The owner of many foreign cars, Stevens imported his first vehicles—three Mercedes—in 1903. The next year he added two Darracq autos from France. Numbered among his imports was also a 1907 Rolls-Royce Silver Ghost, reportedly the fourteenth Silver Ghost made—a very rare car that survives today.[24] With an understandable display of patriotic spirit, however, Stevens used his own American-made Marmon in the 1916 run, which can be seen in photos bearing New York license number 123-197. Stevens's 1916 Marmon Model 34 was a "touring car of regular production," as Nordyke & Marmon phrased it, although the company neglected to specify whether the auto was its $2,700 five-passenger touring car or its $2,750 seven-passenger version.[25] In stock form, the bigger Marmon weighed an extra 90 pounds—3,540 pounds total— but both touring cars shared a 136-inch wheelbase.

Slightly modified for the trip, Stevens's Marmon had had its tonneau, or rear passenger compartment, removed both to lighten the car and to provide for "the placing of an auxiliary gas tank in the rear so that there would be plenty of fuel in the long run across the desert," the company explained. "The Marmon carried the standard gas tank in the cowl, which was ordinarily filled via a spout under the hood," according to historian Betts. "But the transcontinental car had an extension fitted which protruded through the hood to facilitate filling the tank without lifting the hood."[26]

For night driving, the car carried two spotlights—one on each windshield post— and had a desert water bag hanging from each windshield post. Photos reveal that the car also carried a can of gas or oil on the left running board and, it appears, a jack, several boxes, and as many as four spare tires on the open rear deck. The boxes no doubt contained tools and spare parts; the automaker, however, neglected to list all the equipment on board. From a pole on the left rear of the car, the drivers flew a thirteen-star American flag.

With the tonneau gone, there was also room for a jump seat behind the two front-seat occupants. This seat—a precarious perch, virtually without protection from the elements—was presumably where the local pilots, or guides, sat, for, according to the *San Francisco Chronicle*, "three people traveled in the car at all times, two of the regular drivers and a friendly pilot picked up at the different points where the changes of drivers occurred."[27]

The Marmon company was regarded as an industry leader in engineering, thanks in part to its exploits on the race track. In one prominent instance, well-known driver Ray Harroun won the first Indianapolis 500, in 1911, driving the yellow, long-tailed Marmon Wasp racer. Further cementing its reputation for engineering excellence, the Marmon company's 1916 introduction of the Model 34 "ranks as probably the greatest single step-change in domestic motor car design and additionally marked the strong beginning of the automotive styling age," concludes a book titled *The Marmon Heritage*. The advanced construction of its body and engine, the design of its suspension, and the use of both aluminum and thin, high-tensile steel made the 1916 Marmon "a really scientific car," *Automobile* raved.[28]

"The machine is built of aluminum," the *Wyoming Tribune* blithely stated—and this sweeping generalization was close to the mark. The engine casting, body, radiator shell, and fenders were all of aluminum—even the steel rear axle used an aluminum differential case. The Marmon company riveted steel running boards directly to frame side rails that, at 10 inches, were unusually tall, thereby allowing the use of "thin stock" in the frame, which both lightened and strengthened the car, the automaker claimed. The rigid frame allowed for an unusually light body, built in three pieces with sills or a subframe—cowl, front seat, and rear seat. "Thus properly speaking there is no separate body; both body and chassis are a unit and reduplication of strain-bearing parts is thus eliminated completely," *Automobile* said. Because of its construction, the Marmon 34 was "1100 pounds lighter than cars of equal size and power," the automaker advertised.[29]

With a 3¾ x 5⅛-inch bore and stroke, Marmon's new 6-cylinder aluminum engine displaced 339.7 cubic inches, developing 74 horsepower at 2,500 rpm, claimed the automaker. In a test on the Indianapolis Motor Speedway, a 1916 Marmon equipped with this engine—"the first automobile motor to be placed in regular production with an aluminum cylinder casting"—accelerated from 10 to 50 mph in third gear in 17.6 seconds, *Automobile* reported. Even the pistons were aluminum, running in iron sleeves. A pump supplied oil through passages drilled into the crankshaft to lubricate the crankshaft main bearings and through a hollow rocker-arm shaft to the overhead valve train. As *Automobile* noted, "one reason that the overhead valve motor has not been more popular is the difficulty in lubricating the parts properly." On the Marmon, however, "altogether the valve system is lubricated much more efficiently than is usual on L head [valve-in-block] motors."[30]

Marmon's unusual rear suspension used two transversely mounted leaf springs, which reduced the tendency of the car to roll on turns without producing an overly stiff ride, one of *Automobile*'s reviewers remarked. "To test this springing the writer drove the car over moderate gravel and dirt roads at speeds from 10 to 50 m.p.h. with a single 140 lb. passenger in the rear seat and no bump was sufficiently severe to separate him from the cushion." To reduce the amount of routine maintenance required for its car, Marmon eliminated most of the grease cups so common on early automobiles. These threaded cups required car owners or hired mechanics, first, to keep them well-filled with grease, and then to screw them downward frequently in order to pump grease to the parts needing it. The Marmon company sealed most of the typical chassis lubrication points and also advertised its springs as "self-lubricating." In contrast to most 1916 cars, "only four grease cups are used, and these are on the steering connections."[31]

FIRST ATTEMPT FLOPS

Stevens was not the first person to cross the country in a Marmon. As a test, the factory took one of its early experimental models "right across the continent," although they unfortunately did so "at an unfavorable time of the year, encountering roads in the worst possible state," *Automobile* said in its December 23, 1915, review of the new car.[32] In addition, as automotive historian Charles Betts points out, the Marmon company had made its first attempt to set a transcontinental speed record in June 1916, although the trip received little or no publicity—which was probably just as well. According to Betts, Olle Holman, who was a passenger on one leg of the successful July run, later reported that the Marmon used in the trip a month earlier struck a tree just west of Fremont, Ohio, putting an abrupt end to that attempt.

> At the time Bill Binz was following the transcontinental car with an ordinary Marmon phaeton, with instructions that should anything go amiss he was to take parts or pieces off his car in order to keep the record car moving. But the transcontinental car jumped a ditch and hit a big oak tree, damaging the car so badly that it had to be towed back to Toledo. On arrival at Toledo, Bill called the factory to report the damage and was instructed to ship the car back to Indianapolis.[33]

Despite the Marmon's failed first attempt, auto enthusiasts were treated to a flurry of well-publicized transcontinental runs in the summer of 1916. During June and July, "vaudeville star" Claire Rochester drove from coast to coast in a 1917 Apperson Roadaplane, in part to raise $30,000 for the nighttime illumination of the Statue of Liberty.[34] From July 15 to July 22—just before Stevens's trip—thirty-eight Saxon cars, in what was truly an "automobile relay," traveled coast to coast in 6 days, 21 hours, 10 minutes, beating the mark Cannon Ball Baker had set in May 1916 in a V-8 Cadillac. Between July 3 and August 1, Walter A. Weidely and Hinnie Scholler drove from San Diego to New York City in a 12-cylinder Pathfinder car that had had its first and second gears removed. A publicity stunt, this high-gear crossing set no speed records.[35]

"SEALED" CAR SPEEDS WESTWARD

Driver Fred Barbour started the successful Marmon transcontinental dash from the base of the Maine Memorial in the northeast section of Columbus Circle, at 59th and Broadway in New York City, at 1:30 A.M. Monday, July 24, 1916. Flash photos show Fred E. Moskovics, who helped design the Marmon 34 and would later head the Stutz Motor Car Company, shaking hands with the driver (see Fig. 89). To keep the drivers from switching or repairing parts during the July attempt, representatives of the Automobile Club of America had placed seals in a dozen locations on the Marmon's machinery and had also recorded various unspecified "marks of identification."[36]

The seals would prevent repairs being made to the differential, transmission, springs, the single universal joint—even the radiator cap was sealed. As the *Rome Daily Sentinel* observed, the organizers of the trip took such precautions "so that there would be no question of the identity of the car which reached San Francisco." For the same reason, after the run the Marmon company distributed a list of thirty-two auto agents or agencies, reporters or newspapers, telegraph operators, and pilots who could confirm the Marmon's passage through various points—one of whom was Louis Disbrow, a famous automobile racer.[37]

The Marmon company was evidently reacting to Bobby Hammond's loss of face when, two months earlier, he arrived in New York City claiming to have driven from San Francisco in record-breaking time. But Hammond had neglected to collect signatures along much of the way—a standard practice—and thus could not document his route. Tellingly, none of the auto journals or newspapers covering the Marmon trek recognized Hammond's time as legitimate.[38]

The Marmon's route lay across central New York state to Buffalo, south around Lake Erie to Cleveland, and across northern Ohio and Indiana. The car would then

strike the Lincoln Highway near Merrillville, Indiana, and follow it "with few devia-
tions" to San Francisco, according to the *Marmon News* (see Fig. 90). Barbour drove
the 295 miles to Syracuse, where at 10:30 A.M. Monday he turned the wheel over to
Stevens, who reached Buffalo at 2:50 P.M. "Through Buffalo the police piloted the car
at 40 miles an hour, holding up traffic and stopping pedestrians," the *Rome Daily Sentinel* reported.[39]

Stevens continued driving through Erie, Pennsylvania, to end his 352-mile relay
in Cleveland at about 7:30 P.M. Monday, according to the Rome newspaper and one
Marmon ad, although other ads put the arrival time at 7:55 P.M. "There was some delay in Cleveland on account of the car getting caught in a parade and bad luck at railroad crossings," the company said. "At one crossing the car was held twelve minutes."[40] Binz, the driver from the Chicago Marmon agency, took over in Cleveland.
He drove 330 miles overnight (see Fig. 91) into Day 2, Tuesday, July 25, and at 6:45 A.M.
on Tuesday reached Merrillville, just nine miles south of Gary, Indiana. According to
the automaker:

Fig. 89. Fred E. Mosko-
vics (standing) shakes
hands with the Marmon
driver—unidentified in
this photo but presum-
ably Fred Barbour, who
drove the first relay. His
passenger is also
unidentified. The boy
with outstretched arms
on the prow of the bat-
tleship Maine, in the
background, represents
Victory; other figures
on the monument repre-
sent the Atlantic and
Pacific coasts. (AAMA)

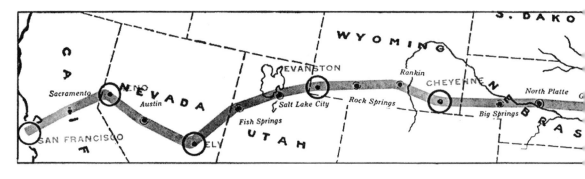

Fig. 90. The Marmon's coast-to-coast route. (Automobile, August 17, 1916)

The time made on this stretch was limited to the time which could be made by Stevens in getting from Cleveland to Merrillville by train. The train stop near Merrillville is Gary, and it was impossible for Stevens to get to Gary until 6:45 Tuesday morning. The Marmon car reached Merrillville exactly on time and after taking on supplies another car flashed over the hill bearing Stevens, the driver, who was to take the car to Omaha. The car left the station as per schedule at 7:00 A.M.[41]

Fresh from his train ride, Stevens drove across Illinois, passing south of Chicago to avoid congestion, crossed the Mississippi River into Iowa, and reached Cedar Rapids at 3:45 P.M. on Tuesday (see Fig. 92). At Marshalltown, the next city of any size, Stevens

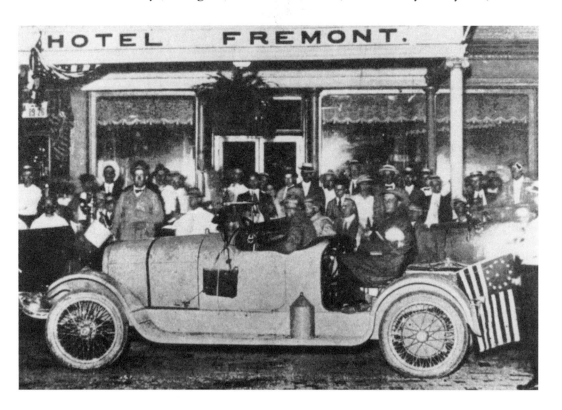

Fig. 91. A flash photo captures the Marmon, with William Binz at the wheel, during a brief stop in Fremont, Ohio. (Horseless Age, August 15, 1916)

was traveling too fast to stop to be interviewed. Thus the *Marshalltown Evening Times-Republican* could say only that "the Marmon car, trying for a speed record from coast to coast, passed thru this city late Tuesday afternoon."[42]

UNION PACIFIC HOLDS TRAIN IN OMAHA

Completing his 559-mile relay, Stevens arrived in Omaha, Nebraska, at 1:05 A.M. on Wednesday, July 26, right on the schedule for Day 3, according to the Marmon company's timetable. Allowing for the one-hour time difference, the car averaged 31.6 mph in covering the 1,536 miles from New York City in an elapsed time of 48 hours, 35 minutes. At Omaha, Stevens jumped on a westbound Union Pacific passenger train that had arrived 35 minutes earlier and, by special arrangement, had waited for him.

Barbour then took the wheel for the longest leg of the trip—577 miles across the Nebraska prairie to Cheyenne, Wyoming. Late Wednesday morning, a "long, grey streak" rocketed through North Platte, Nebraska, traveling east to west, reported the *North Platte Telegraph* (see Fig. 93). "So fast did the object travel that it was just possible to identify it as a speeding road car and to distinguish three huddled figures clinging to the machine. Two of the men on the car were the crew that is taking the machine through this section of the country. The third was Joe Filion, who pilots the machine from North Platte to Pine Bluffs, Wyo."[43]

With Barbour at the wheel, the Marmon "went through this city Wednesday morning on a world's record trip," according to *North Platte's Semi-Weekly Tribune*:

It reached here at 10:41 A.M., twenty-two minutes ahead of schedule, changed pilots and drivers and took on supplies. The car carries three men to each town, driver, pilot and machinist[,] and H. G. Smith of the Goodrich Rubber Co., of Kansas City, was here to make

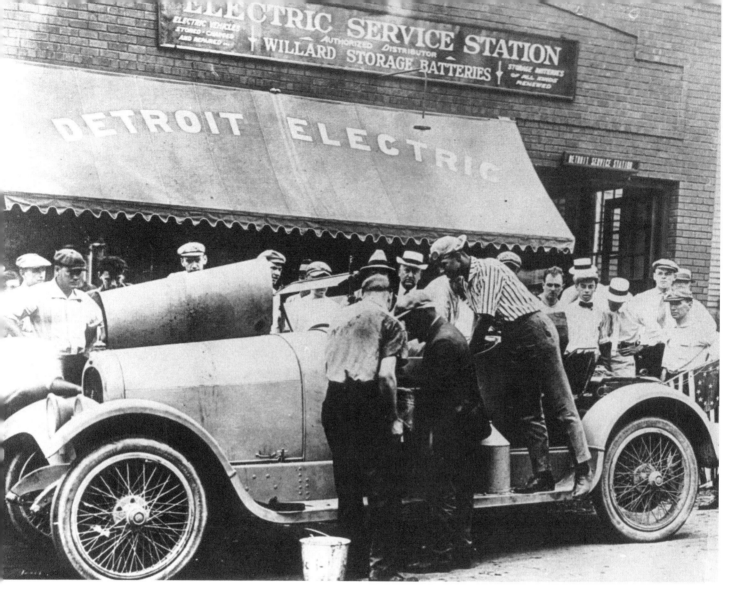

Fig. 92. Mechanics
scramble to service the
car at Cedar Rapids,
Iowa. (AACA)

these changes and secure a pilot. Joseph E. Fillion, Jr., accompanied the party to Pine Bluffs as pilot.

About twenty local people met the car at the South [Platte] river where a number of photographs were taken by H. A. Brooks. The members of the party were very complimentary in their remarks concerning the condition of the Lincoln Highway.[44]

The newspaper may have been mistaken in its comment that a new driver took over in North Platte. The Marmon company maintained that Barbour drove all the way from Omaha to Cheyenne, where he arrived at 4:50 P.M. on Wednesday, to average 34.5 mph during a trip that lasted 16 hours, 45 minutes (see Fig. 94). The car thus had averaged 32.3 mph from New York to Cheyenne, where it was "about thirty minutes" ahead of schedule, the automaker claimed.[45] Thursday's *Wyoming Tribune* heralded the auto's arrival: "Clipping off one hour [from] the auto record between Omaha and Cheyenne on a transcontinental race to lower the world's speed record from New York to San Francisco[,] a Marmon six-cylinder car passed through Cheyenne last evening far ahead of its original schedule, which was drawn for the purpose of lowering the record."[46]

Unfortunately, the *Tribune*, and likewise the competing *Cheyenne State Leader*, failed to compensate for the time difference between Cheyenne and Omaha, which led them to understate Barbour's time by one hour. Thus, he presumably only tied the existing record speed between the two cities. According to Thursday's *State Leader*, Stevens had traveled to Cheyenne by train "and was waiting here when his car arrived yesterday afternoon at 4:50. After a brief stop at the Plains garage, Stevens climbed into the machine and pulled out at 5:30." During the short stop in Cheyenne, the *San Francisco Examiner* stated, the tires "were changed as a matter of precaution."[47]

In his third stint at the wheel, Stevens drove 416 miles overnight through mountainous southern Wyoming, crossing the Continental Divide and—despite fighting muddy roads for 20 miles near Rawlins—reaching Evanston at 11:30 A.M. on Thursday, July 27. He telegraphed the factory: "Delay on account of much rain. Roads muddy. Car in best of condition."[48]

Fig. 93. Helpers abound at this gas and oil stop near North Platte, Nebraska. (NAHC)

Fig. 94. In sending this photograph to Motor Age, the Marmon company identified it only as "The Marmon 34 at Cheyenne, Wyo." (WDCR)

A new driver, Walter Bieling, then took the wheel to drive the four miles from Evanston to the Utah border and the 75 miles beyond to Salt Lake City. From there, he would drive into Nevada. Traveling in the Wasatch Mountains through Parley's Canyon, however, "they encountered a terrific electrical storm that converted the roadway into a sea of mud and made the going difficult and dangerous," the *San Francisco Chronicle* related.[49] Bieling reportedly arrived in Salt Lake at 1:55 P.M. on Thursday, meaning that he had averaged 32.6 mph from Evanston. Such a fast clip casts doubt, however, either on the reports of rain or on his reported arrival time. From Salt Lake City, Bieling drove southwest into the desert—and into the night.

"A COLLISION WAS UNAVOIDABLE"

Somewhere in the darkness of the Utah desert, however, the Marmon went astray. According to the company, "three hours were lost west of Salt Lake City because the pilot became confused in the route through the desert."[50] Supplementing these meager details, the *Rome Daily Sentinel* also added information about another Utah mishap. As the paper reported it:

> A friend of the pilot who had been engaged met the car west of Salt Lake and the car went on in darkness through the desert. By midnight a place which was supposed to have been reached was not found. At 1 o'clock the pilot admitted he was wrong and two valuable hours were spent in getting back on the right road.
>
> A second accident occurred in Utah as the car went racing over a narrow road. The driver of the record smashing machine gave an oncoming car as much room as possible, but a collision was unavoidable. When Mr. Stevens's car came to a halt it lacked one of its wheels. Another was quickly put on and the machine drove off, nobody having been hurt in the accident.[51]

Belying this report of quick repairs, a timetable accompanying the Rome newspaper story indicates a "delay of seven hours for repairs" at Salt Lake City.[52] This suggests that the collision occurred on the road through Parley's Canyon, forcing the long stop in Salt Lake City. In what is evidently another version of the same mishap, *Automobile* and *Motor Age* make no mention of a collision: "A wire from Salt Lake City reported that a torque rod socket had been broken in Parley's Can[y]on, 16 miles from Salt Lake City. Repairs were soon made, however, and Bieling left with the car at 7:40 P.M. from Salt Lake City."[53] Given the car's 1:55 P.M. arrival in Salt Lake City, though, the repairs "soon made" actually consumed nearly six hours, according to this account.

In reporting on the accident, the two journals appear to be referring to the "torque rod" that extended from the front of the transmission to a ball-and-socket joint on one of the frame cross members and was intended to help brace the amidships transmission. Other accounts, however, mention damage to a different part, although one similar in name—the steel torque tube, which protected the driveshaft. *Automobile* and *Motor Age* further cloud the picture by indicating that the broken wheel to which the *Rome Daily Sentinel* refers occurred in Nevada: "Rain and washouts delayed the car just before entering Ely, and due to poor roads a broken wheel resulted along the same stretch."[54] Salt Lake City's four daily newspapers fail to clear up the mystery of why the Marmon lingered in Salt Lake: they missed the story of the car's arrival altogether.

Fig. 95. Bieling pulls to a stop in Ely, Nevada, against a backdrop evincing local support for the Lincoln Highway, the transcontinental route that the Marmon generally followed. (NAHC)

Ely was Bieling's destination, and he arrived there to end his 451-mile, nearly 21-hour trip from Evanston at 7:55 A.M. on Friday, July 28, Day 5 of the trip (see Fig. 95).[55] The car left Ely at 8:10 A.M., according to the automaker, whereas the *White Pine News* of East Ely indicated that "the car arrived in Ely at 8:05 A.M., where all needed supplies were procured, the crew changed and the start made again at 8:15."[56] Another new driver, Robert Creighton, took the wheel to drive west across central Nevada on a 350-mile trip to Reno through Austin, Alpine (which the Marmon company calls "Alpine Ranch"), and Fallon. His travel time of 22 hours, 36 minutes, was the longest of the nine relays. According to the *Marmon News*, Creighton certainly encountered his share of troubles: "Aside from being delayed by the rough trails, a short circuit left him without lights. He located the trouble, however, and remedied it so that delay from this source was not considerable. Breaking through a bridge several miles out of Fallon caused a further delay of 3½ hours."[57] Neither the automaker nor the newspapers provided further information about the bridge accident, although the *San Francisco Call* may be alluding to the mishap when it says that "some time also was lost in the Fallon Sink, Nev., as the road was in bad shape."[58]

Creighton reached Reno at 5:31 A.M. Saturday, July 29—3,240 miles from New York City via the Lincoln Highway and just 236 miles out of San Francisco. Meeting the car at Reno, Stevens resumed the journey at 5:40 A.M. "Reaching the California line faster time was made, and the run down the Sierra mountains was negotiated at a good clip," the *San Francisco Chronicle* recounted.[59] As his average speed shows, though, Stevens's run from Reno to San Francisco was actually the second slowest of the nine relays on the cross-country trip (see Table 16).

CROSSING SHOWS "REMARKABLE REGULARITY"

Stevens reached Sacramento, California, at 12:22 P.M. and Vallejo at 3:10 P.M., where H. B. Rector of San Francisco, the Marmon distributor for northern California, was awaiting their arrival. In Vallejo, the Marmon and crew boarded a special ferry to

TABLE 16. Marmon Relays, July 24–29, 1916

City to City	Driver	Mileage for Each Relay	Cumulative Mileage[a]	Time	Average Speed
New York City–Syracuse, N.Y.	Fred Barbour	295	295	9h-00m	32.8 mph
Syracuse, N.Y.–Cleveland	S. B. Stevens	352	647	10h-25m	33.8 mph
Cleveland–Merrillville, Ind.	William Binz	330	977	10h-50m	30.5 mph
Merrillville, Ind.–Omaha, Neb.	S. B. Stevens	559	1,536	18h-20m	30.5 mph
Omaha, Neb.–Cheyenne, Wyo.	Fred Barbour	577	2,113	16h-45m	34.5 mph
Cheyenne, Wyo.–Evanston, Wyo.	S. B. Stevens	416	2,529	18h-40m	22.3 mph
Evanston, Wyo.–Ely, Nev.	Walter Bieling	451	2,980	20h-25m	22.1 mph
Ely, Nev.–Reno, Nev.	Robert Creighton	350	3,330	22h-36m	15.5 mph
Reno, Nev.–San Francisco	S. B. Stevens	236	3,566	11h-29m	20.6 mph
				5d-18h-30m	25.1 mph

SOURCES: For drivers and their relays, "Marmon Coast-to-Coast Record," *Automobile*, Aug. 3, 1916. For distances, table in the September 1916 issue of the *Marmon News*, repr. in Charles L. Betts, Jr., "The Marmon Transcontinental Record," *Antique Automobile*, May–June 1966, p. 30.

[a] See note a to Table 15, p. 220.

Fig. 96. The Marmon arrives on the cobblestones outside San Francisco's ferry building. (NAHC)

cross San Pablo and San Francisco bays into San Francisco (see Figs. 96 and 97). At 5:00 P.M. on Saturday, the car checked in at Lotta's Fountain, Third and Market streets, to end the fastest transcontinental automobile crossing yet seen.

"When the car reached San Francisco it showed little effect of the hard run," the *San Francisco Chronicle* declared. "The motor was shooting as perfectly as though the grind had been an average day's run." More remarkable, the Marmon's engine "was kept running continuously right across the continent," the newspaper asserted—apparently in error, as the Marmon company made no such claim.[60] The crossing time of 5 days, 18 hours, 30 minutes (138½ hours) cut almost two days—41 hours, 22 minutes—from the record Baker had set in May. It also cut 26 hours, 40 minutes, from the Saxon relay record set two days before the Marmon left New York City.

With five drivers, the Marmon had covered 3,476 miles at an average speed of

25.1 mph, or 602 miles per day, for its elapsed time. To average 25 mph, the automaker explained, "most of the actual driving must be done at 45 miles an hour or more—and this speed must be maintained day and night with stops only to secure supplies. All sorts of roads and conditions are to be encountered, and all the delays of passing vehicles on the roads and through towns." Maintaining such an average while limiting the top speed to 50 mph "gives a remarkable demonstration of regularity," *Automobile* commented.[61]

The car was idle for up to 7 hours for repairs in Salt Lake City and for 3½ hours when it broke through the Nevada bridge, or 10½ hours total—probably more, in fact, but the automaker doesn't provide any information about how much time the car spent at refueling or relay points. Thus, for a running time of no more (and probably less) than 5 days, 8 hours, the Marmon averaged 27.2 mph, or nearly 652 miles per day. The drivers reportedly experienced just two punctures.

Rector, the Marmon distributor, "will place the car on display in his showrooms for the next few days," the *Chronicle* said at the finish of the trip. An Automobile Club

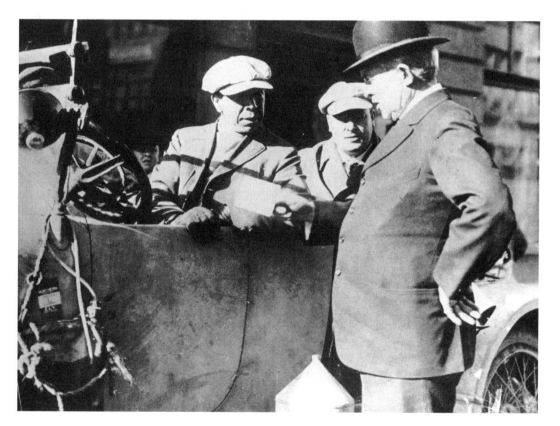

Fig. 97. Samuel B. Stevens reaches San Francisco, completing his fourth and final stint behind the wheel. Some auto journals contend that this photo depicts Stevens handing his military dispatch to Major General James Franklin Bell, but such accounts fail to explain why a high-ranking officer would be wearing a business suit. The back-seat passenger—presumably a local pilot—is unidentified. (NAHC)

of America official would then inspect the seals on various parts of the car. Afterward, Stuart Lake would drive Stevens's Marmon back home to Rome, New York, the *Rome Daily Sentinel* reported—although *Motor West* claimed that Stevens's Marmon was shipped home by rail. "Moving pictures of the trip have been taken and will soon be shown in theaters throughout the country," added the *Sentinel*, which was the only source that mentioned such film footage. Unfortunately, the newspaper did not provide a further description of the movies.[62]

AUTOMAKER EXPLAINS BROKEN SEALS

In San Francisco, ACA representative J. W. Pearson discovered that three of the twelve seals that had been placed on the car in New York City were missing—one each on the driveshaft torque tube, the left front spring, and the differential case (see Fig. 98). Another seal on the torque tube was broken but still in place. But all four of these seals "were so placed that they came in contact with the road, and were in this way either broken or torn away," the Marmon company explained. "Identification marks showed conclusively that these parts were not changed or repaired." In addition, the original wheels "were missing at the end because the wheels, rather than the tires, were changed" in Cheyenne to save time.[63]

The Marmon "was the only car that ever attempted the trip with the parts so sealed and identified," the automaker would claim in its 1920 book, *Nordyke & Marmon Company: An Institution*. In fact, although the Marmon company was among the first to take such precautions, the ACA had stamped the axles and other parts of the cars that participated in the 1909 New York–Seattle race. "Wax impressions of these stamps were forwarded to Seattle so that the examiners could ascertain absolutely if the parts bore the genuine stamps they received in New York," *Motor Age* explained at the time.[64]

As he told the *San Francisco Examiner*, the 42-year-old Stevens saw some lessons in the run:

> The mere establishing of a new transcontinental record and thereby being hailed all over the world as a speed maniac would not of itself have appealed to me at my age. The transcontinental run in a Marmon car was an effort to demonstrate what it would be possible for a motorist to accomplish providing the original means of communication between the East and the West were interrupted in some way.
> It also shows the possibility of the rapid mobilization of troops as an adjunct to train

service, and further demonstrates the advisability of organizing at once a National Motor Reserve similar to the very fine Automobile Reserve Corps which you have here in San Francisco, only on a national scale.[65]

Further, Stevens credited the Union Pacific Railroad and other companies for making the swift time possible, the *Examiner* reported:

> Stevens said that it would have been hopeless for him to have started with the car and finished with the car [as driver] had it not been for the splendid co-operation which he received from the railroad officials along the line, and also from the Western Union Telegraph Company officials, who kept him and the car in constant touch with the officials of the American Defense Society, the B. F. Goodrich Rubber Company factory and the Goodrich and Marmon stores all along the line of travel. . . .
>
> When the various railroad officials and the general manager of the telegraph company learned that Stevens' trip was in the interest of preparedness they extended him unusual courtesies. Stevens sent telegrams and received an answer repeatedly in from six to ten minutes.[66]

Fig. 98. J. W. Pearson and "Mr. Ridley"— although the Marmon company neglects to say which is which— inspect the Marmon's seals in San Francisco. (NAHC)

Police were also "willing and ready to help," as they did in speeding Stevens through Buffalo, New York, at 40 mph. The trustees of the American Defense Society quickly wired their congratulations to Stevens, and

> to those patriotic Americans who in co-operating with you made possible this needed lesson of American enterprise, bringing San Francisco nearer to New York by a period of two whole days. Under most adverse conditions you have demonstrated to the citizens of this country the possibility of a new transcontinental mobilization of troops independent of railways. It remains now for this nation to lay the lesson of your achievement to heart by the immediate organization of an adequate motor reserve.[67]

"WONDERFUL STRIDES IN AUTOMOBILE SPEED"

Ignoring the question of preparedness, other observers saw in the Marmon's performance a variety of implications. According to the *White Pine News*, of East Ely, Nevada, the transcontinental run

> proved beyond a question that the Lincoln Highway is the right way to travel. . . . The advantages of the Lincoln Highway as a military road have long been appreciated by many, but the car will doubtless be the cause of greater and keener interest being taken in the route by the United States government to the end that it will be made a boulevard all the way and as such of great value in time of war.[68]

Horseless Age preferred to see in the Marmon's accomplishment an example of what the modern automobile could do:

> Transcontinental runs are rapidly being relegated to the commonplace in motoring, but with each essay at covering the roads from the Atlantic to the Pacific the speed, sturdiness and flexibility of the modern automobile under unusually severe road conditions are strikingly demonstrated. Within the past month the continent has been crossed three times by automobiles [by the Saxon relay, the Marmon, and the Pathfinder high-gear car] under varying conditions and engaged in tests that have brought about surprising records.[69]

The growing reliability and comfort of auto travel led the *San Francisco Call* to draw from the Marmon's trip another noteworthy conclusion:

> The automobile is coming in direct competition with the fastest express trains. The Cadillac and Buick motor cars, which hold the coast and valley route records between San Francisco and Los Angeles, were sent along at a faster clip than the speediest iron monsters running between these two cities. Now the coast to coast record has gone a-glimmering.[70]

Expanding on this idea, *MoToR* wrote in its September 1916 issue:

If you are traveling by rail from the Atlantic to the Pacific you can make the trip in about four days and a half, providing you make good connections. Taking a 5:30 P.M. train from New York you land in Chicago twenty-four hours later and at 8 o'clock that evening you are on one of the fast trains bound for the Pacific coast, where you will land about three days later.

By automobile it is nearly as fast, now that the Marmon has set up the new mark of 5 days 18 hours 30 minutes, but of course you do not travel so comfortably, nor is such a trip an every-day occurrence in the motor world. But the record simply shows you the wonderful strides being made nowadays in automobile speed.

Thirteen years ago Dr. H. N. Jackson and S. K. Crocker, driving a Winton, traveled from the Pacific to the Atlantic in sixty-four days. They were the pioneers and their record was then a seven-day wonder. Since that time months have been clipped off the ocean-to-ocean mark until now we are pushing the railroads in the matter of time.[71]

As is reflected in its post-run advertising (see Fig. 99), the Nordyke & Marmon Company saw in Stevens's trip implications relating to the design of its auto. "This epoch-making run by the Marmon 34 demonstrates again the soundness of its advanced scientific construction—the extensive use of aluminum, the deep section frame, the new rear spring suspension, the self-oiling chassis lubrication system and other features."[72] Many firms that supplied parts to the Marmon company were also quick to advertise their contributions to the record-setting run. The standard parts included 34 x 4½-inch Goodrich Silvertown tires on Houk wire wheels; Sheldon springs; Hartford shock absorbers; Hyatt, New Departure, and U.S. bearings; AC spark plugs; Stromberg carburetor; Bosch magneto, generator, and starter; Van Sicklen speedometer; and Thermoid clutch and brake linings. The engine used Lynite aluminum alloy, Non-Gran bronze bushing material and Monogram oil.[73]

STEVENS CHALLENGES AUTOMAKERS

In later years, Stevens encouraged the development of better autos by creating the Stevens Challenge Cup in 1927. "What the manufacturers know about automobile performance they learned from racing and . . . endurance touring contests," explained Stevens, by then one of the oldest members of the Society of Automotive Engineers. "Many claims for speed abilities of standard stock cars have lately been made. Flash speed as against sustained speed means very little. It is the latter quality that really counts"—and it was the latter quality that Stevens exhibited to break the transconti-

Fig. 99. Marmon's advanced design made the transcontinental record possible, the automaker claimed. (Saturday Evening Post, September 16, 1916)

nental speed record in 1916. By 1927, the year Stevens announced his award, buyers of automobiles were demanding more sedans, coupes, and other cars with closed bodies and were consequently buying fewer open touring cars. In recognition of this trend, Stevens's traveling trophy went to the regular-production closed car maintaining the highest speed above 60 mph during a 24-hour run on the Indianapolis Motor Speedway.[74] Stutz was the first winner of the Stevens Challenge Cup.

Stevens died of "heart disease" on November 16, 1935, at age 61. "I remember him as an old man in the 1930s," writes historian Ned Comstock of Rome, "wearing a stained smock, peering uncertainly through steel-rimmed spectacles at his micrometer, fussing endlessly with his automobiles."[75] The fate of the Marmon transcontinental car, chassis number 1816016, is not as well documented.[76] A victim of the Great Depression, the Marmon company made its last autos—a V-16 model that sold for about $5,000, depending on the body style—in 1933. For decades afterward, however, a company related to the original Nordyke & Marmon Company manufactured commercial vehicles, including buses, four-wheel-drive trucks, and over-the-road trucks, bearing the Marmon and Marmon-Herrington names. The last Marmon truck rolled off the assembly line in Garland, Texas, on February 5, 1997.[77]

MARMON RUN INTERESTS MILITARY

Stevens's 1916 Marmon crossing did not lead to immediate changes in the military use of automobiles. But it undoubtedly influenced government planners, who were coming to believe that "large bodies of troops can be mobilized by motor cars before the railroads operating in the respective districts can get sufficient cars ready to transport them," the New York Times reported in August.[78] Stevens's trip did, however, pique the military's interest in the automobile. Six weeks after the Marmon run, an automobile relay that again carried a War Department message duplicated its effort and bettered its time. The relay left Plymouth, Massachusetts, on September 16 and, traveling by way of the Yellowstone Trail, arrived in Seattle five days later. It was just 72 minutes behind its schedule—"due to an accident to one of the automobiles."[79]

It would, however, be years before the Lincoln Highway or any other transcontinental road could handle heavy military loads. On July 7, 1919, an Army convoy left Washington, D.C., to "determine by actual experience the feasibility of moving an army across the continent." Some eighty autos and heavy trucks and nearly three hundred soldiers would travel to San Francisco, mostly along the Lincoln Highway. The vehicles raised clouds of dust on dry stretches, sank in the mud and slid or overturned on wet stretches, and broke through scores of flimsy wooden bridges everywhere.[80] The 62-day ordeal was calamitous, according to a young lieutenant on the convoy, Dwight D. Eisenhower. In *At Ease: Stories I Tell to Friends*, Eisenhower recounts his experiences as part of the convoy in a chapter titled "Through Darkest America." The hardships—"some days when we had counted on sixty or seventy or a hundred miles, we would do three or four"[81]—inspired President Eisenhower's 1956 signing of a funding bill to speed the creation of a 42,000-mile U.S. interstate highway system, intended in part to serve the military in times of war.

Another president, Woodrow Wilson, signed his name to the first federal-aid highway bill in July 1916, the month of the Marmon crossing. The rainstorms that slowed the Marmon's progress in Wyoming, Utah, and Nevada demonstrated the urgent need for such assistance, as coast-to-coast travel in one respect had changed very little since 1903: motorists were still at the mercy of the weather. As of 1916, the Lincoln Highway was paved throughout New Jersey and most of Pennsylvania and Ohio. From Indiana on west, however, the route remained primarily dirt or sand. In many such areas, America's premier transcontinental road didn't deserve to be called a "highway."

"NO LONGER A PLAYTHING OF THE RICH"

In overcoming poor roads, the Marmon journey underscored the great improvements to the automobile since the first transcontinental crossing in 1903. Gone were the days when an automaker sent its product from coast to coast simply to prove "that the automobile is a reliable means of locomotion and no longer a plaything of the rich."[82] This point was no longer in question. A modern transcontinental crossing was more a race than an endurance contest. So fast and reliable was a well-engineered American-built auto in 1916, the Marmon trip proved, that it could run virtually nonstop for six days with only minor mechanical problems—and those due to bad roads.

This is not to say that in 1916 every American auto could have done what the Marmon did. The popular Studebaker, for instance, was crudely designed in comparison to the Marmon, as engineer Carl Breer learned upon joining Studebaker in 1916. Studebaker's 6-cylinder engine was notorious for hard starting and rough running. Breer's solution was to install a simple baffle above the updraft carburetor, which distributed the fuel more evenly to the cylinders, as well as incorporating other changes that boosted the engine's horsepower from 26 to 65.[83]

During his 1903 trek, Dr. H. Nelson Jackson reported that "in more remote places, where natives had never even seen a train, they mistook our machine for a railroad coach which somehow had got off the rails."[84] Some observers mistook the Marmon for a locomotive as well, but only because of its speed. By 1916, challengers were cutting not weeks and days but hours and minutes off the transcontinental speed record. Record-seeking coast-to-coast drivers, once intrepid explorers, were becoming modern motor tourists—speeding over the land but not engaging with it, instead stopping only for gas, oil, and food.

So fast was the Marmon's crossing that its coast-to-coast record "would be creditable," *Automobile Topics* claimed, even "if the car had been a racing machine in the hands of professionals."[85] Did somebody say "professionals"? Officials with the Hudson Motor Car Company were evidently listening, for later in 1916 Hudson hired professional racer Ralph Mulford to help set a record even more creditable than the Marmon's.

HUDSON SUPER-SIX SMASHES RECORDS TO GOTHAM AND BACK

8

Mulford came over the brow of a hill at sixty miles an hour and saw dead ahead of him a bridge, a herd of cattle blocking the way. He had to decide quickly whether he should go over the embankment or take his chances on running into the cattle.

—*Des Moines (Iowa) Register*

IN SEPTEMBER 1916, speed demon Ralph Mulford and two other race-car drivers set out to travel across the continent and back in record time. *Indianapolis News* reporter William F. Sturm, who had traveled with Cannon Ball Baker during his 1915 Stutz and 1916 Cadillac coast-to-coast junkets, organized the Hudson trip and again rode in the car as a passenger. Hudson dealer Arthur H. Patterson and Charles H. Vincent, an engineer with the Hudson Motor Car Company of Detroit, joined Mulford as relay drivers in what a San Francisco newspaper dubbed "one of the greatest events in the history of automobiling."[1]

248

The great event got off to an inauspicious start, however. A few days before the successful start was made, another Hudson left San Francisco, only to crash off a bridge, temporarily halting the attempt. Once on their way, the three men took turns driving a loaded car—besides baggage, its passengers often included Sturm, a guide, and a mechanic—from San Francisco to New York City and back, covering 6,952 miles in 10 days, 21 hours, 4 minutes (or, including the time spent idle in New York City, 11 days, 13 hours, 22 minutes). It was the first well-publicized transcontinental round trip since 1905–6, when Percy Megargel and David Fassett drove across the country and back in a 2-cylinder Reo touring car, a journey that took not ten days but nearly ten months.

The Hudson's eastbound journey cut the coast-to-coast record by more than half a day. Vincent drove the farthest—nearly 1,000 miles at one sitting, covering a day and two nights—Patterson the longest (in total hours), and Mulford perhaps the hardest. When the dust settled, the Hudson's journey had proven conclusively that American stock autos "can do any kind of long distance traveling under all kinds of road conditions," the *San Francisco Examiner* declared.[2] The speed with which the Hudson traveled also signaled that the automobile and eventually the motor truck would actively compete with U.S. railroads.

MULFORD MAKES HEADLINES

At the time, it was Mulford—rather than the implications of the record-setting trip—who attracted the most attention. Mulford had been much in the news for his exploits in Duesenberg, Lozier, and Peugeot race cars.[3] Moreover, he had long maintained that his Lozier, not Ray Harroun's Marmon Wasp, won the 1911 Indianapolis 500. Three circumstances suggest that Mulford was correct, writes automotive historian Russ Catlin. First, a "horrendous pile-up" that took place directly in front of them forced scorers and judges to dive for cover midway through the race. Drivers had also complained that scorers wandered off at other times during the event and had miscounted laps throughout the race. Second, the electric timing wire broke twice during the race, thereby increasing the possibility of a miscount. Three, Catlin argues that "Mulford took the finish flag alone and, on instruction from his pit," made three "safety laps" to ensure his victory. But when he finally stopped his car, "Harroun and the Marmon were receiving the winner's laurels." Mulford and the other drivers who took safety laps claimed that scorers counted these laps against the cars' final times.[4] Understandably, Mulford perhaps took pleasure in 1916 by defeating another Marmon—that driven by Samuel Stevens's relay team some seven weeks earlier—for transcontinental honors.

In 1916, Mulford was making headlines by racing Hudsons. On April 10, 1916, at Daytona Beach, Florida, he set a stock-car record by driving a Hudson Super-Six at an average speed of 102.53 mph over a one-mile course.[5] On May 1, 1916, Mulford drove the same Hudson in a one-car contest on the wood-surfaced Sheepshead Bay Motor Speedway in Brooklyn, New York. There, Mulford averaged 75.8 miles per hour to cover 1,819 miles in 24 hours, thus breaking a 1908 endurance record. Perhaps anticipating its upcoming double transcontinental trip, in a June 1916 ad in *Motorist* Hudson heralded the 24-hour mileage of their Super-Six as equivalent to the distance between New York City and Denver, or "more than two-thirds across the continent" (see Fig. 100). The Hudson that Mulford drove in the 1916 speed runs, both of which were supervised by the American Automobile Association, used a custom racing body on a stock chassis that was specially geared to a 2.61:1 ratio, according to press accounts. Despite such modifications, the AAA still considered the vehicle to be a stock car. "Man and machine covered more miles in two rounds of the clock than ever any man or any car have done before," *Automobile* said in an editorial about the 24-hour race. "In thinking of this run the splendid endurance of the man is the uppermost thought . . . but the endurance of the car must not be forgotten, as this is quite as splendid."[6]

And then, on August 11, 1916, Mulford's Super-Six beat five other cars—all with engines ranging from 231 to 300 cubic inches—to win his class on a winding, 12.5-mile course at Pikes Peak. The Hudson—with its 289-cubic-inch engine—climbed the 7.5 percent grade in 18:24.7 minutes, more than five minutes ahead of the second-place Duesenberg. The next day, Mulford placed second among sixteen racers in an open-class event won by a car fitted with a 402-cubic-inch 8-cylinder airplane engine.[7]

Patterson and Vincent were also experienced drivers. Patterson, a Hudson agent in Stockton, California, who also took part in the August 1916 Pikes Peak climb, had raced Hudsons on his own before joining the factory-sponsored racing team that the company formed in 1916. He had set a nonstop record in Santa Monica—just one of the many victories that led the *San Francisco Bulletin* to call him the "holder of numerous California records."[8] Before joining Hudson, Vincent had worked as a Thomas-Detroit mechanic and test driver and as an experimental engineer with the Ferro Machine & Foundry Company of Cleveland, makers of automobile and marine engines.

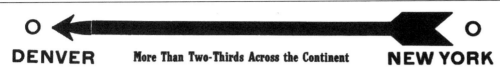

Fig. 100. Detail of a Hudson ad hailing "the greatest motor ever built." (Motorist, June 1916)

He worked on the Super-Six engine while he was at Hudson. Joining Packard in autumn 1916, Vincent helped design the V-12 Liberty airplane engine—a standard model built in several factories to supply allied warplanes in World War I. Vincent also directed testing at the Packard Proving Grounds in Utica, Michigan, until 1947.[9]

STIRRED TO ACTION

"Recent boasts of rival cars crossing the continent in fast time stirred the Super-Six to action," according to H. O. Harrison, the Hudson agent in San Francisco and nearby Oakland. In reality, the Hudson company, which had built its first 6-cylinder engine some years earlier, simply wanted to sell more cars, and it did so by promoting a new 6-cylinder engine that it introduced in its 1916 line (see Fig. 101). "The new type of Super-Six motor, as yet only a few months old (having come out this year), is controlled exclusively by Hudson patents," the automaker advertised. "All Motordom has therefore been against it."[10] It was the old we're-so-good-the-other-manufacturers-are-out-to-get-us argument. Back of it all was Hudson President Roy D. Chapin, who in 1905,

Fig. 101. At automobile shows, Hudson displayed this cutaway model of its new Super-Six engine. (NAHC)

1576-

when he was the Olds sales manager, helped to organize a cross-country race of two curved-dash Oldsmobiles.[11]

One of Chapin's purposes in 1905 was "to show the crying need for good roads," because good roads would boost car sales. In 1916, as vice president of the Lincoln Highway Association, Chapin had similar goals in mind. "From the very first he realized that the development of the rural sections of America was largely dependent on the condition of the highways," according to the 1926 book *Automotive Giants of America*. By the time America entered World War I in 1917, Chapin was such an authority on roads that he was named to head a committee "entrusted with the war-time energizing of highway transportation" and thus initiated a development that "has had a far-reaching effect on the entire problem of highway traffic."[12]

Three of the four record-setting coast-to-coast trips earlier in 1916 had been made on the Lincoln Highway.[13] The exception was Cannon Ball Baker, who drove the more southerly route that he favored. Naturally (given Chapin's involvement with the road), the plan was that the Hudson would also follow the Lincoln Highway, it was widely reported. The drivers did indeed take this well-marked route through all of California, Wyoming, and Nebraska, as well as in parts of Nevada and northern Indiana. But they left the highway between Indiana and New York City and strayed so often from it elsewhere that they actually traveled other routes more than half the time (see Table 17). It was just as well for Lincoln Highway backers, because the United States Tire Company would later boast that in the course of the Hudson trip its tires survived a vicious thrashing over "the worst roads on the American Continent."[14]

Although the tire maker reveals that Patterson chose the United States "royal cord" tires for the trip, Sturm was responsible for "the complete organization and arrangements made for handling the event," according to the *San Francisco Examiner*. "Supplies were stationed along the route and train connections were arranged so that each relay driver was ready to take the wheel upon arrival of the car." In addition to organizing the run, Sturm later wrote, "it was my good fortune to be able to be in the car for thousands of miles in the round trip."[15] As had relay drivers on other record-setting trips, between stints in the car the Hudson drivers rested aboard trains.

HIGH PERFORMANCE, LOW VIBRATION

The Hudson company said little about how it prepared and equipped the Hudson, although Hudson's San Francisco agent claimed, incredibly, that the run was made "without special preparation." In fact, like most other transcontinental cars, the Hudson had been modified, "with the top removed and extra gasoline and oil tanks under the seat," according to the *Des Moines (Iowa) Register*.[16] The car, which carried tire chains (but never used them, Sturm said), featured a spotlight on each windshield post and was fitted with a front bumper.

TABLE 17. West-to-East Route of the Hudson Super-Six

San Francisco start:
  12:01 A.M., Wednesday, September 13, 1916

California
  Placerville
Nevada
  Carson City
  Lahontan
  Fallon
  Frenchman
  Austin
  Carlin
  Elko
Utah
  Ogden
Wyoming
  Evanston
  Rock Springs
  Laramie
  Cheyenne
Nebraska
  North Platte
  Omaha
Iowa
  Council Bluffs
  Panora
  Panther
  Des Moines
  Grinnell
  Davenport
Illinois
  Moline
  Joliet
Indiana
  South Bend
Ohio
  Cleveland
Pennsylvania[a]
New York
  Buffalo
  Syracuse
  Albany

New York finish:
  6:32 A.M., Monday, September 18, 1916

SOURCES: Newspapers and auto journals.

[a] The Hudson passed through Pennsylvania, but news reports did not mention the cities along the route.

The record-setting Hudson was a 6-cylinder "light weight 7-passenger phaeton," the automaker said. "Previous records were made with roadsters and stripped cars, but the Hudson at all times carried three, and sometimes four, passengers, and with its baggage weighed in excess of 5,000 pounds."[17] By comparison, the Super-Six—an open touring car that sold for $1,475—weighed 3,200 pounds empty. The stock model had a 125½-inch wheelbase and used 35 x 4½ wheels—wire wheels, on the coast-to-coast car, which carried Michigan license number 5056M.[18]

First produced in 1909 as 1910 models, the Hudson cars were named for the company's principal financier, Joseph L. Hudson, "who owned Detroit's most successful department store."[19] The company had experimented with V-8 and V-12 designs for its 1916 models but instead introduced an improved flathead (valve-in-block) 6-cylinder engine. The engine's 3½ x 5-inch cylinders displaced 289 cubic inches—a modest-sized 6-cylinder by 1916 standards—and produced 76 horsepower, the company advertised. The new Hudson engine was a "super" version of the automaker's old power plant of the same size, which produced just 48 horsepower, according to automotive historian Maurice Hendry:

> The theme was higher performance and efficiency. To increase rpm, great pains were taken in reducing engine friction. Similar care went into enlarging gas passages and valves, and perfecting cam designs and carburetion to improve the breathing. Vibration at the higher rpm was minimized by the large dimensions and special design of the four-bearing crankshaft. Developed and patented by Hudson technician Stephen I. Fekete . . . it featured a special counterbalancing method using eight counterweights of unique design. Their positions were determined by careful calculations so as to balance inertia forces at all speeds, eliminate bending and make the shaft "float" in its bearings even at 3,000 rpm.[20]

"Last spring the wonder record for the one-way trip made by a famous eight was 2⅓ days longer than the time required by the Super-Six," Hudson boasted following Mulford's record-setting trip—the "famous eight" referring to Cannon Ball Baker's Cadillac V-8.[21]

HUDSON PICKS UP WHERE MARMON LEFT OFF

According to Sturm's schedule, the Hudson would reach New York City in 5 days, 10 hours, or less, newspapers reported—for a time at least 8½ hours ahead of the record set on July 29, 1916, by five relay drivers in a Marmon (see Chapter 7). "But in statements made before he started East," said the *San Francisco Chronicle*, Sturm "firmly believed that this time would be materially bettered."[22] The *Chronicle's* automobile editor, Leon J. Pinkson, and William C. Kiefer, San Francisco general agent of Wells Fargo and Company, acted as starters by sending off the Super-Six from its starting point near the *Chronicle* building at Lotta's Fountain, Third and Market streets, where the Marmon had ended its record-setting run. The Hudson's speedometer had been set to zero, Pinkson wrote. "Smiling at the old superstition of the thirteenth being an unlucky day, A. H. Patterson, the Stockton dealer, who drove the car on the first leg of the cross-continent journey, was checked out of San Francisco from in front of the *Chronicle* building at exactly 12:01 o'clock on Wednesday morning" (see Fig. 102).[23] Patterson would drive through California and most of Nevada, to Elko, where Mulford would take the wheel.

The September 13 departure was actually the Hudson's second attempt to set a coast-to-coast record, according to the *Daily Appeal* of Carson City, Nevada, among other sources.[24] Mulford and company muffed their first attempt. On Wednesday, Sep-

Fig. 102. A flash photo captures Sturm (foreground) and Patterson (at the wheel) near the San Francisco Chronicle building moments before the start. The unidentified cigar-smoking passenger in back is probably a local guide. What looks like a large flashlight on the windshield post is actually a searchlight. (NAHC)

tember 6, a week before the successful departure, the *Churchill County Standard*, of Fallon, Nevada, reported the arrival in town "last Monday" of a Hudson Super-Six automobile that was attempting to break the coast-to-coast speed record that a Marmon auto set earlier in the year. Although probably mistaken in reporting that Sturm was driving the Hudson, the *Standard* went on to describe the car's stop in Fallon:

> Arrangements had been made for a pilot out of here and "Chick" Thomas came over from Austin to direct them over the route, but the driver concluded that they would make the trip without guidance and left here at 11 o'clock [A.M.] and an hour and a half later was reported at Frenchman's station, having made the 35 miles across what is usually termed the worst piece of road on the Lincoln Highway in an hour and a half.[25]

Somewhere beyond Austin, however, the car met with a mishap. Reporting that "one manufacturer" had been frustrated in its attempt to make a trip from San Francisco to the East Coast and back, Sturm's newspaper, the *Indianapolis News*, explained that "the car . . . was wrecked shortly after its first start by going over a bridge and this start has been delayed until another car can be made ready."[26]

Behind the wheel on September 13 for the Hudson's second start, Patterson drove the short distance down Market Street to the boat landing, where the car and crew boarded a ferry for a 35-minute ride across San Francisco Bay. As the sponsors of such trips typically did, the Hudson company had lined up checkers—people who would certify when the transcontinental auto passed through their towns. Hudson had assembled perhaps the most eclectic group of checkers ever. *Automobile* published a list that included, besides the usual reporters, editors, and auto-club members, a blacksmith, a lumber dealer, a clergyman, an undertaker, and two dentists.[27] Quite possibly all were Hudson owners.

PATTERSON'S PACE "SENSATIONAL"

The Lincoln Highway offered motorists routes both north and south of Lake Tahoe, situated on the California-Nevada border. Speeding away from the coast, Patterson and Sturm drove the south fork through Placerville, California, and over the Sierra Nevada to reach Carson City, Nevada, at 7:34 A.M. on Wednesday. "Over California's world-famous highways the car sped. Local records were shattered," Sturm later wrote in an article for the *San Francisco Chronicle*.[28] Patterson in fact averaged an impressive 33.5 mph in traveling 253 miles from San Francisco.[29] His pace into Carson City "over the summit of the Nevada mountains is one of the sensational features of the trip," raved the *San Francisco Examiner*. "This section was one of the most difficult on the journey across the continent and the high speed maintained by Patterson on this stretch was a big factor" in breaking the coast-to-coast record.[30]

Patterson paused eight minutes in Carson City, according to the *Carson City Daily Appeal*, which mistook a following car—perhaps carrying a pilot—for a second transcontinental racer: "Both cars stopped only long enough to replenish with gasoline and water and enable the drivers and assistants to eat a light lunch furnished at the car." According to the *Churchill County Standard*, from Carson City the car would travel northeast through Lahontan, bypassing Reno and temporarily abandoning the Lincoln Highway. From Fallon, Patterson would travel through Frenchman, Austin, and Carlin to end his relay at Elko, the newspaper reported (see Table 18).[31]

TABLE 18. Drivers for the Relays on the Hudson Trip, September 13–18, 1916

City to City	Driver
San Francisco–Elko, Nev.	A. H. Patterson
Elko, Nev.–Laramie, Wyo.	Ralph Mulford
Laramie, Wyo.–Omaha, Neb.	Patterson
Omaha, Neb.–South Bend, Ind.	Mulford
South Bend, Ind.–New York City	C. H. Vincent

SOURCE: Hudson press release, which ran in many newspapers.

"WHY DIDN'T YOU STOP OUT HERE?"

From Austin, motorists following the Lincoln Highway would continue east and then northeast to reach Salt Lake City, traveling south of the Great Salt Lake. The Hudson, however, traveled northeast from Austin to Elko, and then through Utah around the north side of the Great Salt Lake, passing through Ogden but bypassing Salt Lake City altogether. In Elko, a crowd of spectators gathered while Mulford and his mechanic waited impatiently for Patterson to appear. The *Elko Daily Free Press* for Thursday, September 14, described the scene in detail:

> Boyish in appearance, with keen, sharp eyes, well-knit frame and elastic step, Ralph Mulford, one of the most famous of the world's auto drivers, paced up and down in front of Simcox's garage in company with his mechanician, Louis Kalinskey, last night about eight o'clock, every now and then casting an anxious glance up towards the Carlin road and making some remark that "I wish she'd get here." And Louis concurred with Ralph in wishing the same thing.
> Reason for their anxiety: a Hudson Super-Six car, stripped of top and driven by A. H.

Patterson of Stockton with L. Kuhn as mechanician, had left San Francisco at 12:01 of the 13th on a record breaking run to New York. . . . And Ralph and Louis were to take the car from this city to Laramie, where Patterson would again pick it up and drive to Omaha. . . .

There was a goodly crowd gathered and all were speculating on when it would arrive, when Ralph and Mrs. C. L. Fike heard a roar up the road and saw the flash of lights on the sky. With a shout of joy, the boyish driver hurried into his driving togs and prepared to take the speeding monster on its way. On around the ball park with clattering Klaxons and lights glittering, the big Hudson, in a cloud of dust, tore for the main road, came up opposite the Simcox garage, hesitated a second, swung to the right abruptly on two wheels and tore madly towards the garage door.

"Hey, stop her right here," shouted Mulford, indicating the red gasoline pump at the edge of the sidewalk. On came the car, past Mulford into the house and stopped with a smoking of tires as the brakes gripped the bands. "What's the matter with you—why didn't you stop out here?" shouted the excited Ralph. A dirt-stained, grimy face peered out from behind the steering wheel and said: "Rear wheel and muffler bent a bit—guess you'll have to fix them. What in——time is it?"

Two men climbed out of the car, were told the time by a hundred watches and Patterson, the driver, exclaimed with pride: "Just twenty hours and twenty-nine minutes from 'Frisco!" Calling the editor of the *Free Press* to him, he asked that a book be signed showing that the time of arrival was 8:29, number of miles traveled according to the speedometer, 578, and that the city where [the] stop was made was Elko. Mrs. C. L. Fike, W. H. Peace and C. F. Clark, city editor of the *Free Press*[,] signed the book, and Patterson tore for the Western Pacific depot where he caught the 8:25, luckily for him, late, to Salt Lake, where he will journey on to Laramie to pick Mulford up if he gets that far.

Mechanicians swarmed all over the big machine; some put in water, some got in the others' way and all seemed to be at a loss what to do next. Mulford then got busy and with orders, began the work of getting the car ready for its next trip. Wheels were changed and brakes adjusted—three times Mulford told the mechanics to take off the old broken muffler and replace it with a new one from a spick and span Hudson on the floor, and three times they managed to get the muffler—the old one—off and shook a little dirt out of it and put it back. It was on his mind, and when nearly everything was ready, he asked about the muffler and somebody told him that the old one had been put back on. There were several chunks of explosive language ejaculated into the atmosphere from the gun of Mulford, and he demanded that the new muffler be put on and this time, after much grunting and lying underneath the car, Louis got it on, wired the brother up tight and they were ready to go.

The car was backed to the little red pump that pays dividends to Sim and Johnny Rockefeller, and she was loaded up with "joy juice." Mulford, a racing cap over his head and ears and bundled up in a driving coat, piled in, followed by Kalinskey, his mechanician, and Jimmy Hays, the local expert, who was to pilot them to Ogden. With a roar from her big engine, the car jumped into low at exactly 10:16, slipped over into second like a flash and was running 35 miles an hour before twenty feet had been traveled. And the last seen of Mulford and his Hudson Super-Six, they went around the corner by the Pioneer block in a cloud of dust, traveling somewhere in the neighborhood of forty miles an hour.[32]

By covering the distance to Elko in 20 hours, 28 minutes (not 29, as he said), Patterson averaged 28.2 mph. According to the *Salt Lake (City) Tribune*, he was 6½ hours ahead of schedule. The Hudson beat railroad time from the West Coast to Elko, the *San Francisco Chronicle* reported, for Patterson "dropped off packages of the *Chronicle* addressed to the *Chronicle* dealers in the principal cities through which he passed and in all cases the papers arrived hours before the regular shipments that go by train."[33]

As Sturm described it, Mulford drove all night to reach Ogden on roads that were just "fair."[34] The Hudson covered the 842 miles from San Francisco to Ogden in 32 hours, 29 minutes, at a clip of 25.9 mph. Thursday's *Ogden Standard* recorded Mulford's arrival:

> There was panting, chugging and coughing at the garage of the Ogden Motor Car company at 2331 Hudson avenue, at 9:30 o'clock this morning. The noise was not unlike that common to the garage, but had a distinctive character in that it attracted attention to its source, which was described as being a big Hudson car, which the company handles exclusively in this territory, and which was the vehicle being used by Ralph Mulford, famed the country over as a speed king, and two other companions in an endurance run from San Francisco to New York.
>
> The automobilists were at the garage just one hour during which they purchased the supplies necessary to carry them to the next stopping point—Evanston, Wyo. They were piloted out of the city by L. L. Haines, local manager of the company. Mr. Haines will accompany the autoists as far as Evanston, returning to the city tomorrow.[35]

Driving "the Hudson Super-Six in which he and Mrs. Botterill recently crossed the continent," Salt Lake City auto dealer Frank Botterill also met Mulford in Ogden to pilot him to Evanston.[36] From Evanston, Mulford drove throughout the day Thursday and into Friday, again following the Lincoln Highway, through coal-rich Rock Springs and across southern Wyoming to Laramie.

FIERY "TALE" OF WONDER

"The Hudson Super-Six automobile making the trip from San Francisco to New York to break the record passed through Rock Springs at 5:54 on Thursday afternoon, having made the trip from Ogden in seven hours and five minutes," reported the *Rock Springs Miner*. "In the car were Ralph Mulford and Mr. Sturm. Dan Ganiard of the Western Auto Transit Co. of this city piloted them from Evanston to Laramie." The Hudson "racing car" reached Laramie at 5:00 A.M. on Friday, September 15, and stayed just twenty minutes, reported the *Laramie Republican*, which was obviously unaware of the driver's renown. "A man named Mulford brought the car from Elko, Nev. The party were about two hours behind time, having encountered some very hard roads between Rock Springs and this city, caused by the recent heavy rains in that vicinity. It is expected the lost time will be more than made up across Nebraska."[37]

And so it was, according to Sturm, who makes no mention of rain. Rather, he wrote: "Like a comet the car sped through Wyoming, leaving a fiery tail of wonder behind it. The rough desert going stretched out detaining hands, washes [washouts] bade the car pause and the intense cold, augmented by the speed of the car, proved a big inconvenience to the drivers. But . . . the car pressed on." Sturm exaggerated the wonderful speed of the Hudson comet, however, for the auto's average speed of only 18.1 mph between Ogden and Cheyenne confirms that the roads were as poor as the Laramie newspaper described. Moreover, the 30-hour drive on desert roads from Elko to Laramie had taken its toll on Mulford, according to the *Des Moines Register*. "He said the terrible monotony of that drive, the glare of the sun and the dust, was more exhausting than his twenty-four-hour drive, when he made the world's record in the Hudson Super-Six chassis, traveling 1,819 miles."[38]

Patterson was at the wheel with Sturm beside him when the Hudson reached Cheyenne at 7:53 A.M. on Friday, the car having at that point covered 1,246 miles from San Francisco, as the *Cheyenne State Leader* noted. The local *Wyoming Tribune* reported that the Hudson "passed through Cheyenne at a clip estimated at 65 miles an hour . . . [and] slowed up in front of W. E. Dinneen's garage while a small box of provisions was loaded. Plans had been made to prop up the rear wheels of the machine and install a new wheel here but the drivers signaled that they would not make the change and continued on their way." Somehow, though, the *Tribune* had got the idea that it was witnessing a nonstop run, leading it to append a few colorful, and clearly inaccurate, details:

> The machine will not be stopped once on its transcontinental race, unless a break down occurs. It is sealed so that it cannot be stopped. Repairs are made on the run, the machine being throttled down to its slowest speed while these repairs are in progress, and the driving being continued night and day.[39]

Provided they were able to maintain their present pace, the Hudson drivers "will equal the best time made by the fastest straight through trains between the two coast metropolises," the *Cheyenne State Leader* predicted. In fact, "as the car flew East she gathered speed," Sturm recalled. "The desert lands merged almost intangibly into the prairies of Nebraska, with the grazing cattle and huge fields of grain." Sturm also

TABLE 19. Average Speed of the Hudson Super-Six

City	Mileage	Local Arrival Time	Elapsed Time	Average Speed	Cumulative Average Speed
Carson City, Nev.	253	7:34 A.M., Sept. 13	7h-33m	33.5 mph[a]	33.5 mph
Elko, Nev.	578	8:29 P.M., Sept. 13	20h-28m	25.1 mph	28.2 mph
Ogden, Utah	842	9:30 A.M., Sept. 14	32h-29m	22.0 mph	25.9 mph
Cheyenne, Wyo.	1,246	7:53 A.M., Sept. 15	54h-52m	18.1 mph	22.7 mph
Omaha, Neb.	1,844	2:05 A.M., Sept. 16	72h-04m	34.8 mph	25.6 mph
Des Moines, Iowa	2,029	10:06 A.M., Sept. 16	80h-05m	23.1 mph	25.3 mph
South Bend, Ind.	2,491	12:07 A.M., Sept. 17	94h-06m	33.0 mph	26.5 mph
Buffalo, N.Y.	2,971	2:35 P.M., Sept. 17	107h-34m	35.6 mph	27.6 mph
New York City	3,476	6:32 A.M., Sept. 18	123h-31m	31.7 mph	28.1 mph

SOURCES: Arrival times have generally been taken from local newspapers; distances are primarily from a table printed in *Motor World*, Sept. 20, 1916, p. 14. Sources also include auto journals, San Francisco newspapers, and Hudson ads.

[a] Average speeds are from the previous city to the present one. The Hudson started in San Francisco.

noted the "significant fact that Omaha was reached in three days and four minutes"—at 2:05 A.M. Saturday, September 16, given the two-hour time difference between San Francisco and Omaha.[40] The Hudson had therefore covered the 1,844 miles from San Francisco at a pace of 25.6 mph. Arriving at Omaha, the car was eight hours ahead of Sturm's schedule, according to the *Des Moines Register*, and nearly eighteen hours ahead of the Marmon's pace between Omaha and San Francisco. The car did indeed gather speed further east, as Sturm asserted, but only after making a two-hour repair stop near Des Moines (see Table 19).

CRASH INJURES MULFORD AND DAMAGES CAR

Taking the wheel from Patterson in Omaha, Mulford left the Lincoln Highway in Iowa and Illinois on his drive to South Bend, Indiana. He would travel through Council Bluffs, Panora, Des Moines, Grinnell, and Davenport, following both the River-to-River Road and central Iowa's Panora Speedway—"probably the fastest fifty miles in Iowa, being almost free from turns and practically level," the Panora newspaper boasted. "Twenty miles of the Speedway is now graveled between Panora and Des Moines."[41]

Perhaps because the speedway allowed such fast running, Mulford ran into trouble midway between Panora and Des Moines, on the very graveled stretch the Panora paper mentioned. According to the *Des Moines Register*:

> At Panther, Ia., Mulford came over the brow of a hill at sixty miles an hour and saw dead ahead of him a bridge, a herd of cattle blocking the way. He had to decide quickly whether he should go over the embankment or take his chances on running into the cattle. He chose the latter course and killed two cows. That delayed him over two hours, but despite this stop he drove on to South Bend, Ind., where Charles H. Vincent took the wheel.[42]

Mulford "was hurt about the head" and received "a few other scratches," reported the *Guthrie County Vedette* in Panora, about fourteen miles west of Panther. "He was brought to Panora where Dr. Sones patched him up. The Miller Garage made repair on the car, and after a delay of two hours [he] was on his way."[43] Some accounts, however, put the delay at three hours.

The record is unclear about whether Mulford's passengers were also injured. The crash, however, damaged the Hudson's radiator, windshield, and headlamps, according to various accounts. "The run would have been made much quicker had it not been that a cow stuck her hoof through the radiator of the car in Iowa," remarked one report.[44] The front bumper was evidently destroyed as well, for when the Hudson arrived back in San Francisco it sported a skinny bumper, mounted higher than the stout, squarish bumper that it originally carried.

The Hudson drivers faced another danger when cresting hills: "They figured that the road followed the telephone poles when they went up a hill and they didn't know if there'd be a turn on the other side," according to Mulford's son, Ralph K. Mulford, Jr., "Going as fast as they were going, they followed the telephone wire, figuring that's where the road would be."[45] Fortunately, it usually was.

THROUGH CLEVELAND A-WHOOPING

A group of mechanics and assistants joined reporters in checking Mulford into Des Moines at 10:06 A.M. on Saturday. "The service men filled the gas and water tanks, gave the car lubricating oil and changed a tire for Mulford," the *Des Moines Capital* reported. "He was off for the east in just five minutes." Although a poor reproduction, a photo in the *Des Moines Register* shows that the Hudson arrived in Des Moines after its accident with its headlights, windshield, and spotlights intact—unless they had been replaced at Panora. The car appears to be missing its front bumper, however. Despite the crash and the subsequent delay for repairs, Mulford drove 326 miles across Iowa in 10½ hours to average 31 mph overall, or 37.6 mph for his actual running time, the *Register* noted.[46]

According to the Hudson company, at 3:00 P.M. on Saturday Mulford reached Davenport, where he crossed the Mississippi River into Moline, Illinois. He raced across that state on a route that went south of the Lincoln Highway, through Joliet, arriving there at 8:25 P.M., according to *Motor World*. At 12:07 A.M. Sunday, September 17, after twenty-two hours of driving, Mulford pulled into South Bend, putting the Hudson only 985 miles from New York City by its chosen route. Between San Francisco and South Bend, a distance of some 2,491 miles, the Hudson had averaged 26.5 mph. From South Bend, Vincent set off on the 480-mile drive to Buffalo, New York, where Mulford would take the wheel for the last leg of the journey.

East of South Bend, at Elkhart, Indiana, the Lincoln Highway turned southeast. But the Hudson parted company with the transcontinental road by continuing east along the Lake Erie shoreline to Cleveland and across the northwestern tip of Pennsylvania to Buffalo. From there, Mulford would follow the popular route through central New York—east to Syracuse and Albany, and then south along the Hudson River valley into New York City. The Hudson Super-Six drivers routinely slowed down in cities, according to the *New York Tribune*. "In Cleveland, however, the car was paced by motorcycle police and it dashed through a-whooping. Of course, all speed laws were fractured at night. They had to be to keep up the average."[47]

THE CAR'S HERE—WHERE'S RALPH?

Vincent reached Buffalo, 2,971 miles from San Francisco, at 2:35 P.M. on Sunday, September 17, ready to turn over the wheel to Mulford. Mulford, however, was late arriving, and at 3:10 P.M. Vincent drove on. As the *San Francisco Chronicle* explained it, "Mulford's train was twenty minutes late in reaching Buffalo and the car proceeded without him. He continued on to Albany, thinking he would catch the record breaker; but here, too, he was too late, and he never got his hand on the wheel again, Vincent driving the entire last lap, a distance of 910 miles, without leaving the seat." (Another source, perhaps more reliable, puts the distance from South Bend to New York at 985 miles.)[48] Vincent had to contend with more towns on his route than the other drivers

Fig. 103. The record-setting Hudson attracted a small knot of New Yorkers despite the early hour. Mulford is at the wheel, flanked by Vincent, who actually drove the final leg of nearly 1,000 miles. In the back, Sturm, wearing goggles, is on the far side; to his right is Louis Kalinskey. In the background is the Columbus Monument. (NAHC)

had encountered on theirs, according to one press account, yet he still averaged 33.5 mph from South Bend to New York City.

Heading south from Albany, Vincent drove through his second straight night, reaching Columbus Circle at 59th and Broadway at 6:31 A.M. on Monday, September 18 (see Fig. 103). James A. Hemstreet of the American Automobile Association checked him in at this time, according to most news accounts, although two reports said 6:32 A.M. This must, in fact, be the correct time because, as was almost universally reported, Mulford, Patterson, and Vincent left San Francisco at one minute past midnight on September 13 and traveled coast to coast in 5 days, 3 hours, 31 minutes. Their time cut an impressive 14 hours, 59 minutes, from the Marmon's seven-week-old record. As Sturm later summed it up:

COAST TO COAST BY AUTOMOBILE

Ask a man to average twenty-five miles an hour for ten hours over an average road and he will tell you he does not wish to put his car on the scrap heap. Yet on its trip to New York the Hudson averaged 28.14 miles an hour. Were road conditions manufactured to include every variety possible they could not have more closely met requirements.[49]

Despite the variable roads that Sturm described, only three tire punctures slowed the auto, both the *New York Herald* and the *New York Tribune* reported.

With a notable lack of excitement, New York City's daily newspapers ran short, stuffy summaries of the trip—all nearly identical and obviously based on a Hudson press release. The absence of any vivid, first-hand descriptions of the car's arrival suggests that the New York press corps generally ignored it. While their lack of enthusiasm was perhaps due to the early hour, more likely it was because the press had come to regard such runs more as publicity stunts than as genuine news. In San Francisco, however, where the round-trip transcontinental run both started and ended, the large dailies paid much closer attention to the event.

TREK HINTS AT POSSIBILITIES

Of course, the trip *was* a publicity stunt, a colorful spectacle that helped Hudson advertise its new engine and the other refinements it had introduced in its 1916 models. All the same, by cutting the coast-to-coast speed record by more than half a day despite its heavy load, Hudson underscored the automobile's potential usefulness in moving people and products across the continent quickly and reliably. Was the new time low enough to compete with the speed of the railroads? No, according to New York-based *Automobile*, which noted that "the best railroad time across the continent is 3 days, 21 hr., 45 min., according to railroad officials here."[50] Even so, the railroads might have done well not to rest too firmly on their laurels.

The record—which "will probably remain undisturbed for some time to come," predicted the *San Francisco Bulletin*—was what the *San Francisco Chronicle* called "a wonderful compliment to the sturdiness of the car and the power and flexibility of the motor."[51] The *San Francisco Examiner* had even more to say:

This latest demonstration of the speed and endurance of the modern motor vehicle is another proof of the possibilities of these machines for long distance transportation. In maintaining a speed of over twenty seven miles an hour for the trip across the continent the drivers of the Hudson machine had to hold their car at top speed on the good stretches of road and send it through the rough stretches at as high a speed as the roads would permit.

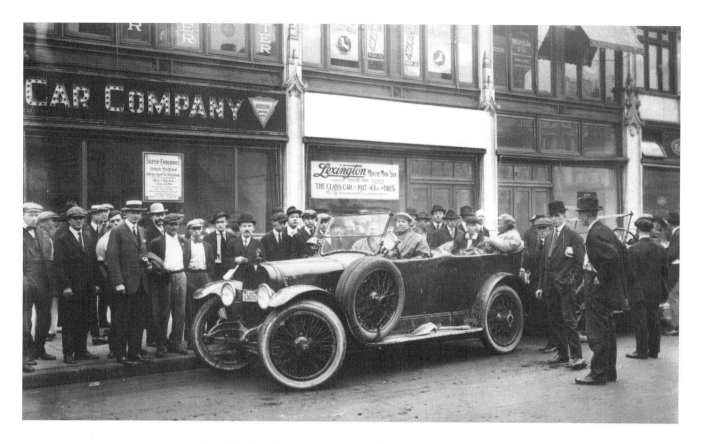

Fig. 104. Mulford pulls up to the local Hudson agency soon after arriving in New York City. The front bumper is missing, destroyed in the Iowa collision. (AAMA)

Considering the great variety of the country and road conditions over which they had to travel the time established makes the record one of the most unusual events in the history of automobile racing. . . . The contrast between this time and the early cross continent automobile records shows the wonderful advance which has been made in motor car construction as well as highway construction.[52]

FASTER STILL?

After a break of 16 hours, 18 minutes, in New York City "to replenish gasoline and lubricating oil and give the drivers a chance for some rest,"[53] Mulford, Patterson, and Vincent headed back to San Francisco. Hemstreet, the AAA official who had checked them in at 6:32 Monday morning, checked them out at 10:50 that night (see Figs. 104 and 105). "After an all-day inspection yesterday," revealed Tuesday's *New York Tribune*, "the car pulled out on the return trip, to see if the record might be improved upon." Exactly what repairs or maintenance the auto received in New York City the papers never specified. On its trip east, the car had carried bundles of newspapers; on its trip west, "the Hudson brought back a package sent by the president of the Wells Fargo Company to the head of the local branch of the big express company," the *San Francisco Bulletin* reported.[54]

Was it possible to go faster still? The frequent setting of coast-to-coast records had already proven beyond question the automobile's speed and endurance, as the *San Francisco Examiner* observed. The Hudson's performance thus "indicates that the future speed records for the cross continent trip will depend largely on the conditions of the Lincoln Highway," the paper concluded. "With this great highway improved in Nevada and Utah the time of motor travel across the country will be greatly lowered."[55] The Hudson drivers no doubt shared that precise sentiment after being delayed by poor roads in Nevada on their return trip to San Francisco.

With a few exceptions, returning home the drivers merely reversed their west-to-east route. They would still follow the River-to-River Road and Panora Speedway

Fig. 105. Equipped with a new bumper and makeshift top, the Super-Six is ready for its return trip to San Francisco. Mulford is at the wheel, and Sturm, with notebook in hand, stands beside the spare tire. The other men are unidentified. (AAMA)

across Iowa, for instance, but this time they would pass to the north of Iowa's capital city. "Service men from the Hudson-Jones Auto company and newspaper men will meet the car tomorrow to check it past Des Moines," the *Des Moines Capital* wrote on Tuesday, September 19. The car also revisited Panora, where Mulford and the Hudson were patched up after their run-in with the cattle. The citizens of Panora clearly had not forgotten the Hudson and its crew. As Thursday's *Guthrie County Vedette*, Panora's local paper, reported: "On the return trip the car passed through here at about 11:30 last night, several hours behind time, but even at that hour was greeted by a crowd of fans who had remained up to see them pass."[56]

MUD AND SPEED COPS

In general, the press paid little attention to the return trip because the Hudson failed to lower its eastbound time. The run through the East and Midwest was apparently uneventful, for the most part. "In Nebraska Patterson had quite a bit of trouble in avoiding 'speed-cops,'" the *San Francisco Chronicle* said, "but he succeeded in escaping from them." Patterson again drove the stretch from Elko to San Francisco, a distance he had covered in 20 hours, 28 minutes, on the trip to New York City. This time, however, it took him more than 35 hours. "From Elko, Nevada, to Carson [City] . . . the motor was forced to pull the car through a sea of deep and sticky mud which buried the wheels to the hubs," the *San Francisco Bulletin* remarked. "This going naturally checked the speed of the car, but the motor did not falter, according to the drivers, and pulled the record-breaker through without mishap" (see Fig. 106).[57] According to Sturm:

> Coming back to San Francisco from Elko on that thirty-five-hour grind every mile of which was real work . . . the alkali flats, water-covered, held out a detaining hand to grasp the tires; but the engine whirred, the wheels revolved and on we went. In spite of the soap-like going it was never necessary to put on chains. . . .
>
> The reader cannot appreciate the hardships through which a driver passes. Imagine being compelled to sit up in a comfortably furnished home for thirty-five hours and thirty-seven minutes. There is no more refined torture than wanting to sleep and not being permitted to. Yet Patterson had to do this thing, not in comfort, but in the most disagreeable surroundings.
>
> We left Elko at 2 in the morning of Saturday [September 23] and were deluged with muddy water without intermission practically up to Carson City. Pulling out one's finger nails, as was the practice of the ancients, had nothing on this ride for Patterson. And his experience was the experience of all the drivers.[58]

Fig. 106. Returning west, Patterson steers the mud-covered Hudson through rugged terrain at an undisclosed location. Sturm shares the front seat. The back seat passengers are unidentified. (RKM)

The men traveled through mud and water for 247 miles, according to the *Indianapolis News*, in a special dispatch sent once the car reached San Francisco. Quite possibly, Sturm was the author:

> All traffic was suspended, but the record car managed to creep along. On a stretch of high ground, while traveling forty-five miles an hour, a front wheel collapsed and Sturm was a victim of the accident, suffering injuries to three ribs. However, the car was jacked up, a new wheel put on and the journey resumed in an hour. Sturm's injuries are not serious and a physician says he will be able to take a deep breath in a week or two. . . . The transcontinentalists passed several machines mired in the mud, waiting for it to dry up.[59]

Press accounts from 1916 give no evidence that Sturm drove the Hudson. But when he died in 1937, his longtime employer, the *Indianapolis News*, implied that the Nevada accident occurred while Sturm was behind the wheel and Patterson was his passenger: "Pounding on through drenching rains, Sturm received several broken ribs when a front wheel collapsed and threw him into the steering wheel. But the two went on, determined to set a record."[60] If he actually drove the car, however, Sturm neglected to mention it at the time.

Patterson had better luck eluding "speed cops" in Nebraska than he did just west of his hometown, Stockton. "He was not so fortunate in California," the *San Francisco*

Chronicle revealed, "for at Livermore he was nabbed for exceeding the speed law, and he lost some fifteen minutes in going through the formality of being arrested and putting up bail money."[61]

AN OVATION AND A PARADE

Patterson got a better reception in San Francisco, just 39 miles from Livermore, where a cheering crowd awaited him (see Fig. 107). His arrival at Lotta's Fountain at 1:23 P.M. on Sunday, September 24, ended the fastest double transcontinental auto trip of the era. Unfortunately, though, bad roads in Nevada had prevented the drivers from breaking their own record. "Under similar road conditions as were met in the going trip the return would have been under 5 days," a Hudson ad proclaimed.[62]

But the car's return trip of 5 days, 17 hours, 33 minutes, at an average pace of 25.27 mph still beat the Marmon's July 1916 record by 57 minutes. And the round-trip time of 10 days, 21 hours, 4 minutes, cut a whopping 283 days from the record set during the first double transcontinental trek, the calamitous 1905–6 wintertime crossing made by Percy Megargel and David Fassett at the wheel of a Reo. Including the New York City layover, the Hudson took 11 days, 13 hours, 22 minutes, to travel from San Francisco to the East Coast and back. The automaker simply doubled the Hudson's San Francisco–New York City mileage (3,476) to arrive at a round-trip distance of 6,952 miles.

Monday's *San Francisco Bulletin* recounted the Hudson's finish:

No record-breaking crew has ever received the ovation that was given A. H. Patterson, who drove the car on the last lap of the journey, and W. J. [*sic*] Sturm, the popular and capable manager of the record-smashing trip, when the car was checked in by C. H. Kiefer of Wells Fargo, at Third and Market streets.

Fully 1000 motor-car enthusiasts were on hand to greet the record-breakers and it was with difficulty that Patterson pulled up to the finishing line. The crowd quickly closed in on the car, and the crew were highly complimented on the splendid showing made.

Aside from a heavy coating of mud and traces of long exposure in the open and in all kinds of weather, the Super-six showed no visible traces of the hard test to which it had been subjected. The motor was running as smoothly and showed the same power as when the start was made despite the ten days of continuous gruelling and difficult work it performed. . . .

There was a big parade today at noon about the main streets of the city. Owners of Hudson Super-sixes did honor to the record-breaker by parading behind the transcontinental car. Following the demonstration, the record-breaker was placed on exhibition at the headquarters of the Harrison Company, and will remain there for the rest of the week.[63]

Fig. 107. Outside the San Francisco Hudson agency, a crowd celebrates the arrival of the transcontinental car. Draped on the Hudson is a banner reading "From San Francisco to New York and Return." (RKM)

THREE RECORDS GONE

The automaker claimed that "counting all stops, and slowing down to the speed restrictions of 350 cities, towns and villages each way, the average time from San Francisco to New York and back to San Francisco was almost 700 miles a day."[64] This was perhaps true for the Hudson's unspecified running time. For its round-trip elapsed time, however, the car averaged 639 miles per day and 26.63 mph, compared to the Marmon's 602 miles per day at 25.10 mph.

The *Chronicle* pictured "Tom Wilkinson of the United States Tire Company congratulating the drivers." The Hudson Super-Six traveled coast to coast and back on "a single set of United States Royal Cord tires," the tire manufacturer asserted. But Sturm indicated otherwise: "Had we not had a few punctures and had to change wheels and tires we would have been able to negotiate the entire trip on one set of tires."[65] The automaker did not report the car's gas and oil consumption.

According to Sturm, organizer of the Hudson run, "To Patterson goes the credit for driving the greatest number of hours on the trip and to Charles Vincent the credit for the greatest mileage. Vincent drove the car out of South Bend for Buffalo on the way to New York. He was to meet Mulford there, but we had been moving as fast as

Fig. 108. Headlines
breathlessly proclaim the
Hudson achievement.

the train, and Mulford's train being late, Vincent had to drive the car on into New York, making his entire distance over 900 miles."[66]

Slyly playing up the feat, Patterson told reporters that the Hudson actually broke three speed records—between San Francisco and New York, between New York and San Francisco, and for the round trip. And he was right. Hudson easily outdid the previous best west-to-east time of 15 days, 2 hours, 12 minutes, set by Lester L. Whitman and four other drivers in 1906. In July 1916, the Marmon relay had set the New York–San Francisco speed record (and the fastest coast-to-coast time to that point), which the Hudson broke by almost an hour. And the Reo's 1905–6 trek—the best-publicized double transcontinental crossing prior to the Hudson's 1916 trip—had consumed nearly 10 months.

"VALUABLE TO EVERY AUTO OWNER"

"Twenty years ago the motor industry was in its infancy," Sturm wrote in 1916, reflecting on the implications of the Hudson run. "Today, in spite of rough roads it rivals the railroad trains on their ribbons of steel in its speed across the country." Many observers agreed. The Hudson's San Francisco–New York time was "so much faster than any previous record for the transcontinental journey that it stands out as one of the greatest events in the history of automobiling," said the *San Francisco Examiner*. "Speedway records have proved endurance and remarkable speed, but this fast time across the continent required not only those qualities, but efficiency over practical road conditions, and, therefore, is valuable to every owner of an automobile."[67] The fast time was valuable to the Hudson company as well, which was no doubt delighted by the publicity (see Fig. 108).

The Hudson dash also foreshadowed the rise of long-distance bus lines and the trucking industry. As the *Examiner* correctly observed:

Nothing could better demonstrate the possibilities of the automobile as a means of transportation than this round trip record. When a motor vehicle can make the trip from San Francisco to New York and back in a little over ten days it shows what could be done in case of emergency or with better roads.

If the Lincoln highway was completed clear across the continent the motor vehicle would be used as a vehicle for transporting passengers or freight and the present remarkable demonstration indicates that the motor car manufacturers are making machines that can do any kind of long distance traveling under all kinds of road conditions.[68]

The Hudson's fast trip apparently left some Midwesterners—and probably Americans everywhere—anxiously scanning the horizon, half expecting Ralph Mulford to rocket into view. Just days after the westbound Hudson roared through town, the Panora, Iowa, newspaper reported that a local motorist had driven his Packard across the state in record time. Added the newspaper, almost breathless with hopeful anticipation: "It is said that Ralph Mulford may take a shot at the new record in a Hudson super six."[69]

STURM JUMPS TO CHALMERS

Largely on the strength of his three transcontinental trips in 1915 and 1916, Sturm in 1917 became manager of contests and trials for the Chalmers Motor Car Company— evidently a part-time job, for he continued writing for the *Indianapolis News*. As a contrast to his work for Hudson, Sturm's first stunt for Chalmers was to seek a low-speed record. Sturm had the first- and second-speed gears removed from the transmission of a new Chalmers, which was then driven around outlying Detroit as slowly as possible, "illustrating the ability of the car to throttle down at low speed on high gear." The car covered 71.7 miles in 24 hours—at 2.99 mph.[70]

Over the years, Sturm managed several race drivers, including Frank Lockhart, who was killed in the crash of his Stutz Black Hawk while attempting to set a land speed record at Daytona Beach on April 25, 1928. Sturm also managed British racers Henry O. D. Segrave, Sir Malcolm Campbell, and Kaye Don, as well as Americans Cannon Ball Baker, Ray Keech, and Ralph Mulford. As automobile-racing editor of the *Indianapolis News*, Sturm "covered every Indianapolis Speedway race since the track was opened in 1909" until 1936. Born August 25, 1883, in Columbus, Indiana, he died of a "throat ailment" on August 26, 1937, at the age of only 54.[71]

END OF THE GOLDEN AGE

Mulford, a pilot as well as an auto racer, helped direct the inspection department of the Wright-Martin aircraft factory in New Brunswick, New Jersey, during World War I. "In later years, he was responsible for the development and testing of the modern passenger-type automobile we enjoy today," said an obituary following Mulford's death in Worcester, Massachusetts, on October 24, 1973, at the age of 87.[72] "It's a wonder to me how many of us old-time drivers survived auto racing's early years," Mulford mused in a 1969 article.[73]

The last Hudson appeared in 1957, but it was a Hudson in name only. Dwindling sales had forced the automaker to merge with Nash-Kelvinator Corporation in 1954, and the "Hudsons" produced from 1955 to 1957 were actually slightly restyled Nashes. Hudson, however, went down swinging, for racer Marshall Teague's "Fabulous Hudson Hornet" won twelve of the thirteen AAA stock-car events it entered in 1953.[74]

The Hudson's back-to-back five-day transcontinental dashes in 1916 represented the end of an era as well. Because of the outbreak of World War I, the Hudson's 1916 performance brought to a close the golden age of record-setting coast-to-coast auto trips, an age that had begun in 1903 when the first auto crossed America—in 63 days.

CONCLUSION

REGULAR COAST-TO-COAST air-mail flights were a decade away when, in 1909, three men in a Mitchell auto ferried a mock "war dispatch" from New York City to San Francisco. This military exercise—designed to win congressional funding for a U.S. Army automobile corps—illustrated how autos could serve the nation should an enemy seize or cripple America's railroads and silence its telegraph wires.

In 1910, seven years after their 72-day transcontinental trip in an Oldsmobile, Lester L. Whitman and Eugene I. Hammond, assisted by three relay drivers, repeated the feat in a Reo touring car. This time, they completed the journey in slightly less than eleven days, thereby trimming four days off the record set in 1906 by Whitman and Clayton S. Carris at the wheel of a Franklin auto. The speedy trip generated an incalculable amount of publicity for the Reo Motor Car Company and for several years discouraged other automakers from challenging the mark.

Seeking recreation, not records, forty "luxury loving" men, women, and children boarded a dozen Premier autos in 1911 for a 45-day sightseeing trip from Atlantic City to Los Angeles. It was the first time that an auto caravan and group of amateur drivers had crossed the country. The wealthy "Premier Motor Tourists" spent thousands of dollars on food, gasoline, lodging, and other necessities along their route through fourteen states. Their trip served notice that an entirely new industry was springing up to meet the needs of "autoists," to use the term then in vogue. In an effort to promote commerce, the forty tourists visited President William Howard Taft and at least five governors to lobby support for a federal road-building program. Their appeal resonated with some of the country's largest daily newspapers. "The tour of the . . . Premier cars from the Atlantic to the Pacific has proved that a highway across the United States would mean the sale of thousands more automobiles," observed the *Los Angeles Times*.[1]

Beyond hinting at the economic might and far-reaching influence of the fledgling automotive industry, the 1911 Premier caravan signaled what some commentators saw as larger societal change. "There is a general feeling that the Pacific and Atlantic coasts have been brought closer together and transcontinental touring by pleasure parties is now expected to become common since the first tour of this kind has been such an unqualified success," *Motor Age* asserted. "It has been proven that there are no unsurmountable difficulties in the way."[2]

Another lesson taught by the Premier Motor Tourists concerned the usefulness of trucks. The Premier caravan's baggage car—an automobile modified to look like a prairie schooner—carried a full load of luggage, food, and spare parts over most of the overland route. Had it traveled the entire distance between coasts, it would have become only the second "truck" (in the sense of a cargo-carrying vehicle) to have completed a transcontinental trip.

Later in 1911, a New York City touring agency assembled a fleet of Garford automobiles to conduct a second transcontinental sightseeing tour—with a twist. Whereas the Premier tourists were private owners who joined the trip by invitation only, the Raymond and Whitcomb Company's tour was open to the public. Tickets cost $875 apiece to board the nation's first "transcontinental automobile train," which steamed across the country on a 52-day, 4,000-mile schedule that closely followed an itinerary the Raymond and Whitcomb Company had published prior to the trip. As a profit-making venture, the Raymond and Whitcomb tour foreshadowed the rise of long-distance passenger bus lines, as well as the subsequent decline in passenger rail service. "The project marks the gasoline car as a common carrier of inter-State traffic," the *New York Times* observed, "and is for that reason most significant."[3]

The hardships faced by the Premier and Garford coast-to-coast tourists—routine hazards included deep mud, washouts, and bridgeless rivers—sparked a hue and cry for better roads. Partly in response to these trips, the privately funded Lincoln Highway Association was organized in 1912 and mapped out the Lincoln Highway the following year. But, as even its backers conceded, a trip along the Lincoln Highway remained "a sporting proposition" for many years to come.[4] Although more a trail than a highway between Omaha and the West Coast, the Lincoln Highway—the first ocean-to-ocean roadway—quickly became the most popular route for transcontinental motoring. Inspired as much by the 1911 Premier and Garford caravans as by Murdock's family tour of 1908, and at last having a marked route to follow, American motorists embraced the notion of touring long distances for pleasure.

Consequently, the sponsors of record-setting coast-to-coast trips in 1915 and 1916—automakers who were, of course, eager to boost sales—set their sights on demonstrating the higher speed and greater reliability of the modern automobile. In May 1915, Erwin G. "Cannon Ball" Baker single-handedly drove a Stutz Bearcat roadster across the country in eleven and a half days—the fastest crossing ever by a solo driver. What's more, an independent testing laboratory that inspected his Bearcat upon Baker's arrival in New York City from San Diego, California, found his car to be in generally good condition despite the hard usage it had received over primarily dirt roads.

Baker's trip and a number of city-to-city speed records set in 1915 "are valuable to the motor industry in that they point out to the buying public the absolute dependability of the modern automobile which now devours distance with an ease and speed that rivals even the railroad train," concluded the auto journal *MoToR*. "They have demonstrated most forcibly that it is possible to travel hundreds of miles over give-and-take roads at railroad speed and without mechanical mishaps of any sort."[5]

Whereas Baker averaged 327 miles per day during his 1915 Stutz run, the following year he sped from coast to coast at an average pace of 450 miles per day behind the wheel of a 1916 Cadillac. His performance settled all doubts about the speed and dependability of Cadillac's new V-8 engine—although in view of the car's dismal gas mileage—10 miles per gallon—the automaker was less successful in proving the thriftiness of its new power plant. Granted, Baker spent more time driving and less time sleeping in 1916 than he had a year earlier, but his Cadillac record of seven and a half days trimmed a full four days off his Stutz solo-driver record. Furthermore, as the letters he mailed from points along his route indicated, Baker traveled faster from coast to coast by automobile than did the U.S. mail by rail.

By placing seals on the engine, transmission, and other vital mechanical parts, backers of another 1916 transcontinental motor trip stressed the reliability of America's first "really scientific car." The high speed of the new Marmon 34—innovative among American autos for its extensive use of weight-saving aluminum—rivaled that of some coast-to-coast passenger trains, newspapers marveled. According to some observers, the Marmon's performance demonstrated the military's need both for a National Motor Reserve and a "great national highway"—one boasting more improvements than the privately financed Lincoln Highway could hope to offer—to serve the country's wartime needs. Congress got the message, passing a federal-aid highway bill in 1916.

To close out the pre–World War I era of transcontinental speed dashes, the Hudson Motor Car Company staged "one of the greatest events in the history of automobiling": the breaking of the Marmon's record on both legs of a double transcontinental trip. Hudson's five relay drivers lowered the one-way crossing time to slightly more than five days. Furthermore, the car scarcely missed a beat during almost eleven days of nearly continuous hard driving from San Francisco to New York City and back again. The Hudson trip underscored—and even added an exclamation point to—the emerging belief that the automobile (and eventually the motor truck) could actively compete with the railroads.

From H. D. Ashton to Frank X. Zirbes, the daring drivers who set transcontinental records between 1909 and 1916 helped sell prewar America on the utility of the automobile. Their hardships fueled a cry for better roads, their breakdowns showed manufacturers how to improve automotive designs, and their adventures inspired ordinary Americans to follow in their tire tracks.

Five of the eight runs described in this volume were speed runs, designed at least partly to prove that recent advances in both road construction and auto engineering made the automobile not only an enjoyable but also a practical means of transportation. Automobiles improved faster than the roads they traveled upon, however. The lightweight, 4-cylinder Reo that set a 1910 speed record of just under eleven days evolved into heavier 6- and 8-cylinder machines that were at least twice as powerful and capable of crossing the continent in a mere five days. For example, Cadillac's V-8 engine developed 77 horsepower; the 4-cylinder Reo's only 30. And a journey that had taken the Reo 10 days, 18 hours in 1910 took the Hudson Super-Six less than half as long—5 days, 3 hours—in 1916 (see Table 20).

The differences between the Mitchell crossing of 1909 and the five-day Hudson crossing of 1916—subjects of the first and last chapters in this book—vividly illustrate the changes that eight years had wrought. Sponsors of the Mitchell trip were satisfied that the car's 31-day crossing convincingly demonstrated that an automobile could carry military messages between coasts should an enemy disable America's railroads and telegraph wires. By contrast, the Marmon and Hudson, both of which crossed the continent in 1916 in under six days, were "pushing the railroads in the matter of time." The ease and speed with which automobiles could be pressed into service during a

TABLE 20. Comparison of Autos on Coast-to-Coast Speed Runs, 1910–1916

	H.P.	Weight	Weight-to-Power Ratio (lbs./H.P.)[a]	Average Daily Mileage	Average Speed	Time
Reo Thirty (1910)	30	2,350	78:1	331	13.78 mph	10d-18h-12m
Stutz Bearcat (1915)	60	—	—	327	13.75 mph	11d-7h-15m[b]
Cadillac V-8 (1916)	77	—	—	451	18.80 mph	7d-11h-52m
Marmon 34 (1916)	74	3,495[c]	47:1	602	25.10 mph	5d-18h-30m
Hudson Super-Six (1916)	76	3,200	42:1	639	26.63 mph	5d-3h-31m[d]

[a] Dividing the car's weight by its horsepower yields the number of pounds per horsepower, which provides the basis for a theoretical comparison of autos that vary greatly in weight and engine size.

[b] Cannon Ball Baker's 1915 Stutz dash failed to break the Reo's 1910 speed record. Baker, however, drove alone, whereas a relay team of five drivers took turns at the wheel of the Reo.

[c] Records do not indicate whether the coast-to-coast Marmon was a five-passenger touring car (3,450 pounds) or the seven-passenger model, which weighed 90 pounds more (3,540 pounds). The weight of 3,495 pounds splits the difference between the two figures.

[d] Time on the fastest leg of the transcontinental round trip.

time of national emergency—first evident during the Marmon run—clearly constituted one significant advantage the automobile offered over the railroads.

By 1916, the era had passed when an amateur could do what the first person to drive across the United States, Dr. H. Nelson Jackson, did in 1903: pack an automobile with tools, food, and a tent and depart on a record-setting transcontinental trip. High-speed driving and quick thinking behind the wheel had become more valuable traits in a driver than the ability to grind valves, read a compass, or work a block and tackle.

Although numerous transcontinental speed runs took place after World War I, an increasing number of automakers stressed gas and oil economy, rather than speed, on such trips. Moreover, these postwar crossings seemed routine in comparison to their prewar counterparts and consequently received less press coverage—perhaps partly because reporters also found it difficult to conduct interviews with drivers who rocketed across the country, stopping only for gas. Nonetheless, following World War I and until the mid-1930s, when interest in transcontinental runs waned, a handful of drivers made virtual careers out of making coast-to-coast trips to publicize various makes of automobiles, trucks, or buses. By far the biggest stars were Cannon Ball Baker, Ab Jenkins, Bob McKenzie, and Louis B. Miller.

During the eight years from 1909 through 1916, the period we have called the "age of acceptance," Americans embraced the automobile in growing numbers. Other writers have examined Henry Ford's quest for a "universal car," built as efficiently as possible on a moving assembly line and therefore cheap enough for almost anyone to own. But consumers didn't part with their money merely because they could afford to buy an automobile: they needed to see how an automobile would earn its keep. Whereas the earlier transcontinental trips merely proved that it was possible to drive across the country in an automobile, from 1909 onward such trips increasingly illustrated how pleasurable coast-to-coast travel could be.

In short, each of the eight journeys described in *The Record-Setting Trips* represented a public test of the automobile's performance and reliability. The machines scored admirably well in convincing the public that automobile travel—once a daring exploit demanding courage, stamina, and perhaps a touch of foolishness—was rapidly becoming a practical matter, well within the reach of the ordinary individual. Because the automobile is today a fixture in our lives, however, we seldom stop to consider what a coast-to-coast auto trip meant in an age when a spring thunderstorm would turn a "highway" into a virtual mortar trough. Perhaps it is the very routine nature of long-distance driving—our sense of diminishing frontiers—that excites our fascination with the pioneer trips made early in the twentieth century, when the automobile was new and the trails it tamed were primitive and steeped in adventure.

APPENDIX:
THE TRIPS
AT A GLANCE

The 1909 Mitchell Trip

DRIVERS	Frank X. Zirbes, Malcolm E. Parrott*
PASSENGER	B. B. Rosenthal
CAR	4-cylinder, 30-horsepower 1910 Mitchell Model T touring car
CITY–CITY	New York City–San Francisco
DATES	Noon, August 19–2:00 P.M., September 19, 1909
DISTANCE	3,693 miles
ELAPSED TIME	31 days, 5 hours
RUNNING TIME	—
AVERAGE SPEED (*for elapsed time*)	4.93 mph
FIRSTS	First car to carry a military dispatch from coast to coast.

*There's some question about how much, if any, driving Parrott did.

281

The 1910 Reo Trip

DRIVERS   Dave Fassett, C. E. "John" Griffith, Eugene I. Hammond,
                   Percy J. Haycock, Lester L. Whitman

CAR   4-cylinder, 30-horsepower 1911 Reo Thirty touring car

CITY–CITY   New York City–San Francisco (and on to Los Angeles)

DATES   12:01 A.M., Aug. 8–3:13 P.M., Aug. 18, 1910 (New York City–
                   San Francisco)

DISTANCE   *New York City–San Francisco*: 3,557 miles
                   New York City–Los Angeles: 4,118 miles

ELAPSED TIME   *New York City–San Francisco*: 10 days, 18 hours, 12 minutes
                   New York City–Los Angeles: 12 days, 21 hours, 39 minutes

RUNNING TIME   Approximately 9 days, 18 hours, or less (New York City–
                   San Francisco)

AVERAGE SPEED   13.78 mph (New York City–San Francisco)
(*for elapsed time*)

FIRSTS   Cut transcontinental record by 4 days, 8 hours.

The 1911 Premier Caravan

DRIVERS   John Guy Monihan, Ray F. McNamara, and ten other drivers in a
                   twelve-car caravan

PASSENGERS   Family and friends; the drivers and passengers numbered about
                   forty

CARS   Twelve 4- and 6-cylinder Premier autos (one outfitted as a
                   baggage truck), 1909, 1910, and 1911 models, ranging from
                   30 to 60 horsepower

CITY–CITY   Atlantic City, N.J.–San Francisco and Los Angeles

DATES   *Start*: 8:00 A.M., June 26, 1911
                   Reached San Francisco: 8:30 P.M., Aug. 3, 1911
                   Reached Los Angeles: 2:00 P.M., Aug. 10, 1911

DISTANCE	*To San Francisco*: 4,075.5 miles
	To Los Angeles: 4,617.6 miles
ELAPSED TIME	*To San Francisco*: 38 days, 15 hours, 30 minutes
	To Los Angeles: 45 days, 9 hours
RUNNING TIME	*To San Francisco*: 31 calendar days
	To Los Angeles: 35 calendar days
AVERAGE SPEED (*for elapsed time*)	*To San Francisco*: 4.39 mph
	To Los Angeles: 4.24 mph
FIRSTS	First auto caravan and first group of amateur drivers to cross the country.

The 1911 Garford Automobile Train

DRIVERS	Anton L. Westgard (pilot), H. D. Ashton (conductor), and five hired chauffeurs
PASSENGERS	Eight travelers who paid $875 apiece; paying travelers, tour guides, and drivers totaled eighteen persons, including three women
CARS	Four 4-cylinder, 36-horsepower 1911 Garford touring cars and a Garford baggage truck
CITY–CITY	New York City–Los Angeles
DATES	10:30 A.M., Oct. 2–6:00 P.M., Nov. 23, 1911
DISTANCE	4,025.6 miles
ELAPSED TIME	52 days, 10 hours, 30 minutes
RUNNING TIME	43 calendar days
AVERAGE SPEED (*for elapsed time*)	3.21 mph
FIRSTS	First public transcontinental automobile tour.

The 1915 Stutz Trip

DRIVER	Erwin G. "Cannon Ball" Baker
PASSENGER	William F. Sturm, observer
CAR	4-cylinder, 60-horsepower 1915 Stutz Bearcat roadster
CITY–CITY	San Diego–New York City
DATES	Midnight, May 7–10:15 A.M., May 18, 1915
DISTANCE	3,728.4 miles
ELAPSED TIME	11 days, 7 hours, 15 minutes
RUNNING TIME	Approximately 148 hours
AVERAGE SPEED (*for elapsed time*)	13.75 mph
FIRSTS	Broke coast-to-coast record for a single driver; second-fastest crossing; Stutz was first automaker to submit its coast-to-coast auto to an independent testing lab following the trip.

The 1916 Cadillac Trip

DRIVER	Erwin G. "Cannon Ball" Baker
PASSENGER	William F. Sturm, observer
CAR	V-8, 77-horsepower 1916 Type 53 Cadillac roadster
CITY–CITY	Los Angeles–New York City
DATES	12:01 A.M., May 8–2:53 P.M., May 15, 1916
DISTANCE	3,380.7 miles
ELAPSED TIME	7 days, 11 hours, 52 minutes
RUNNING TIME	5½ days
AVERAGE SPEED (*for elapsed time*)	18.10 mph
FIRSTS	Cut 3 days, 6 hours, 20 minutes from existing transcontinental record (set in 1910); set record for single driver.

The 1916 Marmon Trip

DRIVERS	Fred Barbour, Walter Bieling, William Binz, Robert Creighton, Samuel B. Stevens
CAR	6-cylinder, 74-horsepower 1916 Marmon 34 touring car
CITY–CITY	New York City–San Francisco
DATES	1:30 A.M., July 24–5:00 P.M., July 29, 1916
DISTANCE	3,476 miles
ELAPSED TIME	5 days, 18 hours, 30 minutes
RUNNING TIME	No more than 5 days, 8 hours
AVERAGE SPEED (*for elapsed time*)	25.10 mph
FIRSTS	Set transcontinental record by cutting 26 hours, 40 minutes from the Saxon relay mark, set shortly before the Marmon trip.

The 1916 Hudson Trip

DRIVERS	Ralph Mulford, A. H. Patterson, Charles H. Vincent
PASSENGERS	William F. Sturm, trip organizer; mechanics; pilots
CAR	6-cylinder, 76-horsepower 1916 Hudson Super-Six 7-passenger phaeton
CITY–CITY	San Francisco–New York City; New York City–San Francisco
DATES	*San Francisco–New York City*: 12:01 A.M., Sept. 13–6:32 A.M., Sept. 18, 1916 *New York City–San Francisco*: 10:50 P.M., Sept. 18–1:23 P.M., Sept. 24, 1916
DISTANCE	3,476 miles each way, 6,952 miles total
ELAPSED TIME	*San Francisco–New York City*: 5 days, 3 hours, 31 minutes *New York City–San Francisco*: 5 days, 17 hours, 33 minutes *Total excluding New York City layover*: 10 days, 21 hours, 4 minutes *Total including New York City layover*: 11 days, 13 hours, 22 minutes

RUNNING TIME   —

AVERAGE SPEED   *San Francisco–New York City*: 28.14 mph
(*for elapsed time*)   *New York City–San Francisco*: 25.27 mph
    Overall: 26.63 mph (excluding New York City layover)

FIRSTS   Cut 14 hours, 59 minutes from the Marmon's 1916 coast-to-coast record; also set a record between San Francisco and New York City, between New York City and San Francisco, and for a double transcontinental trip.

NOTES

Introduction

1. "Sharp Criticisms by the Editors/Automobile Trip Across the Continent May Result in a Revolution in Travelling," editorial, *San Francisco Call*, reprinted in the *New York Herald*, July 6, 1899, p. 8, col. 6.

2. "Coast to Coast in 15 Days 6 Hours," *New York Herald*, Aug. 18, 1906, p. 5, col. 2.

3. One year later, in 1909, Alice Ramsey drove three female companions across the country in a Maxwell touring car. In 1915 silent film actress Anita King became the first person of either sex to make a documented solo transcontinental auto trip, and the following year Amanda Preuss drove her V-8 Oldsmobile coast to coast in a time that rivaled the men's speed record. These trips and others are detailed in Curt McConnell, *"A Reliable Car and a Woman Who Knows It": The First Coast-to-Coast Auto Trips by Women, 1899–1916* (Jefferson, N.C.: McFarland & Co., 2000).

4. "One Man's Family Tour from Coast to Coast," *Automobile*, May 28, 1908, p. 733.

5. More information about these early trips may be found in Curt McConnell, *Coast to Coast by Automobile: The Pioneering Trips, 1899–1908* (Stanford, Calif.: Stanford University Press, 2000).

6. "Arrival of Overlanders in New York," *Automobile*, Aug. 29, 1903, pp. 205–6.

7. "Ocean to Ocean Race," *New York Tribune*, May 9, 1905, p. 5, col. 6.

8. "Dr. Jackson's Success," editorial, *Motor Age*, July 23, 1903, p. 6.

Chapter 1

1. "Progress of the Ranger," *Motor Age*, Sept. 9, 1909, p. 32.

2. "War Car Awaits Marching Orders," *New York Times*, Aug. 15, 1909, sec. 4, p. 4, col. 4.

3. "Ocean-to-Ocean Run for a Soldier," *Motor World*, Aug. 12, 1909, p. 832.

4. U.S. Signal Corps annual report for 1903, cited in "Automobile in Warfare," editorial, *Automobile*, March 5, 1904, p. 288; Frank Gaynor, ed., *The New Military and Naval Dictionary* (New York: Philosophical Library, 1951), pp. 233–34.

5. "Motor Cars Meet War Tests," *Motor World*, Aug. 26, 1909, p. 927.

6. "Mitchell War Car Speeding Westward," *New York Times*, Aug. 22, 1909, sec. 4, p. 4, col. 6; Joseph E. G. Ryan, "Mitchell Ranger Reaches Chicago," *Chicago Inter Ocean*, Aug. 25, 1909, p. 5, col. 4.

7. "Mitchell Ranger Reaches 'Frisco,'" *Racine (Wis.) Daily Journal*, Sept. 20, 1909, p. 2, col. 2; "Automobiles in Government Dispatch Service," *Motor Field*, September 1909, p. 68.

8. *New York Times*, Aug. 22, 1909, sec. 4, p. 4, col. 7.

9. *Racine (Wis.) Daily Journal*, Sept. 20, 1909, p. 2, col. 2.

10. "Motors and Motorists," *Kansas City Star*, Aug. 22, 1909, p. 10A, col. 2. Some press accounts join the *Kansas City Star* in dating this race to 1908; others say 1907.

11. "Motor Cycles in Long Run," *New York Times*, July 3, 1903, p. 6, col. 3; "Motor Cycle Reliability Run," *Automobile*, July 11, 1903, p. 35.

12. "Fast Track Work at St. Paul," *Automobile*, July 4, 1907, p. 30; "Thomas Wins Chicago's Twenty-Four Hour," *Automobile*, July 18, 1907, p. 80.

13. "Winning of a 24 Hour Record Race," *Automobile*, Aug. 15, 1907, pp. 221–25.

14. James W. Gilson, *From Ocean to Ocean: How the Mitchell Ranger Carried the First Transcontinental War Dispatch* (Racine, Wis.: Mitchell Motor Car Company, 1909?), p. 7; "Autoists Bearing Army Message Here," *Omaha (Neb.) Daily News*, Aug. 30, 1909, p. 6, col. 1; "War Courier Ahead of Schedule," *Motor World*, Aug. 26, 1909, p. 978; *New York Times*, Aug. 22, 1909, sec. 4, p. 4, col. 7.

15. "Mitchell Rangers Rushed to Chicago," *South Bend (Ind.) Tribune*, Aug. 24, 1909, p. 9, col. 4; *Racine (Wis.) Daily Journal*, Sept. 20, 1909, p. 2, col. 2; *From Ocean to Ocean*, p. 7.

16. *Chicago Inter Ocean*, Aug. 25, 1909, p. 5, col. 4.

17. The biographical information on Lewis is from "She's Coming Fine; Day Ahead of Time," *Racine (Wis.) Daily Journal*, Aug. 24, 1909, p. 8, col. 1; and Beverly Rae Kimes and Henry Austin Clark, Jr., *Standard Catalog of American Cars, 1805–1942*, 2d ed. (Iola, Wis.: Krause Publications, 1989), p. 938.

18. *From Ocean to Ocean*, pp. 5–6.

19. "Military Mitchell Begins Its Transcontinental Trip," *Automobile*, Aug. 26, 1909, p. 373.

20. *Racine (Wis.) Daily Journal*, Aug. 24, 1909, p. 8, col. 1.

21. "Speed War Auto West," *Chicago Daily News*, Aug. 25, 1909, "latest sporting edition," p. 2, col. 7.

22. Mitchell ad in the *Nevada State Journal* (Reno), Sept. 19, 1909, p. 8, col. 1.

23. "Dispatch Bearer Arrives in Reno," *Nevada State Journal* (Reno), Sept. 17, 1909, p. 8, col. 1.

24. "Winton Chicago–New York Run Postponed," *Horseless Age*, Aug. 23, 1899, p. 8; "A Message by Automobile," *Automobile*, September 1899, p. 8.

25. See Curt McConnell, *Coast to Coast by Automobile: The Pioneering Trips, 1899–1908* (Stanford, Calif.: Stanford University Press, 2000), pp. 30–58.

26. "To Break All Records," *Ashtabula (Ohio) Beacon-Record*, June 18, 1906, p. 3, col. 3.

27. The information and quotations in this paragraph are from "Studebaker War Car Proves Its Utility," *Motor Age*, March 19, 1908, p. 15; and from "Chicago Triumph for Leading Auto," *Chicago Daily Tribune*, Feb. 26, 1908, p. 3, col. 1. For more about the 1908 New York–Paris auto race, see Curt McConnell, *Coast-to-Coast Auto Races of the Early 1900s* (Warrendale, Pa.: Society of Automotive Engineers, 2000).

28. *Racine (Wis.) Daily Journal*, Aug. 24, 1909, p. 8, col. 1.

29. *Racine (Wis.) Daily Journal*, Sept. 20, 1909, p. 2, col. 2. A specifications table, "Details of Cars on the American Market for 1910—American Gasoline Pleasure Cars," that appeared in the February 3, 1910, issue of *Automobile* puts the weight of the Mitchell Model T at 2,300 pounds.

30. Specifications for the Mitchell Model R and Model T can be found in *From Ocean to Ocean*; "1910: The Mitchell," *Cycle and Automobile Trade Journal*, October 1909, pp. 126–32; "Mitchell Gasoline Pleasure Cars," *Cycle and Automobile Trade Journal*, March 1910, p. 190; "Motor Car Development:

Three Mitchell Chassis," *Motor Age*, Oct. 21, 1909, pp. 24–27; and "Details of Cars on the American Market for 1910—American Gasoline Pleasure Cars," *Automobile*, Feb. 3, 1910, n.p.

31. "Mitchell Six [*sic*] for Long Trip," *Motor Age*, Aug. 19, 1909, p. 35; *Automobile*, Aug. 26, 1909, p. 373; *South Bend (Ind.) Tribune*, Aug. 24, 1909, p. 9, col. 4.

32. *Kansas City Star*, Aug. 22, 1909, p. 10A, col. 2.

33. "Motors and Motorists," *Kansas City Star*, Sept. 5, 1909, p. 11A, col. 2; "Dispatch Car Left Goshen," *Goshen (Ind.) Daily News–Times*, Aug. 24, 1909, p. 1, col. 4; "Army Auto in This City," *Carson City (Nev.) Daily Appeal*, Sept. 17, 1909, p. 1, col. 5.

34. *Automobile*, Aug. 26, 1909, p. 373.

35. *Racine (Wis.) Daily Journal*, Aug. 24, 1909, p. 8, col. 1; "Mitchell Ranger Is Off for San Francisco," *Automobile Topics*, Aug. 28, 1909, p. 1417.

36. "Along Auto Row," *Omaha (Neb.) Sunday Bee*, Aug. 29, 1909, sec. 2, p. 5, col. 4. Nearly identical accounts ran as "Army Despatch Car Goes Through City," *Cedar Rapids (Iowa) Daily Republican*, Aug. 27, 1909, p. 2, col. 2, and "Trans-Continental Dispatch Car," *Rawlins (Wyo.) Republican*, Sept. 11, 1909, p. 1, col. 6.

37. *Automobile Topics*, Aug. 28, 1909, p. 1417.

38. *Racine (Wis.) Daily Journal*, Aug. 24, 1909, p. 8, col. 1.

39. "U.S. Army Car on Dash West," *Erie (Pa.) Dispatch*, Aug. 23, 1909, p. 8, col. 2.

40. *Goshen (Ind.) Daily News–Times*, Aug. 24, 1909, p. 1, col. 4.

41. *South Bend (Ind.) Tribune*, Aug. 24, 1909, p. 9, col. 4.

42. *Chicago Inter Ocean*, Aug. 25, 1909, p. 5, col. 4. The *Chicago Daily News*, however, reported the visitors "checking in at Chicago shortly after 1 o'clock," Aug. 25, 1909, "latest sporting edition," p. 5, col. 7.

43. *Chicago Inter Ocean*, Aug. 25, 1909, p. 5, col. 4.

44. Joseph E. G. Ryan, "Flag to Flag Donor Wahlgreen [*sic*] in City . . . Mitchell Ranger, War Car Bearing Dispatches to Major General Weston in Frisco, in Ligonier, Ind., Last Night—Here Today," *Chicago Inter Ocean*, Aug. 24, 1909, p. 5, col. 5; *Chicago Daily News*, Aug. 25, 1909, "latest sporting edition," p. 2, col. 7.

45. *From Ocean to Ocean*, p. 10.

46. Articles documenting the 1907 New York–Chicago record include "Franklin Lowers Chicago–New York Mark," *Automobile*, Aug. 29, 1907, p. 296; and "Chicago–New York Record Broken," *Motor Age*, Aug. 29, 1907, p. 4.

47. "Mitchell Ranger Completes Its Long Run," *Motor Age*, Sept. 23, 1909, p. 12.

48. *Chicago Inter Ocean*, Aug. 25, 1909, p. 5, col. 4; *Cedar Rapids (Iowa) Daily Republican*, Aug. 27, 1909, p. 2, col. 2; "War Dispatch Auto in City," *Chicago Daily Tribune*, Aug. 25, 1909, p. 9, col. 3.

49. "War Dispatch Auto Departs," *Chicago Daily Tribune*, Aug. 26, 1909, p. 8, col. 4.

50. *From Ocean to Ocean*, p. 13.

51. "Blizzard Rages in Path of Auto," *Racine (Wis.) Daily Journal*, Sept. 13, 1909, p. 1, col. 5.

52. *Cedar Rapids (Iowa) Daily Republican*, Aug. 27, 1909, p. 2, col. 2.

53. Ibid.

54. *Racine (Wis.) Daily Journal*, Sept. 13, 1909, p. 1, col. 5.

55. "Dispatch Car in City Short Time," *Marshalltown (Iowa) Evening Times-Republican*, Aug. 28, 1909, p. 6, col. 4; "Trans-Continental War Dispatch Car Is Here," *Omaha (Neb.) World-Herald*, Aug. 29, 1909, sec. 2, p. 6E, col. 1; "Dispatch Car at Omaha," *Council Bluffs (Iowa) Daily Nonpareil*, Aug. 29, 1909, p. 6, col. 3.

56. *Racine (Wis.) Daily Journal*, Sept. 13, 1909, p. 1, col. 5.

57. Ibid.; *Kansas City Star*, Sept. 5, 1909, p. 11A, col. 1; *From Ocean to Ocean*, p. 16.

58. *Kansas City Star*, Sept. 5, 1909, p. 11A, col. 2; *Motor Age*, Sept. 9, 1909, p. 32. Although the Mitchell's route took it far north of Kansas City, the *Star* explained that it was following the run because a Mitchell had been entered in its upcoming Star Trophies Tour, an endurance contest.

59. "Army Dispatch Auto Has Reached Cheyenne," *Wyoming Tribune* (Cheyenne), Sept. 3, 1909, p. 1, col. 6; "Automobile Carrying Army Dispatches to the Pacific," *Sunday State Leader* (Cheyenne, Wyo.), Sept. 5, 1909, p. 2, col. 3.

60. *Motor Age*, Sept. 23, 1909, p. 12.

61. *From Ocean to Ocean*, p. 25.

62. "Weston in Distress," *New York Times*, June 10, 1909, p. 5, col. 2; "Weston's Shoes Wear Out," *Chicago Daily Tribune*, June 14, 1909, p. 11, col. 5.

63. "Government Car Is in Reno on Way to Coast," *Reno (Nev.) Evening Gazette*, Sept. 16, 1909, p. 1, col. 3.

64. *From Ocean to Ocean*, p. 16.

65. *Racine (Wis.) Daily Journal*, Sept. 13, 1909, p. 1, col. 5.

66. "Army Car Arrives from Transcontinental Trip," *San Francisco Chronicle*, Sept. 20, 1909, p. 1, col. 5.

67. *Motor Age*, Sept. 23, 1909, p. 12.

68. "Rangers' Progress," *Automobile*, Sept. 16, 1909, p. 470; *Racine (Wis.) Daily Journal*, Sept. 13, 1909, p. 1, col. 5; *Reno (Nev.) Evening Gazette*, Sept. 16, 1909, p. 1, col. 3.

69. *San Francisco Chronicle*, Sept. 20, 1909, p. 1, col. 5; *Motor Age*, Sept. 23, 1909, p. 12; *Reno (Nev.) Evening Gazette*, Sept. 16, 1909, p. 1, col. 3.

70. *From Ocean to Ocean*, p. 19; "Ranger Expected in Reno Tonight," *Nevada State Journal* (Reno), Sept. 16, 1909, p. 2, col. 3; *Nevada State Journal* (Reno), Sept. 17, 1909, p. 8, col. 1.

71. *Nevada State Journal* (Reno), Sept. 17, 1909, p. 8, col. 1.

72. "Army Auto Passes through This City," *Carson City (Nev.) News*, Sept. 18, 1909, p. 1, col. 6.

73. *Carson City (Nev.) Daily Appeal*, Sept. 17, 1909, p. 1, col. 5.

74. *Motor Age*, Sept. 23, 1909, p. 12.

75. "'War Car' Arrives at Midnight, Breaking Cross-Continent Record," *Sacramento (Calif.) Union*, Sept. 19, 1909, p. 1, col. 5; *San Francisco Chronicle*, Sept. 20, 1909, p. 4, col. 1; "Signal Corps Auto Crosses Continent," *San Francisco Examiner*, Sept. 20, 1909, p. 4, col. 1.

76. *Sacramento (Calif.) Union*, Sept. 19, 1909, p. 1, col. 5.

77. *San Francisco Chronicle*, Sept. 20, 1909, p. 4, col. 1; *San Francisco Examiner*, Sept. 20, 1909, p. 4, col. 1.

78. *San Francisco Examiner*, Sept. 20, 1909, p. 4, col. 1; *Automobile*, Sept. 23, 1909, p. 508.

79. *San Francisco Chronicle*, Sept. 20, 1909, p. 4, col. 1; *Automobile*, Aug. 26, 1909, p. 373.

80. *San Francisco Chronicle*, Sept. 20, 1909, p. 4, col. 1; *From Ocean to Ocean*, p. 23; *Motor Age*, Sept. 23, 1909, p. 12.

81. *San Francisco Chronicle*, Sept. 20, 1909, p. 1, col. 5.

82. "Cross Country in War Time Test," *San Francisco Call*, Sept. 20, 1909, p. 12, col. 2.

83. *San Francisco Examiner*, Sept. 20, 1909, p. 4, col. 1.

84. *Automobile*, Aug. 26, 1909, p. 373.

85. *San Francisco Chronicle*, Sept. 20, 1909, p. 1, col. 5; *From Ocean to Ocean*, p. 21.

86. *San Francisco Chronicle*, Sept. 20, 1909, p. 1, col. 5.

87. This statement is based on telephone conversations with and a letter of December 12, 1994, from Dennis Copeland, an archivist at the Presidio Army Museum. Stephen Haller, park historian for Golden Gate National Recreation Area, was also unable to find copies of the communiqué.

88. Entry for John Francis Weston in *Who Was Who in American History: The Military* (Chicago: Marquis Who's Who, 1975).

89. *Reno (Nev.) Evening Gazette*, Sept. 16, 1909, p. 1, col. 3; *From Ocean to Ocean*, p. 30.

90. *San Francisco Call*, Sept. 20, 1909, p. 12, col. 2; "Mitchell Ranger Reaches San Francisco," *Automobile Topics*, Sept. 25, 1909, p. 1679; *San Francisco Examiner*, Sept. 20, 1909, p. 4, col. 1.

91. *Motor Age*, Sept. 23, 1909, p. 12.

92. "Coast-to-Coast War Game," *Motor World*, Sept. 30, 1909, p. 29.

93. "Mitchell Military Car Ends Trip," *Automobile*, Sept. 23, 1909, p. 508; *Racine (Wis.) Daily Journal*, Sept. 20, 1909, p. 2, col. 2.

94. "Auto Owners as Defenders," *Reno (Nev.) Evening Gazette*, Sept. 11, 1915, p. 6, col. 5.

95. "Glidden Tour Dangers," *New York Times*, April 10, 1910, p. 4, col. 3. The dates of Zirbes' trek and other details are from "Many Tours Planned Throughout the Country," *Motor Field*, May 1910, p. 82. The annual Glidden Tours, organized by the American Automobile Association beginning in 1905, gave drivers a time limit to travel a route over public roads. Penalties accrued for late arrivals. Drivers also lost points for making repairs, and the judges who conducted post-run inspections deducted points for any mechanical deficiencies they spotted. Glidden Tour rules limited entrants to owners driving only stock autos.

96. *Motor Field*, May 1910, p. 82.

97. "Wisconsin, Racine," *Automobile Topics*, June 11, 1910, p. 647.

98. Information on the Mitchell company's production and bankruptcy is from Kimes and Clark, *Standard Catalog of American Cars, 1805–1942*, 2d ed., p. 938.

Chapter 2

1. Lester L. Whitman, *Coast to Coast in a Reo: 10 Days, 15 Hours, 13 minutes* (Lansing, Mich.: R. M. Owen & Company, 1910), pp. 5, 17. The correct time for the crossing is, however, 10 days, 18 hours, 12 minutes.

2. W. H. B. Fowler, "Feat of Reo Car Surprises Even Auto Men," *San Francisco Chronicle*, Aug. 21, 1910, p. 41, col. 1. Detailed accounts of Whitman's 1903, 1904, and 1906 transcontinental trips can be found in Curt McConnell, *Coast to Coast by Automobile: The Pioneering Trips, 1899–1908* (Stanford, Calif.: Stanford University Press, 2000).

3. "Reo Record-Breaking Trip," *New York Times*, Aug. 21, 1910, sec. 4, p. 8, col. 3, which also gives the men's hometowns; *Coast to Coast in a Reo*, p. 6; "Reo Crosses Continent from Ocean to Ocean and Establishes Record for Trip," *Motor Age*, Aug. 25, 1910, p. 4. The *New York Times* calls Griffith "John Griffith," whereas Whitman says "C. E. Griffith." Similarly, the *Times* says "Percy Haycock," while Whitman calls him "P. J. Haycock."

4. *Car Classics 1974 Yearbook*, n.p.; Beverly Rae Kimes, "Reo Remembered: A History," *Automobile Quarterly*, vol. 14, no. 1 (1976), p. 18.

5. Specifications for the Reo Thirty are from "Details of Passenger Automobiles on the American Market for 1911," *Automobile*, Jan. 5, 1911, pp. 78–79; *Reo, 1911* (Lansing, Mich.: R. M. Owen & Co., 1910?).

6. *Coast to Coast in a Reo*, p. 6.

7. Ibid.

8. "On Long Auto Record," *New York Tribune*, Aug. 9, 1910, p. 9, col. 1.

9. *Motor Age*, Aug. 25, 1910, p. 5.

10. *Reo, 1911*, p. 15.

11. Reo ad in *American Magazine*, October 1910, p. 88.

12. *Coast to Coast in a Reo*, pp. 7–8.

13. Ibid., p. 9; and W. H. B. Fowler, "Reo Car Cuts Deep Into New York Record," *San Francisco Chronicle*, Aug. 19, 1910, p. 9, col. 5.

14. "Reo Thirty Breaks Sea to Sea Record," *Los Angeles Times*, Aug. 21, 1910, sec. 7, p. 10, col. 3; "Less Than 11 Days Used for Journey," *San Francisco Call*, Aug. 19, 1910, p. 3, col. 4; "Whitman in Reo Makes New Transcontinental Record," *Horseless Age*, Aug. 24, 1910, p. 278.

15. See Curt McConnell, *Coast to Coast by Automobile: The Pioneering Trips, 1899–1908* (Stanford, Calif.: Stanford University Press, 2000), pp. 88–90.

16. "A Record Auto Run and What It Means," *New York Times*, Aug. 19, 1906, p. 7, col. 3.

17. *Coast to Coast in a Reo*, p. 8; *San Francisco Chronicle*, Aug. 19, 1910, p. 9, col. 5; *Motor Age*, Aug. 25, 1910, p. 4; *San Francisco Call*, Aug. 19, 1910, p. 3, col. 3.

18. "Auto Hits Farmer," *Marshalltown (Iowa) Evening Times-Republican*, Aug. 13, 1906, p. 1, col. 6.

19. *Los Angeles Times*, Aug. 21, 1910, sec. 7, p. 10, col. 3.

20. "New York to San Francisco," *Goshen (Ind.) Daily Democrat*, Aug. 9, 1910, p. 1, col. 6. The distance of 75 miles corresponds to the most direct route shown in a 1936 H. M. Gousha map of Ohio.

21. Ibid.

22. "Reo Reached Goshen," *Goshen (Ind.) Daily Democrat*, Aug. 10, 1910, p. 1.

23. *Coast to Coast in a Reo*, p. 9.

24. Ibid., pp. 9–10.

25. "5 Days Are Cut Off Overland Auto Record," *Los Angeles Examiner*, Aug. 22, 1910, p. 7, col. 1.

26. "New York City to Council Bluffs," *Council Bluffs (Iowa) Daily Nonpareil*, Aug. 12, 1910, p. 5, col. 5; *San Francisco Chronicle*, Aug. 19, 1910, p. 9, col. 5.

27. *Coast to Coast in a Reo*, p. 10.

28. *Council Bluffs (Iowa) Daily Nonpareil*, Aug. 12, 1910, p. 5, col. 5.

29. In his *Coast to Coast in a Reo* account, Whitman does not give the Reo's actual mileage to Chicago—a trip of some 1,000 to 1,200 miles, depending on the route taken. For this calculation, the distance is assumed to be 1,000 miles.

30. *Coast to Coast in a Reo*, p. 10.

31. Untitled blurb, *Columbus (Neb.) Telegram*, Aug. 12, 1910, p. 1, col. 5.

32. "Whitman's Auto Meets with Mishap," *North Platte (Neb.) Telegraph*, Aug. 18, 1910, p. 1, col. 5. This article was reprinted in the weekly *Telegraph* "From Friday's Daily"—that is, from the *North Platte Evening Telegraph* of Aug. 12, an edition that is missing from the Nebraska State Historical Society's holdings.

33. *Coast to Coast in a Reo*, p. 10.

34. *New York Times*, Aug. 21, 1910, sec. 4, p. 8, col. 3; "Makes Fast Time," *North Platte (Neb.) Semi-Weekly Tribune*, Aug. 16, 1910, p. 1, col. 3.

35. *Coast to Coast in a Reo*, p. 11.

36. "Four Days from New York," *Wyoming Tribune* (Cheyenne), Aug. 15, 1910, p. 4, col. 5.

37. "On Their Way to the Pacific Coast," *Laramie (Wyo.) Daily Boomerang*, Aug. 13, 1910, p. 6, col. 5.

38. "Will Pilot Car Across the State," *Laramie (Wyo.) Republican*, Aug. 13, 1910, p. 3, col. 4. For more information about Murdock's historic journey, see McConnell, *Coast to Coast by Automobile*, pp. 266–302.

39. See Curt McConnell, *"A Reliable Car and a Woman Who Knows It": The First Coast-to-Coast Auto Trips by Women, 1899–1916* (Jefferson, N.C.: McFarland & Co., 2000), pp. 23–59.

40. "Transcontinental Car Due in Ogden Today," *Salt Lake (City) Herald-Republican*, Aug. 14, 1910, p. 6, col. 2; "Breaking Coast-to-Coast Record," *Salt Lake (City) Tribune*, Aug. 14, 1910, sec. 2, p. 4, col. 3.

41. *Coast to Coast in a Reo*, p. 11.
42. Ibid., p. 11; "Making Good Time," *Rawlins (Wyo.) Republican*, Aug. 18, 1910, p. 1, col. 3.
43. *Coast to Coast in a Reo*, p. 12.
44. *San Francisco Chronicle*, Aug. 19, 1910, p. 9, col. 5.
45. *Coast to Coast in a Reo*, p. 12.
46. Ibid., p. 13.
47. "Record Run to the Coast," *Ogden (Utah) Daily Standard*, Aug. 15, 1910, p. 2, col. 5.
48. *Coast to Coast in a Reo*, pp. 13–14.
49. Ibid., pp. 14–15.
50. *Los Angeles Examiner*, Aug. 22, 1910, p. 7, col. 1.
51. *Coast to Coast in a Reo*, p. 15.
52. "Reo Breaking Auto Records," *Nevada State Journal* (Reno), Aug. 18, 1910, p. 8, col. 2.
53. *Coast to Coast in a Reo*, p. 15.
54. *San Francisco Chronicle*, Aug. 19, 1910, p. 9, col. 5.
55. *Motor Age*, Aug. 25, 1910, p. 5; *San Francisco Call*, Aug. 19, 1910, p. 3, col. 3.
56. *Motor Age*, Aug. 25, 1910, p. 5; *Coast to Coast in a Reo*, p. 16.
57. *San Francisco Chronicle*, Aug. 19, 1910, p. 9, col. 5.
58. *Coast to Coast in a Reo*, pp. 16–17.
59. "Auto Record Across Continent Smashed," *Los Angeles Examiner*, Aug. 19, 1910, p. 1, col. 4; Stuart Gayness, "Reo Car Makes New Record," *San Francisco Examiner*, Aug. 19, 1910, p. 8, col. 2; *Los Angeles Examiner*, Aug. 22, 1910, p. 7, col. 1.
60. Reo ad in *Saturday Evening Post*, March 4, 1911, pp. 36–37; *Los Angeles Times*, Aug. 21, 1910, sec. 7, p. 1, col. 6.
61. *Reo, 1911*, p. 15.
62. *Los Angeles Examiner*, Aug. 22, 1910, p. 7, col. 1.
63. *San Francisco Examiner*, Aug. 19, 1910, p. 8, col. 2.
64. *San Francisco Chronicle*, Aug. 21, 1910, p. 41, col. 1.
65. *San Francisco Call*, Aug. 19, 1910, p. 3, col. 3.
66. W. H. B. Fowler, "Reo Continues Its Run to Los Angeles," *San Francisco Chronicle*, Aug. 20, 1910, p. 9, col. 3.
67. *Los Angeles Examiner*, Aug. 22, 1910, p. 7, col. 1; *Los Angeles Times*, Aug. 21, 1910, sec. 7, p. 1, col. 4.
68. *Los Angeles Times*, Aug. 21, 1910, sec. 7, p. 10, col. 2.
69. Ibid., p. 10, col. 4.
70. The 1910 record time is from David W. Rice, "The Fernando Nelson Trophy," *Horseless Carriage Gazette*, November–December 1995, p. 16.
71. *Los Angeles Examiner*, Aug. 22, 1910, p. 7, col. 1.
72. *San Francisco Chronicle*, Aug. 19, 1910, p. 9, col. 5.
73. R. R. L'Hommedieu, "Record Making Reo Speeds on to Los Angeles in Try for More Laurels," *San Francisco Call*, Aug. 20, 1910, p. 13, col. 3; *San Francisco Call*, Sept. 27, 1910, p. 11, col. 5, photo and caption.
74. On the 1924 Reo bus trip, see "Reo Motor Bus Starts Transcontinental Trip," *Automotive Industries*, July 24, 1924, p. 221; "Cross-Country Bus Run On," *Bus Transportation*, August 1924, p. 385; "Long Trip by Bus Arousing Wide Interest," *San Francisco Chronicle*, Aug. 24, 1924, p. 6A, col. 1; "Big Bus Ends Cross Country Test as Stage," *San Francisco Chronicle*, Aug. 26, 1924, p. 8, col. 1; and Reo ad in *Bus Transportation*, November 1924, back cover.
75. *San Francisco Chronicle*, Aug. 24, 1924, p. 6A, col. 1.

76. "E. I. Hammond Dies; Set Mark in Auto," *New York Times*, Nov. 21, 1948, p. 88, col. 7; John S. Hammond II, *From Sea to Sea in 1903 in a Curved Dash Oldsmobile* (Egg Harbor City, N.J.: Laureate Press, 1985), p. 160.

77. *Los Angeles Times*, Aug. 21, 1910, sec. 7, p. 1, col. 5, p. 10, col. 4.

78. See Curt McConnell, "Bluff by Bluster? Blisterin' Bobby Begs Believability," *Antique Automobile*, September–October 2000, pp. 3–7.

Chapter 3

1. "10 Ocean-to-Ocean Autos Due Today," *Indianapolis Star*, July 2, 1911, p. 16, col. 2.

2. "National Auto Highway," *New York Times*, July 23, 1911, sec. 4, p. 8, col. 7.

3. "Owners Enjoying Their Long Tour," *Motor Age*, July 13, 1911, p. 10; "Eastern Autoists on Tour," *Reno (Nev.) Evening Gazette*, Aug. 1, 1911, p. 6, col. 3. On the origin of the idea of a coast-to-coast trip, see "Premier Fleet Starts Long Cruise," *Automobile*, June 29, 1911, p. 1454.

4. John Guy Monihan, "The Record of a Transcontinental Trek," *Automobile*, Feb. 15, 1912, p. 479.

5. *Automobile*, Feb. 15, 1912, p. 484; Premier ad, *Automobile*, Dec. 28, 1911, p. 141; "Long Ocean to Ocean Trail Is Blazed," *Motor Age*, Aug. 17, 1911, p. 9.

6. "Offers Auto Trophy . . . Ocean to Ocean Travelers Will Pass Sunday in Iowa Town," *Chicago Daily News*, July 8, 1911, p. 2, col. 2; John Guy Monihan, "The Record of a Transcontinental Trek, Part III," *Automobile*, March 14, 1912, p. 695.

7. Premier Motor Manufacturing Company, *Ocean to Ocean Tour of the Premierites Told by Wire and Photo*, 2d ed. (Indianapolis: 1911), p. 48 of 52 unnumbered pages. For convenience, quotations from this booklet have been assigned page numbers.

8. Ibid., pp. 1, 42.

9. The photo taken at the Colorado-Wyoming border appears in R. S. Monihan, "Ocean to Ocean —by Automobile!" *American Heritage*, April 1962, pp. 60–61.

10. Information about Jenkins's inventions and patents comes from two sources: Wheeler Preston, *American Biographies* (New York: Harper & Brothers, 1940), p. 538; and "Auto Party Stays over Another Day," *Salt Lake (City) Herald-Republican*, July 26, 1911, p. 12, col. 5. Jenkins took out about four hundred patents between 1896 and 1930, according to Georges Sadoul, *Dictionary of Film Makers*, trans., ed., and updated by Peter Morris (Berkeley, Calif: University of California Press, 1972), p. 127, col. 2.

11. *Salt Lake (City) Herald-Republican*, July 26, 1911, p. 12, col. 5.

12. "Ocean-to-Ocean Tour," *New York Times*, Aug. 27, 1911, sec. 4, p. 9, col. 2; "Touring Party in Moving Pictures," *Salt Lake (City) Herald-Republican*, July 27, 1911, p. 14, col. 6; *New York Times*, Aug. 27, 1911, sec. 4, p. 9, col. 2; "Ocean to Ocean Autos Arrive Here," *Zanesville (Ohio) Daily Courier*, July 3, 1911, p. 5, col. 4.

13. "Amateur Motorists Start for the Coast," *New York Times*, June 27, 1911, p. 10, col. 3.

14. *Ocean to Ocean Tour*, p. 3; "12 Autos Leave," *Atlantic City (N.J.) Daily Press*, June 27, 1911, p. 1; *Zanesville (Ohio) Daily Courier*, July 3, 1911, p. 5, col. 4; "Owners Touring from Coast to Coast," *Motor Age*, July 6, 1911, p. 14.

15. "Ocean to Ocean Auto Party," *Elko (Nev.) Daily Free Press*, July 29, 1911, p. 1, col. 3.

16. "Tourists from Atlantic City Reach Denver," *Denver Republican*, July 16, 1911, p. 7, col. 1.

17. *Automobile*, Feb. 15, 1912, p. 484.

18. Ibid.

19. "Ocean to Ocean Tourists Arrive," *Deseret Evening News* (Salt Lake City), July 22, 1911, p. 12, col. 2.

20. "Millionaires to Get Hearty Hand," *Salt Lake (City) Herald-Republican*, July 26, 1911, p. 3, col. 2; *Ocean to Ocean Tour*, p. 5; "Cars in Ocean to Ocean Auto Run Parked in Front of State Capitol," *Harrisburg (Pa.) Patriot*, June 28, 1911, p. 7, col. 3, photo and caption.

21. "Ocean-to-Ocean Tour," *New York Times*, July 2, 1911, sec. 3, p. 8, col. 2.

22. Ibid.

23. "Autos on Long Trip," *Washington Post*, June 29, 1911, p. 14, col. 3.

24. For an account of the 1909 New York–Seattle race, see Curt McConnell, *Coast-to-Coast Auto Races of the Early 1900s: A History of Three Races That Changed the World* (Warrendale, Pa.: Society of Automotive Engineers, 2000), pp. 137–215.

25. "Lone Man 'Holds Up' Automobile Tourists," *Indianapolis News*, July 4, 1911, p. 9, col. 3.

26. *Indianapolis Star*, July 2, 1911, p. 16, col. 1; "On a 4,000-Mile Joy Ride," *Denver Times*, July 16, 1911, p. 21, col. 5.

27. "Coast to Coast Trip by 11 Autos," *Zanesville (Ohio) Signal*, July 3, 1911, p. 8, col. 5; John Guy Monihan, "The Record of a Transcontinental Trek, Part II," *Automobile*, Feb. 22, 1912, p. 530.

28. *Indianapolis News*, July 4, 1911, p. 9, col. 3.

29. "Premier Tourists 'Held Up,'" *Indianapolis Star*, July 3, 1911, p. 10, col. 5.

30. *Indianapolis News*, July 4, 1911, p. 9, col. 3.

31. "Pseudo Copper Delays Auto," *Indianapolis Sun*, July 3, 1911, p. 7, col. 5.

32. "Premier Caravan on Westward Way," *Automobile*, July 6, 1911, p. 43; *Motor Age*, July 6, 1911, p. 14; *Indianapolis Star*, July 2, 1911, p. 16, col. 2; "See National Auto Road Need," *Indianapolis Star*, July 4, 1911, p. 9, col. 4; "Autos Start on to Coast," *Indianapolis Sun*, July 5, 1911, p. 6, col. 2.

33. Mechanical specifications for the Premier autos are from *Ocean to Ocean Tour*, p. 2; *Automobile*, Feb. 15, 1912, pp. 480 (chart), 485.

34. Beverly Rae Kimes and Henry Austin Clark, Jr., *Standard Catalog of American Cars, 1805–1942*, 2d ed. (Iola, Wis.: Krause Publications, 1989), p. 1199. According to Kimes and Clark, Premier cofounder and designer George A. Weidely left the company in 1914 in order to manufacture and sell Weidely auto engines, although Premier cars continued to be produced through the 1926 model year. At his death in 1942, at age 56, McNamara was an engineer in the Chrysler Corporation's parts division. See "Ray M'Namara: Executive of Chrysler Corp., 56, Once Cross-Country Racer," *New York Times*, Oct. 16, 1942, p. 19, col. 2.

35. For information on the 1910 Glidden Tour, see "Premier and Moline the Glidden Tour Winners," *Automobile*, July 7, 1910, pp. 4–5; "Contest Board Declares Premier Gliddenites Are Not Stock," *Automobile*, July 28, 1910, p. 172; "Premier Injunction Denied," *Automobile*, Sept. 15, 1910, p. 455; and "End of the Glidden Tour," *Cycle and Automobile Trade Journal*, August 1910, p. 98.

36. A. L. Westgard, "From Coast to Coast by Automobile," *Collier's*, Jan. 14, 1911, p. 14.

37. The Premier Motor Manufacturing Company later published a booklet, *Motoring Across a Continent*, summarizing the McNamara-Westgard tour. See "Motor Car Literature," *Motor Age*, June 22, 1911, p. 33.

38. "Prairie Schooner Is Added to Tour Ranks," *Indianapolis Star*, July 5, 1911, p. 6, col. 6.

39. "Ocean-to-Ocean Auto Tourists Take Trail," *Indianapolis News*, July 5, 1911, p. 13, col. 4; "Ocean to Ocean Autoists Arrived in Rawlins Two Days Behind Their Schedule," *Carbon County Journal* (Rawlins, Wyo.), July 21, 1911, p. 1, col. 3.

40. *Ocean to Ocean Tour*, p. 14.

41. "Ocean to Ocean Tourists," *Lafayette (Ind.) Daily Courier*, July 5, 1911, p. 7, col. 5.

42. "Making Run to Coast," *Chicago Daily News*, July 6, 1911, "5 o'clock edition," p. 6, col. 7. Other reports state that the tourists stayed at Chicago's Auditorium Hotel.

43. "Easterners Visit City Parks," *Chicago Inter Ocean*, July 8, 1911, p. 5, col. 6.

44. *Denver Times*, July 16, 1911, p. 21, col. 5.

45. *Chicago Daily News*, July 8, 1911, p. 2, col. 2.

46. "Touring Autoists Visit Davenport," *Davenport (Iowa) Democrat and Leader*, July 9, 1911, p. 4, col. 1.

47. "Autoists Continue on Trip to Coast," *Davenport (Iowa) Daily Times*, July 10, 1911, p. 8, col. 4.

48. "Amateurs in Tour from Sea to Sea," *Des Moines (Iowa) Evening Tribune*, July 10, 1911, p. 1, col. 3.

49. *Automobile*, Feb. 22, 1912, p. 531.

50. "Coast-to-Coast Tourists on the Famous Highway," *Des Moines (Iowa) Capital*, July 10, 1911, p. 1, col. 7; p. 6, col. 5.

51. *Des Moines (Iowa) Capital*, July 10, 1911, p. 1, col. 7; *Des Moines (Iowa) Evening Tribune*, July 10, 1911, p. 1, col. 3; "Autoists Resume Journey to Ocean," *Des Moines (Iowa) Register and Leader*, July 11, 1911, p. 2, col. 6.

52. "Forty Philadelphia Tourists in Autos," *Omaha (Neb.) World-Herald*, July 11, 1911, p. 10, col. 6.

53. *Indianapolis Star*, July 2, 1911, p. 16, col. 2; *Automobile*, Feb. 15, 1912, p. 482.

54. *Omaha (Neb.) World-Herald*, July 11, 1911, p. 10, col. 6; *Automobile*, Feb. 15, 1912, p. 482.

55. Ibid., pp. 481–82.

56. Ibid., p. 483.

57. *Ocean to Ocean Tour*, p. 18; *Automobile*, Feb. 22, 1912, p. 532.

58. *Automobile*, Feb. 15, 1912, p. 484; *Ocean to Ocean Tour*, p. 24.

59. *Automobile*, Feb. 15, 1912, p. 482; Leon J. Pinkson, "Autos End Ocean to Ocean Trip," *San Francisco Call*, Aug. 4, 1911, p. 11, col. 4.

60. *Ocean to Ocean Tour*, p. 22.

61. "Millionaire Auto Tourists Give Western Roads Boost," *Rocky Mountain News* (Denver), July 16, 1911, p. 7, col. 3.

62. *Rocky Mountain News* (Denver), July 16, 1911, p. 7, col. 3.

63. *Denver Republican*, July 16, 1911, p. 7, col. 1.

64. *Automobile*, Feb. 15, 1912, p. 484.

65. Ibid.

66. "Ocean to Ocean Tourists Reach City," *Laramie (Wyo.) Daily Boomerang*, July 19, 1911, p. 1, col. 7.

67. *Automobile*, Feb. 15, 1912, p. 482.

68. Ibid., p. 480.

69. Monihan says 8,000 feet, but Gousha road maps from 1940 and 1962 give Tie Siding's elevation as 7,753 feet.

70. *Laramie (Wyo.) Daily Boomerang*, July 19, 1911, p. 1, col. 7.

71. *Ocean to Ocean Tour*, p. 26.

72. "Insufficient Hotel Rooms," *Laramie (Wyo.) Daily Boomerang*, July 20, 1911, p. 1, col. 2.

73. *Automobile*, Feb. 22, 1912, p. 533.

74. Ibid.

75. Ibid., pp. 533 and 485.

76. *Motor Age*, Aug. 17, 1911, p. 8; *Ocean to Ocean Tour*, p. 28.

77. *Automobile*, Feb. 22, 1912, p. 533.

78. Ibid.

79. *Automobile*, Feb. 15, 1912, p. 481.

80. "Great Auto Party Welcomed by City," *Salt Lake (City) Herald-Republican*, July 25, 1911, p. 12, col. 1.

81. "'Ocean to Ocean' Motorists Arrive," *Salt Lake (City) Herald-Republican*, July 24, 1911, p. 7, col. 3.

82. "Ocean to Ocean Tourists Arrive in Dusty Caravan," *Deseret Evening News* (Salt Lake City), July 24, 1911, p. 7, col. 5.

83. *Salt Lake (City) Herald-Republican*, July 24, 1911, p. 7, col. 3.

84. W. H. B. Fowler, "Big Motoring Party from Atlantic Coast Reaches City," *San Francisco Chronicle*, Aug. 4, 1911, p. 4, col. 1.

85. *Deseret Evening News* (Salt Lake City), July 24, 1911, p. 7, col. 5.

86. *Salt Lake (City) Herald-Republican*, July 24, 1911, p. 7, col. 3.

87. Ibid., July 25, 1911, p. 12, col. 1.

88. "Auto Tourists Leave for Coast," *Deseret Evening News* (Salt Lake City), July 26, 1911, p. 2, col. 1; *Salt Lake (City) Herald-Republican*, July 27, 1911, p. 14, col. 6.

89. *Deseret Evening News* (Salt Lake City), July 26, 1911, p. 2, col. 1.

90. "Pennsylvania Autoists Spend Day in Ogden," *Ogden (Utah) Morning Examiner*, July 27, 1911, p. 6, col. 2.

91. "Speeding Auto Party Met at Brigham City," *Salt Lake (City) Herald-Republican*, July 28, 1911, p. 6, col. 2.

92. *Automobile*, March 14, 1912, p. 691, and Feb. 15, 1912, p. 482.

93. *Ocean to Ocean Tour*, p. 34. In his three-part series that *Automobile* published in early 1912, Monihan called it the Belvidere Hotel.

94. *Ocean to Ocean Tour*, p. 36.

95. "Gambling House Is Raided," *Elko (Nev.) Daily Free Press*, July 29, 1911, p. 1, col. 5.

96. *Reno (Nev.) Evening Gazette*, Aug. 1, 1911, p. 6, col. 3; "Ocean to Ocean Automobilists Reach Reno After Long Journey," *Nevada State Journal* (Reno), Aug. 1, 1911, p. 1, col. 1.

97. *Reno (Nev.) Evening Gazette*, Aug. 1, 1911, p. 6, col. 3.

98. "With the Auto Drivers," *Reno (Nev.) Evening Gazette*, Aug. 4, 1911, p. 4, col. 2.

99. *Reno (Nev.) Evening Gazette*, Aug. 1, 1911, p. 6, col. 3; *Automobile*, March 14, 1912, p. 692.

100. *Nevada State Journal* (Reno), Aug. 1, 1911, p. 1, col. 1.

101. *San Francisco Call*, Aug. 4, 1911, p. 11, col. 4. In listing San Jose among the towns through which the Premier caravan passed en route to San Francisco, the *Call* possibly meant "Mission San Jose," a city north of San Jose. San Jose was too far south to be on the caravan's direct route; the tourists would stop in San Jose on their trip south from San Francisco to Los Angeles.

102. Ibid.; *San Francisco Chronicle*, Aug. 4, 1911, p. 4, col. 1.

103. *Salt Lake (City) Herald-Republican*, July 24, 1911, p. 7, col. 3; "Ocean-to-Ocean Tour," *New York Times*, July 30, 1911, sec. 4, p. 8, col. 7.

104. "Sea-to-Sea Motorists Welcomed," *Los Angeles Examiner*, Aug. 11, 1911, p. 13, col. 4.

105. Bert C. Smith, "Premier Cars Reach Goal of First Long Tour," *Los Angeles Times*, Aug. 11, 1911, sec. 3, p. 1, col. 5.

106. *Los Angeles Examiner*, Aug. 11, 1911, p. 13, col. 6.

107. Bert C. Smith, "Tires of Ocean-to-Ocean Cars Dipped in Pacific," *Los Angeles Times*, Aug. 14, 1911, sec. 2, p. 3, col. 1.

108. "Cars Dip in the Ocean," *New York Times*, Aug. 13, 1911, sec. 3, p. 8, col. 3.

109. Chester Lawrence, "Ocean-to-Ocean Autos Dip in Pacific," *Los Angeles Examiner*, Aug. 14, 1911, p. 1, col. 4.

110. *Los Angeles Times*, Aug. 14, 1911, sec. 2, p. 3, col. 1.

111. *Los Angeles Examiner*, Aug. 14, 1911, p. 2, col. 6; "10,000 Cheer Atlantic Dipped Autos When Driven into Pacific at Venice," *Los Angeles Herald*, Aug. 14, 1911, p. 12, col. 1.

112. *Los Angeles Times*, Aug. 14, 1911, sec. 2, p. 3, col. 1; *Los Angeles Examiner*, Aug. 14, 1911, p. 2, col. 6; "Famous Tour in Moving Pictures," *Automobile Topics*, Dec. 23, 1911, p. 301.

113. *Los Angeles Times*, Aug. 14, 1911, sec. 2, p. 3, col. 1.

114. *San Francisco Chronicle*, Aug. 4, 1911, p. 4, col. 1.

115. Side trips, including the distance the drivers traveled from their homes to the starting point in Atlantic City, raised the overall average to 4,761 miles, the Premier company claimed.

116. *A Complete Official Road Guide of the Lincoln Highway*, 5th ed. (Detroit: Lincoln Highway Association, 1924; repr. Tucson, Ariz.: Patrice Press, 1993), p. 13.

117. C. Francis Jenkins, "A Transcontinental Highway," letter, *Scientific American*, June 15, 1912, p. 535; *Automobile*, Feb. 15, 1912, p. 482.

118. *Automobile*, Feb. 15, 1912, pp. 479, 481; *Motor Age*, July 13, 1911, p. 10.

119. *Motor Age*, July 13, 1911, p. 10; *Chicago Daily News*, July 8, 1911, p. 2, col. 2.

120. "Premier Party Gathers Honor," *Los Angeles Times*, Aug. 12, 1911, p. 9, col. 1.

121. Chester Lawrence, "Ocean to Ocean Auto Trip May Pave Way for a National Boulevard," *Los Angeles Examiner*, Aug. 13, 1911, sec. 7, p. 1, col. 7.

122. *Complete Official Road Guide of the Lincoln Highway*, 5th ed. (1924), p. 41; John Guy Monihan, "Across America by Auto," *Harper's Weekly*, Jan. 6, 1912, p. 11.

123. McNamara's comments on road conditions come from three verbatim accounts: Ray McNamara, "Two Ocean-to-Ocean Highways," *Motor Age*, Sept. 14, 1911, pp. 20–21; "Automobile Touring Across the American Continent the Real Thing," *New York Times*, Sept. 17, 1911, p. 8C; and "McNamara on Transcontinental Tours," *Automobile Topics*, Sept. 30, 1911, pp. 1319–21.

124. *Automobile*, Feb. 15, 1912, p. 484.

125. *San Francisco Call*, Aug. 4, 1911, p. 11, col. 5.

126. *Automobile*, March 14, 1912, p. 695.

127. *Automobile*, Feb. 15, 1912, p. 482; *Harper's Weekly*, Jan. 6, 1912, p. 11; *Complete Official Road Guide of the Lincoln Highway*, 5th ed. (1924), pp. 41, 43, 109.

128. "News of the Week Condensed," *Automobile*, Nov. 23, 1911, p. 924. This is the booklet titled *Ocean to Ocean Tour of the Premierites Told by Wire and Photo*, cited throughout this chapter.

129. Untitled blurb, *Automobile*, Nov. 2, 1911, p. 785.

130. Premier ads in *Automobile*, Dec. 28, 1911, p. 141, and in *Motor Age*, Oct. 5, 1911, p. 76; *Ocean to Ocean Tour*, p. 1.

131. *Automobile Topics*, Dec. 23, 1911, p. 301.

132. "Ocean-to-Ocean Tour's Lessons," *Automobile Topics*, Dec. 9, 1911, p. 191.

133. *New York Times*, July 30, 1911, sec. 4, p. 8, col. 7, and Sept. 17, 1911, p. 8C, col. 1.

134. "H. O. Smith, Premier Factory Chief, Here," *Los Angeles Times*, Nov. 26, 1911, sec. 7, p. 1, col. 5.

135. "Great Tour Ends by Pacific Waters," *Los Angeles Herald*, Aug. 13, 1911, sec. 3, p. 8, col. 1; Bert C. Smith, "Sea to Sea Motor Tour Means National Highway," *Los Angeles Times*, Aug. 13, 1911, sec. 7, p. 4, col. 1.

136. "Transcontinental Stone Road Project," *Automobile*, Sept. 12, 1912, p. 518; Lincoln Highway Association, *The Lincoln Highway: The Story of a Crusade That Made Transportation History* (New York: Dodd, Mead & Co., 1935), p. 15.

137. *Complete Official Road Guide of the Lincoln Highway*, 5th ed. (1924), p. 107.

138. President Wilson's signing of the federal-aid highway bill is from "Signs Good Roads Bill, *New York Times*, July 12, 1916, p. 6, col. 4. Lincoln Highway paving figures are from *A Complete Official Road Guide of the Lincoln Highway*, 5th ed. (1924), p. 108.

139. "Transcontinental Movement Progressing," *Automobile*, May 15, 1913, p. 1015.

140. *Motor Age*, Aug. 17, 1911, p. 8.

Chapter 4

1. "Long Tour Planned," *Motor Age*, Aug. 24, 1911, p. 13.

2. "Coast-to-Coast Tours in Favor," *New York Times*, Sept. 24, 1911, sec. 4, p. 8, col. 1; "Ocean to Ocean Auto Touring Party Arrives," *Omaha (Neb.) World-Herald*, Oct. 22, 1911, p. 8N, col. 2.

3. *New York Times*, Sept. 24, 1911, sec. 4, p. 8, col. 1.

4. Ibid.

5. Ibid.; "R. & W. Tourists Spend Night and Day in Trinidad," *Trinidad (Colo.) Chronicle-News*, Nov. 2, 1911, p. 2.

6. "Transcontinental Tour Information," *Automobile Topics*, Sept. 23, 1911, p. 1289.

7. "'The Trail to Sunset,'" *MoToR*, December 1911, p. 60. The full citation for the AAA booklet is Anthon L. Westgard, *Strip Maps of the "Trail to Sunset" Transcontinental Automobile Route: Chicago–Los Angeles via Santa Fe Trail* (New York: American Automobile Association, 1911).

8. "On Tour in Autos from New York to 'Frisco," *South Bend (Ind.) Times*, Oct. 14, 1911, p. 10, col. 3.

9. *New York Times*, Sept. 24, 1911, sec. 4, p. 8, col. 1.

10. For the information on Eubank's background, see *Who Was Who in America, 1951–1960* (Chicago: Marquis Who's Who, 1963), p. 265.

11. Victor Eubank, "Log of an Auto Prairie Schooner," *Sunset*, February 1912, p. 188.

12. *Sunset*, February 1912, p. 190.

13. "Automobile Train Leaves for the Coast," *New York Herald*, Oct. 3, 1911, p. 12, cols. 1, 3.

14. "Doing the Big Automobile Tour," photo in the *New York Times*, Oct. 8, 1911, p. 8C, col. 3.

15. *New York Times*, Oct. 8, 1911, p. 8C, col. 4.

16. "'The Trail to Sunset'—A Transcontinental Tour to Be Made by 10 Garford Touring Cars Accompanied by a Garford Truck," *Elyria (Ohio) Evening Telegram*, Aug. 28, 1911, p. 2, col. 1; *Motor Age*, Aug. 24, 1911, p. 13.

17. "Coast to Coast Automobile Tour," *La Junta (Colo.) Tribune*, Nov. 4, 1911, p. 2, col. 2.

18. *New York Herald*, Oct. 3, 1911, p. 12, col. 3.

19. *Elyria (Ohio) Evening Telegram*, Aug. 28, 1911, p. 2, col. 1.

20. "Coast-to-Coast Auto Party Stops Off Here," *Erie (Pa.) Dispatch*, Oct. 10, 1911, p. 1, col. 6.

21. "Autoists on Trip to Coast in City," *Cleveland Leader*, Oct. 11, 1911, p. 8, col. 3; "Transcontinental Auto Train Arrives," *Elyria (Ohio) Evening Telegram*, Oct. 11, 1911, p. 1, col. 3.

22. "Autoists Are Entertained in This City," *Elyria (Ohio) Evening Telegram*, Oct. 12, 1911, pp. 1, 8.

23. "Gossip of the Automobilists and Notes of the Trade," *New York Times*, Oct. 15, 1911, p. 8C, col. 5.

24. Specifications and historical details are from "The Improved Garford G-8 Chassis For 1911," *Motor Age*, Dec. 22, 1910, pp. 22–23; "Details of Passenger Automobiles on the American Market for 1911," *Automobile*, Jan. 5, 1911, pp. 80–81; and Beverly Rae Kimes and Henry Austin Clark, Jr., *Standard Catalog of American Cars, 1805–1942*, 2d ed., (Iola, Wis.: Krause Publications, 1989), p. 601.

25. *South Bend (Ind.) Times*, Oct. 14, 1911, p. 10, col. 3.

26. "Auto Train Here in 4,200 Mile Journey," *Chicago Inter Ocean*, Oct. 15, 1911, p. 8, col. 5.

27. *New York Times*, Sept. 24, 1911, sec. 4, p. 8, col. 1.

28. A. L. Westgard, "Long Distance Touring in America," *Club Journal* (American Automobile Association), April 17, 1909, p. 7.

29. "To Spend Night Here," *Hutchinson (Kan.) News*, Oct. 27, 1911, p. 9, col. 3.

30. *Sunset*, February 1912, p. 191.

31. "Big Truck Travels Overland," *Motor Age*, March 30, 1911, p. 24; "Saurer Finishes Trip," *Motor Age*, Aug. 10, 1911, p. 12. Several other articles from *Motor Age* provided background information on the journey: "Saurer Truck on Long Tour," March 16, 1911, p. 42; "Progress of Saurer Truck," April 27, 1911, p. 31; "Truck Near Journey's End," May 4, 1911, p. 37; "Long Truck Run Ends," May 18, 1911, p. 32; "Saurer Headed East," June 29, 1911, p. 19; and "Saurer Reaches Chicago," July 6, 1911, p. 38. Background information was also drawn from a series of articles published in *Automobile*: "Roads and Routes," March 23, 1911, pp. 804–5; "Roads and Routes," March 30, 1911, p. 846; "Saurer Truck Nearing Its Goal," April 27, 1911, p. 1019; "The Week's Doings in Detroit," July 20, 1911, p. 121; and "Saurer Truck Reaches New York," Aug. 3, 1911, p. 205.

32. *Motor Age*, April 27, 1911, p. 31.

33. *Motor Age*, July 6, 1911, p. 38.

34. See the following articles from the *New York Times*: "Three Continental Trips," June 16, 1912, sec. 7, p. 14, col. 7; "Pathfinder Due Tuesday," Sept. 22, 1912, sec. 8, p. 10, col. 7; "More Roads for Autoists," Sept. 25, 1912, p. 11, col. 2; "Second Route Completed," Oct. 6, 1912, sec. 9, p. 13, col. 3; and "Midland Auto Trail," Oct. 13, 1912, sec. 7, p. 15, col. 1.

35. "Likes River to River Highway Through Iowa," *Omaha (Neb.) World-Herald*, Oct. 23, 1911, p. 2, col. 5.

36. "Trans-Continental Tourists in City," *Davenport (Iowa) Daily Times*, Oct. 17, 1911, p. 4, col. 3; "Westgaard [*sic*] Tourists Pass through Town," *Grinnell (Iowa) Herald*, Oct. 20, 1911, p. 1, col. 7.

37. "Garford Tourists on Santa Fe Trail," *Automobile*, Oct. 26, 1911, p. 734.

38. "Route of Ocean to Ocean Auto Party in Atchison To-Day," *Atchison (Kan.) Daily Globe*, Oct. 24, 1911, p. 1, col. 6.

39. "Seeing America By Motor," *Kansas City (Mo.) Star*, Oct. 25, 1911, p. 2, col. 2.

40. *Kansas City (Mo.) Star*, Oct. 25, 1911, p. 2, col. 2.

41. Ibid.

42. *Sunset*, February 1912, pp. 191–92.

43. "Auto Caravan Is Delayed by Snow," *Newton (Kan.) Evening Kansan-Republican*, Oct. 28, 1911, p. 1, col. 1.

44. "Westgard and Party," *Hutchinson (Kan.) News*, Oct. 28, 1911, p. 8, col. 4. The "Harvey system" refers to a chain of hotels and restaurants, including railway dining cars and lunchrooms, established by Frederick Henry Harvey, who was employed with the Sante Fe Railroad. Harvey's goal was to provide travelers with good, solid food—much of it grown on the Fred Harvey Farm, in Newton, Kansas—and comfortable, congenial accommodations at a reasonable price. In their heyday, around the time of World War I, there were over 80 Harvey Houses scattered throughout the Southwest.

45. *Hutchinson (Kan.) News*, Oct. 28, 1911, p. 8, col. 4. By "dragging," Westgard refers to the dragging of a heavy timber behind an automobile or team of horses, a popular early method of smoothing dirt highways.

46. *Hutchinson (Kan.) News*, Oct. 28, 1911, p. 8, col. 5.

47. "Motorists Found a Sticky Trail," *Dodge City (Kan.) Globe*, Nov. 2, 1911, p. 1, col. 3.

48. *New York Times*, Sept. 24, 1911, sec. 4, p. 8, col. 2.

49. *La Junta (Colo.) Tribune*, Nov. 4, 1911, p. 2, col. 2.

50. *Trinidad (Colo.) Chronicle-News*, Nov. 2, 1911, pp. 1, 2.

51. *Sunset*, February 1912, p. 193.

52. *Trinidad (Colo.) Chronicle-News*, Nov. 2, 1911, pp. 1, 2.

53. "Seeing America First and Mud Afterward," *Santa Fe New Mexican*, Nov. 6, 1911, n.p.

54. "Auto Tourists to Resume Trip This Morning," *Albuquerque (N.M.) Morning Journal*, Nov. 7, 1911, p. 3, col. 2.

55. *Sunset*, February 1912, p. 193.

56. Ibid., pp. 188, 192.

57. Ibid., p. 194.

58. *New York Times*, Sept. 24, 1911, sec. 4, p. 8, col. 2.

59. *Sunset*, February 1912, p. 194.

60. Ibid.

61. "Auto Tourists Reach Phoenix," *New York Times*, Nov. 12, 1911, sec. 4, p. 8, col. 6. In its account of Sunday, Nov. 12, the *New York Times* assumed that the Garford auto train had adhered to its schedule and had arrived in Phoenix on Saturday, Nov. 11. The article therefore treats the arrival as a fact. Thanks to delays, however, the cars did not actually reach Phoenix until Tuesday, Nov. 14.

62. "Eastern Tourists Coming to City by Automobile," *San Diego Union*, Nov. 19, 1911, n.p.; "Westgard Party Left This Morning," article from the *Yuma (Ariz.) Daily Examiner* reprinted in the *Arizona Sentinel* (Yuma), Nov. 23, 1911, p. 5.

63. *Arizona Sentinel* (Yuma), Nov. 23, 1911, p. 5. For the information about the Yuma Irrigation Project, see Henry G. Alsberg and Harry Hansen, eds., *Arizona: The Grand Canyon State*, 4th ed. (New York: Hastings House, 1966), p. 273.

64. A. L. Westgard, "National Highway from Atlantic to Pacific," *Los Angeles Times*, Nov. 26, 1911, sec. 7, p. 3, col. 5; *Sunset*, February 1912, p. 195.

65. *San Diego Union*, Nov. 19, 1911, n.p.

66. "Continental Auto Tourists Declare Local Route Is Best of All," *San Diego Union*, Nov. 22, 1911, p. 12, col. 1.

67. *San Diego Union*, Nov. 22, 1911, p. 12, col. 1.

68. F. L. Copley, "Garford Tourist Train Sets New Continental Record," *Los Angeles Evening Herald*, Nov. 25, 1911, p. 13, col. 1; Bert C. Smith, "Garford Cars Cover the Long Trail to Sunset," *Los Angeles Times*, Nov. 26, 1911, sec. 7, p. 2, col. 1.

69. Bert C. Smith, "Garford Cars Complete Ocean-to-Ocean Tour," *Los Angeles Times*, Nov. 24, 1911, sec. 3, p. 1, col. 6.

70. "Garford Tells of Motor Tour," *Los Angeles Times*, Nov. 24, 1911, sec. 3, p. 4.

71. *Sunset*, February 1912, pp. 192–93.

72. *Los Angeles Times*, Nov. 24, 1911, sec. 3, p. 1, col. 3; "Will Entertain Tourists at Banquet," *Pasadena (Calif.) Star*, Nov. 23, 1911, p. 14, col. 1.

73. "Men of Affairs Welcome Ocean-to-Ocean Tourers," *Los Angeles Times*, Nov. 24, 1911, sec. 3, p. 3, col. 2.

74. Ibid.

75. "End Long Trip at Pasadena Last Evening," *Pasadena (Calif.) Star*, Nov. 24, 1911, p. 3, col. 1; *Los Angeles Evening Herald*, Nov. 25, 1911, p. 13, col. 1.

76. *Pasadena (Calif.) Star*, Nov. 24, 1911, p. 3, col. 1.

77. The background information on Rodgers's trip is from "Rodgers Off in Race, Flying Eighty Miles," *New York Times*, Sept. 18, 1911, p. 1, col. 5; and, from the Nov. 6, 1911, edition, C. P. Rodgers, "Rodgers Ends Long Flight," p. 1, col. 7, and p. 2, col. 1; "20,000 See Rodgers Land," p. 2, col. 1; and "Story of Rodgers's Flight," p. 2, col. 2.

78. "Garford Cars on Ocean-to-Ocean Trip Reach Los Angeles," *Elyria (Ohio) Evening Telegram*, Nov. 27, 1911, p. 1, col. 3, and p. 5, col. 1.

79. *Los Angeles Times*, Nov. 26, 1911, sec. 7, p. 2, col. 2.

80. "Midwinter Auto Tours in California," in unnumbered advertising section of *Sunset*, February 1912.

81. *New York Times*, Sept. 24, 1911, sec. 4, p. 8, col. 1.

82. *Los Angeles Times*, Nov. 26, 1911, sec. 7, p. 1, col. 6.

83. Ibid.; "Ocean-to-Ocean Tour," *Larned (Kan.) Chronoscope*, Nov. 2, 1911, p. 1, col. 3.

84. As described in "Covers 10,000 Miles," *New York Times*, Dec. 7, 1913, sec. 9, p. 9, col. 6.

85. "Stutz Stunt Encourages Transcontinental Touring," *Motor West*, June 15, 1915, p. 18.

86. A. L. Westgard, "Motor Routes to the California Expositions," *MoToR*, March 1915, n.p.

87. The quotation concerning Westgard is from "Westgard—Chief of Pathfinders," an undated clipping from an unidentified magazine—perhaps *American Motorist*—in the Westgard photo file at the Free Library of Philadelphia's Automobile Reference Collection. The full citation for his book is Anthon L. Westgard, *Tales of a Pathfinder* (New York: A. L. Westgard, 1920). For background on Eubank's later years, see *Who Was Who in America, 1951–1960*, p. 265.

88. *Sunset*, February 1912, p. 191.

89. Ibid.

90. Ibid., p. 195.

Chapter 5

1. "Baker Starts Flying Trip Across Country," *Indianapolis News*, May 7, 1915, p. 18, col. 6.

2. "Came from Coast Here in Eight Days," *Greenville (Ill.) Advocate*, May 17, 1915, p. 3, col. 4.

3. Russ Catlin, "The Inimitable Mister Baker," *Automobile Quarterly*, vol. 13, no. 1 (1975), p. 41.

4. The Automobile Club of America's "Certified Test No. 19," as reproduced in the back of the twenty-page publicity booklet the Stutz factory published following the trip: W. F. Sturm, *Stutz: 11 Days 7 Hours 15 Minutes—A Story* (Indianapolis: Stutz Motor Car Co., 1915?), p. 17. Page numbers, absent in the original, have been assigned in this and all later references to the factory's publicity booklet.

5. Biographical information about Baker is from Scripps-Howard syndicated columnist Ernie Pyle, "Hoosier Vagabond," *Indianapolis Times*, Aug. 16, 1940, p. 13, col. 2; Kenneth Hufford, "5,500,000 Famous Miles," *Indianapolis Star Magazine*, May 24, 1953, pp. 16, 18; and *Automobile Quarterly*, vol. 13, no. 1 (1975), p. 39, which says that in his vaudeville days Baker could keep five—not eleven, as Pyle contends—punching bags moving at once. Pyle became famous as a correspondent during World War II.

6. His *New York Times* obituary, "Erwin G. Baker, Early Car Racer" (May 11, 1960, p. 39, col. 5), says Baker first raced his motorcycle at Crawfordsville, Indiana, in "about 1904." In a 1975 article for *Automobile Quarterly* based on "countless conversations with the Cannon Ball," automotive historian Russ Catlin agrees that Baker's first race took place at Crawfordsville but gives the date as July 4, 1908. Many other retrospective pieces, however, say 1906.

7. On Baker's July 1911 victories, see the *Indianapolis News*, "Baker Loses Hoodoo and Wins Four Races," July 4, 1911, p. 13, col. 1; and "Improved Track Helps Demon Motorcyclists," July 5, 1911, p. 12, col. 5. See also the *Indianapolis Star*, "Baker Lowers Track Record," July 4, 1911, p. 9, col. 5, and, in the July 5 edition, "Taft Greets Winner of Special Motorcycle Race," p. 6, col. 3, photo and caption, and "Fast Time Marks Motorcycle Races," p. 11, col. 4.

8. In "Baker Cuts in Two Coast-to-Coast Mark" (*Indianapolis News*, May 18, 1915, p. 12, col. 2), reporter W. F. Sturm says that Baker traveled 3,378.9 miles on his 1914 motorcycle trip. Baker's own account, however, says 3,497 miles ("Motorcyclist Tells of How He Broke All Coast-Coast Records," *Salt Lake (City) Herald-Republican*, June 28, 1914, p. 4, col. 6, of sports section).

9. "Ocean-to-Ocean Record," *New York Times*, May 15, 1914, p. 13, col. 7.

10. *Salt Lake (City) Herald-Republican*, June 28, 1914, p. 4, col. 6, of sports section.

11. Merle Crowell, "'Cannonball' Baker—Who Lives a Life of Thrills," *American Magazine*, September 1923, p. 186.

12. *American Magazine*, September 1923, p. 184.

13. Ibid.

14. Ibid.

15. "New Auto Record Run from San Diego," *New York Times*, May 19, 1915, p. 11, col. 5; "New Transcontinental Record," *Automobile*, May 20, 1915, p. 911.

16. Ernie Pyle, "Hoosier Vagabond," *Indianapolis Times*, Aug. 15, 1940, p. 15, col. 2.

17. Hartford Suspension Company ad in *Automobile*, June 24, 1915, p. 1 of ad section.

18. "Sturm's Death Recalls Early Race Exploits to Automotive Veterans," *Indianapolis News*, Aug. 26, 1937, sec. 2, p. 4, col. 6.

19. *Greenville (Ill.) Advocate*, May 17, 1915, p. 3, col. 4; *Stutz: 11 Days 7 Hours 15 Minutes*, p. 3. On the Stutz booklet, see n. 4 to this chapter.

20. *Indianapolis News*, Aug. 26, 1937, sec. 2, p. 4, col. 6; W. F. Sturm, "Fastest One-Man Auto Drive Ever Made Across America," *American Chauffeur*, February 1916, p. 65.

21. Ibid.

22. Ibid.

23. *Automobile*, May 20, 1915, p. 911.

24. "Baker Ready for Long Dash Across Continent," *Indianapolis News*, May 5, 1915, p. 10, col. 7; *Stutz: 11 Days 7 Hours 15 Minutes*, p. 3.

25. *Stutz: 11 Days 7 Hours 15 Minutes*, pp. 3–4.

26. *Indianapolis News*, May 7, 1915, p. 18, col. 6. In the *Stutz* booklet, Sturm spells the name of the *San Diego Union*'s city editor as "Gwellow" and calls him the managing editor.

27. Beverly Rae Kimes and Henry Austin Clark, Jr., *Standard Catalog of American Cars, 1805–1942*, 2d ed. (Iola, Wis.: Krause Publications, 1989), p. 1394.

28. The Wisconsin Motor Manufacturing Company of West Allis, Wisconsin, made engines for the Stutz autos. For more about this early engine maker, see Curt McConnell, "Wisconsin Engines: State of the Engine, State of the Art," *Automobile Quarterly*, vol. 40, no. 1 (March 2000), pp. 82–97.

29. The SAE formula requires squaring the cylinder bore, multiplying by the number of cylinders, and then dividing the result by 2.5. The 1915 Stutz Bearcat had a cylinder bore of 4.75 inches, the square of which is 22.5625. Multiplying that figure by four (for 4 cylinders) yields 90.25, which divided by 2.5 gives the SAE horsepower—36.1.

30. For Stutz specifications, see the following articles in *Automobile*: "Small Four Runabout Is Newest Stutz," Oct. 1, 1914, p. 634; "Passenger Cars for 1915 Listed with Their Principal Specifications," Dec. 31, 1914, pp. 1226–27; May 20, 1915, p. 911; "A.C.A. Tests Transcontinental Stutz," May 27, 1915, p. 954; and "One Set of Goodyear Tires on Transcontinental Stutz," June 3, 1915, p. 1008.

31. *Stutz: 11 Days 7 Hours 15 Minutes*, p. 19.

32. "Stutz Establishes New Transcontinental Record," *Horseless Age*, May 19, 1915, p. 666; "Covers 3,728 Miles in Eleven Days," *Automobile Topics*, May 22, 1915, p. 123.

33. *Stutz: 11 Days 7 Hours 15 Minutes*, pp. 3, 4.

34. Leather Tire Goods Company ad, *Automobile Trade Directory*, April 1916, p. 80.

35. *Stutz: 11 Days 7 Hours 15 Minutes*, p. 3.

36. "Baker Making History on Continental Trip," *Indianapolis News*, May 8, 1915, p. 11, col. 1.

37. *Stutz: 11 Days 7 Hours 15 Minutes*, p. 4.

38. *Indianapolis News*, May 7, 1915, p. 18, col. 6.

39. *Stutz: 11 Days 7 Hours 15 Minutes*, p. 5.

40. Ibid.

41. *Indianapolis News*, May 8, 1915, p. 11, col. 1.

42. "Stutz Gets A.C.A. Certified Test," *Automobile Topics*, June 5, 1915, p. 304.

43. *Stutz: 11 Days 7 Hours 15 Minutes*, pp. 5–6, 7.

44. *American Magazine*, September 1923, p. 184; *Indianapolis News*, May 8, 1915, p. 11, col. 1; *Stutz: 11 Days 7 Hours 15 Minutes*, p. 6.

45. *American Magazine*, September 1923, p. 186.

46. *Stutz: 11 Days 7 Hours 15 Minutes*, pp. 6, 7.

47. Sturm has neglected to compensate for El Paso time running one hour ahead of San Diego time. If he is using the correct elapsed time, the car actually arrived in El Paso at 2:15 A.M. Sunday. If he is using the correct arrival time, 1:15 A.M., the car's actual elapsed time must be 2 days, 15 minutes.

48. *Stutz: 11 Days 7 Hours 15 Minutes*, p. 7.

49. Ibid., p. 8.

50. Ibid.

51. W. F. Sturm, "Ahead of Record in Coast-to-Coast Dash," *Indianapolis News*, May 10, 1915, p. 10, col. 2.

52. *Stutz: 11 Days 7 Hours 15 Minutes*, p. 9.

53. Ibid., pp. 9–10.

54. W. F. Sturm, "Baker Nears Kansas in Coast-to-Coast Run," *Indianapolis News*, May 11, 1915, p. 13, col. 4.

55. *American Magazine*, September 1923, p. 186.

56. *Indianapolis News*, May 11, 1915, p. 13, col. 4; *Automobile Quarterly*, vol. 13, no. 1 (1975), p. 39.

57. *Indianapolis Times*, Aug. 16, 1940, p. 13, col. 1.

58. *Stutz: 11 Days 7 Hours 15 Minutes*, pp. 10, 11.

59. Ibid., p. 11.

60. W. F. Sturm, "Baker Due Here Sunday on Dash to Atlantic," *Indianapolis News*, May 12, 1915, p. 12, col. 7.

61. Ibid.

62. "Baker in Dodge," *Dodge City Kansas Journal*, May 13, 1915, p. 1, col. 2.

63. *Stutz: 11 Days 7 Hours 15 Minutes*, pp. 11–12; *Automobile Topics*, June 5, 1915, p. 304, which renders the name "F. M. Kim."

64. "He Is a Real Live Cannonball, Too," *Dodge City (Kan.) Daily Globe*, May 12, 1915, p. 1, col. 4.

65. "Baker Is Going Some; 1655 Miles in 3 Days," *Dodge City (Kan.) Daily Globe*, May 11, 1916, p. 1, col. 6, and May 12, 1915, p. 4, col. 2. On the 1914 motorcycle races in Dodge City, see "Glen Boyd, of Denver, Won 300-Mile Motorcycle Race in Record Breaking Time," *Dodge City (Kan.) Daily Globe*, July 6, 1914, p. 1, col. 4.

66. W. F. Sturm, "Baker Shoots Through Kansas on Way East," *Indianapolis News*, May 13, 1915, p. 13, col. 1.

67. *Stutz: 11 Days 7 Hours 15 Minutes*, p. 12; *Automobile Topics*, May 22, 1915, p. 123; "Pauses Here in Cross-Continent Dash to Break Record," *Kansas City Post*, May 16, 1915, p. 3C, col. 2.

68. W. F. Sturm, "Coast-to-Coast Driver Is Due Here Saturday," *Indianapolis News*, May 14, 1915, p. 22, col. 5.

69. W. F. Sturm, "Flying Baker Is Due in Indianapolis Today," *Indianapolis News*, May 15, 1915, p. 11, col. 1.

70. *Greenville (Ill.) Advocate*, May 17, 1915, p. 3, col. 4; *Indianapolis News*, May 15, 1915, p. 11, col. 1.

71. *Stutz: 11 Days 7 Hours 15 Minutes*, p. 13.

72. Ibid.

73. W. F. Sturm, "Baker Likely to Break Ocean-to-Ocean Mark," *Indianapolis News*, May 17, 1915, p. 10, col. 5.

74. "Coast to Coast Autoists Here," *Donora (Pa.) American*, May 21, 1915, n.p.

75. *Stutz: 11 Days 7 Hours 15 Minutes*, p. 13.

76. "Transcontinental Tourists in Town," *Trenton (N.J.) Evening Times*, May 18, 1915, p. 2.

77. "Coast to Coast Run in 11 Days," *New York Herald*, May 19, 1915, p. 9, col. 7.

78. "Tourists Return from Cross-Country Jaunt," *Indianapolis News*, May 20, 1915, p. 14, col. 5.

79. *Indianapolis Times*, Aug. 16, 1940, p. 13, col. 1.

80. *New York Times*, May 19, 1915, p. 11, col. 5.

81. *Indianapolis News*, May 20, 1915, p. 14, col. 5, and May 18, 1915, p. 12, col. 2; "Baker Breaks Record," *Indianapolis Star*, May 19, 1915, p. 10, col. 3.

82. *Stutz: 11 Days 7 Hours 15 Minutes*, p. 17. A summary of the ACA report appeared as "A.C.A. Tests Stutz Transcontinental Car," *Horseless Age*, May 26, 1915, p. 697; and *Automobile Topics*, June 5, 1915, p. 303, published a verbatim reprint of the report.

83. "Certified Test No. 19," in *Stutz: 11 Days 7 Hours 15 Minutes*, pp. 17, 18.

84. Ibid.; "Stutz Features New Bodies Mounted on Two Four-Cylinder Chassis," *Automobile*, Aug. 5, 1915, p. 240.

85. Stutz Motor Car Company ad in the *New York Times*, May 23, 1915, sec. 7, p. 10, col. 7.

86. Wisconsin Motor Manufacturing Company ad in the *Commercial Car Journal*, July 15, 1915, p. 73.

87. Stromberg Motor Devices Company ad in *Automobile Topics*, May 29, 1915, p. 229.

88. Houk Manufacturing Company ad in *Automobile*, June 3, 1915, p. 96.

89. *Automobile Quarterly*, vol. 31, no. 1 (1975), p. 41.

90. March 25, 1916, letter of the Lincoln Highway Association, Special Collections Library, Harlan Hatcher Graduate Library, University of Michigan, Ann Arbor.

91. Kimes and Clark, *Standard Catalog of American Cars, 1805–1942*, 2d ed., pp. 662, 1394–95.

92. "Stutz Stunt Encourages Transcontinental Touring," *Motor West*, June 15, 1915, p. 18.

93. "Cross Country Runs Prove Automobile's Reliability," *MoToR*, October 1915, p. 56.

Chapter 6

1. "Coast-to-Coast Record Is Shattered by Baker," *Indianapolis News*, May 16, 1916, p. 16, col. 1; "'Cannon Ball' Baker Passes Thru City on Coast-to-Coast Automobile Dash," *Trinidad (Colo.) Chronicle-News*, May 10, 1916, p. 1, col. 1.

2. "New Coast to Coast Record Established," *Salt Lake (City) Tribune*, July 21, 1916, p. 1, col. 4, of auto section.

3. "Cadillac Has Again Broken a World Record," *Dayton (Ohio) Daily News*, May 16, 1916, p. 8, col. 4.

4. Russ Catlin, "The Inimitable Mister Baker," *Automobile Quarterly*, vol. 13, no. 1 (1975), p. 44. For information on speed limits, see the "General Information" sections on specific states in *The Complete Official Road Guide of the Lincoln Highway* (Detroit: Lincoln Highway Association, 1916; repr. Sacramento, Calif.: Pleiades Press, 1995).

5. Merle Crowell, "'Cannonball' Baker—Who Lives a Life of Thrills," *American Magazine*, September 1923, p. 182.

6. Ibid., p. 180.

7. Ibid., p. 184.

8. Cadillac ad in the *Saturday Evening Post*, June 17, 1916, p. 55.

9. "New Road Record a Remarkable Test," *Omaha (Neb.) World-Herald*, May 21, 1916, p. 12E, col. 5.

10. Specifications for the Cadillac Type 53 roadster can be found in "1916 Passenger Automobiles Listed with Their Technical Specifications," *Automobile*, Dec. 30, 1915, pp. 1248–49; "A Transcontinental Record," *Automobile*, May 18, 1916, p. 909; and Beverly Rae Kimes and Henry Austin Clark, Jr., *Standard Catalog of American Cars, 1805–1942*, 2d ed. (Iola, Wis.: Krause Publications, 1989), p. 199.

11. Duncan Curry, "Cross Country Auto 5½ Days," *San Francisco Examiner*, May 16, 1916, p. 6, col. 4.

12. "Baker Is Going Some; 1655 Miles in 3 Days," *Dodge City (Kan.) Daily Globe*, May 11, 1916, p. 1, col. 6.

13. "Auto Makes Record in Run from Pacific," *New York Times*, May 16, 1916, p. 7, col. 2; *Automobile*, May 18, 1916, p. 909.

14. *Automobile*, May 18, 1916, p. 909.

15. *Trinidad (Colo.) Chronicle-News*, May 10, 1916, p. 1, col. 1.

16. "Cadillac Endurance Run," *La Junta (Colo.) Tribune*, May 13, 1916, p. 4, col. 3.

17. *Dodge City (Kan.) Daily Globe*, May 11, 1916, p. 1, col. 6.

18. *New York Times*, May 16, 1916, p. 7, col. 2.

19. *Dodge City (Kan.) Daily Globe*, May 11, 1916, p. 1, col. 6. "Going some"—an early twentieth-century colloquialism—meant "driving fast."

20. "Smashing Records," *Hutchinson (Kan.) Daily News*, May 13, 1916, p. 11, col. 4; "Baker Breaking Record," *Hutchinson (Kan.) Daily Gazette*, May 12, 1916, p. 4, col. 1.

21. *Indianapolis News*, May 16, 1916, p. 16, col. 1.

22. "Baker and Sturm Are Far Ahead of Record," *Indianapolis News*, May 15, 1916, p. 12, col. 1.

23. *Indianapolis News*, May 16, 1916, p. 16, col. 1.

24. "Coast-to-Coast Record Breakers Return Home," *Indianapolis News*, May 20, 1916, p. 10, col. 8.

25. *Indianapolis News*, May 15, 1916, p. 12, col. 1.

26. *Indianapolis News*, May 16, 1916, p. 16, col. 1.

27. *Dayton (Ohio) Daily News*, May 16, 1916, p. 8, col. 4.

28. "Crossed Continent in Seven Days and Half," *Columbus (Ohio) Evening Dispatch*, May 16, 1916, p. 6, col. 3; *Indianapolis News*, May 15, 1916, p. 12, col. 1. The *Dayton (Ohio) Daily News* offered an imaginative variation on the strapped-in story. Mistakenly assuming that Sturm and Baker took turns driving, the *Daily News* reported that "while one was driving, the other was strapped on the car getting what sleep he could."

29. "Makes New Auto Record," *Philadelphia Inquirer*, May 16, 1916, p. 10, col. 7.

30. "In Auto, Beats His Mail 'Cross Country," *New York Tribune*, May 16, 1916, p. 3, col. 4.

31. *New York Times*, May 16, 1916, p. 7, col. 2.

32. "Monday to Monday, Coast to Coast," *MoToR*, June 1916, p. 87.

33. *Indianapolis News*, May 16, 1916, p. 16, col. 1.

34. *New York Times*, May 16, 1916, p. 7, col. 2.

35. *Automobile*, May 18, 1916, p. 909; *Trinidad (Colo.) Chronicle-News*, May 10, 1916, p. 1, col. 1.

36. *New York Times*, May 16, 1916, p. 7, col. 2; *New York Tribune*, May 16, 1916, p. 3, col. 4.

37. *Indianapolis News*, May 16, 1916, p. 16, col. 1; *New York Times*, May 16, 1916, p. 7, col. 2.

38. *Automobile*, May 18, 1916, p. 909.

39. *New York Times*, May 16, 1916, p. 7, col. 2.

40. Cadillac ads in the *Saturday Evening Post*, June 17, 1916, p. 55, and in the *Omaha (Neb.) World-Herald*, May 21, 1916, p. 11E.

41. *Automobile*, May 18, 1916, p. 909.

42. Electric Storage Battery Company ad in *MoToR*, September 1916, p. 194.

43. Cadillac ad in *MoToR*, August 1916, p. 37.

44. "Baker and Sturm in Detroit," *Indianapolis News*, May 18, 1916, p. 12, col. 6.

45. *Indianapolis News*, May 20, 1916, p. 10, col. 8.

46. *New York Times*, May 16, 1916, p. 7, col. 2.

47. *Indianapolis News*, May 16, 1916, p. 16, col. 1.

48. *Automobile Quarterly*, vol. 13, no. 1 (1975), p. 38.

49. Scripps-Howard syndicated columnist Ernie Pyle, "Hoosier Vagabond," *Indianapolis Times*, Aug. 15, 1940, p. 15, col. 1; Welton W. Harris II, "Hoosier 'Cannonball' Loved Speed," *Indianapolis News*, May 12, 1994, p. D1.

50. "Cannonball Baker," *Indianapolis News*, May 12, 1960, p. 10, col. 2.

Chapter 7

1. Marmon ad in *Automobile*, Aug. 17, 1916, p. 93. The Marmon company started production in 1905, although Howard C. Marmon had built and sold six cars, "mostly to friends," the previous year. See Beverly Rae Kimes and Henry Austin Clark, Jr., *Standard Catalog of American Cars, 1805–1942*, 2d ed. (Iola, Wis.: Krause Publications, 1989), p. 885.

2. "Marmon Coast-to-Coast Record," *Automobile*, Aug. 3, 1916, p. 168; "Cross Continent Record Broken by S. B. Stevens," *Rome (N.Y.) Daily Sentinel*, July 31, 1916, p. 5, col. 2; Marmon ad in *Automobile*, Aug. 17, 1916, p. 94. According to his *New York Times* obituary, Stevens was born on June 24, 1874; thus he had just turned 42 at the time of the 1916 crossing. See "S. B. Stevens Dies on Way to Coast," *New York Times*, Nov. 17, 1935, sec. 2, p. 11, col. 4.

3. "News and Notes of Auto Makers and Dealers," *New York Times*, Aug. 20, 1916, sec. 3, p. 8, col. 3.

4. "Breaking Auto Record," *Salt Lake (City) Herald-Republican*, July 27, 1916, p. 6, col. 1; *Rome (N.Y.) Daily Sentinel*, July 31, 1916, p. 2, col. 1. Many other newspapers besides the *Salt Lake (City) Herald-Republican* used the phrase "millionaire auto enthusiast" in describing Stevens.

5. Samuel B. Stevens, "The Garage of an Enthusiast," *MoToR*, August 1904, reprinted in the *Rome (N.Y.) Daily Sentinel*, Aug. 27, 1904, n.p.

6. *Rome (N.Y.) Daily Sentinel*, Aug. 27, 1904, n.p.; *New York Times*, Nov. 17, 1935, sec. 2, p. 11, col. 4; "Mr. Stevens's New Trophies," *Rome (N.Y.) Daily Sentinel*, Feb. 5, 1906, n.p. The 1906 *Sentinel* account doesn't say so, but the trophies Stevens displayed probably included those won by the drivers he often hired to race his cars.

7. *New York Herald* article, reprinted as "S. B. Stevens President," *Rome (N.Y.) Daily Sentinel*, Nov. 24, 1906, n.p.; *Chicago Inter Ocean*, June 18, 1909, p. 7, col. 1, photo and caption.

8. *New York Times*, Nov. 17, 1935, sec. 2, p. 11, col. 4; "All Records over Lincoln Highway Are Smashed," *White Pine News* (East Ely, Nev.), Aug. 6, 1916, p. 1, col. 5.

9. For Stevens's association with Fiat, see the *New York Times*, Nov. 17, 1935, sec. 2, p. 11, col. 4 (which also details Stevens's experiments involving aluminum pistons and rods). See also Kimes and Clark, *Standard Catalog of American Cars, 1805–1942*, 2d ed., p. 38. From 1892 to 1898 Stevens pursued a course in manufacturing from the Lawrence Scientific School, a separate school within Harvard College, according to an August 29, 1995, letter from Virginia L. Smyers of the Harvard University Archives. "Apparently Mr. Stevens left before receiving his degree," Smyers wrote.

10. On the activities of the American Defense Society, see the following articles in the *New York Times*: "New Defense Band Opens Local Office," Aug. 5, 1915, p. 5, col. 5; "Extend Defense Campaign," Aug. 19, 1915, p. 9, col. 5; "Plans to Win Congress," Sept. 16, 1915, p. 3, col. 2; "To Fight Bryan's Policy," Nov. 8, 1915, p. 8, col. 5; "Enroll for America First," Jan. 7, 1916, p. 8, col. 2; and "Teach Every One to Shoot," Feb. 19, 1916, p. 7, col. 3.

11. *Marmon News* account, in Charles L. Betts, Jr., "The Marmon Transcontinental Record," *Antique Automobile* (Antique Automobile Club of America), May–June 1966, p. 26.

12. Roger J. Spiller, ed., *Dictionary of American Military Biography* (Westport, Conn.: Greenwood Press, 1984), p. 1211.

13. "General Wood Groomed as G.O.P. Candidate," *Omaha (Neb.) World-Herald*, May 21, 1916, p. 9, col. 7; Spiller, ed., *Dictionary of American Military Biography*, p. 1211.

14. Spiller, ed., *Dictionary of American Military Biography*, pp. 80–81.

15. *Marmon News* account, in Betts, "The Marmon Transcontinental Record," *Antique Automobile*, May–June 1966, p. 26; *Rome (N.Y.) Daily Sentinel*, July 31, 1916, p. 5, col. 2.

16. "Defense Body Lauds Record Stevens Set," *San Francisco Examiner*, Aug. 6, 1916, p. 4, col. 2, of auto section.

17. "War Car Awaits Marching Orders," *New York Times*, Aug. 15, 1909, sec. 4, p. 4, col. 4.

18. "Motorcycle Relay Riders on Their Way," *Motorcycling & Bicycling*, July 19, 1915, reprinted in Floyd Clymer, *A Treasury of Motorcycles of the World* (New York: McGraw-Hill, 1965), pp. 198–200.

19. *Rome (N.Y.) Daily Sentinel*, July 31, 1916, p. 2, col. 1; "Marmon 34 Lowers Coast-to-Coast Mark," *Motor Age*, Aug. 3, 1916, p. 14; "Marmon Car Thru City," *Marshalltown (Iowa) Evening Times-Republican*, July 26, 1916, p. 9, col. 4.

20. *Rome (N.Y.) Daily Sentinel*, July 31, 1916, p. 2, col. 1.

21. *Marmon News* account, in Betts, "The Marmon Transcontinental Record," *Antique Automobile*, May–June 1966, p. 28.

22. Betts, "The Marmon Transcontinental Record," *Antique Automobile*, May–June 1966, p. 29.

23. *Rome (N.Y.) Daily Sentinel*, July 31, 1916, p. 5, col. 1; *Marmon News* account, in Betts, "The Marmon Transcontinental Record," *Antique Automobile*, May–June 1966, p. 26.

24. Ned Comstock, "Once Owned by Roman, 1907 Silver Ghost a Treasured Car," *Rome (N.Y.) Daily Sentinel*, Oct. 12, 1979, n.p.

25. Marmon ad in *Automobile*, Aug. 17, 1916, p. 93.

26. Betts, "The Marmon Transcontinental Record," *Antique Automobile*, May–June 1966, pp. 26–27 (quoting the *Marmon News*), 29.

27. Leon J. Pinkson, "Marmon Cuts Transcontinental Record Two Days," *San Francisco Chronicle*, July 30, 1916, p. 51, col. 1.

28. George Philip Hanley and Stacey Pankiw Hanley, *The Marmon Heritage* (Rochester, Mich.: Doyle Hyk Publishing Company, 1990), p. 145; "Lowers Omaha-Cheyenne Auto Record Full Hour," *Wyoming Tribune* (Cheyene), July 27, 1916, p. 4, col. 5; "New Marmon Is Unique Car," *Automobile*, Dec. 23, 1915, p. 1140.

29. *Wyoming Tribune* (Cheyenne), July 27, 1916, p. 4, col. 5; Marmon ad in the *Saturday Evening Post*, Sept. 16, 1916, p. 80.

30. "Marmon Features Continued for 1916," *Automobile*, July 1, 1915, pp. 12–15; *Automobile*, Dec. 23, 1915, pp. 1140–46.

31. Ibid.; Marmon ad in *Automobile*, Dec. 30, 1915, p. 311; Marmon ad in the *San Francisco Chronicle*, July 30, 1916, p. 51, col. 5.

32. *Automobile*, Dec. 23, 1915, p. 1146.

33. Betts, "The Marmon Transcontinental Record," *Antique Automobile*, May–June 1966, p. 29. Betts's account of the failed first attempt is based on information provided by Olle Holman.

34. For information on the Apperson run, see "Latest Apperson Model in Test Run," *Omaha (Neb.) Sunday Bee*, July 2, 1916, p. 3E, col. 3; "First Roadaplane Crosses Continent," *Detroit News Tribune*, July 16, 1916, p. 9, col. 7; and "First Roadaplane Across Country," *Motorist*, August 1916, p. 30.

35. On the Pathfinder's crossing, see "Pathfinder Car Goes Thru Town Hittin' on High," *Cedar Rapids (Iowa) Daily Republican*, July 26, 1916, p. 2, col. 1; "New World Auto Record," *Rome (N.Y.) Daily Sentinel*, Aug. 5, 1916, p. 6, col. 2; "Making New Records in Transcontinental Runs," *Horseless Age*, Aug. 15, 1916, pp. 108–9; Pathfinder ad in *MoToR*, September 1916, p. 17; and "Highing from Coast to Coast," *MoToR*, September 1916, pp. 77, 162.

36. "Broken Marmon Seals Due to Road Contact," *Automobile*, Aug. 24, 1916, p. 335.

37. *Rome (N.Y.) Daily Sentinel*, July 31, 1916, p. 5, col. 2. *Automobile* published the list of names in "A.C.A. Seals on Marmon Car," Aug. 17, 1916, p. 289.

38. See Curt McConnell, "Bluff by Bluster? Blisterin' Bobby Begs Believability," *Antique Automobile* (Antique Automobile Club of America), September–October 2000, pp. 3–7.

39. *Marmon News* account, in Betts, "The Marmon Transcontinental Record," *Antique Automobile*, May–June 1966, p. 26; *Rome (N.Y.) Daily Sentinel*, July 31, 1916, p. 5, col. 1.

40. Marmon ad in *Automobile*, Aug. 17, 1916, p. 94.

41. *Marmon News* account, in Betts, "The Marmon Transcontinental Record," *Antique Automobile*, May–June 1966, p. 27.

42. *Marshalltown (Iowa) Evening Times-Republican*, July 26, 1916, p. 9, col. 4.

43. "Some Traveling," *North Platte (Neb.) Telegraph*, July 27, 1916, p. 4, col. 5.

44. "Local and Personal," *North Platte (Neb.) Semi-Weekly Tribune*, July 28, 1916, p. 1, col. 3. Note the variant spellings of the pilot's name: "Filion" in the *North Platte Telegraph*, but "Fillion" in the *Semi-Weekly Tribune*.

45. Marmon ad in *Automobile*, Aug. 17, 1916, p. 94.

46. *Wyoming Tribune* (Cheyenne), July 27, 1916, p. 4, col. 5.

47. "Omaha-Cheyenne Auto Record Gone," *Cheyenne (Wyo.) State Leader*, July 27, 1916, p. 8, col. 1; *San Francisco Examiner*, Aug. 6, 1916, p. 4, col. 2, of auto section.

48. *Marmon News* account, in Betts, "The Marmon Transcontinental Record," *Antique Automobile*, May–June 1966, p. 28.

49. *San Francisco Chronicle*, July 30, 1916, p. 51, col. 1.

50. Marmon ad in *Automobile*, Aug. 17, 1916, p. 95.

51. *Rome (N.Y.) Daily Sentinel*, July 31, 1916, p. 5, col. 1.

52. Ibid., p. 5, col. 2.

53. *Automobile*, Aug. 3, 1916, p. 206; *Motor Age*, Aug. 3, 1916, p. 14, with slight differences in wording.

54. Ibid.

55. The distance between Evanston and Ely was actually 369 miles along the Lincoln Highway in 1916, according to *The Complete Official Road Guide of the Lincoln Highway* (Detroit: Lincoln Highway Association, 1916; repr. Sacramento, Calif.: Pleiades Press, 1995). The Marmon company is perhaps including detours in its mileage figures; Bieling may also have followed another route.

56. "Marmon Car Making Record Run from New York to 'Frisco," *White Pine News* (East Ely, Nev.), July 30, 1916, p. 1, col. 3.

57. *Marmon News* account, in Betts, "The Marmon Transcontinental Record," Antique *Automobile*, May–June 1966, p. 28.

58. Frank Herman, "Fast Time Is Made in Run from Coast to Coast," *San Francisco Call and Post*, July 31, 1916, p. 11, col. 1.

59. *San Francisco Chronicle*, July 30, 1916, p. 51, col. 1.

60. Ibid.

61. Marmon ad in the *New York Times*, Aug. 20, 1916, sec. 3, p. 8, col. 5; Marmon ad in *Automobile*, Aug. 3, 1916, p. 206.

62. *San Francisco Chronicle*, July 30, 1916, p. 51, col. 2; *Rome (N.Y.) Daily Sentinel*, July 31, 1916, p. 5, col. 2."Marmon Crosses Country in Five Days, 18 Hours," *Motor West*, Aug. 15, 1916, p. 10.

63. *Automobile*, Aug. 24, 1916, p. 335; *New York Times*, Aug. 20, 1916, sec. 3, p. 8, col. 3; *Marmon News* account, in Betts, "The Marmon Transcontinental Record," *Antique Automobile*, May–June 1966, p. 26.

64. Nordyke & Marmon Company, *Nordyke & Marmon Company: An Institution* (Indianapolis [?], 1920), p. 59; "Ford Coast-to-Coast Car," *Motor Age*, Oct. 7, 1909, p. 16.

65. *San Francisco Examiner*, Aug. 6, 1916, p. 4, col. 2, of auto section.

66. Ibid.

67. *Rome (N.Y.) Daily Sentinel*, July 31, 1916, p. 5, col. 1.

68. *White Pine News* (East Ely, Nev.), Aug. 6, 1916, p. 1, col. 5.

69. *Horseless Age*, Aug. 15, 1916, p. 108.

70. *San Francisco Call*, July 31, 1916, p. 11, col. 1.

71. *MoToR*, Sept. 16, p. 78.

72. Marmon ad in *Automobile*, Aug. 17, 1916, p. 93.

73. See the ads for the Nordyke & Marmon Company and its suppliers in *Automobile*, Aug. 17, 1916, pp. 93–108, and Aug. 31, 1916, pp. 67, 84.

74. "Seeks Auto Speed Trophy," *New York Times*, April 17, 1927, sec. 2, p. 21, col. 4.

75. Ned Comstock, quoted in the *Rome (N.Y.) Daily Sentinel*, Oct. 12, 1979, n.p. For Stevens's obituary, see the *New York Times*, Nov. 17, 1935, sec. 2, p. 11, col. 4.

76. The chassis number is given in Betts, "The Marmon Transcontinental Record," *Antique Automobile*, May–June 1966, p. 29.

77. "Marmon Production Comes to an End," *SAH Journal* (Society of Automotive Historians), July–August 1997, p. 4.

78. "Troops in Auto Beat Railroad," *New York Times*, Aug. 6, 1916, sec. 2, p. 2, col. 4.

79. On the 1916 Plymouth-Seattle automobile relay, see "Auto Racers Hour Late," *Des Moines (Iowa) Register*, Sept. 17, 1916, p. 5, col. 2. See also "Racers Cross Rockies," *Des Moines (Iowa) Register*, Sept. 16, 1916, p. 2, col. 6; "Relay Automobiles Ahead of Schedule," *Salt Lake (City) Tribune*, Sept. 16, 1916, p. 1, col. 5; and "Army Auto Reaches Seattle Destination," *Joliet (Ill.) Sunday Herald-News*, Sept. 17, 1916, p. 12, col. 5.

80. "The 1919 Transcontinental Motor Convoy," *Overview: Eisenhower Foundation Newsletter*, Fall 1984, p. 1.

81. Dwight D. Eisenhower, *At Ease: Stories I Tell to Friends* (Garden City, N.Y.: Doubleday, 1967), p. 159.

82. "Arrival of Overlanders in New York," *Automobile*, Aug. 29, 1903, pp. 205–6.

83. Carl Breer, *The Birth of Chrysler Corporation and Its Engineering Legacy* (Warrendale, Pa.: Society of Automotive Engineers, 1995), p. 34.

84. H. Nelson Jackson, "Honk! Honk! New York or Bust!" *American Legion Monthly*, February 1936, p. 48.

85. "Marmon Makes New Record to Coast," *Automobile Topics*, Aug. 5, 1916, p. 1278.

Chapter 8

1. "Motor World Is Stirred by Fast Continental Run," *San Francisco Examiner*, Sept. 24, 1916, p. 33, col. 4.

2. Stuart Gayness, "To Gotham and Back by Auto; 10 Days," *San Francisco Examiner*, Sept. 25, 1916, p. 11, col. 4.

3. For an outline of some of the events Mulford won prior to the Hudson trip, see Charles L. Betts, "Auto Racing Winners, 1895–1972," in Albert R. Bochroch, *American Automobile Racing: An Illustrated History* (Middlesex, Eng.: Penguin Books, 1977), pp. 209–14.

4. Russ Catlin, "Who Really Won the First Indy 500?" *Automobile Quarterly*, vol. 7, no. 4 (1969), p. 384.

5. "Hudson Covers Mile at 102.5 M.P.H.," *Automobile*, April 13, 1916, p. 703; "A Mile in 35.11 Seconds," *New York Times*, April 16, 1916, sec. 3, p. 3, col. 5; "The Record-Breaking Hudson Super Six on Ormond–Daytona Beach," *Automobile*, April 20, 1916, p. 732, photos and caption.

6. "24-Hour Record Gained by Hudson," *Automobile*, May 4, 1916, pp. 799, 834; "1819 Miles," editorial, *Automobile*, May 4, 1916, p. 823. See also "Mulford's Driving a Factor in Hudson 24–Hour Record," *Automobile*, May 11, 1916, p. 842, as well as the Hudson ad in the *Saturday Evening Post*, June 10, 1916, p. 27.

7. "Hudson, Chalmers Win at Pike's Peak," *Automobile*, Aug. 17, 1916, p. 292; "Climbing Through Snow," *New York Times*, Aug. 20, 1916, sec. 3, p. 8, col. 7.

8. George V. C. Bacon, "Hudson Sets New Sea-to-Sea Records," *San Francisco Bulletin*, Sept. 19, 1916, p. 5, col. 3. On Patterson's racing background, see Maurice D. Hendry, "Hudson: The Car Named for Jackson's Wife's Uncle," *Automobile Quarterly*, vol. 9, no. 4 (1971), p. 365.

9. Beverly Rae Kimes, ed., *Packard: A History of the Motor Car and the Company* (Princeton, N.J.: Princeton Publishing Co., 1978), pp. 177, 686.

10. Hudson ads in the *San Francisco Chronicle*, Sept. 19, 1916, p. 5, col. 3, and in the *San Francisco Examiner*, Sept. 25, 1916, p. 7, col. 3.

11. For an account of this race, see Curt McConnell, *Coast-to-Coast Auto Races of the Early 1900s: Three Contests That Changed the World* (Warrendale, Pa.: Society of Automotive Engineers, 2000), pp. 1–46.

12. "Ocean to Ocean Race," *New York Tribune*, May 9, 1905, p. 5, col. 6; B. C. Forbes and O. D. Foster, *Automotive Giants of America* (New York: B. C. Forbes Publishing Co., 1926), p. 27.

13. The four record-setting trips exclude a poorly documented May 1916 crossing made by Bobby Hammond in an Empire auto. Hammond's trip, which most observers dismiss as unsubstantiated, was purportedly made on the Lincoln Highway.

14. United States Tire Company ad in the *San Francisco Examiner*, Sept. 24, 1916, p. 5, col. 3, of auto section.

15. *San Francisco Examiner*, Sept. 25, 1916, p. 11, col. 4; W. F. Sturm, "Sidelights on Hudson's Run," *San Francisco Chronicle*, Oct. 1, 1916, p. 46, col. 1.

16. *San Francisco Chronicle*, Sept. 19, 1916, p. 5, col. 3; "Super-Six Breaks Continent Record," *Des Moines (Iowa) Register*, Sept. 19, 1916, p. 2, col. 1.

17. Hudson ad in *Motorist*, October 1916, p. 38.

18. Specifications for the Hudson Super-Six can be found in "1916 Passenger Automobiles Listed with Their Technical Specifications," *Automobile*, Dec. 30, 1915, pp. 1248–49; the *San Francisco Chronicle*, Oct. 1, 1916, p. 46, col. 5; and in numerous Hudson ads. The license tag is visible in photos.

19. Beverly Rae Kimes and Henry Austin Clark, Jr., *Standard Catalog of American Cars, 1805–1942*, 2d ed. (Iola, Wis.: Krause Publications, 1989), p. 690.

20. Hendry, "Hudson," *Automobile Quarterly*, vol. 9, no. 4 (1971), p. 365.

21. Hudson ad in *Motorist*, October 1916, p. 38.

22. Leon J. Pinkson, "Coast to Coast Auto Record Smashed," *San Francisco Chronicle*, Sept. 19, 1916, p. 7, col. 3.

23. "Hudson Super-Six Record Is Praised," *San Francisco Chronicle*, Sept. 24, 1916, p. 45, col. 1. More precisely, Lotta's Fountain is situated at the intersection of Geary, Kearny, and Market streets, near Third Street.

24. "Second Attempt to Break Record," *Carson City (Nev.) Daily Appeal*, Sept. 13, 1916, p. 4, col. 2.

25. "Hudson Super-Six Trying to Beat Marmon Record," *Churchill County Standard* (Fallon, Nev.), Sept. 6, 1916, p. 1, col. 2.

26. "Auto Racing News and Notes About Flyers in General," *Indianapolis News*, Sept. 16, 1916, p. 12, col. 5.

27. "Hudson Coast-to-Coast Record," *Automobile*, Sept. 21, 1916, p. 470.

28. *San Francisco Chronicle*, Oct. 1, 1916, p. 46, col. 1.

29. For the distance Patterson traveled, see "Cross Continent Record Smashed by a Hudson," *Motor World*, Sept. 20, 1916, mileage table on p. 14. Unless otherwise noted, this table is the source for subsequent references to the distance between cities.

30. Stuart Gayness, "S.F. to N.Y. Auto Mark Smashed," *San Francisco Examiner*, Sept. 19, 1916, p. 8, col. 6.

31. The *Carson City (Nev.) Daily Appeal*, Sept. 13, 1916, p. 4, col. 2; *Churchill County Standard* (Fallon, Nev.), Sept. 6, 1916, p. 1, col. 2.

32. "World Famous Driver Here," *Elko (Nev.) Daily Free Press*, Sept. 14, 1916, p. 1, col. 3, and p. 3, col. 2.

33. "Hudson Super-Six Sets New Record," *Salt Lake (City) Tribune*, Sept. 24, 1916, p. 3, col. 1, of auto section; *San Francisco Chronicle*, Sept. 19, 1916, p. 7, col. 3.

34. *San Francisco Chronicle*, Oct. 1, 1916, p. 46, col. 1.

35. "Endurance Run Being Made Across the Continent," *Ogden (Utah) Standard*, Sept. 14, 1916, p. 7, col. 5.

36. *Salt Lake (City) Tribune*, Sept. 24, 1916, p. 3, col. 1, of auto section.

37. Untitled blurb, *Rock Springs (Wyo.) Miner*, Sept. 16, 1916, p. 4, col. 3; "The Hudson Racers Little Behind Time," *Laramie (Wyo.) Republican*, Sept. 15, 1916, p. 7, col. 5.

38. *San Francisco Chronicle*, Oct. 1, 1916, p. 46, col. 3; "More of Record Across Continent," *Des Moines (Iowa) Register*, Sept. 24, 1916, p. 4, col. 1.

39. "Hudson Super-Six Dashes Through City at 65 Miles [an] Hour," *Wyoming Tribune* (Cheyenne), Sept. 15, 1916, p. 1, col. 6.

40. "Hudson Making Record Run Across Continent," *Cheyenne (Wyo.) State Leader*, Sept. 16, 1916, p. 8, col. 8; *San Francisco Chronicle*, Oct. 1, 1916, p. 46, col. 3.

41. "Barndollar Returns," *Guthrie County Vedette* (Panora, Iowa), Sept. 28, 1916, p. 8, col. 3.

42. *Des Moines (Iowa) Register*, Sept. 24, 1916, p. 4, col. 1.

43. "Super-Six Breaks Record," *Guthrie County Vedette* (Panora, Iowa), Sept. 21, 1916, p. 1, col. 3.

44. "New Auto Record in Coast-to-Coast Run," *Indianapolis News*, Sept. 18, 1916, p. 8, col. 6.

45. Ralph K. Mulford, Jr., in a November 7, 1995, telephone interview with the author.

46. "Mulford Going West in Record Drive," *Des Moines (Iowa) Capital*, Sept. 19, 1916, p. 2, col. 5; *Des Moines (Iowa) Register*, Sept. 16, 1916, p. 2, col. 2.

47. "Hudson Sets New Time Across U.S.," *New York Tribune*, Sept. 19, 1916, p. 6, col. 4.

48. *San Francisco Chronicle*, Sept. 19, 1916, p. 7, col. 2. According to the distances listed in *Motor World*, Sept. 20, 1916, p. 14, Vincent actually drove 985 miles between South Bend and New York City.

49. *San Francisco Chronicle*, Oct. 1, 1916, p. 46, col. 2. Many news accounts mistakenly reported the Hudson's average speed as 27.14 mph, rather than 28.14 mph, over the 3,476-mile route.

50. *Automobile*, Sept. 21, 1916, p. 470.

51. *San Francisco Bulletin*, Sept. 19, 1916, p. 5, col. 3; *San Francisco Chronicle*, Sept. 19, 1916, p. 7, col. 3.

52. *San Francisco Examiner*, Sept. 19, 1916, p. 8, col. 6.

53. "Hudson Is at 'Frisco Completing Round Trip," *Motor World*, Sept. 27, 1916, p. 44.

54. *New York Tribune*, Sept. 19, 1916, p. 6, col. 4; George V. C. Bacon, "Hudson Super '6' Back from Record Drive," *San Francisco Bulletin*, Sept. 25, 1916, p. 8, col. 3.

55. *San Francisco Examiner*, Sept. 19, 1916, p. 8, col. 6.

56. *Des Moines (Iowa) Capital*, Sept. 19, 1916, p. 2, col. 5; *Guthrie County Vedette* (Panora, Iowa), Sept. 21, 1916, p. 1, col. 3.

57. Leon J. Pinkson, "Hudson Sets Ocean-to-Ocean Mark," *San Francisco Chronicle*, Sept. 25, 1916, p. 7, col. 2; *San Francisco Bulletin*, Sept. 25, 1916, p. 8, col. 3.

58. *San Francisco Chronicle*, Oct. 1, 1916, p. 46, col. 1. Sturm may be rounding off the Elko departure time. By leaving there at 2:00 A.M. on September 23, Patterson would have reached San Francisco in 35 hours, 23 minutes, not 35 hours, 37 minutes, as Sturm states.

59. "New Record in Coast-to-Coast Round Trip," *Indianapolis News*, Sept. 25, 1916, p. 15, col. 1.

60. "Sturm's Death Recalls Early Race Exploits to Automotive Veterans," *Indianapolis News*, Aug. 26, 1937, sec. 2, p. 4, col. 6.

61. *San Francisco Chronicle*, Sept. 25, 1916, p. 7, col. 2.

62. Hudson ad in *Motorist*, October 1916, p. 38.

63. *San Francisco Bulletin*, Sept. 25, 1916, p. 8, col. 3. The 1916 San Francisco city directory gives the name of the Wells Fargo general agent as William C. Kiefer.

64. Hudson ad in *Motorist*, October 1916, p. 38.

65. *San Francisco Chronicle*, Sept. 25, 1916, p. 7, col. 3, photo and caption; *San Francisco Examiner*, Sept. 24, 1916, p. 5, col. 3, of auto section; *San Francisco Chronicle*, Oct. 1, 1916, p. 46, col. 5.

66. *San Francisco Chronicle*, Oct. 1, 1916, p. 46, col. 1.

67. Ibid.; *San Francisco Examiner*, Sept. 24, 1916, p. 33, col. 4.

68. *San Francisco Examiner*, Sept. 25, 1916, p. 11, col. 4.

69. *Guthrie County Vedette* (Panora, Iowa), Sept. 28, 1916, p. 8, col. 3.

70. "News of Men in the Industry," *Automobile*, April 19, 1917, p. 761. On the Chalmers low-speed stunt, see "Chalmers 24-Hr. High Gear Run for Minimum Speed," *Automobile*, April 19, 1917, p. 764; and "71.7 Miles in 24 Hr. on High Gear," *Automobile*, April 26, 1917, p. 817.

71. "W. F. Sturm Dies at 53 [*sic*]," *Automotive Industries*, Sept. 4, 1937, p. 298; "William F. Sturm, Auto Race Authority and Writer, Is Dead," *Indianapolis News*, Aug. 26, 1937, p. 1, col. 6. On Sturm's life, see also Charles L. Betts Jr., "In Pursuit of the Ultimate Speed," *Automobile Quarterly*, vol. 3, no. 3 (1964), pp. 275–76; "Sturm Services Set for Saturday," *Indianapolis News*, Aug. 27, 1937, sec. 2, p. 7, col. 2.

72. Charles Betts, "Ralph K. Mulford," *Antique Automobile*, January–February 1974, p. 50. See also "Champion Driver Compares Auto Racing with Flying," *Wright-Martin Aircraftings*, Dec. 28, 1918, p. 5; and "Ralph Mulford: Famed Racing Driver," *Boston Evening Globe*, Oct. 26, 1973, p. 34.

73. Ralph Mulford, "Racing with Lozier," *Automobile Quarterly*, vol. 7, no. 4 (1969), p. 366.

74. On Hudson's later years, see John A. Gunnell, ed., *Standard Catalog of American Cars, 1946–1975*, 2d ed. (Iola, Wis.: Krause Publications, 1987), p. 402; and John Moody, *Moody's Industrial Manual* (New York: Moody's Investors Service, 1955), p. 2630.

Conclusion

1. Bert C. Smith, "Sea to Sea Motor Tour Means National Highway," *Los Angeles Times*, Aug. 13, 1911, sec. 7, p. 4, col. 1.

2. *Motor Age*, Aug. 17, 1911, p. 8.

3. *New York Times*, Sept. 24, 1911, sec. 4, p. 8, col. 1.

4. *The Complete Official Road Guide of the Lincoln Highway* (Detroit: Lincoln Highway Association, 1916; repr. Sacramento, Calif.: Pleiades Press, 1984), p. 33.

5. "Cross Country Runs Prove Automobile's Reliability," *MoToR*, October 1915, p. 56.

ILLUSTRATION

CREDITS

AACA   Antique Automobile Club of America Library & Research Center, Hershey, Pennsylvania

AAMA   Reprinted with permission of the American Automobile Manufacturers Association, Detroit

DBG   Courtesy of Dan B. Greer

FLP   Automobile Reference Collection, Free Library of Philadelphia

LCHS   Courtesy of the Lorain County Historical Society, Elyria, Ohio

MSU   Michigan State University Archives and Historical Collections, East Lansing

NAHC   National Automotive History Collection, Detroit Public Library

NAM   Courtesy of the William F. Harrah Foundation National Automobile Museum, Reno, Nevada

OHS   Ohio Historical Society, Archives-Library Division, Columbus

RKM   Courtesy of Ralph K. Mulford, Jr.

UMSC   University of Michigan Special Collections, Ann Arbor

WDCR   Wyoming Division of Cultural Resources, Cheyenne

INDEX

Cole, F. W., 59, 62

Colfax, Iowa, 90, *117*

Collinsville, Ill., *206*, 209

Columbia, Mo., *177*, 190, *206*

Columbus, Mo., *206*

Columbus, Neb., *42*, 49, 51, *117*

Columbus, Ohio, 81, *177*, *207*, 210

Cook, Hugh F., *73*, 116, 119

Cooley's Ranch, Ariz., *136*

Coppers, C. W., 148

Council Bluffs, Iowa: Garford motor train, 142; Hudson trip, *253*; Mitchell trip, *13*, 20; Reo trip, *40*, 41, *42*, 43, *44*, 47, 48, 49, 50, 51

Creighton, Robert, 219, *220*, 236, 237

Creston, Wyo., *13*, 22, 23

Crocker, Sewall K., 1, 2, 39, 243

Cumberland, Wyo., *42*, 55

Darracq automobile, 225

Davenport, Iowa: Garford motor train, *135*, 140, 142; Hudson trip, *253*; Premier caravan trip, 88, 89–90, *117*, 142

Davis, Harry, *73*, 105

Dayton, Ohio, *177*, 191, *195*, *206*, 210

Daytona Beach, Florida, speed trials, 220, 250, 273

Death Valley (Thayer Junction), Wyo., 23

Del Monte, Calif., 113, *118*

Denver, 42, 77, 78, 94, 96, 98, *117*, 141

Des Moines, Iowa: Garford motor train, *135*, 142, 143; Hudson trip, *253*, *261*, 262, 268; Premier caravan trip, 90, *91*; Reo trip, 42

Des Moines (Iowa) Register, 248, 253, 261, 262, 263

Devil's Canyon (Ariz.), 177

Disbrow, Louis, 228

Dixon, Ill., *13*, 19

Dodge City, Kan.: Cadillac trip, 202, 205, *206*, 207, 208; Garford motor train, *135*, 143, 145, 146; Stutz trip, *176*, 188, 189, 190

Dodge City (Kan.) Daily Globe, 165, 189–90, 205, 207

Dorris automobile, 109–10

Douglas, Ariz., *176*, 179

Duesenberg race cars, 249, 250

Eisenhower, President Dwight D., 34, 246

El Centro, Calif., 155, *176*, 177

El Paso, Texas, 165, *176*, 179, 181–82, *184*, *185*, *195*

electric autos, 6, 220

Elko, Nev.: Hudson trip, *253*, 255, *257*, 258, 259, 260, *261*, 268; Premier caravan trip, 107, 111, *118*

Ely, Nev., *236*, *237*

Elyria, Ohio, *13*, 15, 16, 17, *137*

Emporia, Kan.: Cadillac trip, *206*, 208; Garford motor train, *135*, 144, 145, 146; Stutz trip, *176*, 190, *195*

Erie, Pa., *13*, 16, *42*, 134, *135*, 136, 229

Eubank, Victor: biographical details, 129, 163; camping, 151; Garford motor train, 129, 139, 140–64; importance of Garford motor train according to, 164; mileage reports, 139, 158; overnight stops, reports on, 139, 143; photo of, *130*; road condition reports, 140–41, 144, 147, 150, 153

Eureka, Nev., 109, *118*

European automobiles, 9, 225

Evanston, Wyo.: Hudson trip, *253*, 259; Marmon trip, 231, 232, 234, *237*; Mitchell trip, *13*, 22, 23; Premier caravan trip, 104; Reo trip, *42*, 53, 55

Falcon-Knight automobile, 217

Fallon, Nev., 236–37, *253*, 256, 257

family road trips, 2, 70

Fassett, David F.: photo of, *60*; Reo trip (1905–1906), 2, 36, 249, 270; Reo trip (1910), 36, 45, 47, 56, 58, *60*, 67, 68

federal road building and highway funding, 124–25, 246, 275–78

Flagstaff, Ariz., *206*

Flanders automobile, 154

Fletcher, J. H., 172

Hemstreet, James A., 193, 264, 266
Hendry, Maurice, 254
Hewes, C. L., 26
High Hill, Mo., *206*, 209
highway funding and construction, 124–25,
  246, 275–78
Holly, Colo., 205, *206*
Holtville, Calif., *176*, 177
Homer, W. H., 26, 27, 29, *30*
Horne, Horace, *130*, *133*
Horseless Age, 38, 174, 242
Houk Manufacturing Co., 197–98, 243
Hudson automobile, 250, 274
Hudson, Joseph L., 254
Hudson Motor Car Co., 247, 248, 251, 254, 274,
  278
Hudson Super-Six automobile (1916):
  description and performance, 199, 250,
  253–54, 270; photos of, *252*, *255*, *264*, *266*,
  267, *269*, *271*
Hudson trip (1916), 217, 247, 248–80, 278;
  breakdowns, mishaps, and repairs, 249, 256,
  258, 260, 262, 266–67, 269; compared to other
  trips, 1910–1916, 271–72, *279*; crowds, press,
  and publicity, 249, *251*, 257, *264*, 265, 268,
  270, *272*; drivers and passengers, 249–50, *257*;
  east-west trip, 267–70; finish of, 264–65;
  mileage, *261*, 270–72, 285; planning and
  strategy, 253; preparations and purpose,
  251–53, 272–73; route of, 252–53, *253*,
  267–68; speed and safety, 263, 268, 269–70;
  start of, 249, 255–56; summary, 285–86;
  times, running and elapsed, 254–55, 256,
  259, *261*, 265, 267–72, 285–86; weather
  and road conditions, 260, 265, 267, 270;
  west-east trip, *253*, 255–66
Hutchinson, Kan., *135*, 143, 145, *206*, 208

Indianapolis, 81–84, *84–85*, *117*, *177*, *206*
Indianapolis 500, 226, 249
Indianapolis Motor Speedway, 125, 226, 273
Indianapolis News: Baker, Erwin G. "Cannon

Ball," 167, 217; Cadillac trip, 209, 210;
  Hudson trip, 248, 256, 269, 273; Premier
  caravan trip, 80, 82, 86; Sturm, W. F., and,
  171, 273; Stutz trip, 170, 172, 178, 184, 188,
  189, 191, 192, 194
Indianapolis Star, 80, 82, 86, 91, 167, 217

Jackson automobile, 9
Jackson, Dr. H. Nelson, 1, 2, 23, 39, 41, 42,
  215–16, 243, 247, 279
Jenkins, Ab, 199, 279
Jenkins, C. Francis, *73*, 75, 106, 119, 122–23
Jersey City, N.J., *207*, 211
Joliet, Ill., *42*, 46, *253*, 263
Julesburg, Colo., *13*, 19, 21, *42*, 43, *95*, *117*

Kalinsky, Louis, 257–58, *264*
Kansas City, Mo., *135*, 143, 144, 145, *176*, 190,
  206, 208, 209, 214
Kearney, Neb., *13*, *42*, 50, 51, 75, *93*
Kemmerer, Wyo., 103, 104, *117*
Kendallville, Ind., *42*, 46
kerosene, 6
Kimes, Beverly Rae, 173
Kingman, Ariz., *206*
Krarup, Marius C., 1, 78

La Junta, Colo., *135*, 146, *147*, 205, *206*, 207
Lafayette, Ind., 87, *117*
Laguna, N.M., *136*, 150
Lahontan, Nev., *253*, 257
Lake, Stuart N., 223
Lake Tahoe (CA/NV), 42, 58, 111, 118, 256
Lancaster, Pa., *177*, 192
Laramie, Wyo.: Hudson trip, *253*, 257, 258, 259,
  260; Mitchell trip, *13*, 22, 23; Premier caravan
  trip, 96, 98–101, *100*, *117*; Reo trip, *40*, 41, *42*,
  44, 52–53, 54
Larimer, Shirley, 46
Las Vegas, N.M., *136*, 148, 205, *206*
Legg, John, *130*
Legg, Sarah, 126, 144

Monihan, John Guy: arrival and final cere-
monies of Premier caravan trip, 113, 115, 119;
biographical details, 71, *74*; feasibility of transcontinental touring, comments on, 69, 72, 98,
109, 121, 125; financial appropriations, accu-
sations of, 119; photo of, *71*; road conditions
for Premier caravan trip, comments on,
76–78, 90, 96, 98, 101–3, 108, 110, 121; sched-
uling and timing of Premier caravan trip,
80, 88, 105, 107; supplies and preparations,
comments on need for, 93, 95, 120; telegrams
written by, 93, 95, 96, 98, 107, 108, 122
Montello, Nev., *13*, 24, *40*, 41, *42*, *44*, 56, *79*,
107
Moskovics, Fred E., 228, *229*
motion pictures: Marmon trip, 240; Premier
caravan trip, 75–76, 106, 122–23, *123*
MoToR, 163, 199, 211, 214, 220, 243, 277
Motor Age: Garford motor train, 131, 138, 160,
161; Marmon trip, 224, 235, 240; Mitchell
trip, 3, 12, 27, 31; Premier caravan trip, 75,
76, 98, 119; Reo trip, 36, 38, 45, 57, 58; Saurer
truck trip, 141
motor reserve, 219, 221, 224, 241, 242, 277
Motor West, 163, 199, 240
Motor World, 6, 31, 263
motorcycle racing, 165, 167–68, 189–90, 223
Mulford, Ralph: biographical details, 249–50,
273, 274; Hudson trip, 247, 248, 255, 257–64,
266, 268, 271–72, 273; injury of, 262; photos
of, *264*, *266*, *267*
Murdock, Jacob M., 2–3, 166, 193
Murphy, John J., *74*, *79*, *89*, 90
Murphy, Mrs. John J., *74*, *89*

National electric automobile, 220
National Highways Association, 163
National Motor Reserve, 219, 221, 224, 241, 242,
277
national transcontinental highway. *See also*
Lincoln Highway: Garford motor train's
promotion of, 127, 156, 159, 162; Jenkins,
C. Francis, 119; Marmon trip's promotion of,

219, 277–78; Monihan, John Guy, on, 109;
Premier caravan trip's promotion of, 70,
124–25, 275–76; southern route for, 162;
Westgard, Anthon L., 156, 162
Nation's Ranch, N.M., *136*, 150, 151
Needles, Calif., 205, *206*
New York City: Baker motorcycle race, 167;
Cadillac trip, *207*, 211–12; Garford motor
train, 130, 131, *132*, 134, *135*; Hudson trip,
253, *257*, *261*, 263–65, *264*, *266*, 271, 272;
Marmon trip, 228, *237*; Mitchell trip, 1, 5, 8,
11, 13, *15*, 16, *17*, 18, 22; New York–Paris
auto race (1908), 11; Reo trip, 36, *39*, *40*, *61*;
Stutz trip, *177*, 192, *193*, *195*; Whitman's
1904, 1906, and 1910 trips compared, *61*
New York Herald, 2, 131, 194, 220, 265
New York Motor Club, 220
New York Times: Cadillac trip, 211; Garford
motor train, 127–28, 131, 132, 138, 151, 160,
276; Marmon trip, 245; Mitchell trip, 6, 9,
223; national transcontinental highway, 70;
Premier caravan trip, 75, 76, 113; Reo trip,
36; Stutz trip, 194; Weston trip, 22
New York Tribune, 211, 213, 265, 266
Newton, Kan., 145, *206*, 208
Niagara Falls, 134, 135
Nordyke & Marmon Co., 218, 219, 221, 224,
226, 227, 237, 240, 241, 243, 245
North Platte, Neb.: Hudson trip, *253*; Marmon
trip, 231, 232, *233*; Mitchell trip, *13*, 20;
Premier caravan trip, 95, 96; Reo trip, *40*,
41, *42*, *44*, 48, 49, 50, 51, 65

Oakland, Calif., *13*, *42*, 58, 112
O'Brien, Tom, 91, 92
Office of Public Roads, U.S. Department of
Agriculture, 128, 141, 162
Ogallala, Neb., *42*, 50
Ogden, Utah: Hudson trip, *253*, 257, 258, *261*;
Mitchell trip, *13*, 23; Premier caravan trip,
106–7, *117*, *118*; Reo trip, *40*, 41, *42*, *44*, 53,
55, 56, *61*, 65; Whitman's 1904, 1906, and
1910 trips compared, *61*

R. M. Owen & Co., 37, 38, *39*, 41, 59, 61

Racine (Wis.) Daily Journal, 5, 7, 10, 12, 15, 19, 20, 23, 28, 32

railroads: Cadillac trip, 212–13; Garford motor train, 128–29, 146, 162; Hudson trip, 249, 265; Marmon trip, 218, 241, 242–43; Mitchell trip, 5, 21, 22; Stutz trip, 165–66

Ramsey, Alice, 53

Raton, N.M., *136*, 146, 148, 205, *206*

Rawlins, Wyo.: Marmon trip, 231, 232; Mitchell trip, *13*, 22, 23, *28*; Premier caravan trip, 96, *117*; Reo trip, *42*, 53, 54

Raymond and Whitcomb Co.: Ashton, H. D., touring department manager, 128; banquet for Garford motor train, speakers at, 159; Gibson, H. D., vice president and general manager, 138, 140; headquarters in New York City, photo of, *134*; sponsorship of Garford motor train, 126–27, 140, 161–62, 276; touring plans, 161–62, 163

Rector, H. B., 237, 239

Reno (Nev.) Evening Gazatte, 22, 23, 24

Reno, Nev.: Marmon trip, 236, 237, *237*; Mitchell trip, *13*, 24, *25*, *28*; Premier caravan trip, 109, *118*; Reo trip, *40*, 41, *42*, *44*, 56, 57, 58, *61*, 65; Whitman's 1904, 1906, and 1910 trips compared, *61*

Reo automobile, 2, 67

Reo Motor Car Co., 38, *39*, 40, 43, 59, 61, 62, 68

Reo Thirty automobile (1910): description and performance, 37–40, 67; photos of, *39*, *48–50*, *52*, *54*, 55, *57*, *59*, *60*, *63*, *64*

Reo trip (1910), 35–68, 272, 275; breakdowns, mishaps, and repairs, 36, 41, 46–48, 51–52, 56, 65–66; compared to other trips, *279*; crowds, press, and publicity, 37, 59, 68; drivers and assistants, 35–36, *40*; finish of, 58–60; mileage, 48, 61, 64, 282; planning and strategy, 36, 43, 68; preparations and purpose, 37–38; record set by, 60–62, 68; route, *42*; speed and safety, 35–36, 39, 43–45, 62–63, 67; start of, 38–40; summary, 282; times,

running and elapsed, 43–49, 60–62, 64–66, 193, 282; weather and road conditions, 36, 46, 54–56, 57, 58, 60

Reye, George H., 130, *131*

Richmond, Ind., 81, *206*, 210

Rickenbacker automobile, 217

River-to-River Road (Iowa), 49, 90, 142, 261, 267

road funding and construction, 124–25, 246, 275–78

road signs, 159

Robson, Sarah, 148

Rochester, Claire, 227

Rock Springs, Wyo.: Hudson trip, *253*, 259, 260; Mitchell trip, *13*, 22, 23; Premier caravan trip, 103, *117*; Reo trip, 55

Rodgers, Calbraith P., 159, 164

Rolls-Royce Silver Ghost, 225

Rome (N.Y.) Daily Sentinel, 219, 220, 222, 224, 228, 229, 235, 240

Roosevelt Dam (Ariz.), 152, 154

Roosevelt, President Theodore, 221, 222

Rosenthal, Lieutenant B. B.: biographical details, 9–10; comments on Mitchell trip, 19, 21–22, 23, 24, 26; condition following Mitchell trip, 26–27; photos of, *8*, *14*, *15*, *17*, *25*, *30*; responsibilities on Mitchell trip, 5, 7; running time for Mitchell trip, 18; temporary departure from Mitchell trip, 23, 24

Roswell, N.M., *176*, 182, 183, *195*

Ryan, Joseph E. G., 28, 33

Ryan, Mike, 130, *131*

Sacramento, Calif.: Marmon trip, 237; Mitchell trip, *13*, 25, 26; Premier caravan trip, 112, *118*; Reo trip, *40*, 41, *42*, *44*, 58, 65

Salt Lake City, 103–6, *117*, 234, 235, 257

Salt River Canyon (Ariz.), 152, *153*

San Bernardino, Calif., 204, *206*

San Diego: Baker motorcycle race, 167; Garford motor train, *136*, 155, 156; Stutz trip, 165, 172, 175, *176*, 177, *195*

190, 191, 196–99; doughnut-shaped cushions, 178, *179*; fences driven through, 166, 187–88; finish of, 192–95; mileage, 166, 176–77, 178, 182, 190, 194, *195*, 284; planning and strategy, 168–69; route, 175, *176–77*; speed and safety, 166–67, 168, 181, 194, 199; start of, 172; summary, 284; times, running and elapsed, 166, 178, 182, 190, 192–93, 194, 277, 284; weather and road conditions, 165–66, 168, 177–78, 180–81, 184–85, *185*, 188–89, 191–92

Summerford, Ohio, *207*, 210

Sunset: The Pacific Monthly, 129 et seq.

Syracuse, Kan., *135*, 146, *206*

Syracuse, N.Y., *42*, 134, *135*, 229, *237*, *253*, 263

Taft, President William Howard, 70, 79–80, 109, 112, 113, 167–68, 275

Tahoe Tavern, Calif., 111, *118*

Tama, Iowa, *13*, 19, 20

Templar automobile, 217

Thayer Junction, Wyo., *13*, 22, 23

Thomas automobile, 9

Thomas, C. J., 58

Thomas, G. J., 36

Toledo, Ohio, *13*, 42

Tombstone, Ariz., *176*, 179, *180*

Touring Club of America, 85, 124–25

tourism, 124–25, 161–63, 275–77

transcontinental highway. *See* national transcontinental highway

travelers, advice to, 121–22, *163*

Trenton, N.J., *177*, 192, *207*, 211

Trinidad, Colo., *135*, *136*, 146, *147*, 148, 205, *206*

Truckee, Calif., *42*, 58, *111*

trucks, 141, 217, 245, 249, 272, 276

Tucson, Ariz., *176*, 179

United States Tire Co., 105, 253, 271

"universal car" (Ford), 280

U.S. Department of Agriculture's Office of Public Roads, 128, 141, 162

Utica, N.Y.: Garford motor train, 134, *135*;

Mitchell trip, *13*, 15, 16, 17; Reo trip, 38, *40*, 41, *42*, 44

V-8 Cadillac. *See* Cadillac V-8 automobile (1916)

Vallejo, Calif., 237

Valparaiso, Ind., *13*, *42*, 47, 65

Vandalia, Ill., *177*, 191

Velie automobile, 91

Venice, Calif., 114–16, *115*, *118*

Vincent, Charles H.: biographical details, 250–51; Hudson trip, 248, 249, *257*, 261, 263–64, 266, 271–72; photos of, *264*

Wadsworth, Nev., *13*, 24

Washington, D.C., 79–80, *81*, 88, *117*, 245

Waverley electric auto, 220

Weber Canyon (Utah), 55–56

Weehawken, N.J., *207*, 211

Weller, Harry D., *74*, 105, 114

Westgard, Anthon L.: baggage truck, help with, 147; banquet following end of Garford motor train trip, 159; biographical details, 128, 162–63; comments about Garford motor train, 134, 140–42, 144, 148, 155; national highway, support for, 156; photo of, *131*; pilot of Garford motor train, role as, 128

Westgard, Helen, 129, *134*

Weston, Edward Payson, 22

Weston, Major General John F., 6, 29

White automobile, 6

Whitman, Lester L.: biographical details, 35–36, 67; Denver, passage through, 78; Franklin trip (1904), 2, *61*, 78, 275; Franklin trip (1906), 2, 35–36, 43, 47, 60, *61*, 66, 272, 275; Oldsmobile trip, 2; photos of, *39*, *49*, *59*, *60*; Reo trip, 35–38, 41–43, 45–51, 53–60, *61*, 63–69, 275

Whittier, Calif., 156, 157

Williams, Ariz., 205, *206*

Wilson, President Woodrow, 125, 221–22, 246

Winnemucca, Nev., *13*, 24, 57

Winton, Alexander, 11